Microsoft C/C++ Pro...
2nd Edition

Who This Book Is For

Programmers who have prior C experience and want to develop and **extend** their programming expertise to object-oriented C++ and add new **performance** to their programs.

What's Inside

- Full coverage of I/O class libraries
- Function and operator overloading
- C++ for Windows
- Compile-time polymorphism
- Linking C++ to C and assembly language programs
- Memory management with C++

Disk Contents

The *Microsoft C/C++ Programming* disk contains all the programs described in **the book** (and four more programs that do not appear in the book). This means you **can start** advancing your skills immediately. You'll be able to add these C++ projects **to your** repertoire:

- A QuickSort program
- A dynamic C++ mouse interface
- Windows dialog box and clipboard
- Stack classes and objects

Microsoft C/C++ Programming
Second Edition

Steve Holzner

Brady Books

New York London Toronto Sydney Singapore Tokyo

Brady Books

Published by Brady Books
A division of Prentice-Hall Computer Publishing
15 Columbus Circle
New York, NY 10023

Manufactured in the United States of America
10 9 8 7 6 5 4 3 2 1

Library of Congress Cataloging-in-Publication Data

Holzner, Steven.
    Microsoft C/C++ programming / Steven Holzner. — 2nd ed.
      p. cm.
    Includes index.
    1. C (Computer program language) 2. C++ (Computer program
language) I. Title.
QA76.73.C15H6592 1992
005.13—dc20
      92-20069
      CIP

ISBN 0-156686-005-9

To Burt Gabriel

— S. H.

Contents

CHAPTER 2

Welcome to C++: Classes and Objects 59

CHAPTER 3

Functions, Operators, and Overloading 115

CHAPTER 4

C++ Inheritance and Polymorphism 181

CHAPTER 5

C++ I/O Class Libraries 217

CHAPTER 6

Welcome to C++ for Windows 271

APPENDIX A

Using Assembly Language with C++   531

APPENDIX B

About the Diskette   549

Index   553

Limits of Liability and Disclaimer of Warranty

Trademarks

Introduction

Programming on a small scale is usually an enjoyable experience. Small, bite-sized programs don't have the same propensity for gathering errors that large ones do and are quick to compile and run — it's a rare programmer who hasn't had some some fun with small-scale programming and gotten the satisfaction of seeing things work the first time. In fact, as originally created, computers — and especially microcomputers — were only designed to work with small-scale programs. The few hobbyists that had their own computers were lucky if they had more than a few kilobytes of RAM.

But times change, and nowhere faster than in the computer field. As technology developed, the cost of equipment started to fall. Disks became larger, more and more RAM became available, and CPUs keep getting faster. In microcomputing, what had been a hobby became an industry — an industry in which customers today demand more and more functionality from their hardware and software. Following the hardware, programs have grown tremendously in size over the last decade, and it rapidly became apparent that creating a program ten times bigger was not going to be ten times easier. With the standard programming languages, there seems almost to be an inverted economy of scale: as fast as a program increases in size, it becomes unwieldy and unmanageable at double that rate. Errors proliferate and penetrate all parts of the program. One section of code conflicts with another. Debugging a large program becomes less and less an exercise and more and more a career.

This is mostly because the standard programming languages were designed for small-scale projects (by today's standards). The parts of a program often have access to all the other parts of the program, especially if many of its variables are global. The way you store and use data in the whole program has to be kept in mind as you work on any part of the code. And, when you start to debug, you find yourself debugging 10,000 lines of interdependent code and data — the whole program at once — instead of manageable pieces.

In fact, as programs became bigger, the solution became just that — cutting them up into manageable pieces. For example, in assembly language, everything in a file is global; that is, accessible by other parts of the program (but you don't often write large programs in assembly language). In early BASIC, you could cut your code up using GOSUB subroutines, but all data was still global between the subroutine and the main body of the program. Languages like Fortran started supporting functions and subroutines with purely local data and let you transfer data between them by passing it explictly or with COMMON statements. The C language appeared, with its strong emphasis on typing (and, for that matter, data structures), which helps makes sure what you send to and receive from other parts of the program is what you wanted. As programs became larger and larger, the programmer's strategy became to divide and conquer, a process now referred to as *encapsulation*.

Even the idea of data local to a specific function wasn't enough; as programs became more complex, programmers often found that other functions also needed access to that data. They wanted to wrap whole sections of the program — data and code — together into something beyond a simple function: something now called an *object*. For example, if you think of a large program as, say, a workshop, then programmers wanted the ability to stock it with self-contained tools. That is, they didn't want to be concerned with the internal data and functions necessary in, say, an oscilloscope — they wanted to be able to simply have an oscilloscope, ready for use. In a real oscilloscope, the internal data and functions are purely *private*, that is, we don't see what's going on inside. All we see is that we have an oscilloscope, ready for use. That's exactly the stage that programming has now arrived at: we want to be able to package both data and functions together so the internal details of complex parts of our program simply slip out of sight (the idea, quite literally, is out of sight, out of mind). And, that can only be done when we package *both* data and the functions that maintain and work with that data together. In this way, we're able to break a large, unwieldy program into a collection of easily-thought-of tools and resources (which is how we think of it anyway). And, in this way, C++ is the language we're looking for as our programs grow.

C++ lets us create our own objects, programming constructions that let us wrap tasks into easily handled concepts (like a stack or a screen handler). Objects in C++ will take us a step farther than functions in C, making programs even more modular and encapsulated. In addition, we'll find that we can *overload* the standard operators (e.g., + or -) in C++ to work on our new objects so that they seem almost a part of the language. For example, one popular type of C++ object is a character string, which C lacks proper support for (i.e., support for strings in C is maintained by library functions and is not integral to the language). In C++, however, we'll be able to set up string that we can use like this:

```
stringA = stringB + stringC
```

Here, we're simply concatenating two strings; if stringB was "abc" and stringC was "def," then the statement above would assign "abcdef" to stringA. The data for each string object (e.g., "abc") is kept internally. And, when we apply operators like + or = to such strings, it will be the object's internal functions that actually handle what goes on. As far as we know, we are simply able to work with character strings as above — the details don't concern us. This will become even more evident when we start to work with Windows programming; the amount of internal detail that remains hidden is staggering — all we see is the functionality. In other words, the spirit of C++ is to let us create and use our own tools and resources, letting the programmer be king and providing an easy framework in which to implement your program's design.

Our Approach

This book is designed expressly for you if you've had some Microsoft C programming experience and want to move on to Microsoft C++. In other words, we're going to assume you know some C before beginning since most programmers turn to C++ only after they have some C under their belts. However, we don't require much C knowledge, and, to make sure we're up to speed in

C, we'll spend the first chapter reviewing it before plunging into C++. Then, when we start exploring C++, we'll really take off.

Because Microsoft C++ is a language for programmers and because this is a book for would-be programmers, we are going to orient it toward seeing our programs work. In other words, we want to see what the language can do for us, not the other way around. We're not going to work through long, academic arguments about abstractions — those kinds of discussions would be out of place. This is a book for programmers, not theoreticians. We intend to unleash the full power of C++ in its own environment, and that power is outstanding.

However, we should know from the beginning that there is a good deal we have to learn before we can really use C++. There is no way around learning the difference between a class and an object and between overloading functions and overriding them. All in all, we'll have to learn about many things: virtual functions, abstract classes, built-in I/O classes, nested classes, pure virtual functions, constructors, copy constructors, destructors, inheritance, and more. In other words, we're going to get serious about learning C++ — and there's a lot to learn.

For that reason, we'll fill this book with dozens of ready-to-run examples. There's no better way to learn than by example, and we'll see some good ones here. In addition, we'll develop the longer examples line by line, using arrows to indicate where we are as we work through a program. There'll be frequent figures, notes, and — especially — tips. The tips are included to give you something extra. A tip might be a method of making a program run twice as fast; it might be about some other part of C++ that is unexpectedly handy at the present moment; it might even give us some insights about what's going on behind the scenes in C++. Whatever it is, the tips will show us some aspects of C++ from the professional programmer's point of view — giving us a little extra power, a little extra control.

That's our approach: learning C++ by seeing it work, by starting near the beginning and building our expertise carefully. We'll go from the most basic — the very foundations of object-oriented programming — up to the most powerful in C++, from the most simple to the most unexpected. Let's take a moment now to see what's ahead.

What's in This Book

The C++ language itself is capable of wonderful speed and precision — and we're going to put it to work. To start, we'll spend some time reviewing the Microsoft C language in the first chapter of this book. This first chapter is not meant to teach Microsoft C, of course, but only to refresh your memory. From there, we'll launch ourselves into Microsoft C++. Here's an overview of some of the subjects we'll gain mastery of:

- Classes
- Objects
- Function overloading
- Operator overloading
- How C++ uses memory
- Inheritance
- Compile-time polymorphism
- The I/O class libraries
- Run-time polymorphism
- Virtual functions
- Abstract classes
- Nested classes
- Advanced pointers in C++
- Connecting C++ to assembly language
- Connecting C++ to C
- C++ for Windows

The programming package we'll use is Microsoft C 7.0. This package supports nearly all of ANSI standard C++ version 2.1 (with exceptions that we'll note later). In addition, the Microsoft C package supports two programming platforms: DOS and Windows. This book is carefully designed around that division; since Microsoft C 7.0 supports both, programmers will want to use both, and we'll cover them both here. In a nutshell, we'll *learn* C++ under DOS and then really *see* how much easier it can make things when we use it in Windows. In fact, this is a natural division for us: We can develop small example programs in DOS to get the point of object-oriented programs, but small programs won't let us see how C++ can organize a large program efficiently. On the other hand, Windows programs are notoriously large, and we'll see exactly how C++ saves the day (and makes them much, much smaller). C++ and Windows is an entirely natural combination, good for teaching purposes as well as in its own right (i.e., more and more programmers are developing for Windows these days), so after we become familiar with small-scale examples in DOS, we'll turn to the larger scale in Windows. If you've already programmed in Windows, seeing what C++ can do there will be even more dramatic.

What You'll Need

As mentioned, to use this book, you'll need some knowledge of Microsoft C. Microsoft C++ builds on Microsoft C, and we'll need to have a good foundation before we can tackle it. For this reason, you should read the first chapter of this book to make sure you are familiar with topics we'll need later on. If you don't feel comfortable with the level of C programming we take for granted there, you should turn to an introductory C book before proceeding.

In addition, since this book is designed to be put to work, we're going to need some software: Microsoft C version 7.0 or later. This book is expressly designed to be used with that package. You'll also need an editor or word processor to type in the programs we develop. Almost any editor will do (in particular, you can use the built-in editor in the Programmer's Work Bench that comes with Microsoft C 7+). Microsoft C supports both DOS and Windows; to get the most out of our Windows coverage, you should have Windows version 3+. Although you can write Microsoft C++ programs for Windows 3.0 with a little extra trouble, the default (target) version of Windows is 3.1, and the Windows 3.1 Software Development Kit (SDK) comes with Microsoft C++ 7+. We'll be using Windows 3.1 in this book; if you have Windows 3.0, you'll have to add a few extra switches to your program as outlined in Chapter 7.

That's it: We're ready to unleash the full power of Microsoft C++. We're going to see it at work almost immediately because, in programming, there is no substitute for the real thing. If you want to master C++ and become a power programmer, let's start at once with Chapter 1, where we'll start our review and come up to speed in C. After that, when we're ready, we'll begin our guided tour of C++.

Our Review of C

———

Welcome to C++ — and to object-oriented programming, the next step up from today's function-oriented languages. Programs these days are getting bigger and bigger, and programmers are often left struggling with unwieldy, monolithic blocks of code thousands of lines long. C++ goes a long way toward changing that picture and allowing us to cut a program up the way that's most natural. Using C++, a long program is less a mass of uncoordinated functions and interconnecting data structures than a collection of easily managed ready-to-use tools and resources.

That's the way we usually think of our programs anyway — in terms of self-contained sections that are neatly wrapped up into concepts. For example, you might stock your kitchen with a refrigerator, an oven, and a dishwasher, each thought of as discrete units. When you put food in the refrigerator, you don't want to be concerned with the internal operation of the refrigerator, you simply want your food kept cold. Imagine what your kitchen would be like if you had to deal with every detail of the timers, thermostats, and pumps inside your appliances, setting and adjusting and coordinating them. That's a lot like the way a large-scale program works today in purely function-oriented programs: You can't wrap both data and the internal functions needed to work on and maintain that data into easily managed tools. The function is the standard unit of program design. However, in the real world, no one thinks of functions. People think in terms of objects and their associated utility.

That's what C++ is all about — creating objects that are easily thought about and managed, conceptually much like the operation of refrigerators and ovens. It can take many internal functions to maintain an object like a refrigerator, but until now, there was no way of wrapping the functions up with the data they use and need to form anything bigger than another function. Now, however, programmers can work with objects, which can have both data and functions that are either private to the object — internal data and functions — or available to anyone — called public data and functions. That is, when you set the thermostat of your refrigerator, it causes a great number of things to occur inside the refrigerator, none of which you need to concern yourself with. Those internal functions — and the way they interact with each other — are set into motion when you make changes in the thermostat setting. But, you don't need to see the details, and that's what makes it an appliance worth owning.

In the same way, a programming object provides a carefully designed and intentionally limited interface to the rest of the program. For example, one object we'll develop is a stack that can push and pop values. When you push a value onto the stack, some internal pointer is incremented, limits are checked, and the data is stored, but you don't have to worry about that; from your point of view, you're just using a stack. All you need to know is that you have a stack, ready to be used. Internally, several functions necessary for the stack's maintenance might share the stack's data, but you never see that internal coordination (after you've programmed and debugged the object). All you see is the stack's push and pop capabilities wrapped up into a neat object naturally thought of as a stack. That's what C++ allows us to do.

In this book, then, we're going to learn all about C++ and object-oriented programming in the best way — by seeing it at work. We'll avoid the dry cataloging type of teaching, which piles up layer after layer of formal theory. Instead, we're going to see the language in its own environment, giving us a working knowledge of just what it can do. Here, the programmer is king: the idea behind object-oriented programming is to give more power to the programmer, and we'll see how that works. We're going to work deep into the heart of the C++ language, learning about object-oriented programming, C++ memory control, virtual functions, operator overloading, and even some advanced C++ pointer methods. In other words, we're going to explore the full programming power of C++ — and that power is extraordinary.

C++ itself is actually a superset of C; that is, C++ was originally an extension of C (its first name was C with Classes). That means that we have to know how to program in C before tackling C++. For that reason, the first chapter of this book is a review of the C language. In particular, we'll be using Microsoft software in this book, so we'll be reviewing their version of C.

Knowing our way around C is essential before launching ourselves into C++; that is, the best way to prepare for C++ is to make sure we have a solid foundation in C. And the best way to make sure we have a solid foundation is by reviewing the material we'll need. Let's start immediately with a short history of C and C++.

A Brief History of C and C++

The reason the C language is called C is, simply, that it is the successor to the language called B. That language was developed by Ken Thompson in 1970, working on a DEC PDP-7, which is much less powerful than most modern PCs. The original UNIX operating system ran on that machine, and that's also where B got its start. (B itself was the successor to a language called BCPL, which had been written by Martin Richards.)

However, B was a little restricted. In 1972, Dennis Ritchie and Ken Thompson created the C language to augment B's power. C did not become immediately popular after its creation; in fact, it remained almost an esoteric topic for the next six years. In 1978, however — a historic year for C and C++ programmers — Brian Kernighan and Dennis Ritchie wrote *The C Programming Language* (Prentice Hall). And that simple book changed everything.

Now that word was out, there was an explosion of interest, and C was implemented on 8-bit computers under the CP/M operating system. It wasn't until the introduction of the IBM PC in 1981, however, that C really came into its own. When the PC revolution began, C was in a perfect place to take advantage of it. As the number of PCs shot upwards, so did the number of C users. C broke away from its original UNIX background and became a popular language on microcomputers.

It's worth stressing that it became popular for a very good reason: Programmers liked using it. Unlike many other languages, C gives the programmer a great deal of control over the computer. With that control comes responsibility — there are many things you can do in C that will ruin your program or crash your computer. That is, you have the power to do things in C that other languages would never allow you to do. And programmers liked that very much; they liked finding a language that was a tool, not an obstacle. To programmers, C was much like assembly language without the drawback of having to do everything for yourself; in other words, C seemed much like the perfect combination of control and programming power.

ANSI Standardizes C

All this made for such a popular language that different companies started to bring out their own versions of C, and each one began to go in a different direction. The C revolution was in danger of splintering into many incompatible programming packages. For that reason, the American National Standards Institute (ANSI) created a special subcommittee named X3J11 to create a standard version of C. This was an extremely important development for C and C++ programmers; the language, which had been going off in all directions at the same time, became standardized and coherent once more. For that reason, ANSI C did indeed become standard C, and we'll make many references to ANSI C in this book.

On the other hand, ANSI was interested in codifying C for *all* computers, not just the PC. However, there are many things that are specific to the PC which do not really apply to, say, mainframe computers. For example, one important area is the way the PC handles memory, which is quite unlike any computer that is not 80x86-based. For that reason, most implementations of C now adhere to the ANSI standard as far as it goes, and then they add their own extensions. C compliers for the PC agree in most particulars; however, they start to differ when there is no ANSI standard to agree on. The ANSI standard says nothing about screen graphics, for example, so there is considerable difference between compilers when it comes to drawing pictures.

C++ Appears

As the popularity of C grew, so did the number of applications written in C. In time, C programs grew longer and longer, and some people began to feel that the standard programming constructions just weren't up to the task. One solution to that was to make the program more modular, more compartmentalized, and you can use functions to do that. However, some functions may end up needing to share data, some need to coordinate with others, and again you can end up with dozens of things to keep in mind (and dozens of functions in the program's global scope).

In 1983, Bjarne Stroustrup developed C++. In essence, C++ is much like C, but with a number of important extensions. In other words, all that we know about C still applies, but C++ offers us even more power. Primary among the additions C++ brings to C is the idea of an *object*.

An object is really just like a new kind of structure — except that it can hold both data and functions, both of which can be private to the object if you want them to be. As mentioned above, the driving force behind objects is modularity. Programmers found that when they were struggling with large programs — C++ was originally written to be used when programs got very long, over 2,500 lines — that the more modular their programs were, the better. That's what C++ does. It helps us wrap up sections of our programs into discrete units, each of which serves some (easily remembered) purpose.

Although C++ was originally developed to introduce large-scale modularity to C, there are other parts of C++ that made it attractive even if your program is short. One such aspect is its legendary flexibility; we can redesign just about all of the C operators in C++, as well as do (previously) unheard-of things with functions. For example, through function overloading, we'll be able to call the same function with parameters of different types (e.g., int, float, etc.). C++ will decide which version of the function to use based on the types of the parameters we're passing (in C, naturally, this would be an error).

As time went on, versions of ANSI standardized C++ appeared which included even more improvements; this book is written to the specification of ANSI C++ 2.1, which Bjarne Stroustrup introduced in 1990. On February 28th, 1992, Microsoft introduced Microsoft C++ 7.0, which supports ANSI C++ 2.1 (with exceptions that we'll note) — and that brings us up to date, because we're going to use Microsoft C++ 7.0 (or later versions) in this book. That's it for our brief history; now we're ready to begin our review of C, the first step toward our exploration of C++.

The C Programming Language

Here is the absolute shortest possible (legal) C program:

```
main(){}
```

That's it; that's all we need. This is a working C program. On the other hand, this tiny program produces no visible results at all. What's happening here? As you know, main( ) is the label that tags the beginning of the program; following the parentheses in main( ) is the program body, enclosed in curly braces. The program body here is remarkably small; in fact, we have given it no length at all. Although you can run this program, it does nothing. After compilation and linking (which we'll see how to do in MS C 7+ soon), DOS loads the program and starts at main( ), but all that happens is that control is returned immediately to DOS and the program ends. Usually the curly braces enclose more C statements, like this:

```
#include <stdio.h>

/* Print "Hello, world." */

main()
{
    printf("Hello, world.");

    return 0;
}
```

Here, something is really going on; there is a real program body between the curly braces. (In fact, this is the traditional first program of C books.) This program indicates a few more things about writing C programs — especially about the actual format of the program. The curly braces have been split, and one is directly above the other. The program lines themselves are indented.

This kind of format, while not required, helps make C programs easier to use, and it is commonly used by both C and C++ programmers. In particular, we'll find it helpful to align the curly braces, one on top of the other, and indent the body of the program as we've done above. This is an example of C programming style, and the reason we use it will become clearer as our C++ programs grow more complex.

Another example of the C style is the use of lower case for most of the words in a program. Special reserved words, like #include, are always written in lower case — both C and C++ are sensitive to the case of those words (e.g., printf and PrInTf are two different words to C and C++). Let's dissect each part of this short program to make sure we know exactly what's going on here.

The most important line in the whole program is the line with printf( ):

```
#include <stdio.h>

/* Print "Hello, world." */
```

```
    main()
    {
→       printf("Hello, world.");

        return 0;
    }
```

This is where we tell C that we have something to display, and it is the most common way of printing on the screen. But, printf( ) is not a built-in part of the C language; C, of course, is divided into two major sections: the C language proper, and the C libraries. The C libraries are vast collections of functions like printf( ).

NOTE When we're talking about a function in this book, we'll put a pair of parentheses after its name like this: printf( ).

Here, we are telling the printf( ) function that we want it to print the words "Hello, world." on the screen. A function reads what we pass to it inside the parentheses, does something, and can return data to us. For that reason, it's up to us to let C know how the function behaves — in particular, what kind of data it takes, and what kind it returns, if any. Because there are literally hundreds of functions already available to us in the C libraries, C has header files that hold the information it needs to know about the library functions.

In our case, we can provide C with everything it needs to know about printf( ) by including the correct header file; for printf( ) it's stdio.h. The printf( ) function has a line in that file telling C what kind of data it takes and what kind it returns, and if C is going to use any function in a program, it needs that kind of information about it.

The #include instruction is a preprocessor directive; that is, it is an instruction to the compiler, and it doesn't generate any direct code that appears in the final program. Directives like this one simply tell the compiler to do something. In our case, #include tells the compiler to take the entire file stdio.h and place it in the program here:

```
→   #include <stdio.h>

    /* Print "Hello, world." */

    main()
```

```
{
     printf("Hello, world.");

     return 0;
}
```

The next line in our program is a comment. The compiler treats comments as though they weren't there at all; that is, comments are entirely for our benefit. In this case, our comment tells us what the program is for:

```
#include <stdio.h>

/* Print "Hello, world." */

main()
{
     printf("Hello, world.");

     return 0;
}
```

In C, a comment starts with the characters /*, and, when it's done, ends with the matching characters */. As soon as the compiler sees /* it stops reading and interpreting; only after it sees the closing */ marker will it begin reading the program again. Comments may be placed anywhere in the program, as long as you don't obstruct parts of the program that you want compiled. For example, our program could look like this:

```
#include <stdio.h>    /* The required header file for printf() */

/*    This program prints          */
/*    the words "Hello, world."     */
/*    on the screen.                */

main()                 /* The main function. */
{
    printf("Hello, world."); /* Use printf() to print out message. */
}
```

There is more information here, so what is actually happening is clearer. Note in particular the comment:

```
/*    This program prints          */
/*    the words "Hello, world."     */
/*    on the screen.                */
```

Because the compiler stops interpreting what's between the /* and */ mark-ers, we could have done that this way instead:

```
/* This program prints
the words "Hello, world."
on the screen.          */
```

Both work as comments, but it's more clear that the entire text in the first case is a comment; the C and C++ style is usually to place /* and */ markers on each line of a multi-line comment to avoid confusion. And we'll see later that C++ gives us a new way of handling one line comments.

The next line in our program has the label main( ) in it. As we know, main( ) represents the place where the program starts — and it's a function. Every line of C or C++ that does anything must be inside some function before it can be executed. Functions are used to compartmentalize programming tasks into smaller tasks which are easier to work with. The work done in one function is separate to some degree from the work done in another, which breaks our code into manageable pieces.

In DOS, the main( ) function is the one that we always need even if we don't have any others, because it's the one where our program starts. The state-ments that make up the body of a function follow the name of that function, and are enclosed by curly braces — in our case, the first statement is printf("Hello, world."), like this:

```
#include <stdio.h>

/* Print "Hello, world." */

main()
{
    printf("Hello, world.");

    return 0;
}
```

Whatever is between curly braces is referred to as a block. In particular, the body of a function like this one is always enclosed in curly braces, so it is an example of a block. Keep in mind that the indentation and physical arrange-ment of statements in a block is up to us; we could equally as well have done this:

```
#include <stdio.h>

/* Print "Hello, world." */

main(){printf("Hello, world.");
return 0;}
```

However, we'll find it much more useful to indent and arrange the program body so that it's more readable, as above.

Now we reach the meat of the program, the part where we use the printf( ) function. Here's how it looks:

```
#include <stdio.h>

/* Print "Hello, world." */

main()
{
    printf("Hello, world.");

    return 0;
}
```

This line is a statement. Statements like this end with a semicolon (;), which is called the statement terminator. Each action in C is a statement, and each one ends in a semicolon. This terminator tells the compiler that the present statement is complete.

This is the typical way to use a function — by placing the data we want it to use between the parentheses. The data that is passed to a function makes up the function's arguments. In this case, the printf( ) function only receives one argument, and that is the character string "Hello, world." When this statement is executed, "Hello, world." appears on the screen.

The final line in our program is return 0:

```
#include <stdio.h>

/* Print "Hello, world." */

main()
```

```
    {
        printf("Hello world.");

→       return 0;
    }
```

We include this line because, to C and C++, it looks as though the function main( ) should return an integer value. That is, the return type of a function precedes the function's name, and if we omit it, as we've done here, C and C++ expect the function to return a (default) integer. We could have eliminated that problem by declaring main( ) a function of type void instead:

```
    #include <stdio.h>

    /* Print "Hello, world." */

→    void main()
    {
        printf("Hello world.");
    }
```

Technically, returning a value of 0 from our program is not necessary in Microsoft C++, but it's good programming practice, so we'll usually include this line (i.e., return 0;) at the end of our DOS programs. The usual method is simply to return a value of 0 for normal program termination at the end of the program (or a value of 1 for abnormal program termination). That's it for our first review C program. Now that it's working, let's add some data to it.

Using Data in C

Let's say that we wanted to keep track of the current chapter number of this book in a program. When the program was run, it could display the chapter number like this: "This is Chapter 1." In other words, we'll store the chapter number in a variable. Our program is free to work on that variable, and, in the following chapter, the chapter number could be updated to 2.

One very popular type of variable is the integer, which takes up two bytes of memory storage. Those two bytes (which make up 16 bits of memory) can hold integer numbers ranging from -32,768 to 32,767. That's large enough to hold chapter numbers, so let's set up an integer in memory named chapter_number. We can do that and set it equal to 1 at the same time, like this (this process is called variable initialization):

```
#include <stdio.h>

/* Print "This is Chapter 1." */

main()
{
    int chapter_number = 1;

    printf("This is Chapter %d.\n", chapter_number);

    return 0;
}
```

In our case, the data type of chapter_number is integer, that is, an int. As we set aside space for it, we also direct C to store the value 1 in it, initializing like this: int chapter_number = 1;. There are rules in C and C++ about the naming of identifiers — the names that we can give to functions, variables, or labels — and here they are:

- The first character of the identifier must be a letter or an underscore (_). The first character cannot be a number (because C or C++ might think the whole thing is a number).
- The rest of the characters must be numbers, letters, or an underscore.
- The first 247 letters count (32 for external identifiers).
- Both C and C++ are case sensitive: Upper- and lowercase letters in identifiers are different.

We can also use printf( ) to print the value of chapter_number with the %d *format specifier*, which tells printf( ) to print an integer (as we'll see, format specifiers are largely obsolete in C++):

```
#include <stdio.h>

/* Print "This is Chapter 1." */

main()
{
    int chapter_number = 1;
```

→
```
        printf("This is Chapter %d.\n", chapter_number);

        return 0;
    }
```

Note that we're also indicating that we want the text we're displaying on the screen to be followed by a carriage-return line-feed pair, which lets us skip to the next line on the screen. We do that by including the printf( ) backslash code "\n." Other backslash codes include "\a" for alert (rings a bell), "\t" for tab, and "\r" for a carriage return alone.

Of course, there are other ways of reaching the value inside a variable besides initializing it. For example, we can do this:

```
#include <stdio.h>

/* Print "This is Chapter 1." */

main()
{
    int chapter_number;

    chapter_number = 1;
    printf("This is Chapter %d.\n", chapter_number);

    return 0;
}
```

→

In this case, we didn't initialize chapter_number; instead, we assigned a value to it like this:

```
chapter_number = 1;
```

Assignments always take the value on the right-hand side, 1 in this case, and assign it to the variable on the left. As you know, the expression on the right doesn't have to be a constant like 1 — it can be another variable, or, say, a function. In fact, it can be anything at all as long as C or C++ is able to evaluate it and give that value to the variable on the left side (also called an *lvalue*, a left-side-of-the-assignment value; lvalues must correspond to a location in memory so that you can store data in them).

The = sign is called the assignment operator, and we can use it to put values into variables. Both C and C++ have three different types of primary operators: arithmetic operators, relational and logical operators, and bitwise operators. We're ready to review arithmetic operators at this point, so let's do that next.

Arithmetic Operators in C

Arithmetic operators are the ones that do math for us, such as the familiar operations of addition, subtraction, and so on. If you had three oranges and four apples, and you wanted to add them, you could do it this way:

```c
#include <stdio.h>

/* This program adds apples and oranges. */

main()
{
    int apples, oranges, sum;

    oranges = 3;
    apples = 4;
    sum = apples + oranges;
    printf("Total fruit inventory is %d apples and oranges.\n", sum);

    return 0;
}
```

In this case, the value in the variable apples is added to the value in oranges, and the result is placed in the variable sum (neither the value in apples nor the value in oranges is affected). Then the program prints out the total fruit inventory, seven apples and oranges.

Besides addition, we also have subtraction. Let's say that we started with four apples and then ate one. This program would let us know how many we had left:

```c
#include <stdio.h>

/* This program adjusts apples. */

main()
{
    int apples;

    apples = 4;
```

Operator	Action
–	Subtraction
+	Addition
*	Multiplication
/	Division
%	Modulus
– –	Decrementing
++	Incrementing

Table 1-1. C's Arithmetic Operators

→
```
apples = apples - 1;
printf("You now have %d apples left.\n", apples);

return 0;
}
```

Besides addition and subtraction, of course, there are also multiplication, division, modulo, and other arithmetic operations that we can perform, as shown in Table 1-1. In particular, the *modulus operator*, %, returns the modulus of one number with respect to another; that is, this operator simply returns the remainder of an integer division (for example, the integer division 16 / 3 is 5 with a remainder of 1, and 16 % 3 equals 1).

Because changing the value of a variable by adding or subtracting another value is so common, C and C++ also have a shortcut method that comes in handy (and which works for all the arithmetic operators). All we have to do is to combine the symbols we want to use like this: + and = becomes +=, – and = becomes -=, and so on.

The last two arithmetic operators in the table are the increment and decrement operators, ++ and --. Above, we had a program that displayed the new number of apples after we had eaten one; we could have done that this way:

```
main()
{
    int apples;

    apples = 4;
```
→
```
    --apples;
```

```
        printf("You now have %d apples left.\n", apples);

        return 0;
    }
```

All we had to do was to include the statement --apples to decrement the value in apples by one. Each operator, ++ and --, can be either a postfix or a prefix operator. For example, we could have used either --apples or apples--. Both statements decrement the value of apples, but what is important here is *when* they do it. For example, we can use ++ (or --) as a prefix operator, as in this case:

```
    fruits = --apples;
```

Here, the value of apples is first decremented, then it is assigned to the variable fruits. If apples held 4, then after this statement is executed, apples and fruits will both hold 3. On the other hand, look at this statement:

```
    fruits = apples--;
```

Using ++ (or --) as a postfix operator like this means that it will be applied only after the rest of the statement has been executed. If apples held 4, then 4 would be assigned to fruits. After the statement had been executed, the -- operator would be applied to apples, decrementing it to 3. When we move on to the next line, fruits would be left holding 4, and apples would be left holding 3. If you want to avoid confusion, it's often better to break such cases up into two lines, like this:

```
    --apples;
    fruits = apples;
```

Operator Precedence in C

Every now and then, operator expressions can become complicated, so C and C++ have rules about the way operators combine. For example, in the expression 9 + 6 / 3, the division operator, /, has precedence over the addition operator, +, so the result is 9 + 2, or 11. In fact, both the multiplication and division operators have precendence over addition and subtraction. Here are some examples:

3 + 4 * 5   →   23
8 / 2 + 1   →   5
9 * 2 - 1   →   17

In each case, the operator with higher precedence is used first. Table 1-2 shows the operator precedence for the C and C++ operators (the operators with the highest precedence are the highest in the table), and you can refer to it whenever there's a question.

Operator	Description	Associativity
( )	function call	left to right
[ ]	array element	
.	structure member	
->	pointer to a structure member	
!	logical NOT	right to left
~	one's complement	
−	minus (the neg operator)	
++	increment	
--	decrement	
&	address of	
*	contents of	
(type)	typecast operator	
sizeof	returns in bytes	
*	multiply	left to right
/	divide	
%	modulus	
+	add	left to right
−	subtract	
<<	left shift	left to right
>>	right shift	
<	less than	left to right
<=	less than or equal to	

Table 1-2. Operator Precedence in C

Operator	Description	Associativity
>	greater than	
>=	greater than or equal to	
==	equality	left to right
!=	not equal	
&	bit-by-bit AND	left to right
^	bit-by-bit XOR	left to right
¦	bit-by-bit OR	left to right
&&	logical AND	left to right
¦ ¦	logical OR	left to right
?:	conditional	right to left
=	assignment	right to left
*= /= %= +=	compound assignment	
-= <<= >>=	compound assignment	
&= ^= ¦=	compound assignment	
,	comma operator	left to right

Table 1-2. (continued)

The Other C Data Types

We've reviewed the arithmetic operators in C, but so far, we've worked only with one type of variable, integers. However, the world is a place filled with quantities that won't fit into the integer range of -32,768 to 32,767. Some quantities are a great deal larger, some are a great deal smaller. Other quantities have fractional parts associated with them. In C and C++, there are five basic data types: char (1 byte long), int (2 bytes), float (4 bytes), double (8 bytes), and void (0 bytes). We can see the kinds of values they can hold in Table 1-3.

Data Type	Signed?	Bytes	Range
char	signed	1	–128 to 127
int	signed	2	–32,768 to 32,767
float	signed	4	3.4E+–38 [7 digits accuracy]
double	signed	8	1.7E+–308 [15 digits accuracy]
void	neither	0	without value

Table 1-3. The C Basic Data Types

In addition, there are four modifiers that may be used with some of the basic data types. The modifiers are: signed, unsigned, long, and short. These data type modifiers may only be applied to the char and int types, although long may also be applied to double. In Table 1-4, you'll find a list of the possible combinations of the basic data types and the modifiers.

TIP The long double type is ten bytes long, and it corresponds exactly to the internal format of floating point numbers as they're stored in the 80x87. Using assembly language (which is built into MS C 7+), programmers are able to slip these numbers to and from the 80x87 without modification.

NOTE Some of the designations in Table 1-4 are duplicates of each other. For example, int, short, and short int are all names for the same thing.

We can declare our variables to be any of the types listed in that table.

TIP As we'll see, a major change in C++ is that we'll be able to declare our variables almost anywhere a statement can go, which will prove very useful (such as in the initialization section of for loops).

It's worth mentioning at this point that we can also declare constants in C like this:

```
const float pi_val     = 3.14159;
```

Declaration	Signed?	Bytes	Range
char	signed	1	−128 to 127
int	signed	2	−32,768 to 32,767
short	signed	2	−32,768 to 32,767
short int	signed	2	−32,768 to 32,767
long	signed	4	−2,147,483,648 to 2,147,483,647
long int	signed	4	−2,147,483,648 to 2,147,483,647
unsigned char	unsigned	1	0 to 255
unsigned	unsigned	2	0 to 65,535
unsigned int	unsigned	2	0 to 65,535
unsigned short	unsigned	2	0 to 65,535
unsigned long	unsigned	4	0 to 4,294,967,295
signed char	signed	1	−128 to 127
signed int	signed	2	−32,768 to 32,767
signed	signed	2	−32,768 to 32,767
signed long	signed	4	−2,147,483,647 to 2,147,483,647
enum	unsigned	2	0 to 65,535
float	signed	4	3.4E+−38 [7 digits accuracy]
double	signed	8	1.7E+−308 [15 digits accuracy]
long double	signed	10	3.4E−4932 to 1.1E+4932

Table 1-4. C Variable Types with Modifiers

In C++, const also hides the associated object from other files and so prevents external *linkage* (you can override that by declaring a constant as extern const).

TIP We might note that in C++, a pointer declared as a pointer to type const cannot be assigned a pointer to a non-const.

Reading Character Input

The program in Listing 1-1 reads a key you type at the keyboard by using the library function scanf( ), which is the way you read character input in C. The program asks you to type a key and, when you do, it simply types it out again.

Listing 1-1. Example Using scanf( )

```
#include <stdio.h>

/* Read keys from the keyboard with scanf() */

main()
{
    char our_char;

    printf("Please type a character: ");
    scanf("%c", &our_char);

    printf("Thank you. That character was %c.", our_char);

    return 0;
}
```

We start by including the header file stdio.h so that C knows how to handle scanf( ) and printf( ). Next, we set up main( ) and type out a prompt, indicating that we are waiting for a key to be typed at the keyboard:

```
#include <stdio.h>

/* Read keys from the keyboard with scanf() */

main()
{

        printf("Please type a character: ");
          :
          :
```

Now we're ready to read the key that was typed, and to do that, we use scanf( ). To use this function, we set up a format string; in this case, the format string lets C know what kind of input to expect from the keyboard. In our case, we're just expecting a single character, which has the format specification %c. We can store that character as our_char, so we use scanf( ) like this:

```
#include <stdio.h>

/* Read keys from the keyboard with scanf() */

main()
```

```
→       {
            char our_char;

            printf("Please type a character: ");
→           scanf("%c", &our_char);
                :
                :
```

Note that we also declared the variable our_char to hold the keyboard data. In this case, the format string is extraordinarily simple, and just consists of "%c". However, format strings can get complex; if our input characters are separated by spaces, for example, our format string might look like this: "%c %c %c", matching what we receive from the keyboard. In addition, note that we pass the address of our_char to scanf( ), using the & operator:

```
#include <stdio.h>

/* Read keys from the keyboard with scanf() */

main()
{
    char our_char;

    printf("Please type a character: ");
→   scanf("%c", &our_char);
        :
        :
```

In other words, we're passing a pointer to our_char to scanf( ), because scanf( ) needs to reach the value in our_char directly (we'll review pointers in a few pages). After scanf( ) is executed, the character that we typed (actually, its ASCII code) is stored in the variable our_char, and we can print it out again:

```
#include <stdio.h>

/* Read keys from the keyboard with scanf() */

main()
{
    char our_char;

    printf("Please type a character: ");
    scanf("%c", &our_char);
```

→
```
        printf("Thank you. That character was %c.", our_char);

        return 0;
    }
```

It turns out that both scanf( ) and printf( ) are largely obsolete in C++. That is, character input and output are handled in a much more natural way, as we'll see in the next chapter. However, this little program will allow us to review a few more C constructions if we develop it a little.

For example, we might modify it to print out the input character after it's been capitalized. Not all characters that you can type at the keyboard can be legally capitalized, so we can check that the value that was typed, as stored in our_char, is legal. Someone may ask the program to capitalize, say, '5' or '@', in which case we should return an error. We can begin by checking that our_char is not less than 'a'; then we will check that it is not greater than 'z'.

The if Statement

For example, we can compare the character we read to 'a' like this:

```
#include <stdio.h>
#include <ctype.h>

/* Capitalize keys read from the keyboard */

main()
{
    char our_char;

    printf("Please type a lowercase letter: ");
    scanf("%c", &our_char);
```

→
```
    if (our_char >= 'a') printf("In uppercase: %c.", toupper(our_char));

    return 0;
}
```

Here, we check that the value in our_char is greater than or equal to 'a', and, if it is, we print out the uppercase version (using the C library function toupper( )). Note the form of the if statement: We start out with if, followed by a condition, which is enclosed in parentheses. That condition is our_char

>= 'a', and it is true if our_char is greater than or equal to 'a'. If the condition is true, we print the capitalized letter like this:

```
if (our_char >= 'a') printf("In uppercase: %c.", toupper(our_char));
```

Conditions in C or C++ can be either true or false. Properly read, the if statement reads: If our_char is greater than or equal to 'a', then execute the following printf( ) statement. The >= operator is, of course, a relational operator, and it returns a value of true or false.

As far as the program we've been developing goes, we check our_char against 'a', and if it's greater, we print out the capitalized version. Otherwise, we do nothing. There's two obvious problems here — first, we're not checking if our_char is greater than 'z', and second, we're not printing out any error message if the character is less than 'a'. We can rectify the second problem with the second part of the if . . . else statement. Take a look at the program in Listing 1-2.

Listing 1-2. if...else Example

```
#include <stdio.h>
#include <ctype.h>

/* Capitalize keys read from the keyboard */

main()
{
    char our_char;

    printf("Please type a lowercase letter: ");
    scanf("%c", &our_char);

    if (our_char < 'a') printf("Sorry, I cannot capitalize that.\n");
    else printf("Thank you. In uppercase: %c.", toupper(our_char));

    return 0;
}
```

We've improved our program by using the relational operator <, "is less than"; if our_char is less than 'a', we print out an error message. However, we have a problem here; we don't have just two possible outcomes — we have three:

- our_char < 'a'

- our_char > 'z'

- our_char is legal — print out toupper(our_char)

So far, we've only handled the first and last of these conditions, but C allows us to handle all three. In particular, it allows us to chain if...elses together into an if-else-if ladder, and we can see how that works in Listing 1-3.

Listing 1-3. if-else-if Ladder Example

```c
#include <stdio.h>
#include <ctype.h>

/* Capitalize keys read from the keyboard */

main()
{
    char our_char;

    printf("Please type a lowercase letter: ");
    scanf("%c", &our_char);

    if (our_char < 'a')
        printf("Sorry, I cannot capitalize that.\n");
    else if (our_char > 'z')
        printf("Sorry, I cannot capitalize that.\n");
    else
        printf("Thank you. In uppercase: %c.", toupper(our_char));

    return 0;
}
```

There, we check if the character is greater than 'z' or less than 'a' like this:

```c
→    if (our_char < 'a')
        printf("Sorry, I cannot capitalize that.\n");
→    else if (our_char > 'z')
        printf("Sorry, I cannot capitalize that.\n");
            :
```

If it is not, it is legal, so we print out the capitalized version like this, chaining our if...elses together:

```
if (our_char < 'a')
    printf("Sorry, I cannot capitalize that.\n");
else if (our_char > 'z')
    printf("Sorry, I cannot capitalize that.\n");
else
    printf("Thank you. In uppercase: %c.", toupper(our_char));
```

That's it for our review of if...else; now let's take the time to review C's relational and logical operators.

Relational and Logical Operators

You can find a list of C's relational and logical operators in Table 1-5. We've already reviewed a number of these operators, including >=, >, and <. The == operator stands for "is equal to," and, of course, it's popular in if statements. Its counterpart is !=, which means "is not equal to."

The relational and logical operators differ from the arithmetic operators that we've seen so far in one primary way: their operands, and their results, are not numbers but logical values, true or false. For example, C evaluates an expression like (5 == 3) as False.

Numerically, false is represented as 0 in C, and any non-zero value, if it appears as a logical or relational operand, is treated as true. That means that if our_int was 3, the expression (our_int == 3) is true, and has a non-zero value. In fact, even the expression (our_int = 3) has a non-zero value — C evaluates an assignment expression like this from right to left, so not only is our_int given the value 3, but the value of the whole expression itself is 3 — and is therefore true.

The logical operators are of particular value when you want to tie certain conditions together to form one. For example, you might recall that in our earlier capitalizing program, there were two possible ways of disqualifying an incoming character. The character was invalid if either of these conditions were true:

```
our_char < 'a'
our_char > 'z'
```

Type	Operator	Meaning
Relational	>	Is greater than
	>=	Is greater than or equal to
	<	Is less than
	<=	Is less than or equal to
	==	Is equal to
	!=	Is not equal to
Logical	&&	AND
	¦¦	OR
	!	NOT

Table 1-5. Relational and Logical Operators

Using the logical operator ¦¦, the "or" operator, we can make both of these into one condition like this: (our_char < 'a') ¦¦ (our_char > 'z'), which you read as (our_char < 'a') OR (our_char > 'z'). If either of the two conditions are true, the whole condition is true. That means that we can collapse our program's if statements this way:

```
#include <stdio.h>
#include <ctype.h>

/* Capitalize keys read from the keyboard */

main()
{
    char our_char;

    printf("Please type a lowercase letter: ");
    scanf("%c", &our_char);

    if (our_char < 'a' ¦¦ our_char > 'z')
        printf("Sorry, I cannot capitalize that.\n");
    else
        printf("Thank you. In uppercase: %c.", toupper(our_char));

    return 0;
}
```

Here, we have shortened the code to include a single if...else statement. The AND logical operator, &&, is different — for it to be true, both operands must be true (non-zero). For example:

```
if((month == 12) && (day == 25)) printf("Merry Christmas!!\n");
```

Here we are testing to see whether it's Christmas; for that to be true, the variable month must equal 12 AND the day must equal 25. If both conditions are satisfied, then the Merry Christmas message is typed out. Since True and False can be represented by non-zero and zero values, respectively, we can put them together into a table (non-zero, that is, true values, are represented by 1):

OR	0	1		AND	0	1
0	0	1		0	0	0
1	1	1		1	0	1

That's it for our review of variables and operators, which (including the assignment operator) make up the rudiments of data manipulation in C programs. And, now that we've reviewed if statements, we're ready to move up to the other primary method of altering the flow of a program: loops.

The for Loop

The for loop lets us keep performing an action over and over on our data until a condition (which we specify) becomes true. The general form of the for loop looks like this:

```
for(initialization; condition; increment) statement;
```

Here, *initialization* is a statement that is executed when the loop begins, often setting a loop counter to 0, *condition* is the end condition, checked every time the body of the loop is about to execute, and *increment* is a statement that is executed at the end of the loop, just before the condition is tested to see if we should loop again.

When the condition becomes false, the for loop stops and the program continues with the lines of code following it. The body of the loop is made up of *statement* above, and, as is always true in C and C++, that statement can be made up of a block of code that is enclosed in curly braces. For example, we can use a for loop like this:

```
main()
{
    int loop_index;

    for(loop_index = 0; loop_index < 10; loop_index++){
        printf("Hello, world.\n");
    }

    return 0;
}
```

At the beginning of the for loop, the loop counter or index, which we've called loop_index, is set to 0 (this is the initialization statement in our case):

```
         ↓
for(loop_index = 0; loop_index < 10; loop_index++){
    printf("Hello, world.\n");
}
```

then the termination condition is tested:

```
                        ↓
for(loop_index = 0; loop_index < 10; loop_index++){
    printf("Hello, world.\n");
}
```

If it is false, the loop is done and we go on with the program. The condition is tested before the loop executes at all — if the condition here had been loop_index > 0, for example, the loop wouldn't even execute once. However, the condition is loop_index < 10; since loop_index is now 0, the body of the loop is executed, printing "Hello, world.\n" on the screen. At the end of the body of the loop, the increment statement is executed, and loop_index is incremented to 1:

```
                                            ↓
for(loop_index = 0; loop_index < 10; loop_index++){
    printf("Hello, world.\n");
}
```

Next, the termination condition is checked (is loop_index < 10?), and, since loop_index is 1, the body of the loop is executed again. This keeps going until "Hello, world.\n" has been printed out exactly 10 times. That's it for the for loop; let's continue now with a review of the while loop.

The while Loop

The while loop acts a little like a for loop but, unlike a for loop, it doesn't usually have a loop index associated with it. In its general form, it looks like this:

```
while(condition) statement;
```

The while loop continues to execute as long as the condition — which can be any expression — remains true (numerically, non-zero). The statement, of course, can be any block of code as long as you enclose it in curly braces. Note that, like the for loop, the while loop evaluates its condition at the top, so if the condition is false to begin with, the body of the loop will never be executed at all.

Here's a simple while loop example; this program keeps asking you to guess a number until you hit it:

```c
#include <stdio.h>

/* A while loop example */

main()
{
    int our_number = 10, user_guess = 0;

    while(user_guess != our_number){
        printf("Guess my number: ");
        scanf(" %i", &user_guess);
    }
    printf("Good work!!\n");

    return 0;
}
```

This program keeps looping until the read-in value, user_guess, equals our_number:

```
→   while(user_guess != our_number){
        printf("Guess my number: ");
        scanf(" %i", &user_guess);
    }
```

That's it for while loops; now let's take a look at do...while loops.

The do...while Loop

The do...while loop is different from the other two types of loops; here, the body of the loop is always executed at least once, because the condition isn't checked until the end of the loop. The general form looks like this:

```
do{
    statement;
} while(condition);
```

This loop keeps executing while the condition is true. There are times that you'll want the body of the loop to execute at least once, such as when you're allowing choices to be made from a menu (to quit, you'd have to select the quit choice). For example, we can convert our earlier while loop example into a do...while loop example like this:

```
#include <stdio.h>

/* A do...while loop example */

main()
{
    int our_number = 10, user_guess;

    do{
        printf("Guess my number: ");
        scanf(" %i", &user_guess);
    } while(user_guess != our_number);

    printf("Good work!!\n");

    return 0;
}
```

Note that we did not need to initialize user_guess (as we did before) because it is not checked at the top of the loop, only at the bottom — after it holds the actual user's guess:

```
    do{
        printf("Guess my number: ");
        scanf(" %i", &user_guess);
→   } while(user_guess != our_number);
```

That finishes loops; the next step up in program control is writing our own functions.

Writing C Functions

The general form for a function looks like this:

```
return-type function-name (parameter list)
{
    statement(s);
}
```

Let's put together a function named read_char( ); all it will do when called is to read a character from the keyboard and return it like this:

```
#include <stdio.h>

/* Read keys from the keyboard with scanf() */

char read_char(void);

main()
{
    printf("Please type a character: ");
    printf("Thank you. That character was %c.", read_char());

    return 0;
}

→   char read_char(void)
    {
        char our_char;

        scanf("%c", &our_char);
        return our_char;
    }
```

There are a number of points that we should review here. First, at the start of the whole program, we tell C about the function read_char( ) — in particular, that it takes no arguments and that it returns a value of type char — with a function prototype:

```
#include <stdio.h>

/* Read keys from the keyboard with scanf() */

char read_char(void);
    :
```

The keyword void tells C that read_char( ) receives no parameters, and the keyword char indicates that its return value is of type char. If there was no return value, we would have used the prototype void read_char(void).

Later in the program, when C comes across our use of read_char( ), it will know what to expect — it already knows that this is a function that takes no parameters and returns a parameter of type char. The prototype is very important, and we'll include them for all of our C++ functions. A prototype for a function that takes two integer parameters and returns a float value might look like this:

```
float our_func(int a, int b);
```

In the pre-ANSI C days, you could use a partial prototype, without specifying the parameters, like this:

```
float our_func();
```

We should note that although you can still omit the types of the parameters this way in C, C++ requires that you put them in so that it can check to make sure that the types of the variables being passed are correct.

In our program, then, we can use read_char( ) like this:

```
#include <stdio.h>

/* Read keys from the keyboard with scanf() */

char read_char(void);

main()
{
    printf("Please type a character: ");
```

```
→              printf("Thank you. That character was %c.", read_char());
        }
        :
        :
```

Since the return value of read_char( ) is the character that was typed, we can just put it into the printf( ) statement directly; when it's evaluated, its value will be the value it returns. Finally, we define the function read_char( ) itself:

```
#include <stdio.h>

/* Read keys from the keyboard with scanf() */

char read_char(void);

main()
{
    printf("Please type a character: ");
    printf("Thank you. That character was %c.", read_char());

    return 0;
}
```

```
→   char read_char(void)
    {
        char our_char;

        scanf("%c", &our_char);
        return our_char;
    }
```

The definition of a function begins with a line exactly like the function's prototype, except that it is not followed by a semicolon. The body of the function itself is defined after this first line.

We should also examine the variable our_char, which is defined inside read_char( ). Because it is internal to read_char( ), it is not available in the rest of the program; it is a local variable, available to read_char( ) only, which means that you cannot use it in the main( ) function. If, on the other hand, we had defined our_char outside any function, like this:

```
#include <stdio.h>

/* Read keys from the keyboard with scanf() */
```

```
char read_char(void);

main()
{
    printf("Please type a character: ");
    printf("Thank you. That character was %c.", read_char());

    return 0;
}
```

→
```
char our_char;

char read_char(void)
{
    scanf("%c", &our_char);
    return our_char;
}
```

then it is a global variable, and we can use it at any place inside the program. In particular, variables defined inside a function are purely local to that function — this is one of the ways that functions help compartmentalize our programs and make them more modular. Note also that we use the return statement to return a value from read_char( ), like this:

```
char read_char(void)
{
    char our_char;

    scanf("%c", &our_char);
```
→
```
    return our_char;
}
```

TIP   In line with the philosophy of data encapsulation, the C++ style is to use as little global data as possible to avoid possible conflicts, and to make the program simpler to work with or debug.

This is how we return values from functions; in this case, we are returning the value of our_char. Let's take a look now at a more involved function. We might have a function named addem( ) that takes two integer parameters, adds them, and returns the sum as another integer. That program might look like this:

```
#include <stdio.h>

/* A function example with parameters. */

int addem(int a, int b);

main()
{
    int i_1 = 1, i_2 = 2;

    printf("Adding the two numbers gives %d.", addem(i_1, i_2));

    return 0;
}
```

→
```
int addem(int a, int b)
{
    return a + b;
}
```

Here the prototype looks like this:

```
int addem(int a, int b);
```

And the function itself looks like this:

```
int addem(int a, int b)
{
    return a + b;
}
```

Note that we declared the two variables used in addem( ) (i.e., the local names we give to the two integer arguments passed to the function) in the first line:

→
```
int addem(int a, int b)
{
    return a + b;
}
```

This is the third place that you're allowed to declare variables in C (the other two are inside and outside functions). We could have done it this way:

→
```
int addem(a, b)
    int a, b;
```

```
    {
        return a + b;
    }
```

However, this way we run the risk of confusing the variables passed as parameters with the variables internal to the function. The modern C and C++ style is the first way, declaring the variables in the first line. Of course, if the function itself had internal variables in addition to parameters, we could declare them like this:

```
int addem(int a, int b)
{
    int c, d;

    c = a;
    d = b;
    return c + d;
}
```

In this way, we keep the parameters and the internal variables from getting confused. While we're on the subject of parameters, there's one more topic we should review before finishing with functions, and that's how parameters get passed to functions in C (this will be important later in the book).

How C Passes Parameters to Functions

There are two different ways of passing parameters to a function — by value and by reference. When you pass a parameter by value, you pass the value of the parameter; when you pass by reference, you pass the parameter's address. C and C++ pass by value (except for arrays: In that case, it passes the address of the first element of the array). For example, let's take a look at addem( ) again:

```
#include <stdio.h>

/* A function example with parameters. */

int addem(int a, int b);

main()
{
    int integer1 = 1, integer2 = 2;
```

```
        printf("Adding the two gives %d.", addem(integer1, integer2));

        return 0;
}

int addem(int a, int b)
{
        return a + b;
}
```

When we pass integer1 and integer2 to addem( ), we actually pass their values, 1 and 2. That's fine, because that's all addem( ) needs to add them, 1 + 2 = 3, and it can return that value. On the other hand, there's no way that addem( ) can actually affect the values stored in the variables integer1 and integer2 directly, because all it has is a copy of those values.

There's no problem here, but if we want to use a function like scanf( ) to read characters for us, it has to be able to place the values of the characters it reads into the correct variables, which means that we have to pass more than a copy of the current value of the variable to scanf( ). This is when passing by reference (which is the default in a language like FORTRAN) comes in handy; for example, if we pass the address of a variable named our_char to scanf( ), scanf( ) can place the ASCII code it read directly into the variable our_char.

Of course, that's what we're doing when we use & in front of our_char before passing it to scanf( ), because & returns our_char's address. As you know, the address of a variable is a pointer. With that pointer, scanf( ) knows where our_char is in memory, so it can change its value. Using pointers like that is very important in both C and C++, and we'll review that process soon. Next, however, let's look at data storage in arrays and data structures (in particular, this review of data structures will be useful when we create our own objects in C++).

Using Arrays

Let's say that we have to keep track of the test scores of five students; in that case, we could set up an array to hold their scores like this:

```
#include <stdio.h>

/* Record test scores. */
```

```
   main()
   {
→      int scores[5];
          :
   }
```

This statement informs C that we wish to set up an array named scores[ ] that will hold five integers; we say that this an array of type integer. Now we can place the student's scores into that array like this:

```
   #include <stdio.h>

   /* Record test scores. */

   main()
   {
       int scores[5];

→      scores[0] = 92;
:      scores[1] = 73;
       scores[2] = 57;
       scores[3] = 98;
       scores[4] = 89;
          :

          :

   }
```

In other words, we treat the array named scores[ ] as though it were simply a variable with an index. That index can range from 0 to 4, which covers all the five integers that we wish to store in the array. That's how we handle a data set in C — by giving the set one name (the array scores) and an index, which can range over the individual members of the set.

Of course, this is very convenient, because now we can refer to each member of the set with one index whose value we can readily change; this allows us to perform a parallel operation on all members of the set. For example, we could print out all the scores with a for loop like this:

```
   #include <stdio.h>

   /* Record test scores. */

   main()
   {
```

```
        int loop_index, scores[5];

        scores[0] = 92;
        scores[1] = 73;
        scores[2] = 57;
        scores[3] = 98;
        scores[4] = 89;

→       for (loop_index = 0; loop_index < 5; loop_index++)
            printf("Student's score: %d\n", scores[loop_index]);

        return 0;
    }
```

Being able to reach each member of the set with a numeric index like this makes arrays an extraordinarily powerful construction, because the program itself can manipulate that index. We just have to set up the operation we want performed on one member of the set and then let the index vary over all members.

This is pretty good as far as it goes, but it would be a lucky bunch of students that only had one test a term. If we gave them, say, three tests over the duration of the course, we could keep track of their scores in a two-dimensional array like this:

Test Number ↓	Student Number →					
	0	1	2	3	4	
0	92	73	57	98	89	← Row 0: Test 0 Scores
1	88	76	23	95	72	← Row 1: Test 1 Scores
2	94	82	63	99	94	← Row 2: Test 2 Scores

In the program, that might look like this (note the array initialization):

```
#include <stdio.h>

/* Record three tests. */

main()
```

```
    {
       int i, sum, scores[3][5] = {
             { 92 , 73 , 57 , 98 , 89 },
             { 88 , 76 , 23 , 95 , 72 },
             { 94 , 82 , 63 , 99 , 94 }
       };

                :
                :
```

Now, if we like, we can print out the average test score for each test:

```
#include <stdio.h>

/* Record three tests. */

main()
{
    int i, j, sum, scores[3][5] = {
          { 92 , 73 , 57 , 98 , 89 },
          { 88 , 76 , 23 , 95 , 72 },
          { 94 , 82 , 63 , 99 , 94 }
    };

    for (i = 0; i < 3; i++){  /* loop over tests. */
        for (j = 0, sum = 0; j < 5; j++) sum = sum + scores[i][j];
        printf("Average for test %d is %f.\n", i, (float) sum / 5);
    }

    return 0;
}
```

And that's it. Of course, we can also add more dimensions to an array in C; arrays like int big_array[3][4][5] are possible, depending on how many indices your data set has.

Character Strings in C

Now let's take a look at this array of type char:

```
char product_1[8] = {'c','u','c','u','m','b','e','r'};
```

This produces the array product_1[ ], filled like this:

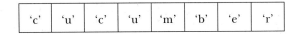

If we wanted to, that means that we could type the word cucumber out with a loop:

```
#include <stdio.h>

/* Print out "cucumber". */

main()
{
    char product_1[8] = {'c','u','c','u','m','b','e','r'};
    int i;

    for (i = 0; i < 8; i++) printf("%c", product_1[i]);

    return 0;
}
```

This program types the word cucumber. In this way, we're able to put individual characters together into a string. String handling in C once again points out the division between the C library functions and the built-in C statements; there is no string type in C (such as ints or floats). Instead, strings are supported only by the library functions. For example, one library function that supports the use of strings is printf( ), which has a format specifier especially for strings — %s. Here are some other ones and what they do:

gets( )	Get a string from the keyboard
strcpy( )	Copy a string
strcat( )	Concatenate two strings
strlen( )	Return the length of a string
strcmp( )	Compare the dictionary order of two strings

The functions that begin with str have their protoypes in string.h (gets( ) is in stdio.h). To use strings, we have to end them with a zero, or null character. In C, that character is expressed with a backslash code like this: '\0'. And, in C, we use double quotes to indicate a string — that is, an array of type char that ends with a null character. In other words, we can initialize our string product_1 like this:

```
#include <stdio.h>

/* Print out "cucumber". */

main()
{
    char product_1[] = "cucumber";
    int i;

    printf("%s", product_1);

    return 0;
}
```

We did not have to indicate the number of characters in the product_1 string (which is now 9 counting the terminating null), because the compiler could count them itself when we initialize that string. Because the C language itself doesn't really have built-in string features, we cannot assign strings using the assignment operator like this:

```
product_1 = "cucumber";      /* NOT LEGAL */
```

TIP Later on, we'll set up our own C++ string type — and take a look at the one Microsoft C++ provides us with, which is named CString — both of which will allow us to use +, =, and other operators directly on strings. In fact, we'll use the CString type (actually, it's a C++ *class*) extensively in the latter part of this book.

On the other hand, most of the normal C capabilities have been duplicated with library functions for strings. To assign one string to another, we can use the string copying function, strcpy( ):

```
strcpy(product_1, "cucumber");
```

We can also concatenate two strings with strcat( ). An example of that might be reading in two strings, concatenating them, and typing the resulting string out. Because that string may be longer than the screen is wide (80 characters), we can test its length with strlen( ) first:

```c
#include <string.h>
#include <stdio.h>

/* Read in a string, assign it, concatenate the two, print it out. */

main()
{
    char read_in_string[80], copy_of_string[80];

    gets(read_in_string);
    strcpy(copy_of_string, read_in_string);
    strcat(copy_of_string, read_in_string);
    if (strlen(copy_of_string) > 80)
        printf("Final string is too long.");
    else
        printf("%s", copy_of_string);

    return 0;
}
```

For example, if we type "test" to this program, it would type back "testtest." In addition, the strcmp( ) function takes the place of the relational operators > and < for strings. It compares the dictionary order of two strings like this: strcmp(string1, string2); if string1 comes before string2 alphabetically, then we say that string1 < string2. The possible returns from strcmp( ) appear in Table 1-6.

Here's a short example program that reads two strings and then types them out in alphabetic order:

```c
#include <string.h>
#include <stdio.h>

/* Read two strings and print them out in dictionary order. */

main()
{
    char string1[80], string2[80];

    gets(string1);
    gets(string2);
    if (strcmp(string1, string2) < 0){
        printf("%s\n", string1);
```

```
        printf("%s\n", string2);
    }
    else{
        printf("%s\n", string2);
        printf("%s\n", string1);
    }

    return 0;
}
```

Of course, we can always construct our strings character by character, treating them as arrays if we wish. For example, you might want to take a look at this program, which converts a positive decimal integer into a hex value and prints it out. Because we strip off the hex digits in reverse order, it's convenient to be able to treat the resulting string like an array and fill it using an index that we can increment or decrement:

```
#include <stdio.h>

main()
{
    unsigned int i = 0, index = 0;
    char out_string[10];

    printf("Type a positive integer please ");
    scanf("%d", &i);

    do{
        out_string[index++] = (i%16 > 9 ? i%16 - 10 + 'a' : i%16 + '0');
    }while(i /= 16);

    printf("That number in hexadecimal is ");
    while(index) printf("%c", out_string[--index]);

    return 0;
}
```

Condition	Return value
string1 < string2	< 0
string1 == string2	0
string1 > string2	> 0

Table 1-6. strcmp( ) Return Values

Notice in particular the line that converts a hex digit into ASCII and places it into the string character by character:

```
out_string[index++] = (i%16 > 9 ? i%16 - 10 + 'a' : i%16 + '0');
```

Here we're using C's conditional operator ?: — if the current hex digit is in the range 0–9, we just want to add the ASCII value '0' to turn it into something we can print. Otherwise, the digit is in the range 0xa–0xf (where the 0x prefix indicates a hex number), and we have to subtract 10 and add 'a' to it.

Using Data Structures in C

It is occasionally useful to associate different types of data together under one name. C provides data structures for just this purpose; data structures let us wrap different data types together under the same name so they can be accessed easily.

TIP   In the next chapter, we'll see that this kind of conglomeration of data can be extended into a conglomeration of data and functions, which is the basis of forming objects in C++.

When we define a data structure, we're setting up a new data type of our own (i.e., to add to the predefined types of char, int, float, double, and void). For example, let's say that we wanted to keep track of the height and weight of some friends. We can set up a structure that looks like this:

```
struct our_record {
    int height;
    int weight;
};
```

After we've defined this structure named our_record, it becomes a new data type; in other words, we've created an entirely new type and we can use it in a program to declare variables like this:

```
#include <stdio.h>

/* Struct example */

main()
```

```
    {
        struct our_record {
            int height;
            int weight;
        };
```

→
```
        struct our_record george, frank;
                :
```

Now we have two variables of type our_record named george and frank. Each has two integers associated with it, height and weight, stored in the order shown above. To reach, say, George's height, we can use the dot operator (formally called the member operator) like this: george.height = 72;. This places a value of 72 (inches) into George's height.

Note that we can declare a number of variables of this structure type in the structure declaration by placing them after the curly braces. For example, we could have declared george and frank like this:

```
#include <stdio.h>

/* Struct example */

main()
{
    struct our_record {
        int height;
        int weight;
```
→
```
    } george, frank;

    george.height = 72;    /* inches */
    george.weight = 180;   /* pounds */

    printf("George is %d inches, %d lbs.", george.height, george.weight);

    return 0;
}
```

We are not limited to using only simple data types as the members of structures. We can use whole arrays inside our structures. One common example is the use of strings; if we wanted to store our friend's names as well as their heights and weights, we could do that by adding a string like this:

```
          struct our_record {
→             char name[20];
              int height;
              int weight;
          } george, frank;
```

TIP Enclosing an array inside a structure is also part of a programmer's trick. When you pass arguments to a function in C, they are passed by value, except for arrays. When you pass an array to a function, it is passed by reference, that is, its beginning address is passed. However, you can pass the whole thing by enclosing it in a structure, because when you pass a structure, the entire structure is passed.

We can also use arrays of structures; this is common when you're formatting records which you want to write to a file. In our case, we can set up an array named friends[ ] made up of ten of these structures this way:

```
          struct our_record {
              char name[20];
              int height;
              int weight;
          } friends[10];          ←
```

We've included space for the person's name, so we can record the data we have on George this way:

```
#include <string.h>
#include <stdio.h>

/* Array of structures example */

main()
{

          struct our_record {
              char name[20];
              int height;
              int weight;
          } friends[10];

→         strcpy(friends[0].name, "George");
→         friends[0].height = 72;    /* inches */
→         friends[0].weight = 180;   /* pounds */
```

```
    printf("%s is %d inches tall, weighs %d lbs.\n", friends[0].name, \
        friends[0].height, friends[0].weight);

    return 0;
}
```

This is very convenient because now the program can let the array index vary over all the records we have. For example, if we had recorded five friends, we could print their data out like this with a for loop:

```
for (i=0; i < 5; i++)
    printf("%s is %d inches tall, weighs %d lbs.\n", friends[i].name, \
        friends[i].height, friends[i].weight);
```

In this way, we have collected different types of data under the same name:

```
friends[i].name
friends[i].height
friends[i].weight
```

In fact, we've done even more than that: We've made an array of these collections, which lets us refer to them by index. That's it for our review of data structures (also called user-defined types). Now let's review a topic that is very important in C (and one that we've already come across): pointers.

Using Pointers

Pointers are one of the most central topics in C, and making sure we have a good foundation here will be very important for us later on in this book. (In particular, we'll see that they form the basis of what is called run-time polymorphism in C++.) So, what is a pointer?

Pointers Are Just Addresses

The answer to that question is very simple: Pointers are just addresses. Every item of data that we store in a program is stored at a particular address in memory. For example, in a program like the following one, our_int is the label given to a location in memory at which the program stores an integer:

```
#include <stdio.h>

/* Example of integer storage. */

main()
```

```
     {
→        int our_int;

         our_int = 1;

         printf("The value of our_int is: %d", our_int);

         return 0;
     }
```

That integer is two bytes long, so if the address it is stored at in memory is, say, 3985, both bytes 3985 and 3986 are set aside to hold our_int. On the other hand, if we were storing a floating point variable, our_float, we would need four bytes.

Declaring a pointer is just the same as declaring any other variable, except that we use the pointer operator, * (also called the indirection operator). For instance, if we wanted to declare a pointer named our_pointer in our program, we could do it like this:

```
#include <stdio.h>

/* Example of integer storage. */

main()
{
→        int our_int, *our_pointer;

         our_int = 1;

         printf("The value of our_int is: %d", our_int);

         return 0;
}
```

In this case, our_pointer is a pointer to a variable of type int. In other words, int is the pointer's base type. As you know, this base type is very important; for example, you can't mix a pointer to an int with a pointer to a float.

TIP   It's possible to declare our_pointer in two ways: int* our_pointer and int *our_pointer. Many programmers use the second method these days to avoid confusion when they declare more than one pointer — int *p1, *p1 declares two pointers to type int, but int* p1, p2 declares only one such pointer; p1. The second variable, p2, is an int.

As it stands, our_pointer doesn't point to anything yet: We have to use another operator to load it with an address. For that, we use the address operator, &. We can use it like this in our program:

```
#include <stdio.h>

/* Example of integer storage. */

main()
{
    int our_int, *our_pointer;

    our_int = 1;
    our_pointer = &our_int;

    printf("The value of our_int is: %d", our_int);

    return 0;
}
```

The statement our_pointer = &our_int; may be read as "our_pointer gets the address of our_int." Now our_pointer points to our_int. Using our_pointer, we can reach our_int with the * operator. Here's how we might print out the value in our_int, using its address as stored in our_pointer:

```
#include <stdio.h>

/* Example of pointer usage. */

main()
{
    int our_int, *our_pointer;

    our_int = 1;
    our_pointer = &our_int;

    printf("The value of our_int is: %d", *our_pointer);

    return 0;
}
```

If you keep in mind that * can be read as "the value at address," then *our_pointer simply means "the value at address our_pointer." We're asking printf( ) to print out the value at address our_pointer, which is our_int. This program produces this result:

```
The value of our_int is: 1
```

It is often helpful to think of pointers simply as variables that are used to hold addresses. For example, we can assign pointers to each other, as we can with variables:

```
#include <stdio.h>

/* Example of pointer usage. */

main()
{
    int our_int, *our_pointer, *our_other_pointer;

    our_int = 1;
    our_pointer = &our_int;
    our_other_pointer = our_pointer;

    printf("The value of our_int is: %d", *our_other_pointer);

    return 0;
}
```

We can even perform addition and subtraction on pointers, as you might expect on variables that hold addresses. For example, what if we had a pointer to the beginning of an integer array and then incremented it? C takes care of this automatically, because it knows the base type of the pointer. If we were to add 1 to our_pointer, C would realize that our_pointer is a pointer to an int, and integers are two bytes long, so it really adds 2 to our_pointer. In the same way, if our_pointer pointed to a float type (four bytes long) an operation like our_pointer = our_pointer + 1 actually adds 4 to our_pointer. In this case, we end up pointing to the next float in memory. We can also use expressions like our_pointer++.

Also, if you're in doubt about the size of a data item (structures included) you can use the C operator sizeof( ). For example, sizeof(our_int) would return a value of 2. On a floating point number, sizeof( ) returns 4. (Note that sizeof( ) is a C operator, not a library function.)

Pointers to Structures

While we're reviewing pointers, we should also note that a special operator is included in C for use with pointers to structures, and it looks like this: -> (called the arrow operator by C programmers). If we set up a structure named our_data that looked like this:

```
struct large_data_struct{
    int key;
    int big_array[20];
} our_data;
```

Then we could declare a pointer named our_pointer to our_data like this:

```
struct large_data_struct *our_pointer;
```

And assign a value to it this way:

```
our_pointer = &our_data;
```

From now on, we can refer to the fields in our_data, like our_data.key, like this:

```
our_pointer->key = 5;   /* same as our_data.key */
```

In other words, our_pointer is a pointer to a structure; to reach a field in the structure it points to, we use the arrow operator, ->. That's the reason the -> operator was developed, to let you pick the individual fields out of the structure you're pointing to. It was added to the * and & operators expressly for those cases when you point to a structure, because & or * alone can't access elements. That is, there is no such thing as *our_pointer.key; we have to use our_pointer->key instead. The arrow operator will prove very useful later in this book, because it also works with pointers to C++ objects.

That's it for our review of pointers. We'll make a quick exploration of file handling and streams next, and then our C review will be complete.

Using Streams and Files in C

C places a great emphasis on portability — on code that can be transferred between different types of computers without many changes. This is one of C's selling points over a language like assembly language: C is portable between different computers to a large extent, and assembly language is definitely not (since it is the native language of the central processor itself).

However, the actual details of different computers can differ enormously — how to work with monitors, keyboards, disk files, printers, or tape drives — and that makes it difficult for a language that seeks to be completely portable.

Stream	Is Connected To
stdout	The screen
stdin	The keyboard
stprn	The printer
stdaux	The screen
stderr	The screen

Table 1-7. Standard Streams and Their Physical Connections

For that reason, C's input/output (I/O) system disconnects us from many of the details of the actual devices.

Theoretically, C's I/O functions work on streams of data. Streams may then be connected to actual devices, which C calls files (in this sense, a C file really stands for a physical device). A stream is a sequence of data, and there are two kinds of streams: text streams, which are streams of ASCII characters; and binary streams, which are streams of raw bytes. Most of the C I/O functions are intended to operate on streams, and streams are flexible because they can be assigned to different devices. As you know, some of these connections are already made for us; when we start our program, five standard streams are set up and connected to various physical devices already. These streams are listed in Table 1-7.

C's I/O functions are designed to work on streams such as those. For example, printf( ) is actually the short form of fprintf( ); fprintf( ) is designed to work with any stream, and printf( ) is dedicated to working with the stdout — that is, the screen — stream (because printing on the screen is so common). As an example, the following program uses fprintf( ) in the same way we'd use printf( ): to print on the screen. To use fprintf( ), we simply specify the stdout stream, which is already connected to the screen:

```
#include <stdio.h>

main()
{
    fprintf(stdout, "Hello, world.\n");

    return 0;
}
```

When we work with a disk file in C, we associate a stream with it by opening that file. Then we'll be able to "print" to that file with fprintf( ), which allows us to choose what stream we want to print to (as opposed to printf( ), which does not). Let's try a small program as an example. This program writes our "Hello, world.\n" string to a disk file named hello.txt:

```c
#include <stdio.h>

main()
{
    FILE *file_pointer;

    if((file_pointer = fopen("hello.txt", "w")) != NULL){
        fprintf(file_pointer, "Hello, world.\n");
        fclose(file_pointer);
    }
    else printf("Error writing hello.txt\n");

    return 0;
}
```

When you run the program, you'll find a 15-byte file named hello.txt on the disk, and typing it reveals our message. Here's the way it works: First we include the I/O function header stdio.h. Next, we associate a stream with a physical file by opening that file for writing with the function fopen( ):

```c
#include <stdio.h>

main()
{
    FILE *file_pointer;

→   if((file_pointer = fopen("hello.txt", "w")) != NULL){
        fprintf(file_pointer,"Hello, world.\n");
        fclose(file_pointer);
    }
    else printf("Error writing hello.txt\n");

    return 0;
}
```

The fopen( ) function does the work of associating a stream with the actual disk file hello.txt. Here we specify both the name of the file ("hello.txt") and the fact that we intend to write to it (by including the character string "w").

File-Opening Option	Means
"r"	Open (existing) file for reading.
"w"	Open (create if necessary) file for writing
"a"	Open (create if necessary) file for appending
"r+"	Open (existing) file for reading and writing
"w+"	Create and open file for reading and writing
"a+"	Open (create if necessary) file for reading and appending
"rb"	Open a binary file for reading
"wb"	Open a binary file for writing
"ab"	Open a binary file for appending
"rt"	Open a text file for reading
"wt"	Create a text file for writing
"at"	Open a text file for appending
"r+b"	Open a binary file for reading and writing
"w+b"	Create a binary file for writing
"a+b"	Open a binary file for appending
"r+t"	Open a text file for reading and writing
"w+t"	Create a text file for reading and writing
"a+t"	Open a text file for reading and writing

Table 1-8. File-Opening Options

There are many file-opening options with the fopen( ) function in C, and you will find them in Table 1-8.

The fopen( ) function returns a pointer to a structure of type FILE, which we name file_pointer. In other words, the name of our stream is file_pointer, and it is connected to the disk file hello.txt. If the file could not be opened, a NULL pointer is returned. NULL is a predefined constant in C (its value is 0), and we can check for it. In that case, the program should terminate and print an error message. We might also note the typical economy of C here — we can both assign the file pointer to file_pointer and check its value in the same statement:

```
if((file_pointer = fopen("hello.txt", "w")) != NULL){
```

If you had wanted to specify a pathname for the file, for example, c:\hello.txt, note that we should make the string in the fopen( ) call "c:\\hello.txt", since a single backslash would be interpreted as part of an escape sequence otherwise.

If the file was opened successfully, we want to write the data string to it. Since we are familiar with printf( ), let's use its analog, fprintf( ). We have to include a format string, as usual, as well as the stream to write to. To indicate the stream, we pass fprintf( ) the file pointer for the file we want to use, file_pointer:

```
#include <stdio.h>

main()
{
    FILE *file_pointer;

    if((file_pointer = fopen("hello.txt", "w")) != NULL){
        fprintf(file_pointer, "Hello, world.\n");
        fclose(file_pointer);
    }
    else printf("Error writing hello.txt\n");

    return 0;
}
```

The fprintf( ) function does the work for us; following it, we close the file (so that DOS may update the file's directory information). To close a file, all you need to do is to pass the file pointer to the fclose( ) function, and that function disconnects the stream we've opened from the actual disk file. That finishes our review of file and stream handling, and with it, our review of C.

Now we're up to speed; our review of C is complete. It's time to start working in C++, and we'll begin doing that in Chapter 2. Note that if you had trouble with the contents of this chapter, the best thing is to work through an introductory C text before continuing. Otherwise, let's get going with our first C++ programs right now.

Welcome to C++:
Classes and Objects

In this chapter, we'll start to see just what makes C++ an improvement over C. We'll see some unique, and very popular, features of C++ first, and then we'll turn to what has made it famous: the ability to work with objects.

The driving force behind objects is *modularity*, a concept that we've already stressed. As mentioned earlier, C++ was originally written to be used when C programs got very long (although there are so many flexible features in it that thousands of programmers prefer it over C for all uses). In programs that long, it's often hard to remember all the details about all the parts; it's much easier if we can connect associated functions and the data they need into a conceptual object, which we can then think of as a single entity. That way, we'll be able to think of the whole object in terms of its overall use, without having to remember all the details of its internal data handling. In fact, an object is very like a new kind of structure, except that it can hold both data and functions.

For instance, one example of an object we'll develop in this chapter is a stack. A stack is a specially dedicated area of memory used for storing data in a particular way; you push values on the stack, and pop them later to retrieve them. When you pop them, they come off in reverse order — if you pushed the values 1, 2, 3, 4, and 5, then popping values off the stack successively would yield 5, 4, 3, 2, and 1.

To make your own stack, you'd need both the memory space used for storage as well as the functions that do the pushing and the popping. The stack may even have some internal functions that monitor the stack. All these details can be distracting if you've got a lot of other things on your mind, and it's easier if you can wrap (the C++ term is encapsulate) them all into one logical idea — a stack.

After we get the ground work done on our first objects, we'll start going into the details of initializing the data in them with C++ *constructors* — and why doing so is essential to the use of objects. Then we'll see how to handle arrays of objects, and how one object can *inherit* the properties of another. All of these are extremely important C++ topics, so let's begin at once. We can start by exploring a few familiar C topics that C++ handles just a little bit better.

Character I/O in C++

Let's begin our tour of C++ by seeing how to manage normal character-based I/O such as printing on the screen and reading from the keyboard. Even though we can still use printf( ) or scanf( ) (because Microsoft C++ includes all of standard Microsoft C), there are even easier, more natural methods available to us now. And, because they are easier to use, C++ programs are often distinctive for their use of them, even when objects are not involved.

The C++ Predefined I/O Streams

We already know about the standard C streams: stdin, stdout, stderr, and stdlog. In C++, there are some additional predefined streams named cin, cout, cerr, and clog; they are tied to the same devices, but we use them in a different way. Let's see an example, showing how to print on the screen using cout. Here's how to print "Hello, world.\n" on the screen using the typical C++ method of sending output to cout:

```
#include <iostream.h>

/* Hello, World. */

main()
{
    cout << "Hello, world.\n";    // Put "Hello, world.\n" on screen.

    return 0;
}
```

We should notice a number of things here. First, to use the predefined C++ streams (which we'll do often), we had to include the header file iostream.h:

```
→  #include <iostream.h>

   /* Hello, World. */

   main()
   {
       cout << "Hello, world.\n";    // Put "Hello, world.\n" on screen.

       return 0;
   }
```

Next, we sent our string to the screen with the << operator:

```
   #include <iostream.h>

   /* Hello, World. */

   main()
   {
→      cout << "Hello, world.\n";    // Put "Hello, world.\n" on screen.

       return 0;
   }
```

In normal C, this is a left shift operator, and it works on integer values by shifting their bits left by a specified number of places. For example, if we had an integer value stored in a variable named data_bits whose binary representation was 0101010101010101 (i.e., 16 bits), then this statement:

```
   data_bits << 1;
```

would leave a value of 1010101010101010 in data_bits: every bit has been shifted left one place. Similarly, the right shift operator, >>, shifts bits right. However, in C++, << and >> do *more* than just shift the bits of operands.

The << and >> operators still function as the left and right shift operators, but in C++, operators can have more than one meaning. In this case, << may also be used to send output to cout, and for that reason it's called the insertor operator (i.e., it inserts data into the cout stream); and >> may also be used to read input from cin, so it's called the extractor. This is called *operator overloading,* and it's an important part of C++.

Say for example that you define some complex data structure, and that you want to be able to define the operation of addition on such structures. In C++, you can overload the + operator to handle it without problem. In fact, almost any of the usual C operators (except for some special ones like ?: or the dot operator, .) can be overloaded in C++, and we'll see how to do that ourselves in Chapter 3. The << operator is already overloaded for us, and in C++ it's used to send character-based output to cout. In fact, we'll use it in the rest of this book to replace the DOS C function printf( ) (Windows will have it's own method of displaying text), as most C++ programmers do, because we don't have to cobble together format strings.

TIP One reason that << is actually a better choice than printf( ) is that printf( ) does not perform reliable type checking on the data being sent to the screen. For example, if you want to print a number but use the "%s" format specifier by mistake, printf( ) will try to interpet the number as a pointer to a string. On the other hand, when you use the << operator, C++ itself checks the type of data you want to print and makes sure that it's handled correctly, as we'll see soon.

In addition, you might notice a new method of using comments in our program. We were able to put a one-line comment into our program (e.g., "// Put Hello, world.\n on screen") by prefacing it with the // symbol. This is a new addition in C++, and it only works for one-line comments; that is, C++ ignores the rest of the line following //. The older /* */ method is still available, of course, but C++ programmers often use the // one-line comments, reserving the /* */ method for multi-line ones.

Getting Our Program to Run

Now that we've got a working C++ program, the next step is getting it to run. There are two options available in Microsoft C++: using the command line compiler or using the Programmer's WorkBench environment. To use the command line compiler, type the above program into a file named hello.cpp. The .cpp extension indicates that this is a C++ file, not just a C file (and the compiler will treat it as such). Next, compile and link the file with the cl command, like this:

```
C:\C700\BIN>cl hello.cpp
```

Microsoft C++ prints this out while generating
hello.exe:

```
C:\C700\BIN>cl hello.cpp

Microsoft (R) C/C++ Optimizing Compiler Version 7.00
Copyright (c) Microsoft Corp 1984-1992. All rights reserved.

hello.cpp

Microsoft (R) Segmented Executable Linker  Version 5.30
Copyright (C) Microsoft Corp 1984-1992.  All rights reserved.

Object Modules [.obj]: hello.obj
Run File [hello.exe]: "hello.exe" /noi
List File [nul.map]: NUL
Libraries [.lib]:
Definitions File [nul.def]: ;
```

TIP   It can take some time even to compile and link small files with Microsoft
C++ because the compiler actually has to compile any included header files
as well (in this case, that's iostream.h). For extra speed, you can create pre-
compiled header files with the /Yc compiler option and use them later with
the /Yu option. Alternatively, you can use the /f (fast compile) switch,
which turns off optimization.

Now we're ready to roll; just type hello to run hello.exe, and you'll get this
result:

```
C:\C700\BIN>hello
Hello, world.
```

That's it; we've gotten our first C++ program to run.

To use the Programmer's WorkBench (PWB), you have two options: You can
type the program above into a file using your own word processor, or you can
use the editor built into PWB. The PWB environment looks like this:

```
┌─────────────────────────────────────────────────────────────────┐
│  File  Edit  Search  Project  Run  Options  Browse  Window  Help │
│ ─────────────────────────────────────────────────────────────── │
│                                                                  │
│                                                                  │
│                                                                  │
│                                                                  │
│                                                                  │
│                                                                  │
│                                                                  │
│                                                                  │
│                                                                  │
│                                                                  │
│                                                                  │
│                                                                  │
│                                                                  │
│                                                      00001.001    │
│ ──────────────────────────────────────────────────────────────  │
│ <F1=Help> <Alt=Menu> <F6=Window>                                 │
└─────────────────────────────────────────────────────────────────┘
```

TIP The numbers at the bottom of the PWB display indicate the current location of the cursor by row (r) and column (c) like this: rrrrr.ccc. This is especially useful after you've tried to create an .exe file and gotten errors; the compiler will indicate what rows of code it found errors in. Using the rrrrr.ccc display in PWB, you can page to that location, or you can use PWB's Search/Goto Mark menu item. When PWB asks what "mark" it should go to in the file, simply type the row number followed by <Enter>.

To enter hello.cpp, you can use PWB's editing capabilities. Start by selecting the New option in PWB's File menu to create a new file. A window will open, and you can enter the text of hello.cpp there. Next, save that file as hello.cpp with the File menu's Save As... item. The screen should look like this:

```
 File   Edit   Search   Project   Run   Options   Browse   Window   Help
──[  2]──────────────── hello.cpp ─────────────

    #include <iostream.h>

    /* Hello, World. */

    main()
    {
        cout << "Hello, world.\n";  // Put "Hello, world.\n" on

        return 0;
    }




                                                    00001.001

 <F1=Help> <Alt=Menu> <F6=Window>
```

Programmer's WorkBench is a platform for program development. It is designed to launch programming tools; the only one it contains itself is an editor. That is, it will have to invoke Microsoft C++ (i.e., using the cl command) to compile and link the file. To allow it to do that, we have to indicate that the file we've just entered (or loaded with the File menu's Open File... item if you've typed in hello.cpp with your own editor) is a C++ file, and that we want to create a DOS .exe file.

To do that, select the Option/Project Templates item. A cascaded menu will open; select the Set Project Template... item in it. The Set Project Template window opens like this:

```
 File  Edit  Search  Project  Run  Options  Browse  Window  Help
─ [  2] ───────────────── hello.cpp ─────────
                          ─ Set Project Template ─────────
          Runtime Support:

            None
            C
            C++


  Project Templates with Runtime Support for: C++

      Generic Options
      DOS EXE
      DOS Overlaid EXE
      DOS p code EXE
      DOS COM


  Current Runtime Support:    C++
  Current Project Template:   DOS EXE


                         <  OK  >  <Cancel>  < Help >
                                              00001.001
```

Here we can specify the type of code and target .exe file we want. Select C++ Runtime Support and DOS EXE as the project template, then select the < OK > item. Now PWB knows that we want a DOS .exe file from our C++ code. Select the Execute item in the Run menu, and PWB will invoke the cl command line compiler, producing hello.exe. After it compiles and links, running the file will produce the same result as before:

```
Hello, world.
```

Again, that's all there was to it; we've gotten our first C++ program to run.

Displaying More than One Data Item

That first program is pretty simple; we just send the string "Hello, world.\n" to the screen. In fact, using <<, we can stack up as many data items to send to the screen as we want, like this:

```
#include <iostream.h>

/* Hello, World. */

main()
{
    cout << "Hello, " << "world." << "\n";

    return 0;
}
```

In this case, we send "Hello, ", followed by "world.", followed by "\n." We can print numbers too, without even having to use a formatting string. As we'll see, C++ can recognize the type of data it is working on, and it can take the appropriate action. For example, look at this program:

```
#include <iostream.h>

/* Print out numbers using cout */

main()
{
    int our_int = 5;
    float our_float = 5.333;

    cout << "The value of our_int is: " << our_int << "\n";
    cout << "The value of our_float is: " << our_float << "\n";

    return 0;
}
```

When we run it, we see this on the screen:

```
The value of our_int is: 5
The value of our_float is: 5.333
```

In other words, C++ handled the rudimentary formatting of these values for us, even though we sent different types of data — i.e., an int and a float — to cout. In this way, C++ will take care of most of the details of screen output for us.

TIP   There are special formatting words that we can send to the predefined I/O streams that will do formatting for us, giving us a good deal of control. These words are called *manipulators*. For example, cout << hex sets the output format of numbers to hexadecimal, and cout << dec sets it to decimal. You can also set the width of a particular numerical field on the screen with setw( ). For example, cout << setw(5) sets the field width to 5. We'll cover all these manipulators in Chapter 5, where we unravel cout and cin in depth.

We've gotten a pretty good handle on sending output to the screen in C++; let's turn now to reading input from the keyboard. In fact, that is as easy as using cout — all we have to do is to use >> and cin.

Using Keyboard Input in C++

Let's develop an example that reads an integer from the keyboard using cin. We start by printing a prompt:

```
#include <iostream.h>

/* Read and print out a number */

main()
{
    cout << "Please type an integer: ";
        :
```

Then we use cin in a manner you might expect, like this:

```
#include <iostream.h>

/* Read and print out a number */

main()
{
    int our_int;

    cout << "Please type an integer: ";
    cin >> our_int;
        :
```

Here we just use the >> operator to read from the keyboard. (Note that even though we are assigning a value to our_int, it appears on the right hand side of the statement.) Finally, we display the result:

```cpp
#include <iostream.h>

/* Read and print out a number */

main()
{
    int our_int;

    cout << "Please type an integer: ";      // prompt
    cin >> our_int;                           // get input
    cout << "The value of that integer is: " << our_int;

    return 0;
}
```

→

Let's call this program int.cpp. When we run it, we see this:

```
Please type an integer:
```

We can type a number, and the program will type it back to us like this:

```
Please type an integer: -5
The value of that integer is: -5
```

That's fine, but less than interesting; we already know what number we've typed without having the program typing it out for us. Let's do a little bit of data manipulation here. In the last chapter, we saw this program briefly, which converts a number from decimal to hex:

```cpp
#include <conio.h>
#include <stdio.h>

main()
{
    unsigned int i = 0, index = 0;
    char out_string[10];

    printf("Type a positive integer please ");
    scanf("%d", &i);

    do{
```

```
        out_string[index++] = (i%16 > 9 ? i%16 - 10 + 'a' : i%16 + '0');
    } while(i /= 16);

    printf("That number in hexadecimal is ");
    while(index) printf("%c", out_string[--index]);

    return 0;
}
```

We can do the same using insertors and extractors like this:

```
#include <iostream.h>

main()
{
    unsigned int i = 0, index = 0;
    char out_string[10];

    cout << "Type a positive integer please ";      // Prompt
    cin >> i;                                        // Numeric input

    do{                          // Convert to hex
        out_string[index++] = (i%16 > 9 ? i%16 - 10 + 'a' : i%16 + '0');
    } while(i /= 16);

    cout << "That number in hexadecimal is ";        // Print it out
    while(index) cout << out_string[--index];

    return 0;
}
```

And that's it; now this program works as before:

```
C:\C700\BIN>hex
Type a positive integer please 16
That number in hexadecimal is 10
```

As with cout and <<, we can handle multiple arguments with cin and >>. **For example, look at this program, where we read two integers and print their values on the screen:**

```
#include <iostream.h>

/* Read and print out two numbers */

main()
```

```
{
    int our_first_int, our_second_int;

    cout << "Please type two integers: ";   // Prompt
    cin >> our_first_int >> our_second_int;   // Get values
    cout << "Those were: " << our_first_int << " and " << our_second_int;

    return 0;
}
```

To run this program, type it into a file named, say, input.cpp; then just create input.exe with the Microsoft command line compiler (i.e., the cl command) or with Progammer's WorkBench and run it. When you do, the screen looks like this:

```
Please type two integers:
```

Since the program wants two integers, we can type 5 and 6, separating them with a space. The program responds this way:

```
Please type two integers: 5 6 ←
Those were: 5 and 6
```

That's it; it was as easy as that to read multiple values from the keyboard — no scanf( ), no format strings. Don't forget that printf( ) and scanf( ) are still available; however, it's usually easier (and safer from a type-checking point of view) to use << and >> instead.

Now we've seen a few functioning C++ programs; even so, the overloaded operators << and >> by themselves do not make C++ radically different — the real difference comes when we define classes and objects and use them. Let's turn to that now, and get to the heart of C++.

Just What Is an Object?

Let's say that we wanted to keep track of the scores of students in various math classes at a college. In this study, let's say that the goal is to compare the average score of several classes to determine the effectiveness of their instructors. To do that, we'd want to associate the test score data with the student's instructor, which means that we might create a data structure like this:

```
struct name_struct {
    char instructor_name[50]
    int scores[40];
} math_class_1;
```

We've also declared a variable of this type, named math_class_1. Now we can reach the name of the instructor like this:

```
strcpy(math_class_1.instructor_name, "Templeton");
```

And we can load individual student's scores like this:

```
math_class_1.scores[5] = 89;
```

When we want to find the average score for math class 1, we could put together a for loop something like this:

```
total = 40;
for (loop_index = 0, sum = 0; loop_index < total; loop_index++){
        sum += math_class_1.scores[loop_index];
}
average = sum / total;
```

Note that to use the structure math_class_1, we have to keep in mind the details about its internal structure. For example, we have to know which student's score we last loaded so that we put the next student's score in the right place:

→   ```
math_class_1.score[5] = 89;
```

In addition, we need to know the total number of students in order to find the average score:

→    ```
total = 40;
for (loop_index = 0, sum = 0; loop_index < total; loop_index++){
        sum += math_class_1.scores[loop_index];
}
average = sum / total;
```

These details can add up in large programs, making the whole thing impenetrable after a while. It would be much better if math_class_1 could handle these details for us. For example, let's suppose that the dot operator could let us address functions as well as data. To store a new student's score, we might have, say, a function named put( ) like this:

```
math_class_1.put(5);
```

This way, the store( ) function can keep track of our position in the array of scores — we don't have to (to read the scores back, we might also have a function named get( )). Similarly, imagine that instead of having to find the average ourselves, we could simply use a function named average( ) that was part of math_class_1 and did the work for us:

```
cout << "Average score =" << math_class_1.average();
```

That's what objects are all about: making sure that the internal details *stay* internal. As you can see, the benefit of connecting put( ) and average( ) to math_class_1 is that they have access to what can then be purely private data: the number of students, and our current location in the array of student's scores. In this way, we can form objects, which are programming entities that we can think of as complete tools or resources. Let's examine the process of creating objects like this next.

C With Classes

The most significant programming improvement of C++ over C is that it can use *classes*. In fact, C++ was originally called C with Classes. Briefly, a class is something like a data structure in C, except that a class can be defined to hold functions as well as data. A class makes up a formal type, just as when you declare the fields of a structure. When you actually declare variables of that type, the variables themselves are the objects. That's how it works in C++; classes are the formal types, objects are the specific variables of that type (this is an important point to remember, and can cause confusion otherwise).

You set up a class just as you might a structure with struct, except that a class definition can also hold function prototypes like this:

```
class our_first_class {
    int private_array[100];
public:
    int public_data;
    void init(void);
    int public_function(int our_param);
};
```

NOTE   All functions in C++ need prototypes.

When you declare variables of this type, those variables will be our objects. In the above case, we're setting up a class named our_first_class. This class includes some data, public_data and private_array[ ], and it also includes two functions, init( ) and public_function( ). If this had been a structure, we could only have included data:

```
struct some_struct {
    int public_data;
    int private_array[100];
};
```

Then we could have declared variables of this structure type, like this:

```
struct some_struct {
    int public_data;
    int private_array[100];
} our_struct;                    ←
```

Or, we could have declared the structure in main( ), like this:

```
struct some_struct {
    int public_data;
    int private_array[100];
};

main()
{
        some_struct our_struct
                :
```
→

Then we could have reached the members of our_struct with the dot operator, like this:

```
struct some_struct {
    int public_data;
    int private_array[100];
};

main()
{
        some_struct our_struct
```

```
→        our_struct.public_data = 5;
              :
```

It works the same way with classes. When we declare a variable of class our_first_class, it is an object, like our_object here:

```
class our_first_class {
    int private_array[100];
public:
    int public_data;
    void init(void);
    int public_function(int our_param);
} our_object;                            ←
```

Alternatively, we could declare our_object in main( ), like this:

```
class our_first_class {
    int private_array[100];
public:
    int public_data;
    void init(void);
    int public_function(int our_param);
};

main()
{
→    our_first_class our_object;
          :
```

Now we can reach the member data of our_object like this, just as we could with our_struct:

```
class our_first_class {
    int private_array[100];
public:
    int public_data;
    void init(void);
    int public_function(int our_param);
};

main()
{
    our_first_class our_object;
```

→
```
        our_object.public_data = 5;
            :
```

However, now we can also refer to functions — called *member functions* — the same way:

```
    class our_first_class {
        int private_array[100];
    public:
        int public_data;
        void init(void);
        int public_function(int our_param);
    };

    main()
    {
        our_first_class our_object;

        our_object.public_data = 5;
```
→
```
        our_object.public_function(5);
            :
```

This is something new; we've associated not only data with our_object, but also functions. And we did that simply by including their prototypes in the declaration of our_first_class:

```
    class our_first_class {
        int private_array[100];
    public:
        int public_data;
```
→
```
        void init(void);
```
→
```
        int public_function(int our_param);
    };
```

You may notice the keyword public in our class declaration. There are two ways of including member data and functions in a class — as *private* or as *public*. By default, all members of a class are private, which is why we don't include that keyword.

If something is private, that means that no part of the program can refer to it outside its object. In our_first_class, private_array[ ] is private, so it cannot be reached by any part of the program except by those functions associated with the objects of that class (i.e., the member functions). Functions can be private as well as data, and it is good to remember the spirit of C++ here — in most cases, as much of the object should be made private as possible to increase the modularity of programs. This is an important part of the C++ style, and it's the reason all member data and functions are private by default (that's the whole idea behind encapsulation).

However, if everything in an object was private, no part of it could be reached from the outside, making it useless. Here, we've declared the int variable public_data public, as well as the functions init( ) and public_function( ). That means that we can reach them from other places in the program like this:

```
our_object.public_data = 5;    // Set public_data
our_object.init();      // Initialize internal our_object routines
our_object.public_function(3);    // Use public_function()
```

In particular, you might notice that we have included an initialization function named our_object.init( ). The data in objects often needs some kind of initialization performed — we'll initialize our stack's internal data pointer soon — and we'll get into more depth on this topic in a few pages. That's the kind of function you need to declare public — those that must be reached from the rest of the program in order to make the object function properly. The functions that should be left private are those that are purely internal to the object, and they're usually used only by other member functions.

Now that we've got an overall idea of what objects are about, let's take the time to work through a specific example and get all the details down.

An Object Example

Let's say that we wanted to write a program to keep track of the number of times the user types a certain character; for example, we might decide to count the number of times the user types 'x'. Before we reached this chapter, we might have set up a structure like this to hold both the character we're watching and the number of times it was typed:

```
struct counter_struct {          // Declare counter_class struct
    char char_to_count;          // Char to watch for
    int number_of_char_seen;     // Number of times char seen
} counter;
```

That is, we've set up a structure named counter; the two fields of counter hold the character to watch for and the number of times we've seen it so far, and we can refer to them in our program like this:

```
counter.char_to_count          // Char to watch for
counter.number_of_char_seen    // Number of times char seen
```

We might also use two functions that manipulate the data in these fields. For example, to initialize the data, we might have a function named init( ), which we can call with the character we've decided to look for:

```
main()
{

    init('x');                       // Initialize counter
        :
```

NOTE   In C++, you cannot initialize a data member when declaring the class, so it's usually done this way or with *constructors*, as we'll see later.

Here we're indicating that the character we're interested in is 'x'. This function would load our data fields like this:

```
void init(char the_char)     // Declare initialization function
{
    counter.char_to_count = the_char;
    counter.number_of_char_seen = 0;
}
```

Next, we could also define a function named add_one( ) that increments counter.number_of_char_seen every time we see the correct character typed:

```
void add_one(void)           // Declare counter-incrementer
{
    counter.number_of_char_seen++;
}
```

In other words, counter has these data fields:

```
counter.char_to_count
counter.number_of_char_seen
```

as well as these associated functions:

```
init()                        // Initialize counter fields
add_one()                     // Increment count
```

If we were keeping track of x's, that might look like this in the program (using add_one( ) every time we saw the character typed):

```
main()
{
    char in_char;

    init('x');                            // Initialize counter

    cout << "Type a few x's and q to quit: ";

    do{                              // Read x's.
        cin >> in_char;
        if(in_char == counter.char_to_count) add_one();
    } while (toupper(in_char) != 'Q');
        :
```

Then, to print the number of x's, we could simply check the value in counter.number_of_char_seen:

```
main()
{
    char in_char;

    init('x');                        // Initialize counter

    cout << "Type a few x's and q to quit: ";

    do{                          // Read x's.
        cin >> in_char;
        if(in_char == counter.char_to_count) add_one();
    } while (toupper(in_char) != 'Q');

    cout << "\nNumber of " << counter.char_to_count << "'s: " << \
        counter.number_of_char_seen;
            :
```

And that's it; the whole program appears in Listing 2-1. In this program, then, we've set up a structure with two fields, as well as setting up two functions to take care of that data:

```
      counter.char_to_count            // Char to watch for
      counter.number_of_char_seen      // Number of times char seen
      init()                           // Initialize counter fields
      add_one()                        // Increment count
```

Listing 2-1. Counter Program with Struct

```
#include <ctype.h>
#include <iostream.h>

/* Counter implemented as a structure */

void init(char the_char);     // Declare initialization function
void add_one(void);           // Declare counter-incrementer

struct counter_struct {       // Declare counter_class struct
    char char_to_count;       // Char to watch for
    int number_of_char_seen;  // Number of times char seen
} counter;

main()
{
    char in_char;
    init('x');                    // Initialize counter

    cout << "Type a few x's and q to quit: ";
    do{                           // Read x's.
        cin >> in_char;
        if(in_char == counter.char_to_count) add_one();
    } while (toupper(in_char) != 'Q');

    cout << "\nNumber of " << counter.char_to_count << "'s: " << \
        counter.number_of_char_seen;

    return 0;
}

void init(char the_char)      // Declare initialization function
{
    counter.char_to_count = the_char;
    counter.number_of_char_seen = 0;
}

void add_one(void)                    // Declare counter-incrementer
```

Listing 2-1. *(continued)*

```
{
    counter.number_of_char_seen++;
}
```

This is frequently the case in programming — we have some specialized data and some specialized functions that work on that data. We've been able to connect the data together into a structure, but the two functions are still separate. And this is exactly the time to take the next step into C++. We can wrap the two functions together with the data and form an object:

```
      counter.char_to_count            // Char to watch for
      counter.number_of_char_seen      // Number of times char seen
→     counter.init()                   // Initialize counter fields
→     counter.add_one()                // Increment count
```

This way, we'll be able to associate the functions that use some data with that data, wrapping it all into a neat package. Even further, if we had some functions that were used only by init( ) and add_one( ), they would become private to the object, disappearing from the program at large altogether (the great utility of this will become apparent in larger programs, as when we start dealing with Windows). That's the idea behind objects — to increase modularity. And now that we've seen the idea, let's see the program itself.

We can start by declaring a class named counter_class:

```
      #include <ctype.h>
      #include <iostream.h>

      /* Counter implemented as an object */

→     class counter_class {               // Declare counter_class class
      public:
          char char_to_count;
          int number_of_char_seen;
          void init(char the_char);
          void add_one(void);
      };
```

Notice that it's just like our earlier structure declaration, except that we've used the public keyword to make everything accessible to the rest of the program, and included the prototypes of the two functions. The next thing to do is to define the two functions themselves:

```
#include <ctyp.h>
#include <iostream.h>

/* Counter implemented as an object */

class counter_class {              // Declare counter_class class
public:
     char char_to_count;
     int number_of_char_seen;
     void init(char the_char);
     void add_one(void);
};
```

→
```
void counter_class::init(char the_char) // Declare initialization
{                                        //  function
     char_to_count = the_char;
     number_of_char_seen = 0;
}
```

→
```
void counter_class::add_one(void)     // Declare counter-incrementer
{
     number_of_char_seen++;
}
     :
```

To indicate that these are member functions of the class counter_class, we use the *scope resolution operator,* ::, this way:

```
void counter_class::init(char the_char) // Declare initialization function
void counter_class::add_one(void)        // Declare counter-incrementer
```

This informs C++ that init( ) is a member function of the class counter_class. That's the way it works: The function prototypes go into the class declaration, and then we're free to define the functions themselves anywhere in the program as long as we use the scope resolution operator :: to indicate which class they're a part of. Note that here we're defining these member functions before reaching the main( ) function. This is not technically necessary; as long as you use the scope resolution operator, ::, you can define member functions anywhere. However, the C++ style is to define them in the beginning of the program, before main( ).

TIP   In fact, C++ programmers occasionally place class and member function definitions both into header files. That way, you only have to include the header files, and thus the classes, that you want. C++ will compile the member functions that it finds in header files like this automatically (C, of course, will not).

Now we're free to set up main( ). We begin by declaring an object of class counter_class named counter and by initializing our object's data:

```
#include <ctyp.h>
#include <iostream.h>

/* Counter implemented as an object */

class counter_class {                    // Declare counter_class class
public:
    char char_to_count;
    int number_of_char_seen;
    void init(char the_char);
    void add_one(void);
};

void counter_class::init(char the_char) // Declare initialization
{                                        //  function
    char_to_count = the_char;
    number_of_char_seen = 0;
}

void counter_class::add_one(void)      // Declare counter-incrementer
{
    number_of_char_seen++;
}

main()
{
    counter_class counter;
    counter.init('x');                 // Initialize counter
        :
```

Then, we find the number of typed x's and print them out like this:

```c
#include <ctype.h>
#include <iostream.h>

/* Counter implemented as an object */

class counter_class {                    // Declare counter_class class
public:
    char char_to_count;
    int number_of_char_seen;
    void init(char the_char);
    void add_one(void);
};

void counter_class::init(char the_char) // Declare initialization
{                                        //  function
    char_to_count = the_char;
    number_of_char_seen = 0;
}

void counter_class::add_one(void)     // Declare counter-incrementer
{
    number_of_char_seen++;
}

main()
{
    counter_class counter;
    counter.init('x');                // Initialize counter
    char in_char;

    cout << "Type a few x's and q to quit: ";
    do{                                // Read x's.
        cin >> in_char;
        if(in_char == counter.char_to_count)
            counter.add_one();
    } while (toupper(in_char) != 'Q');

    cout << "\nNumber of " << counter.char_to_count << "'s: " << \
        counter.number_of_char_seen;

    return 0;
}
```

And that's it; we've developed our first working object, counter, which has both data and functions in it:

```
counter.char_to_count          // Char to watch for
counter.number_of_char_seen    // Number of times char seen
counter.init()                 // Initialize counter fields
counter.add_one()              // Increment count
```

Let's see another example of an object that will be useful in coming chapters — our stack object, capable of pushing and popping data onto and off of its internal (private) data stack. For us, this is the next step up in setting up objects; a stack will have some members that should remain private, as opposed to our counter object, where everything was public.

Our Stack Object

Let's start by examining the way a stack works. A stack is made up of a section of memory that we use to store data in. For example, let's say that this is part of the stack in memory:

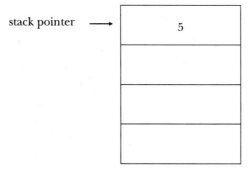

Notice the stack pointer, which points at a particular location called the top of the stack. When we put a value, such as 7, onto the stack, the stack pointer is *decremented* by one place to point to the previous location, and the 7 is placed at that location:

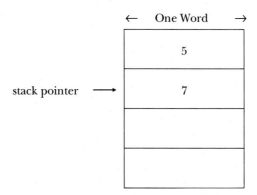

In this way, we push a value onto the stack. We can retrieve these values by popping them off the stack. If we pop one value from the stack, that will be the last value pushed, or 7, and the stack pointer moves up:

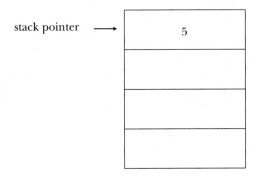

stack pointer   ⟶   5

Popping the stack again yields a value of 5. Note that values come off in the reverse order that they were put on. That's the way our stack will work; if we pushed the values 1, 2, and 3, then popping values off the stack would yield 3, 2, and 1. Stacks like this are very popular programming constructions, but there is no direct support for them in C++. However, we can add that ourselves with a stack class.

It will be easy to design our stack class. First, we'll need some space for the stack itself, and we can set that aside as data internal to our stack object:

```
      class stack_class {
→         int data_buffer[100];
              :
      };
```

Note that we have left it private; only member functions will have access to the stack. This way, the rest of the program doesn't have to bother with it. In addition, we'll have to store the stack pointer (that is, our index in the array data_buffer[ ]), which points at the element that will be popped next:

```
      class stack_class {
          int data_buffer[100];
→         int stack_ptr;      // stack_ptr = -1 → stack is empty
      };
```

This too is private, since only member functions will worry about the value of the stack pointer. The rest of the program only needs to push and pop values; it does not need to worry about the stack pointer itself. Note that in the comment we indicate that when stack_ptr holds -1, the stack is empty. When we push a value, it will go into the first element of the array, data_buffer[0], and stack_ptr will become 0. The next time we push a value, it will go into data_buffer[1], and stack_ptr will become 1 also. When we pop a value, stack_ptr will go back to 0. After we pop that value, too, stack_ptr becomes -1 and there is nothing left on the stack, which means that we can't pop any more values off.

Let's set up the prototypes for the two functions that will actually do the pushing and popping. They should be public so the rest of the program can use them. In addition, we should notice that some stack operations ought to generate an error, such as popping an empty stack, or attempting to push data onto a full stack. For that reason, let's have push( ) and pop( ) return integer values — 0 for failure and 1 for success:

```
     class stack_class {
         int data_buffer[100];
         int stack_ptr;      // stack_ptr = -1 → stack is empty
     public:
→        int pop(int *pop_to);
→        int push(int push_this);
     };
```

Note that, because pop( ) will have to change the value of the argument passed to it, we have to pass a pointer to it (exactly as we do with scanf( )). We should also include an initialization function to set the stack pointer to -1 (i.e., an empty stack) at the beginning of the program:

```
     class stack_class {
         int data_buffer[100];
         int stack_ptr;      // stack_ptr = -1 → stack is empty
     public:
→        void init(void);
         int pop(int *pop_to);
         int push(int push_this);
     };
```

Our class is now ready — that was all there was to it (except, of course, for writing the member functions). Now that our class, stack_class, is set up, we could declare an object of that class named, simply, stack:

```
     class stack_class {
         int data_buffer[100];
```

```
        int stack_ptr;      // stack_ptr = -1 → stack is empty
    public:
        void init(void);
        int pop(int *pop_to);
        int push(int push_this);
    };
    :
    :


    main()
    {
→       stack_class stack;
            :
```

When we want to push data onto the stack, we can do it like this:

```
    class stack_class {
        int data_buffer[100];
        int stack_ptr;      // stack_ptr = -1 → stack is empty
    public:
        void init(void);
        int pop(int *pop_to);
        int push(int push_this);
    };
    :
    :


    main()
    {
        stack_class stack;
→       stack.push(data_value);
            :
```

Conversely, when we want to pop it, we can use pop( ):

```
    class stack_class {
        int data_buffer[100];
        int stack_ptr;      // stack_ptr = -1 → stack is empty
    public:
        void init(void);
        int pop(int *pop_to);
        int push(int push_this);
    };
    :
    :
```

```
main()
{
    stack_class stack;
    stack.push(data_value);
→   stack.pop(&data_value);
        :
```

TIP It's a good idea to have your functions return a value of 0 — i.e., false — for failure, because it's easy to use them in loops and if statements. For example, we'll be able to keep popping values off the stack until we have them all with a simple while(stack.pop(&data_value)) loop. Note also that pushing and popping here is slightly asymmetric; we push a value directly, but have to pass a pointer to pop( ) (exactly the same asymmetry that printf( ) and scanf( ) have). We'll fix that in the next chapter when we start working with passing by reference, another C++ topic.

Now all we need to do is to define the member functions init( ), push( ), and pop( ). The init( ) function is particularly easy, because all it does is to prime the stack by setting the stack_ptr to indicate an empty stack, so let's begin with it:

```
class stack_class {
    int data_buffer[100];
    int stack_ptr;       // stack_ptr = -1 → stack is empty
public:
    void init(void);
    int pop(int *pop_to);
    int push(int push_this);
};

→   void stack_class::init(void){stack_ptr = -1;}
```

Note that in the function init( ), we can reach stack_ptr merely by referring to it as stack_ptr; that is, we do not have to call it stack.stack_ptr. The reason for this is that init( ) is a member function of the object, and stack_ptr is a member variable, so they're in the same scope; that is, the scope of the object itself. In fact, since stack_ptr is private, no statement in the program can refer to stack_ptr outside the stack object, even as stack.stack_ptr. Next, let's define the function pop( ). If the stack is empty, popping is an error, and we should return a value of 0 to indicate that:

```
#include <iostream.h>

/* Stack implemented as an object  */

class stack_class {
    int data_buffer[100];
    int stack_ptr;      // stack_ptr = -1 → stack is empty
public:
    void init(void);
    int pop(int *pop_to);
    int push(int push_this);
};

void stack_class::init(void){stack_ptr = -1;}
```

→
```
int stack_class::pop(int *pop_to)
{
    if(stack_ptr == -1)       // Stack is empty -- return error
        return 0;
            :
```

Otherwise, we have to take data out of the stack; that is, out of the array named data_array[ ]. Notice that we've passed a pointer to pop( ); as mentioned, that is because we want to be able to change the value of the parameter passed to it. In this case, our pointer is named pop_to, and the data it refers to is *pop_to, so we can send the contents of the current stack location there. That stack location is pointed to by stack_ptr; we can place the integer from the array at memory address pop_to and decrement the stack pointer like this:

```
#include <iostream.h>

/* Stack implemented as an object  */

class stack_class {
    int data_buffer[100];
    int stack_ptr;      // stack_ptr = -1 → stack is empty
public:
    void init(void);
    int pop(int *pop_to);
    int push(int push_this);
};

void stack_class::init(void){stack_ptr = -1;}

int stack_class::pop(int *pop_to)
```

```
    {
        if(stack_ptr == -1)        // Stack is empty -- return error
            return 0;
        else                       // Else return data
→           *pop_to = data_buffer[stack_ptr--];
            return 1;
    }
        :
```

Note also that we're returning a non-zero value, 1 in this case, to indicate
success. That's it for pop( ). The only error condition that we had to handle
was when there was nothing left to pop from the stack, and we checked that
simply by checking the value of stack_ptr.

We can check for error conditions when we write push( ) in the same way. Our
stack in memory, data_buffer[100], has enough room for 100 integers, and
stack_ptr can range from -1 for an empty stack to 99 for a completely full one.
When we try to push an integer, it's an error if the stack is full, and we can
check that by comparing stack_ptr to its maximum possible value, 99. If it's
greater than or equal to this value, we should return 0. Otherwise, we have to
increment the stack pointer and place the incoming int onto the stack. Note
that since the stack pointer points to the next integer to be popped, we have
to increment it *before* placing an integer on the stack. We can do that this way:

```
    #include <iostream.h>

    /* Stack implemented as an object   */

    class stack_class {
        int data_buffer[100];
        int stack_ptr;      // stack_ptr = -1 → stack is empty
    public:
        void init(void);
        int pop(int *pop_to);
        int push(int push_this);
    };

    void stack_class::init(void){stack_ptr = -1;}

    int stack_class::pop(int *pop_to)
    {
        if(stack_ptr == -1)        // Stack is empty -- return error
            return 0;
        else                        // Else return data
```

```
        *pop_to = data_buffer[stack_ptr--];
        return 1;
}

int stack_class::push(int push_this)
{
    if(stack_ptr >= 99)      // Stack is full -- return error
        return 0;
    else                     // Else store data
        data_buffer[++stack_ptr] = push_this;
        return 1;
}
```

Again, we return 0 if there was an error, 1 otherwise. Now our class, stack_class, is completely set up, and we can define an object of that class named stack. We're ready to use this object, because we've defined everything it needs, including the member functions. To use it in a program, we simply need to use the dot operator, like this:

```
stack.push(5);
```

This statement pushes a value of 5 onto our stack. Let's write the rest of our program now, seeing our object at work. To do that, we have to define the main( ) function. The first thing to do in main( ) is to declare our object named stack and then to initialize the stack with stack.init( ) (which sets stack_ptr to -1):

```
#include <iostream.h>

/* Stack implemented as an object  */

class stack_class {
    int data_buffer[100];
    int stack_ptr;       // stack_ptr = -1 → stack is empty
public:
    void init(void);
    int pop(int *pop_to);
    int push(int push_this);
};

void stack_class::init(void){stack_ptr = -1;}

int stack_class::pop(int *pop_to)
{
```

```
        if(stack_ptr == -1)      // Stack is empty -- return error
            return 0;
        else                     // Else return data
            *pop_to = data_buffer[stack_ptr--];
            return 1;
    }

    int stack_class::push(int push_this)
    {
        if(stack_ptr >= 99)      // Stack is full -- return error
            return 0;
        else                     // Else store data
            data_buffer[++stack_ptr] = push_this;
            return 1;
    }

    main()
    {
→       stack_class stack;
→       stack.init();
            :
```

Now that we've initialized the stack, we're free to push and pop values. Let's try it out with a loop. Here we can push, say, the numbers from 0 to 9 and print them out as we do so:

```
    #include <iostream.h>

    /* Stack implemented as an object  */

    class stack_class {
        int data_buffer[100];
        int stack_ptr;       // stack_ptr = -1 → stack is empty
    public:
        void init(void);
        int pop(int *pop_to);
        int push(int push_this);
    };

    void stack_class::init(void){stack_ptr = -1;}

    int stack_class::pop(int *pop_to)
    {
        if(stack_ptr == -1)      // Stack is empty -- return error
            return 0;
```

```
        else                        // Else return data
            *pop_to = data_buffer[stack_ptr--];
        return 1;
    }

    int stack_class::push(int push_this)
    {
        if(stack_ptr >= 99)      // Stack is full -- return error
            return 0;
        else                        // Else store data
            data_buffer[++stack_ptr] = push_this;
        return 1;
    }

    main()
    {
        int loop_index;
        stack_class stack;
        stack.init();

        cout << "Pushing values now...\n";
        for(loop_index = 0; loop_index < 10; loop_index++){
            stack.push(loop_index);
            cout << "Pushed value--> " << loop_index << "\n";
        }
            :
```

That's it, we've placed ten numbers on the stack like this:

stack_ptr = 9

| 0 | 1 | 2 | 3 | 4 | 5 | 6 | 7 | 8 | 9 | | | | ...

Now when we pop a value, the first integer that comes off will be 9, and pop( ) will move the stack pointer back one element:

stack_ptr = 8

| 0 | 1 | 2 | 3 | 4 | 5 | 6 | 7 | 8 | | | | | ...

In fact, let's pop all the values with another loop. This time, we have to use stack.pop( ), and we have to pass it a pointer so it can return a value like this:

```
#include <iostream.h>

/* Stack implemented as an object  */

class stack_class {
    int data_buffer[100];
    int stack_ptr;      // stack_ptr = -1 → stack is empty
public:
    void init(void);
    int pop(int *pop_to);
    int push(int push_this);
};

void stack_class::init(void){stack_ptr = -1;}

int stack_class::pop(int *pop_to)
{
    if(stack_ptr == -1)       // Stack is empty -- return error
        return 0;
    else                      // Else return data
        *pop_to = data_buffer[stack_ptr--];
        return 1;
}

int stack_class::push(int push_this)
{
    if(stack_ptr >= 99)      // Stack is full -- return error
        return 0;
    else                     // Else store data
        data_buffer[++stack_ptr] = push_this;
        return 1;
}

main()
{
    int loop_index, popped_value;
    stack_class stack;
    stack.init();

    cout << "Pushing values now...\n";
    for(loop_index = 0; loop_index < 10; loop_index++){
        stack.push(loop_index);
        cout << "Pushed value--> " << loop_index << "\n";
    }

    cout << "Popping values now...\n";
```

```
        for(loop_index = 0; loop_index < 10; loop_index++){
→           stack.pop(&popped_value);
→           cout << "Popped value--> " << popped_value << "\n";
        }

        return 0;
    }
```

That's it; when we pop a value, it is placed in the integer variable popped_value, and then we print it out. On the screen, the output of our program looks like this:

```
Pushing values now...
Pushed value--> 0
Pushed value--> 1
Pushed value--> 2
Pushed value--> 3
Pushed value--> 4
Pushed value--> 5
Pushed value--> 6
Pushed value--> 7
Pushed value--> 8
Pushed value--> 9
Popping values now...
Popped value--> 9
Popped value--> 8
Popped value--> 7
Popped value--> 6
Popped value--> 5
Popped value--> 4
Popped value--> 3
Popped value--> 2
Popped value--> 1
Popped value--> 0
```

Our stack is a success; the numbers are coming off in reverse order. Now that we've gotten some familiarity with objects, let's take the next logical step in organizing our programs — arrays of objects.

How Arrays of Objects Work

Just as we can declare arrays of any variable, so we can declare arrays of objects. We might do that if we have a number of tasks to accomplish that are computationally similar; for example, let's say that we wanted to expand our counter program to count not just x's, but all the letters. We would start by making the counter object into an array:

```
class counter_class {                    // Declare counter_class class
public:
    char char_to_count;
    int number_of_char_seen;
    void init(char the_char);
    void add_one(void);
};

main()
{
        counter_class counter[26];
            :
```

Now we can refer to the objects in this array like this: counter[i]. For example, we could initialize those objects with their init( ) functions this way:

```
class counter_class {                    // Declare counter_class class
public:
    char char_to_count;
    int number_of_char_seen;
    void init(char the_char);
    void add_one(void);
};

main()
{
    counter_class counter[26];
    char in_char;
    int i;
    for(i = 0; i < 26; i++) counter[i].init(i + 'a');
        :
```

Next, we can ask the user to type some letters and keep track of them like this:

```
main()
{
    counter_class counter[26];
    char in_char;
    int i;
    for(i = 0; i < 26; i++) counter[i].init(i + 'a');

    cout << "Type a few letters and 0 to quit: ";
```

```
        do{                                 // Read characters
            cin >> in_char;
→           counter[in_char - 'a'].add_one();
        } while (in_char != '0');
          :
```

Finally, we can type all the data out like this:

```
    main()
    {
        counter_class counter[26];
        char in_char;
        int i;
        for(i = 0; i < 26; i++) counter[i].init(i + 'a');

        cout << "Type a few letters and 0 to quit: ";
        do{                                 // Read characters
            cin >> in_char;
            counter[in_char - 'a'].add_one();
        } while (in_char != '0');

→       for(i = 0; i < 26; i = i + 2){
→           cout << "\nNumber of " << counter[i].char_to_count \
→               << "'s: " << counter[i].number_of_char_seen  \
→               << "  Number of " << counter[i+1].char_to_count \
→               << "'s: " << counter[i+1].number_of_char_seen;
→       }

        return 0;
    }
```

And that's it; the whole program appears in Listing 2-2.

Listing 2-2. Counter Program with an Object Array

```
#include <iostream.h>

/* Counter implemented as an object */

class counter_class {                       // Declare counter_class class
public:
    char char_to_count;
    int number_of_char_seen;
    void init(char the_char);
```

Listing 2-2. *(continued)*

```
    void add_one(void);
};

void counter_class::init(char the_char) // Declare initialization
                                        // function
{
    char_to_count = the_char;
    number_of_char_seen = 0;
}

void counter_class::add_one(void)      // Declare counter-incrementer
{
    number_of_char_seen++;
}

main()
{
    counter_class counter[26];
    char in_char;
    int i;
    for(i = 0; i < 26; i++) counter[i].init(i + 'a');

    cout << "Type a few letters and 0 to quit: ";
    do{                             // Read characters
        cin >> in_char;
        counter[in_char - 'a'].add_one();
    } while (in_char != '0');

    for(i = 0; i < 26; i = i + 2){
        cout << "\nNumber of " << counter[i].char_to_count \
            << "'s: " << counter[i].number_of_char_seen  \
            << "   Number of " << counter[i+1].char_to_count \
            << "'s: " << counter[i+1].number_of_char_seen;
    }

    return 0;
}
```

As far as the rest of our program knows, then, two functions have been added:

```
counter[i].init()
counter[i].add_one()
```

In other words, we've been able to wrap all the details of the counter object up into these two functions. However, we can do better than this; there is no reason that the program should concern itself with initializing the counter — all it really wants to do is to use the counter's utility, not be concerned with the details. C++ provides a special way of automatically invoking an initializing function for objects, and we'll look into that next.

What Are Constructors?

C++ supports class *constructors* to initialize objects for us. Constructors are member functions that are automatically invoked when the object is first set up, initializing the object the way we want it. These functions will be very important throughout the course of this book, so let's examine them here. We can start by looking at our class counter_class, which has a member function named init( ):

```
class counter_class {              // Declare counter_class class
public:
    char char_to_count;
    int number_of_char_seen;
→   void init(char the_char);
    void add_one(void);
};
```

A constructor serves the same purpose as init( ), and it's called automatically, so our program won't have to call init( ) in main( ) anymore. We can change init( ) into a constructor by changing its name to the name of the class itself (note that it does not have any return type):

```
class counter_class {              // Declare counter_class class
public:
    char char_to_count;
    int number_of_char_seen;
→   counter_class(void);
    void add_one(void);
};
```

And that's it; we just set up the constructor as we did the old init( ) function:

```
#include <iostream.h>

/* Counter implemented as an object */
```

```
    class counter_class {           // Declare counter_class class
    public:
        char char_to_count;
        int number_of_char_seen;
        counter_class(void);
        void add_one(void);
    };

→   counter_class::counter_class(void)
    {
        number_of_char_seen = 0;
    }
    :
```

Now, when the program begins and creates counter, the constructor will automatically be invoked. That means that we no longer have to explicitly initialize our counter in the beginning of the program. However, by itself, our constructor cannot initialize the character we're looking for, char_to_count. That is, value in number_of_char_seen always starts at 0, but char_to_count may be any character, such as 'x', and there's no way we can write a constructor that would know that ahead of time. One way of fixing the problem is initializing char_to_count ourselves in the program:

```
#include <ctype.h>
#include <iostream.h>

/* Counter implemented as an object */

class counter_class {           // Declare counter_class class
public:
    char char_to_count;
    int number_of_char_seen;
    counter_class(void);
    void add_one(void);
};

counter_class::counter_class(void)
{
    number_of_char_seen = 0;
}

void counter_class::add_one(void)  // Declare counter-incrementer
{
    number_of_char_seen++;
}
```

```
main()
{
    char in_char;
    counter_class counter;
```

→
```
    counter.char_to_count = 'x';

    cout << "Type a few x's and q to quit: ";
    do{
        // Read x's.
        cin >> in_char;
        if(in_char == counter.char_to_count)
            counter.add_one();
    } while (toupper(in_char) != 'Q');

    cout << "\nNumber of " << counter.char_to_count << "'s: " << \
        counter.number_of_char_seen;

    return 0;
}
```

However, this is less than professional — the idea of objects is to take care of all those details for us. You might recall that our original init( ) function took a parameter (e.g., which we could set to 'x'):

→
```
void counter_class::init(char the_char) // Declare initialization
{                                        //  function
    char_to_count = the_char;
    number_of_char_seen = 0;
}
```

It turns out that we can pass parameters, like 'x', to constructors also, and we'll do that next. (Constructors without parameters are called *default constructors*.)

Passing Parameters to Constructors

Often when we initialize an object, we'll want to initialize it with certain values. We can pass those values to the object's constructor when we set up the object like this:

```
#include <iostream.h>

/* Counter implemented as an object */

class counter_class {             // Declare counter_class class
```

```
public:
    char char_to_count;
    int number_of_char_seen;
    counter_class(char the_char);
    void add_one(void);
};

main()
{
    counter_class counter('x');
        :
```

Now the constructor takes one parameter of type char, and we can write that
function like this:

```
#include <iostream.h>

/* Counter implemented as an object */

class counter_class {              // Declare counter_class class
public:
    char char_to_count;
    int number_of_char_seen;
    counter_class(char the_char);
    void add_one(void);
};

counter_class::counter_class(char the_char)
{
    char_to_count = the_char;
    number_of_char_seen = 0;
}

main()
{
    counter_class counter('x');
        :
```

If we had additional parameters, we could just pass them in order like this:

```
class friends_class {              // Declare friends_class class
    char names[10];
public:
    friends_class(char *f1, char *f2, char *f3);
    friend_func(void);
};
```

```
main()
{
→       friends_class our_friends("Tom", "Dick", "Harry");
        :
```

In other words, passing parameters to a constructor solves most of the problems we might have when initializing an object. We'll see a great deal more about passing parameters to constructors during this book; for now, however, we might note that the revised x-counting program appears in Listing 2-3.

NOTE   In C++, we cannot declare arrays of objects that have constructors, unless those constructors do not take any parameters, i.e., are default constructors.

Listing 2-3. Counter Program with Parameterized Constructor

```cpp
#include <ctype.h>
#include <iostream.h>

/* Counter implemented as an object */

class counter_class {                     // Declare counter_class class
public:
    char char_to_count;
    int number_of_char_seen;
    counter_class(char the_char);
    void add_one(void);
};

counter_class::counter_class(char the_char)
{
    char_to_count = the_char;
    number_of_char_seen = 0;
}

void counter_class::add_one(void)      // Declare counter-incrementer
{
    number_of_char_seen++;
}

main()
```

Listing 2-3. *(continued)*

```
{
    counter_class counter('x');
    char in_char;

    cout << "Type a few x's and q to quit: ";

    do{                              // Read x's.
        cin >> in_char;
        if(in_char == counter.char_to_count)
            counter.add_one();
    } while (toupper(in_char) != 'Q');

    cout << "\nNumber of " << counter.char_to_count << "'s: " << \
        counter.number_of_char_seen;

    return 0;
}
```

While we're on the subject of constructors, we should also note that C++ gives us more freedom here — not only can we set up an object with a constructor when we start using it; we can also get rid of it using a *destructor*.

What Are Destructors?

Destructors (if we declare them) are automatically invoked when we are done with an object. Let's see an example; we could change our stack example so that it includes both constructors and destructors. In fact, that's a good idea here since we can use the constructor to allocate memory space for the stack like this:

```
#include <iostream.h>
#include <malloc.h>

/* Stack implemented as an object   */

class stack_class {
    int *data_buffer;
    int stack_top;        // stack_top = -1 → stack is empty
public:
    stack_class(int mem_required);
```

```
        int pop(int *pop_to);
        int push(int push_this);
    };

    stack_class::stack_class(int mem_required)
    {
        stack_top = -1;          // Can't initalize in a class def'n.
→       data_buffer = (int *) malloc(mem_required);
    }


    main()
    {
→       stack_class stack(200);
            :
```

In this case, we're passing the number of bytes we'll need to the constructor stack_class( ), and allocating that memory with malloc( ):

```
    stack_class::stack_class(int mem_required)
    {
        stack_top = -1;          // Can't initalize in a class def'n.
→       data_buffer = (int *) malloc(mem_required);
    }
```

TIP Although we can use malloc( ) in C++, there are better ways of allocating memory, and we'll see them soon. Most C++ programs would not use malloc( ).

This way, we allocate memory only when we set up an object. In our case, we need an array of 100 integers, which is 200 bytes, so we pass that number to the constructor:

```
    class stack_class {
        int *data_buffer;
        int stack_top;      // stack_top = -1 → stack is empty
    public:
        stack_class(int mem_required);
        int pop(int *pop_to);
        int push(int push_this);
    };

    main()
```

```
      {
→         stack_class stack(200);
              :
```

Similarly, we can deallocate that memory by using free( ) inside a destructor when we're done. Destructors are invoked when the program is done, or we leave the object's scope — as when we exit the function in which the object was declared. This is important in our stack example, because the memory allocated with malloc( ) remains allocated, even when our stack object goes out of scope. (For example, this might happen when a function in our program that sets up a stack object returns.) Now, however, stack_class' destructor will be called when an object of that class goes out of scope, allowing us to clean up. We declare a destructor in the same way as a constructor, but we add a ~ (tilde) character to its name like this:

```
    #include <iostream.h>
    #include <malloc.h>

    /* Stack implemented as an object   */

    class stack_class {
        int *data_buffer;
        int stack_top;        // stack_top = -1 → stack is empty
    public:
        stack_class(int mem_required);
→       ~stack_class(void);
        int pop(int *pop_to);
        int push(int push_this);
    };
              :
```

Now, when the program ends or the stack object goes out of scope, that destructor is invoked. That means that we can deallocate the memory like this:

```
    #include <iostream.h>
    #include <malloc.h>

    /* Stack implemented as an object   */

    class stack_class {
        int *data_buffer;
        int stack_top;        // stack_top = -1 → stack is empty
    public:
```

```
          stack_class(int mem_required);
          ~stack_class(void);
          int pop(int *pop_to);
          int push(int push_this);
     };

     stack_class::stack_class(int mem_required)
     {
          stack_top = -1;         // Can't initialize in a class def'n.
          data_buffer = (int *) malloc(mem_required);
     }
```

→
```
     stack_class::~stack_class(void)
     {
          cout << "Deallocating memory.\n";
```
→
```
          free(data_buffer);
     }
     :
```

And that's it. Note that the constructor and destructor are no longer details that we as programmers have to worry about. As far as programming goes, our stack only adds two new functions to keep in mind:

```
stack.push()
stack.pop()
```

All of the internal details are handled by the object itself (in this case, by the constructor and destructor), and that's the way it should be in C++. The new version of the stack program appears in Listing 2-4.

Listing 2-4. Stack Example with Constructors and Destructors

```
#include <iostream.h>
#include <malloc.h>

/* Stack implemented as an object  */

class stack_class {
     int *data_buffer;
     int stack_top;     // stack_top = -1 → stack is empty
public:
     stack_class(int mem_required);
     ~stack_class(void);
     int pop(int *pop_to);
     int push(int push_this);
};
```

Listing 2-4. *(continued)*

```
stack_class::stack_class(int mem_required)
{
    stack_top = -1;            // Can't initalize in a class def'n.
    data_buffer = (int *) malloc(mem_required);
}


stack_class::~stack_class(void)   // Destructor: get rid of memory
{
    cout << "Deallocating memory.\n";
    free(data_buffer);
}

int stack_class::pop(int *pop_to)
{
    if(stack_top == -1)        // Stack is empty -- return error
        return 0;
    else                       // Else return data
        *pop_to = data_buffer[stack_top--];
        return 1;
}

int stack_class::push(int push_this)
{
    if(stack_top >= 99)        // Stack is full -- return error
        return 0;
    else                       // Else store data
        data_buffer[++stack_top] = push_this;
        return 1;
}

main()
{
    stack_class stack(200);
    int loop_index, popped_value;

    cout << "Pushing values now...\n";      // Push values first

    for(loop_index = 0; loop_index < 10; loop_index++){
        stack.push(loop_index);
        cout << "Pushed value--> " << loop_index << "\n";
    }

    cout << "Popping values now...\n";      // Now pop values
```

(continued)

Listing 2-4. *(continued)*

```
    for(loop_index = 0; loop_index < 10; loop_index++){
        stack.pop(&popped_value);
        cout << "Popped value--> " << popped_value << "\n";
    }

    return 0;
}
```

Now that we've gotten a good start with objects, it's worth pointing out that structures are just like objects in C++; that is, they can have member functions as well as data. This is very different from normal C, where structures can only hold data. The one difference here is that, by default, all the members of a struct are public (in an object, all members are private by default). In addition, unions are the same as structs, except, of course, that the members overlap, and that you cannot use the keyword private in a union; all members of a union are public.

Class Inheritance

There is one more basic C++ concept that we should be familiar with while we're getting introduced to classes and objects. When you're working in C++, you'll frequently find that classes may share many of the same things. For example, you could define a number of classes named, say, tiger, lion, elephant, snake, and antelope. While each of these have obvious differences, they may include many of the same member functions, such as eat( ), sleep( ), breathe( ), and so on. In C++, we can handle this by setting up certain generic classes we call *base classes*. A base class includes the members that all the subsequent *derived classes* have in common. For example, the base class here could be called animal, and it may include the member functions eat( ), sleep( ), and breathe( ). Then, when we wanted to define, say, the class elephant, we could include the class animal to get the basics, adding such functions as trumpet( ) and stampede( ). In general, a class definition looks like this:

```
class class_name : access base_class {
    private data and function list
public:
    public data and function list
} object_list;
```

We can include a base class in the definition of a derived class; in our example, the base class might look like this:

→
```
class animal {
public:
    void eat(void);
    void sleep(void);
    void breathe(void);
};
```

The derived class elephant would then be declared this way:

→
```
class elephant : public animal {
public:
    int trumpet(void);
    int stampede(void);
};
```

The access keyword in front of the base class can be either public or private, and we make it public here. That means that all the private members of animal will be private in elephant, and all the public members will be public. The other option here is private, which makes all the members in animal private in elephant. We'll see much more about inheritance later, in Chapter 4, but for now let's put this together into a program so that we can become familiar with the idea. We'll find inheritance important throughout this book, and especially when we start working with Windows, because Microsoft C++ supplies a number of Windows base classes for us, each of which corresponds to a basic type of window or a window control (such as a text box or a button). Most programs derive their own windows and controls from those base classes, adding to them and tailoring them to their specific needs. In fact, as we'll see later, inheritance is one of the most important concepts in C++ (and one of the defining parts of object-oriented programming).

We can start our short inheritance example by defining our two classes, the base class and the derived class, as well as declaring a derived object named jumbo (that is, the base class is animal, the derived class is elephant, and our object of the derived class is called jumbo):

```
#include <iostream.h>

class animal {
public:
    void eat(void);
    void sleep(void);
```

```
        void breathe(void);
};

class elephant : public animal {
public:
        void trumpet(void);
        void stampede(void);
};

main()
{
        elephant jumbo;
            :
```

Next, we define all the member functions. After we do, the object jumbo has access to all those functions — those that are part of class animal as well as those that are part of class elephant, and we can use them like this:

```
#include <iostream.h>

class animal {
public:
        void eat(void);
        void sleep(void);
        void breathe(void);
};

class elephant : public animal {
public:
        void trumpet(void);
        void stampede(void);
};

void animal::eat(void){cout << "Eating...\n";}
void animal::sleep(void){cout << "Sleeping...\n";}
void animal::breathe(void){cout << "Breathing...\n";}
void elephant::trumpet(void){cout << "Trumpeting...\n";}
void elephant::stampede(void){cout << "Stampeding...\n";}

main()
{
        elephant jumbo;
        jumbo.breathe();
        jumbo.trumpet();
        jumbo.breathe();

        return 0;
}
```

We can use the function breathe( ), which is part of the class animal, because jumbo was derived from that base class, and derived classes (usually) have access to their base class' function, like this:

class elephant

```
class animal

    eat( )
    sleep( )
    breathe( )

    trumpet( )
    stampede( )
```

In addition, of course, we can use the function trumpet( ), which is part of the derived class elephant, because jumbo is an object of that class:

```
main()
{
    elephant jumbo;
    jumbo.breathe();     // Use animal::breathe()
    jumbo.trumpet();     // Use elephant::trumpet()
    jumbo.breathe();     // Use animal::breathe()

    return 0;
}
```

Since we can use the functions in both the class animal and those declared in the class elephant, this program prints out the result:

```
Breathing...
Trumpeting...
Breathing...
```

NOTE   It's worth noting that unions cannot be inherited; that is, a union can't serve as a base type, nor can it be derived from other classes. On the other hand, unions *can* have constructors.

That's it for inheritance, and that's it for this chapter. We've gotten some of the basics of C++ down, and we've put together some functioning C++ objects. The next step is to break through another boundary; in particular, stacks can usually push and pop only integer values, but under C++, we can redefine our member functions to take all sorts of different parameter types. When we use them with parameters of a particular type, C++ will automatically determine which function definition to apply (depending on the parameter types we pass). That way, we'll be able to use our stack with any type of data, not just integers. This is called function overloading. It's one of the big attractions of C++ — and it's one of the topics that the next chapter is all about.

Functions, Operators, and Overloading

The flexibility that C++ brings to programming tasks has made it a programmer's favorite, and we'll see much about that flexibility in this chapter when we cover the new capabilities given to functions in C++. One aspect of that is function overloading; rather than the restrictive data typing we find in other languages (where if you call a function with the wrong data type, your program might crash), C++ is smart enough to check the data type you want to use and to see whether the function you're calling has been defined with that type or not. That is, the same function can be defined a number of times for different variable types in C++; C++ will use the correct version of the function (as determined by the arguments we pass) automatically.

We'll see examples of function overloading in this chapter, as well as many other new topics having to do with functions, such as default parameters, friend functions, and others. Then, after we cover functions, we'll press on to see how we can also overload operators (e.g., +, –, and *). For example, we'll design our own string class in C++, and then we'll be able to redefine the + and = operators so they work on strings (as opposed to using strcat( ) and strcpy( )). In fact, just about every operator in C++ can be overloaded to handle the objects we define. With all this coming up, let's get started at once with a very popular C++ topic — function overloading.

Function Overloading: One Function, Many Uses

Let's say that we had a function named print_this( ) that could send a character to the screen like this:

```
print_this(char the_char)
{
    cout << the_char;
}
```

We could then use print_this( ) this way:

```
print_this('A');
```

However, sometime we might want to print a string — or even an ASCII code. In C, we'd have to define a new function, but in C++, we can *overload* our print_this( ) function so that all of these are perfectly legal:

```
print_this('A');                 // Print 'A'
print_this(65)                   // Print 'A' (ASCII code for 'A' = 65)
print_this("Hello, world.\n");
```

In other words, we can define three versions of print_this( ), and, depending on the argument type we pass (char, char*, or int for an ASCII code), C++ will choose the correct version for us. This is a powerful and very popular asset in C++, and you use it whenever the same code is appropriate for different data types (e.g., we'll enable our stack to handle ints, floats, and so on later).

Overloading print_this( ) is easy; all we have to do is to set up three prototypes matching the three different versions of the function in a new class which we might call printer_class:

```
#include <iostream.h>

/* Function Overloading Example   */

class printer_class {
public:
→       void print_this(char the_char);
→       void print_this(char* the_string);
→       void print_this(int the_ASCII_code);
};
    :
```

Now, C++ can distinguish between them based on their parameter types, char, char*, or int. Next, we simply define the three versions of print_this( ) as we would normal member functions:

```
#include <iostream.h>

/* Function Overloading Example  */

class printer_class {
public:
    void print_this(char the_char);
    void print_this(char* the_string);
    void print_this(int ASC_code);
};
```

```
→  void printer_class::print_this(char the_char){cout << the_char;}
→  void printer_class::print_this(char* the_string){cout << the_string;}
→  void printer_class::print_this(int ASC_code){cout << (char) ASC_code;}
    :
```

Now we can use print_this( ) as we wish, and the program will figure out what version we want depending on what parameter we pass:

```
#include <iostream.h>

/* Function Overloading Example  */

class printer_class {
public:
    void print_this(char the_char);
    void print_this(char* the_string);
    void print_this(int ASC_code);
};

void printer_class::print_this(char the_char){cout << the_char;}
void printer_class::print_this(char* the_string){cout << the_string;}
void printer_class::print_this(int ASC_code){cout << (char) ASC_code;}

main()
{
→      printer_class printem;
→      printem.print_this(97);          // ASCII code for 'a'
→      printem.print_this('b');         // Char
→      printem.print_this("c");         // String

       return 0;
}
```

This program prints out:

abc

Note that C++ does not allow us to overload operators when the operation is already defined — such as addition on integers.

Let's see another example. In particular, we can expand our stack from the last chapter to work on floating point values, not just on integers. When we're done, both of these will be legal in our programs:

```
stack.push(the_int);        // Push an integer value
stack.push(1.3333);         // Push a float value
```

By itself, C++ will select the correct definition of push( ), the one for floats or the one for ints. This means that we'll have to have two internal stacks, however, one for floats and one for ints.

When passing immediate values, such as stack.push(0), there might be some ambiguity, which you should avoid by using typed values only with overloaded functions (otherwise, C++ will generate an error).

We can begin the new, expanded class definition with the new arrays, int_data_buffer[ ] and float_data_buffer[ ] (to avoid using up too much memory on C++'s own stack, let's limit those arrays to 50 elements each):

```
#include <iostream.h>

/* Overloading stack functions  */

class stack_class {
→        int int_data_buffer[50];
→        float float_data_buffer[50];
            :
```

Two stacks also mean that we'll have to have two stack pointers:

```
#include <iostream.h>

/* Overloading stack functions  */
```

```
      class stack_class {
          int int_data_buffer[50];
          float float_data_buffer[50];
→         int int_stack_ptr;        // int_stack_ptr = -1 → stack is empty
→         int float_stack_ptr;      // float_stack_ptr = -1 → stack is empty
            :
```

Now let's write the functions. We'll have to modify our constructor to initialize both stack pointers — but we'll still only need one constructor. However, we'll need two pop( )s and two push( )es, one to handle ints and one to handle floats. We can include their prototypes in the class definition like this:

```
#include <iostream.h>

/* Overloading stack functions   */

class stack_class {
    int int_data_buffer[50];
    float float_data_buffer[50];
    int int_stack_ptr;        // int_stack_ptr = -1 → stack is empty
    int float_stack_ptr;      // float_stack_ptr = -1 → stack is empty
public:
→   stack_class(void);
:       int pop(int *pop_to);
:       int pop(float *pop_to);
:       int push(int push_this);
→       int push(float push_this);
    };
        :
```

Now we can define the member functions themselves. Once again, we use the :: scope resolution operator to let C++ know which class these functions belong to. The constructor has to initialize both int_stack_ptr and float_stack_ptr, and that can be done easily like this (-1 indicates an empty stack):

```
#include <iostream.h>

/* Overloading stack functions   */

class stack_class {
    int int_data_buffer[50];
    float float_data_buffer[50];
    int int_stack_ptr;        // int_stack_ptr = -1 → stack is empty
    int float_stack_ptr;      // float_stack_ptr = -1 → stack is empty
```

```
  public:
      stack_class(void);
      int pop(int *pop_to);
      int pop(float *pop_to);
      int push(int push_this);
      int push(float push_this);
  };

  stack_class::stack_class(void)
  {
→     int_stack_ptr = -1;
→     float_stack_ptr = -1;
  }
      :
```

Next, as before, we can define the pop( ) function this way:

```
  #include <iostream.h>

  /* Overloading stack functions  */

  class stack_class {
      int int_data_buffer[50];
      float float_data_buffer[50];
      int int_stack_ptr;      // int_stack_ptr = -1 → stack is empty
      int float_stack_ptr;    // float_stack_ptr = -1 → stack is empty
  public:
      stack_class(void);
      int pop(int *pop_to);
      int pop(float *pop_to);
      int push(int push_this);
      int push(float push_this);
  };

  stack_class::stack_class(void)
  {
      int_stack_ptr = -1;
      float_stack_ptr = -1;
  }

→ int stack_class::pop(int *pop_to)
  {
      if(int_stack_ptr == -1)        // Stack is empty -- return error
          return 0;
      else                           // Else return data
          *pop_to = int_data_buffer[int_stack_ptr--];
          return 1;
  }
      :
```

This is the integer version; we also have to include the floating point version, which uses float_data_buffer[ ] and float_stack_ptr. We can do that like this:

```
#include <iostream.h>

/* Overloading stack functions  */

class stack_class {
    int int_data_buffer[50];
    float float_data_buffer[50];
    int int_stack_ptr;      // int_stack_ptr = -1 → stack is empty
    int float_stack_ptr;    // float_stack_ptr = -1 → stack is empty
public:
    stack_class(void);
    int pop(int *pop_to);
    int pop(float *pop_to);
    int push(int push_this);
    int push(float push_this);
};

stack_class::stack_class(void)
{
    int_stack_ptr = -1;
    float_stack_ptr = -1;
}

int stack_class::pop(int *pop_to)
{
    if(int_stack_ptr == -1)       // Stack is empty -- return error
        return 0;
    else                          // Else return data
        *pop_to = int_data_buffer[int_stack_ptr--];
        return 1;
}

int stack_class::pop(float *pop_to)
{
    if(float_stack_ptr == -1)     // Stack is empty -- return error
        return 0;
    else                          // Else return data
        *pop_to = float_data_buffer[float_stack_ptr--];
        return 1;
}
:
```

And that's how function overloading looks in general. We can also do the same for push( ):

```
#include <iostream.h>

/* Overloading stack functions  */

class stack_class {
    int int_data_buffer[50];
    float float_data_buffer[50];
    int int_stack_ptr;     // int_stack_ptr = -1 → stack is empty
    int float_stack_ptr;   // float_stack_ptr = -1 → stack is empty
public:
    stack_class(void);
    int pop(int *pop_to);
    int pop(float *pop_to);
    int push(int push_this);
    int push(float push_this);
};
        :
        :
→   int stack_class::push(int push_this)
:   {
:       if(int_stack_ptr >= 49)    // Stack is full -- return error
            return 0;
        else                    // Else store data
            int_data_buffer[++int_stack_ptr] = push_this;
            return 1;
    }

    int stack_class::push(float push_this)
    {
        if(float_stack_ptr >= 49)     // Stack is full -- return error
            return 0;
        else                   // Else store data
            float_data_buffer[++float_stack_ptr] = push_this;
            return 1;
    }
        :
```

Now we can delare an object of this class named stack, which can be used with either integers or floats — that's all there is to it. In the last chapter, we pushed and printed the integers from 0 to 9; now let's do the same with floating point numbers. We can change the loop index we used into a floating point variable, allowing us to push and pop floating point values this way:

```
main()
{
→     stack_class stack;
```

```
→       float loop_index;
        float popped_value;

        cout.setf(ios::showpoint);            // Turn on fixed pt notation

        cout << "Pushing values now...\n";
        for(loop_index = 0; loop_index < 10; loop_index++){
→           stack.push(loop_index);
→           cout << "Pushed value--> " << loop_index << "\n";
        }

        cout << "Popping values now...\n";
        for(loop_index = 0; loop_index < 10; loop_index++){
→           stack.pop(&popped_value);
→           cout << "Popped value--> " << popped_value << "\n";
        }
```

You might also note that we used a member function of cout itself (i.e., cout itself will turn out to be an object, as we'll see in Chapter 5) like this: cout.setf(ios::showpoint). We'll cover this type of action in far greater detail later; all this does is to make C++ display the zeroes that follow floating point numbers (so we can distinguish them from ints). The new program appears in Listing 3-1; this time, the program output looks like this:

```
Pushing values now...
Pushed value--> 0.000000
Pushed value--> 1.000000
Pushed value--> 2.000000
Pushed value--> 3.000000
Pushed value--> 4.000000
Pushed value--> 5.000000
Pushed value--> 6.000000
Pushed value--> 7.000000
Pushed value--> 8.000000
Pushed value--> 9.000000
Popping values now...
Popped value--> 9.000000
Popped value--> 8.000000
Popped value--> 7.000000
Popped value--> 6.000000
Popped value--> 5.000000
Popped value--> 4.000000
Popped value--> 3.000000
Popped value--> 2.000000
Popped value--> 1.000000
Popped value--> 0.000000
```

Listing 3-1. Function Overloading Stack Example

```
#include <iostream.h>

/* Overloading stack functions  */

class stack_class {
    int int_data_buffer[50];
    float float_data_buffer[50];
    int int_stack_ptr;    // int_stack_ptr = -1 → stack is empty
    int float_stack_ptr; // float_stack_ptr = -1 → stack is empty
public:
    stack_class(void);
    int pop(int *pop_to);
    int pop(float *pop_to);
    int push(int push_this);
    int push(float push_this);
};

stack_class::stack_class(void)
{
    int_stack_ptr = -1;
    float_stack_ptr = -1;
}

int stack_class::pop(int *pop_to)
{
    if(int_stack_ptr == -1)     // Stack is empty -- return error
        return 0;
    else                        // Else return data
        *pop_to = int_data_buffer[int_stack_ptr--];
        return 1;
}

int stack_class::pop(float *pop_to)
{
    if(float_stack_ptr == -1)   // Stack is empty -- return error
        return 0;
    else                        // Else return data
        *pop_to = float_data_buffer[float_stack_ptr--];
        return 1;
}
int stack_class::push(int push_this)
{
    if(int_stack_ptr >= 49) // Stack is full -- return error
        return 0;
    else                        // Else store data
        int_data_buffer[++int_stack_ptr] = push_this;
        return 1;
}
```

Listing 3-1. *(continued)*

```cpp
int stack_class::push(float push_this)
{
    if(float_stack_ptr >= 49)     // Stack is full -- return error
        return 0;
    else                          // Else store data
        float_data_buffer[++float_stack_ptr] = push_this;
        return 1;
}

main()
{
    stack_class stack;
    float loop_index;
    float popped_value;

    cout.setf(ios::showpoint);          // Turn on fixed pt notation

    cout << "Pushing values now...\n";
    for(loop_index = 0; loop_index < 10; loop_index++){
        stack.push(loop_index);
        cout << "Pushed value--> " << loop_index << "\n";
    }

    cout << "Popping values now...\n";
    for(loop_index = 0; loop_index < 10; loop_index++){
        stack.pop(&popped_value);
        cout << "Popped value--> " << popped_value << "\n";
    }
    return 0;
}
```

So far, our overloaded functions have only had one parameter — but what if different versions of the function required different numbers of parameters? We can handle that also in C++.

Overloaded Functions with Different Parameter Numbers

Let's say that we wanted to modify our print_this( ) function so that it was primarily a string-printing function. For example, we might use it this way:

```cpp
print_this("No worries.");
```

In addition, let's say that we occasionally wanted to use it to print out strings made up of repetitions of the same character. For example, using it this way:

```
    print_this("No worries.");
→   print_this('a', 5);
```

would print out a string of five a's: "aaaaa". It turns out that overloading the function like this in C++ is no problem: C++ does not require the same number of parameters in the different versions of an overloaded function. All we need to do is to declare the correct prototypes in the class declaration like this:

```
    #include <iostream.h>

    /* Function overloading example */

    class print_class {
    public:
→       void print_this(char *the_string);
→       void print_this(char the_char, int number_repetitions);
    };
        :
```

Then we're set. We simply set up the two versions of the function and make use of them:

```
    #include <iostream.h>

    /* Function overloading example */

    class print_class {
    public:
        void print_this(char *the_string);
        void print_this(char the_char, int number_repetitions);
    };

→   void print_class::print_this(char *the_string){cout << the_string;}

→   void print_class::print_this(char the_char, int number_repetitions)
    {
        int i;

        for (i = 0; i < number_repetitions; i++){cout << the_char;}
    }

    main()
```

```
     {
→        print_class printem;
→        printem.print_this("abc");
→        printem.print_this('a', 5);

         return 0;
     }
```

In this way, C++ allows you to handle similar tasks with the same function in your code — even if those tasks take different numbers of parameters. For example, drawing circles and ellipses on the screen make up two similar tasks, but when you draw a circle, you have to specify two parameters: both its origin and radius. When you draw an ellipse, you have to specify three: the origin, major radius, and minor radius. In C++, we can put these tasks together into one overloaded function called, say, draw_figure( ).

Now let's take a closer look now at the second prototype of print_this( ):

```
   void print_this(char the_char, int number_repetitions);
```

In this case, we can use print_this( ) this way: print_this('a', 5). Frequently, we might want to print out just a single character, however, which means that we might find ourselves using print_this( ) like this often: print_this('x', 1). It turns out that C++ has improved on C here also; in particular, it lets us define *default parameters*. If we gave the second parameter a default value of 1, we could just invoke print_this( ) this way: print_this('x'), which will be exactly the same as print_this('x', 1). We'll examine this process next.

Default Function Parameters

Giving a function a default parameter or parameters is quite easy. All we have to do is to include the value of that default when we declare the function, like this in the case of print_this( ):

```
#include <iostream.h>

/* Function overloading example */

class print_class {
public:
    void print_this(char *the_string);
    void print_this(char the_char, int number_repetitions);
};
```

```
      void print_class::print_this(char *the_string){cout << the_string;}

→     void print_class::print_this(char the_char, int number_repetitions = 1)
      {
          int i;

          for (i = 0; i < number_repetitions; i++){
              cout << the_char;
          }
      }
      :
```

In other words, this line:

```
void print_class::print_this(char the_char, int number_repetitions = 1)
```

means that if we invoke print_this( ) like this: print_this('a', 5), then we'll get aaaaa on the screen. If we use it this way, however: print_this('a'), then we'll get just one character, a, on the screen. That might look like this in the program (keep in mind that it's still overloaded to handle strings as well):

```
#include <iostream.h>

/* Function overloading example */

class print_class {
public:
    void print_this(char *the_string);
    void print_this(char the_char, int number_repetitions);
};

void print_class::print_this(char *the_string){cout << the_string;}

void print_class::print_this(char the_char, int number_repetitions = 1)
{
    int i;

    for (i = 0; i < number_repetitions; i++){
        cout << the_char;
    }
}

main()
{
→   print_class printem;
→   printem.print_this("abc");
```

```
→      printem.print_this('a', 5);
→      printem.print_this('b');

       return 0;
}
```

There is one thing to note here; if we give a parameter a default value, then all parameters following it must have default parameters also. For example, in this declaration:

```
int the_func(int a, int b = 1, int c = 2, char d = 'a')
```

all the parameters following b — the first parameter to get a default — also need defaults. That is because when we start omitting arguments, C++ starts supplying defaults for the rightmost parameter first. For example, all of these are legal and unambiguous:

```
the_func(5, 2, 3, 'z');
the_func(5, 2, 3);
the_func(5, 2);
the_func(5);
```

If the parameters that had defaults could appear in any place, it wouldn't be clear which ones we were omitting (and therefore giving default values to). In this case, it's quite clear. When we start omitting arguments, C++ starts assigning default values from the right and works its way towards the left (i.e., the rightmost parameter is the most expendable).

A Mouse Object

Here's an example of default parameter use: This program sets up a mouse object whose constructor initializes the mouse and displays the mouse cursor in DOS. When you use the function mouse_move( ), you can move the mouse cursor to (row, column) like this: mouser.mouse_move(row, column). However, if you omit row and column, the program will assume that you want to move the cursor to the top left of the screen (i.e., position (1, 1)), and will move it there for you:

```
#include <dos.h>
#include <iostream.h>

// Initialize mouse and place cursor at (1, 1)
```

```
class mouse_class {
public:
    mouse_class();
    void mouse_move(int row, int col);
};

mouse_class::mouse_class()
{
    union REGS in_regs, out_regs;

    in_regs.x.ax = 0;                    // Initialize mouse
    int86(0x33, &in_regs, &out_regs);

    in_regs.x.ax = 1;                    // Show cursor
    int86(0x33, &in_regs, &out_regs);
}
```

→
```
void mouse_class::mouse_move(int row = 1, int col = 1)
{
    union REGS in_regs, out_regs;

    in_regs.x.dx = 8 * (row - 1);       // Move cursor
    in_regs.x.cx = 8 * (col - 1);
    in_regs.x.ax = 4;
    int86(0x33, &in_regs, &out_regs);
}

main()
{
    mouse_class mouser;
```

→
```
    mouser.mouse_move();

    return 0;
}
```

That's all there is to default function parameters. However, while we're discussing C++ functions, there is one more powerful technique we should be aware of here, and that's inline functions.

All About Inline Functions

Another new item in C++ is the use of inline functions. The reason inline functions exist is for speed; when you invoke one in your code, it's expanded right there in the program (this is for efficiency, not for object-oriented programming per se). For example, if we made print_this( ) an inline function, then this line:

```
    :
printem.print_this(97);          // ASCII code
    :
```

would be expanded into the entire contents of the print_this( ) function right there, which looks like this:

```
    :
cout << 97;
    :
```

This saves us a good deal of overhead; in particular, it saves us the code needed to push values onto the stack, call the function, pick parameters off the stack, and then return (with possible return values). To make a member function inline, we just have to declare it that way like this:

```
#include <iostream.h>

/* Function Overloading Example  */

class printer_class {
public:
    void print_this(char the_char);
    void print_this(char* the_string);
    void print_this(int ASC_code);
};
```

→
```
inline void printer_class::print_this(char the_char){cout <<
    the_char;}
```
→
```
inline void printer_class::print_this(char* the_string){cout <<
    the_string;}
```
→
```
inline void printer_class::print_this(int ASC_code){cout <<
    (char)ASC_code;}
```

```
main()
{
    printer_class printem;
    printem.print_this(97);          // ASCII code
    printem.print_this('b');         // Char
    printem.print_this("c");         // String

    return 0;
}
```

NOTE   inline is actually a request to the compiler, not a directive; in other words, the compiler will make the function inline if it can.

Here, we're making all versions of our function print_this( ) into inline functions. They are not called any longer; instead, the whole body of the function is placed right there in the program (something like a macro but with type checking). In other words, the entire code of an inline function is placed into the body of the program each time it is invoked. For that reason, it is best to use inline functions when you're calling a relatively short function.

In fact, in C++, if we place a program's definition (i.e., its code) right after its declaration (i.e., its prototype) in a class declaration, that function automatically becomes an inline function. For example, we could have set up all three versions of print_this( ) in the declaration of the class itself, like this:

```
#include <iostream.h>

/* Function Overloading Example  */

class printer_class {
public:
        void print_this(char the_char) {cout << the_char;}
        void print_this(char* the_string) {cout << the_string;}
        void print_this(int ASC_code) {cout << (char) ASC_code;}
};

main()
{
    printer_class printem;
    printem.print_this(97);         // ASCII code
    printem.print_this('b');        // Char
    printem.print_this("c");        // String

    return 0;
}
```

If we do, each of them is an inline function. That's automatic in C++: Whenever you declare and define a function in a class declaration, it's automatically an inline function. Although that is usually helpful (i.e., in most cases, you only spell out short functions in the class declaration), it's something we should be aware of.

Let's press on now with our discussion of overloading functions. For example, we can even overload constructors (but not destructors), and we're going to examine that process next.

Overloading Constructors

There is nothing special about overloading constructors; in this regard, they are just like other functions. For example, let's say that we had a class named print_class, and we're declaring an object of that class named printem. If we wanted the option of passing a string to our object's constructor, we might do it like this:

```
printem("aaa");
```

On the other hand, we might want to do the same thing by passing a single character with a repetition count this way:

```
printem('a', 3);
```

This works exactly as we'd expect it to. All we have to do is to set up our class and declare our object (let's pass it the string "aaa"):

```
#include <iostream.h>

/* Constructor overloading example */

class print_class {
public:
    print_class(char *the_string);
    print_class(char the_char, int number_repetitions);
};
    :
    :
main()
{
    print_class printem("aaa");
    return 0;
}
```

→

Then, we have to define the two versions of our constructors, and that's it:

```
#include <iostream.h>

/* Constructor overloading example */
```

```
class print_class {
public:
    print_class(char *the_string);
    print_class(char the_char, int number_repetitions);
};
```

→
```
print_class::print_class(char *the_string){cout << the_string;}
```

→
```
print_class::print_class(char the_char, int number_repetitions = 1)
{
    int loop_index;

    for (loop_index = 0; loop_index < number_repetitions; loop_index++){
        cout << the_char;
    }
}

main()
{
    print_class  printem("aaa");
    return 0;
}
```

When we run this program, C++ initializes our object (printem) with the constructor, and the constructor simply prints out "aaa", as it should. On the other hand, we could also initialize this object by passing a single character, like this:

```
#include <iostream.h>

/* Constructor overloading example */

class print_class {
public:
    print_class(char *the_string);
    print_class(char the_char, int number_repetitions);
};

print_class::print_class(char *the_string){cout << the_string;}

print_class::print_class(char the_char, int number_repetitions = 1)
{
    int loop_index;

    for (loop_index = 0; loop_index < number_repetitions; loop_index++){
        cout << the_char;
    }
```

```
   }

main()
{
→      print_class printem('a');
       return 0;
}
```

> **TIP**
>
> One good place to overload constructors is when you're creating a class —
> or classes — that will be used by other people (this is actually called creat-
> ing a *class library*, as we'll see in Chapter 5), and you want to be as flexible as
> possible, giving them the option of initializing objects of that class(es) in
> different ways. That's one of the trademarks of C++: flexibility.

Here, we let the default value for the second parameter (number_repetitions
= 1) take over; this example prints out only one character, a. There is still
more power that we can add to functions in C++, and we're going to turn to
one of those powerful techniques next, when we see how one function can
reach the data stored inside many different objects. This technique is important if you want to share data between objects (when, for example, you have an
array of objects). So far, the member functions of our objects have only been
able to access the data in their own object. Now we'll see how to extend that
over a number of objects.

Sharing Data between Objects with Friend Functions

You may recall that in the last chapter, we set up an example to handle an
array of objects. In particular, we set up a counter object for each letter of the
alphabet like this:

```
counter[26]
```

Then we read characters from the keyboard. Each time we read a certain
letter, we used a function built into the corresponding object, add_one( ), to
increment its internal counter (note that in a real program, we should check
the value of in_char to make sure it's a valid lowercase character before doing
this):

```
cin >> in_char;
counter[in_char - 'a'].add_one();
```

That left us with 26 objects, each of which held the number of a particular letter that had been typed. But what if we wanted to get the total number of letters that had been typed? In that case, we would want to add up the data from many different objects.

This process can be very difficult if the data we want to reach in those objects happens to be private, like this:

```
class counter_class {                    // Declare counter_class class
→       int number_of_char_seen;
    public:
        char char_to_count;
        counter_class(char the_char);
        void add_one(void);
    } counter[26];
```

Until now, we could not access the variable counter unless we were in a member function of the current object — but even then, we could not access another object's counter, which is bad news if we want to add them all up. The solution to this problem is to use *friend* functions. If you declare a function to be a friend of a certain class, it has access to that class' private members. For example, we can set up a function to sum our counter objects' internal data, which we can name total( ). We declare it to be a friend of counter_class like this:

```
class counter_class {                    // Declare counter_class class
        int number_of_char_seen;
    public:
        char char_to_count;
        void init(char the_char);
        void add_one(void);
→       friend int total(int number_of_objects);
    } counter[26];
```

A friend function like this has access to the private data of an object (and you usually use friends when you want to use data from different objects, as we do here). We want to sum up the values in counter[i].number_of_char_seen as the index i ranges from 0 to the total number of counter objects. We can set up the function total( ) this way (note that we do not use the friend keyword here in the function's definition):

```
int total(int number_of_objects)
{
    int i, sum;
```

```
→              for (i = 0, sum = 0; i < number_of_objects; i++)
→                  sum += counter[i].number_of_char_seen;

            return sum;
        }
```

In other words, total( ) is a friend of each of our 26 objects (since it's declared as a friend in the class declaration), and it has access to the private data of each. We can use total( ) like this in our program:

```
#include <iostream.h>

/* Friend function example */

class counter_class {                      // Declare counter_class class
    int number_of_char_seen;
public:
    char char_to_count;
    void init(char the_char);
    void add_one(void);
    friend int total(int number_of_objects);
} counter[26];    // Global so total() can reach this object array

void counter_class::init(char the_char)
{
    char_to_count = the_char;
    number_of_char_seen = 0;
}

void counter_class::add_one(void){number_of_char_seen++;}

main()
{
    char in_char;
    int i;

    for(i = 0; i < 26; i++) counter[i].init(i + 'a');
    cout << "Type a few letters and 0 to quit: ";
    do{                             // Read characters
        cin >> in_char;
        counter[in_char - 'a'].add_one();
    } while (in_char != '0');

→   cout << "\nThe total number of letters was: " << total(26) << "\n";
    return 0;
}

int total(int number_of_objects)
```

```
{
    int i, sum;

    for (i = 0, sum = 0; i < number_of_objects; i++)
        sum += counter[i].number_of_char_seen;

    return sum;
}
```

We just read characters until the user types 0, then we sum the number of characters typed by checking the internal counter in each object. That is how friend functions work. Another example might be an object that holds a master data list of some kind. You could have several friend functions that maintain sublists inside this master data list — each of these sublist objects can maintain their own beginning and ending locations in the master list. In that way, they can share the master list's data.

Note that a friend is *not* a member of the corresponding object. This means that we refer to the private variable number_of_char_seen as counter[i].number_of_char_seen, not just as number_of_char_seen (as we could in a member function):

```
int total(int number_of_objects)
{
    int i, sum;

    for (i = 0, sum = 0; i < number_of_objects; i++)
        sum += counter[i].number_of_char_seen;

    return sum;
}
```

An easy way to think of this is to just remember that, to a function that is a friend of some class, all members of that class are public. It turns out that there's another way for functions to share data in C++, and that's using static class members. Let's take a look at that next.

Sharing Data with Static Class Members

If we declare a member of a class static, then only one copy of that member will exist in memory, no matter how many objects of that class we make. In other words, if we changed our counter class to this, where we declare the counter variable itself as static:

```
class counter_class {            // Declare counter_class class
public:
    char char_to_count;
→   static int number_of_char_seen;    // Make counter static
    counter_class(char the_char);
    void add_one(void);
};
```

then no matter how many objects of this type we make, they will share the same variable number_of_char_seen. In fact, this is the way programmers frequently share data between objects in C++ — by declaring members static. For example, let's say that we wanted to keep track of the number of x's and y's typed. In that case, we can set up two objects, x_counter and y_counter, each of which share the static data member named number_of_char_seen:

```
#include <iostream.h>
#include <ctype.h>

/* Counter implemented as an object */

class counter_class {            // Declare counter_class class
public:
    char char_to_count;
→   static int number_of_char_seen;    // Make counter static
    counter_class(char the_char);
    void add_one(void);
};

counter_class::counter_class(char the_char)
{
    char_to_count = the_char;
    number_of_char_seen = 0;
}

void counter_class::add_one(void){number_of_char_seen++;}

main()
{
    char in_char;
→   counter_class x_counter('x'), y_counter('y');
        :
```

Here we've initialized the two objects' constructors with 'x' and 'y.' Now, x_counter and y_counter share the variable number_of_char_seen. Each time we see an x or a y, we can use the correct version of add_one( ) like this:

```
#include <ctype.h>
#include <iostream.h>

/* Counter implemented as an object */

class counter_class {                       // Declare counter_class class
public:
    char char_to_count;
    static int number_of_char_seen;         // Make counter static
    counter_class(char the_char);
    void add_one(void);
};
    :

    :
main()
{
    char in_char;
    counter_class x_counter('x'), y_counter('y');

    cout << "Type a few letters and q to quit: ";
    do{                                 // Read x's.
        cin >> in_char;
→       if(in_char == x_counter.char_to_count) x_counter.add_one();
→       if(in_char == y_counter.char_to_count) y_counter.add_one();
    } while (toupper(in_char) != 'Q');
        :
```

Since the variable number_of_char_seen has been declared static, these two objects share it; that means that both x_counter.add_one( ) and y_counter.add_one( ) increment the same memory location. In fact, since that memory location, number_of_char_seen, is the same for any object of class counter_class, we can refer to it in code by its class name like this: counter_class::number_of_char_seen (note that this is only the case for static members of a class). In other words, since there is only one memory location named number_of_char_seen associated with this class, C++ allows us to refer to it by the names y_counter.number_of_char_seen, x_counter.number_of_char_seen, or counter_class::number_of_char_seen. In our program, that means that we can print out the number of x's and y's, like this:

```
#include <ctype.h>
#include <iostream.h>

/* Counter implemented as an object */

class counter_class {                       // Declare counter_class class
```

```
public:
    char char_to_count;
    static int number_of_char_seen;            // Make counter static
    counter_class(char the_char);
    void add_one(void);
};

counter_class::counter_class(char the_char)
{
    char_to_count = the_char;
    number_of_char_seen = 0;
}

void counter_class::add_one(void){number_of_char_seen++;}

main()
{
    char in_char;
    counter_class x_counter('x'), y_counter('y');

    cout << "Type a few letters and q to quit: ";
    do{                              // Read x's.
        cin >> in_char;
        if(in_char == x_counter.char_to_count) x_counter.add_one();
        if(in_char == y_counter.char_to_count) y_counter.add_one();
    } while (toupper(in_char) != 'Q');

    cout << "\nNumber of x's and y's: " <<
        counter_class::number_of_char_seen;

    return 0;
}
```

Member functions can also be declared static; in that case, there will only be one copy of that function, and you can refer to it as, say, counter_class::add_one( ), where counter_class is the class name, again independent of the names of any objects this function is a member of.

Let's finish our discussion of functions with one last topic before moving on to operator overloading: passing objects to functions.

Passing Objects to Functions

It turns out that passing objects to functions works as you might expect: C++ passes by value, so a copy of the object is simply sent to the function. Let's see how this works. For example, we might modify the program we developed to count the number of x's typed; at the end of the program, let's pass the object named counter (which holds the number of x's) to a function, print_this( ), which will print out the number of x's seen. To start, we just set up our counting object, which we name counter:

```
#include <iostream.h>
#include <ctype.h>

/* Object passing example */

class counter_class{
public:
    char char_to_count;
    int number_of_char_seen;
    counter_class(char the_char);
    void add_one(void);
};
    :
    :
main()
{
    counter_class counter('x');

}
```

Next, we define the necessary member functions, count x's, and then we pass counter to the printing function print_this( ) to print out counter.number_of_char_seen:

```
#include <iostream.h>
#include <ctype.h>

/* Object passing example */

class counter_class{
public:
    char char_to_count;
    int number_of_char_seen;
    counter_class(char the_char);
    void add_one(void);
};

counter_class::counter_class(char the_char)
{
    char_to_count = the_char;
```

```
        number_of_char_seen = 0;
    }

    void counter_class::add_one(void){number_of_char_seen++;}
    void print_this(counter_class counter_obj);

    main()
    {
        char in_char;
        counter_class counter('x');

        cout << "Type a few x's and q to quit: ";
        do{                            // Read x's.
            cin >> in_char;
            if(in_char == counter.char_to_count) counter.add_one();
        } while (toupper(in_char) != 'Q');
```
→
```
        print_this(counter);

        return 0;
    }
```

In print_this( ), we will take the copy of counter that is passed to us and name it, say, counter_obj:

→
```
    void print_this(counter_class counter_obj)
    {

    }
```

Now we're free to refer to the fields in this copy (and print them out) this way in print_this( ):

```
void print_this(counter_class counter_obj)
{
```
→
→
```
    cout << "Number of " << counter_obj.char_to_count << "'s: " << \
        counter_obj.number_of_char_seen << "\n";
}
```

The full program appears in Listing 3-2. Note that in print_this( ), all we have is a copy of the object to work with, not the original object. In particular, that means that we cannot affect any member of the original object. If we had wanted to do that, we would have needed a pointer to the object (and we'll see how that works soon).

That completes our discussion of functions in this chapter; we've seen over-loaded functions, inline functions, overloaded constructors, static functions, friend functions, and more. Now, however, it's time to turn to the next topic: Operator overloading. As you might expect, now that we can define our own objects, it will be very useful to redefine the standard operators to use those objects, and we'll explore that next.

Listing 3-2. Passing an Object to a Function

```
#include <iostream.h>
#include <ctype.h>

/* Object passing example */

class counter_class{
public:
    char char_to_count;
    int number_of_char_seen;
    counter_class(char the_char);
    void add_one(void);
};

counter_class::counter_class(char the_char)
{
    char_to_count = the_char;
    number_of_char_seen = 0;
}

void counter_class::add_one(void){number_of_char_seen++;}
void print_this(counter_class counter_obj);

main()
{
    char in_char;
    counter_class counter('x');

    cout << "Type a few x's and q to quit: ";
    do{                                 // Read x's.
        cin >> in_char;
        if(in_char == counter.char_to_count) counter.add_one();
    } while (toupper(in_char) != 'Q');

    print_this(counter);

    return 0;
}

void print_this(counter_class counter_obj)
```

Listing 3-2. *(continued)*

```
{
    cout << "\nNumber of " << counter_obj.char_to_count << "'s: " \
        << counter_obj.number_of_char_seen;
}
```

Overloading Unary Operators like ++ and --

We'll begin our discussion of operator overloading by noting that there are some operators that we cannot overload; in particular, we cannot overload the ., ::, .*, and ? operators. However, we can overload the rest, so let's begin with overloading unary operators (i.e., operators that only take one argument like ++ and --). For instance, our counter objects keep track of a certain character. In particular, every time that character is seen, we've been using a member function named add_one( ) to increment the internal data member number_of_char_seen.

We can change that, however, by defining the increment operation, ++, on counter objects. In other words, if we have an object named counter, and want to increment the data member number_of_char_seen, we'll be able just to use a statement like this:

```
counter++;
```

Overloading a unary operator like this is not difficult. To do it, we set up an *operator function.* Such functions must be either members or friends of the objects they work on. A unary operator function looks like this in general:

```
type class_name::operatorX(void)
{
    :
}
```

Here, the X is replaced by the operator's symbol itself (e.g., +, -, ++, --, etc). Note in particular that there is a return type associated with this function. Usually, an operator function returns the type of object that it works on. That's so that expressions like this (where each identifier stands for an object) are possible:

```
b = c + d;
```

Here, we want the results of adding two objects (c + d) to be another object of the same type so that we can assign it to a variable of that type (b). In fact, even the assignment operator can be used like this:

```
a = b = c + d;
```

so we'll also want it to return an object of the same type. In other words, using operator functions should follow the usual rules for expressions in C++: An expression like (c + d) should be of the same type as c and d themselves. That means that when we overload the addition operator, we'll specify that it returns that type.

Overloading a unary operator is easy. In our case, we're overloading ++, so we start by replacing the prototype of add_one( ) with the prototype of our new operator function in the class declaration:

```
#include <iostream.h>
#include <ctype.h>

/* Overload unary ++ */

class counter_class {              // Declare counter_class class
public:
    char char_to_count;
    int number_of_char_seen;
    counter_class(char the_char);
    counter_class operator++(void);
};
    :
```

Now we have to define the operator function itself. The actual member we have to increment is named number_of_char_seen, so we just do this:

```
#include <iostream.h>
#include <ctype.h>

/* Overload unary ++ */

class counter_class {              // Declare counter_class class
public:
    char char_to_count;
    int number_of_char_seen;
```

```
        counter_class(char the_char);
        counter_class operator++(void);
    };

    counter_class::counter_class(char the_char)
    {
        char_to_count = the_char;
        number_of_char_seen = 0;
    }

→   counter_class counter_class::operator++(void)
    {
→       number_of_char_seen++;
            :
```

That's almost it; since this operator function is a member of the class counter_class, we've been able to reach and increment the internal counter without problem. However, there is still one difficulty; we have to allow statements like this:

```
    her_counter = counter++;
```

so our return type will have to be of type counter_class. In particular, now that we've incremented the counter of the object we're working on, we should return that object. But how do we do that? You may have noticed that unary operator functions like this one get passed no parameters; i.e., the declaration looked like this:

```
    counter_class operator++(void);
```

It seems that we have no way of returning an object of type counter_class, because one was never passed to us. However, that's not quite true; our operator function (just like any member function) is *implicitly* passed a pointer to the object it's a member of. In other words, we couldn't refer to members like number_of_char_seen unless we knew what object we were referring to, and the program uses this implicit pointer automatically. In fact, we can use that pointer explicitly in our program if we want to — it's called the *this* pointer, and it points to the object our function is a member of. Using the this pointer, we'll be able to return the current object from our operator function, so let's determine how pointers to objects work next.

Pointers to Objects

In fact, pointers to objects work just as pointers to structures did in C, except now the -> operator can access member functions as well as data. For example, look at our counter object example:

```
#include <iostream.h>
#include <ctype.h>

/* Standard counter object */

class counter_class {              // Declare counter_class class
public:
    char char_to_count;
    int number_of_char_seen;
    counter_class(char the_char);
    void add_one(void);
};

counter_class::counter_class(char the_char)
{
    char_to_count = the_char;
    number_of_char_seen = 0;
}

void counter_class::add_one(void){number_of_char_seen++;}

main()
{
    char in_char;
    counter_class counter('x');

    cout << "Type a few x's and q to quit: ";
    do{
        cin >> in_char;
        if(in_char == counter.char_to_count)counter.add_one();
    } while (toupper(in_char) != 'Q');

    cout << "\nNumber of " << counter.char_to_count << "'s: " << \
        counter.number_of_char_seen;

    return 0;
}
```

To reach the member data and functions of the object counter, we can also just declare a pointer to that object, which we might call obj_ptr, and which we can use like this:

```
    obj_ptr->add_one();
```

Here's the new version of the same program, using a pointer to the object (note that we load the object pointer as we would any pointer; i.e., obj_ptr = &counter):

```
#include <iostream.h>
#include <ctype.h>

/* Object pointer example */

class counter_class {                    // Declare counter_class class
public:
    char char_to_count;
    int number_of_char_seen;
    counter_class(char the_char);
    void add_one(void);
};

counter_class::counter_class(char the_char) // Declare constructor
{
    char_to_count = the_char;
    number_of_char_seen = 0;
}

void counter_class::add_one(void){number_of_char_seen++;}

main()
{
    char in_char;
    counter_class counter('x'), *obj_ptr;
    obj_ptr = &counter;

    cout << "Type a few x's and q to quit: ";

    do{                               // Read x's.
        cin >> in_char;
        if(in_char == obj_ptr->char_to_count)obj_ptr->add_one();
    } while (toupper(in_char) != 'Q');

    cout << "\nNumber of " << obj_ptr->char_to_count << "'s: " << \
        obj_ptr->number_of_char_seen;

    return 0;
}
```

Of course, we can also increment or decrement object pointers, or perform pointer arithmetic on them as we can for any type of pointer. Now that we know how to handle pointers to objects, let's get back to our ++ overloading example.

The this Keyword

As mentioned earlier, 'this' is the name given to the pointer that is implicitly passed to each member function of an object. It is the reason that we can refer to member fields as number_of_char_seen instead of counter.number_of_char_seen in our objects. For example, each of these expressions in these member functions:

```
#include <iostream.h>
#include <ctype.h>

/* Counter implemented as an object */

class counter_class {                   // Declare counter_class class
public:
    char char_to_count;
    int number_of_char_seen;
    counter_class(char the_char);
    void add_one(void);
};

counter_class::counter_class(char the_char)
{
    char_to_count = the_char;
    number_of_char_seen = 0;
}

void counter_class::add_one(void)  // Declare counter-incrementer
{
    number_of_char_seen++;
}

main()
{
    :
    :
}
```

is actually a shorthand version of what's really happening. If this stands for a pointer to the current object, then we can reach members of that object with the arrow operator, ->, as we just saw. That is, this program works the same way, and means the same thing:

```
#include <iostream.h>
#include <ctype.h>

/* Counter implemented as an object */

class counter_class {                    // Declare counter_class class
public:
    char char_to_count;
    int number_of_char_seen;
    counter_class(char the_char);
    void add_one(void);
};

counter_class::counter_class(char the_char)
{
    this->char_to_count = the_char;
    this->number_of_char_seen = 0;
}

void counter_class::add_one(void) // Declare counter-incrementer
{
    this->number_of_char_seen++;
}

main()
{
    :
    :
}
```

Now we can see how to return the object we've been working on in our ++ function; because the pointer was implicitly passed to us (it's actually last on the stack), all we have to do is to return *this in our operator++( ) function:

```
#include <iostream.h>
#include <ctype.h>

/* Overload unary ++ */

class counter_class {                    // Declare counter_class class
public:
    char char_to_count;
```

```
        int number_of_char_seen;
        counter_class(char the_char);
        counter_class operator++(void);
};

counter_class::counter_class(char the_char)
{
    char_to_count = the_char;
    number_of_char_seen = 0;
}

counter_class counter_class::operator++(void)
{
    number_of_char_seen++;
    return *this;              // Use this keyword
}
    :
```

→

TIP   Friends functions do not get a this pointer passed to them; instead, when overloading unary friend operators, you should set up your objects as reference objects, and we'll see how to do that soon. That way, the object itself is passed, not a copy of it. For that matter, static member functions do not get a this pointer implicitly (because you can refer to them with the class name alone, independent of any object). The only parameters passed to them are the parameters passed explicitly, as declared in their prototypes. If you want a pointer to the current object, you'll have to pass it to a static member function (or a friend function) explicitly.

In earlier versions of ANSI C++, this operator function would have overridden ++ as both a postfix and prefix operator. Now, however, the function we've defined will only be called when ++ is used as a prefix like this: ++counter. To overload ++ as a postfix operator, we must declare it as a function receiving an int type argument (actually a dummy argument) and then copy over the function definition, giving it an int argument like this:

```
#include <iostream.h>
#include <ctype.h>

class counter_class {           // Declare counter_class class
public:
    char char_to_count;
    int number_of_char_seen;
    counter_class(char the_char);
```

```
    counter_class operator++(void);
→   counter_class operator++(int);
};

counter_class::counter_class(char the_char)
{
char_to_count = the_char;
number_of_char_seen = 0;
}

counter_class counter_class::operator++(void)
{
number_of_char_seen++;
return *this;          // Use this keyword
}

counter_class counter_class::operator++(int)
{
number_of_char_seen++;
return *this;          // Use this keyword
}

main()
{
  :
  :
}
```

Now we can use expressions like counter++ like this:

```
#include <iostream.h>
#include <ctype.h>

class counter_class {              // Declare counter_class class
public:
  char char_to_count;
  int number_of_char_seen;
  counter_class(char the_char);
  counter_class operator++(void);
  counter_class operator++(int);
};

counter_class::counter_class(char the_char)
{
char_to_count = the_char;
number_of_char_seen = 0;
}
```

```
counter_class counter_class::operator++(void)
{
number_of_char_seen++;
return *this;              // Use this keyword
}

counter_class counter_class::operator++(int)
{
number_of_char_seen++;
return *this;              // Use this keyword
}

main()
{
    char in_char;
    counter_class  counter('x');

    cout << "Type a few x's and q to quit: ";
    do{                                 // Read x's.
        cin >> in_char;
        if(in_char == counter.char_to_count)counter++;
    } while (toupper(in_char) != 'Q');

    cout << "\nNumber of " << counter.char_to_count << "'s: " \
        << counter.number_of_char_seen;
    return 0;
}
```

Our program is a success. That's it for our coverage of overloading unary operators. We'll move on to binary operators (e.g., +, - , *) next.

Overloading Binary Operators like + and –

As we saw, the only item passed to unary operator functions was the implicit pointer this, which pointed at the object we're using the operator on. In this case:

```
counter++;
```

we got a pointer to counter. However, in an expression like the following one, where b and c are objects (and we've overloaded the + operator):

```
b + c;
```

we'll get a this pointer to b, and a copy of c will be passed to us. In other words, unary operator functions get no parameters, but binary operator functions get one parameter, which corresponds to the rightmost operand. In general, it looks like this:

```
type class_name::operatorX(class_name second_operand)
{
   :
}
```

Here, X stands for the binary operator (e.g., +, -, *). For instance, we can create our own string type in C++, and overload operators like + and = to work with our new class. In this example, our goal will be to set up strings like this (where we are passing initialization values to the string's constructors):

```
main()
{
    string data_string("\0"), string1("Hello "), string2("world.\n");
       :
```

After we overload the +, = and even the << operator, we'll be able to do this with our strings:

```
main()
{
    string data_string("\0"), string1("Hello "), string2("world.\n");

→   data_string = string1 + string2;
→   cout << data_string;

}
```

In this case, we should get "Hello world.\n" on the screen. Let's see this in code.

Creating a C++ Character String Class

We can declare + and = as operator functions in the class which we might call string; notice that we do not declare << there — overloading insertors and extractors is slightly more complex, and we'll do that separately:

```
#include <iostream.h>
#include <string.h>
#include <ctype.h>

/* Operator overloading example */

class string {
public:
    char the_string[100];
    string(char *init_string);
→   string operator+(string second_string);
→   string operator=(string second_string);
};
    :
```

Here we've set aside space for the string data itself in our new objects, and then we declare the member functions that will work on that data. There are three such functions — a constructor to initialize the string, and two operator functions, + and =, which will work on these objects.

Note that both + and = only get one parameter — the copy of the second object that's passed. Let's start by defining the operator function operator+( ). When we use +, we'll be adding two string objects this way:

```
main()
{
    string data_string("\0"), string1("Hello "), string2("world.\n");

→   data_string = string1 + string2;
    cout << data_string;

    return 0;
}
```

We don't want to change the value of either string1 or string2 here; we just want to return an object that holds the two strings concatenated together. We might do that by declaring an internal string of the same type, filling it, and then returning it like this:

```
string string::operator+(string second_string)
{
→   string internal_string("\0");

    strcpy(internal_string.the_string, the_string);
    strcat(internal_string.the_string, second_string.the_string);
```

→
```
        return internal_string;
    }
```

Since we already have an implicit pointer to string1 (i.e., this), we can refer to the actual string data in it simply as the_string (which C++, in turn, understands as this->the_string). A copy of the second object, string2, is passed to us, and we name that copy second_string. We can reach the string data in second_string like this: second_string.the_string. All we need to do now is to use the data available to us and create the correct return object, and we do that as shown above.

| TIP | Note that while returning an object like this is safe (since what's really returned is a copy of the object), it would not have been safe to return a pointer to internal_string, because internal_string goes out of scope (and may therefore be overwritten in memory) when we exit string::operator+( ). |

The = operator function is similar. Here's how we want to use it:

```
main()
{
    string data_string("\0"), string1("Hello "), string2("world.\n");
```
→
```
    data_string = string1 + string2;
    cout << data_string;

    return 0;
}
```

In this case, we'll be working with two objects; the pointer named this will be pointing to the left hand object, data_string, and we'll get a copy of an object passed to us. The object passed to us is just the result of adding string1 and string2 (i.e., the object we just returned from the + operator function). We simply want to copy the string data from the object passed to us to the one pointed to by this, and can we do that as shown here:

```
    string string::operator=(string second_string)
    {
```
→
```
        strcpy(the_string, second_string.the_string);
        return *this;
    }
```

Here, since we do want to change the string data in the left hand object (i.e., this is the assignment operator), we overwrite it with strcpy( ) and then return that object. So far, then, our program looks like this:

```
#include <iostream.h>
#include <string.h>
#include <ctype.h>

/* Operator overloading example */

class string {
public:
    char the_string[100];
    string(char *init_string);
    string operator+(string second_string);
    string operator=(string second_string);
};

string::string(char *init_string){strcpy(the_string, init_string);}

string string::operator+(string second_string)
{
    string internal_string("\0");

    strcpy(internal_string.the_string, the_string);
    strcat(internal_string.the_string, second_string.the_string);
    return internal_string;
}

string string::operator=(string second_string)
{
    strcpy(the_string, second_string.the_string);
    return *this;
}
:
```

All that remains now is to overload the << operator so that we can print the result of our operations on the screen. To do that, we'll have to master a technique new in C++ — *references*.

Why to Call by Reference in C++

The normal way of passing parameters in C++ is by value — that is, a copy of the passed parameter is made, and the function we're calling can work on it.

However, we can also pass parameters by reference; in fact, we're already familiar with one way of passing parameters by reference — we can pass a pointer. For example, in this program, we pass a pointer to a character; in the function that we call, we are free to change that character's value like this:

```
#include <iostream.h>
void load_a(char *the_char);

/* Passing pointers */

main()
{
    char the_char = 'z';

    load_a(&the_char);                      // Pass a pointer
    cout << the_char;

    return 0;
}

void load_a(char *passed_char)
{
    *passed_char = 'a';
}
```

In C++ there's another way of passing by reference. We can set up functions so that the default method of passing parameters is to pass by reference, not by value. That is, even though we invoke the function with certain arguments, not pointers:

```
load_a(the_char);
```

the arguments are automatically passed by reference (which really means that an internal pointer to the parameter in memory is passed to the function). Let's look at an example. To set this kind of a function up, we only need to preface the names of the parameters it takes with &, this way:

```
#include <iostream.h>
void load_a(char &the_char);

/* Passing by reference */

main()
```

```
    {
        char the_char = 'z';

        load_a(the_char);                    // Pass by reference
        cout << the_char;

        return 0;
    }
```

→
```
    void load_a(char &passed_char)
    {
        passed_char = 'a';
    }
```

Note that we're no longer passing a pointer; instead, we've changed the way C++ handles this function, making it operate much more like a language that passes parameters by reference. What's happening here is that an internal pointer is passed to load_a( ), so that function has access to the original variable that was passed to it — but from our point of view, the syntax is just the same as if we passed parameters by value. Here, the variable named passed_char, which is internal to load_a( ), has become a reference to the_char, which is back in the main( ) function. Both of these variables refer to the same memory location. In other words, you can think of a reference to a variable (here that's passed_char) as simply another name for that variable (the_char):

```
    #include <iostream.h>
    void load_a(char &the_char);

    /* Passing by reference */

    main()
    {
        char the_char = 'z';
```

→
```
        load_a(the_char);                    // Pass by reference
        cout << the_char;

        return 0;
    }

    void load_a(char &passed_char)
    {
```
→
```
        passed_char = 'a';
    }
```

TIP It might appear as though & now has two uses: to create references, and to find addresses. The way to distinguish between them is this: If &variable is preceded by a type (e.g., int &variable), then we're talking about a reference. If there is no type (e.g., vble_ptr = &variable), then we're talking about an address.

That means that passing by reference is just as efficient as passing a pointer (i.e., it's quicker to pass a pointer than it is to copy over a whole object when passing by value), and the syntax is as simple as when we pass by value. This is one good reason to pass by reference. If you don't want the object you're passing to be changed, you can pass by constant reference like this: function_name(const &object_name).

TIP You can also declare *reference variables*, not just reference parameters. If you use & when declaring a variable, then it is treated as a reference variable, which means that it always gets handled and passed by reference. Note, however, that you have to be careful; for example, returning references to local variables when you return from a function will probably cause your program to crash.

As an example, we can update our stack example to use references. We used to pop values by passing a pointer, like this: stack.pop(&variable_name). Now we can change that by declaring pop( ) to take a reference like this:

```
int stack_class::pop(int& pop_to)
{
    if(stack_ptr == -1)        // Stack is empty -- return error
        return 0;
    else                       // Else return data
        pop_to = data_buffer[stack_ptr--];
        return 1;
}
```

Now variables are automatically passed to pop( ) by reference, not value, so we can pop values like this: stack.pop(variable_name). The new program is in Listing 3-3.

Listing 3-3. Stack Example with References

```
#include <iostream.h>

/* Stack implemented as an object  */

class stack_class {
    int data_buffer[100];
    int stack_ptr;      // stack_ptr = -1 → stack is empty
public:
    stack_class(void);
    int pop(int& pop_to);
    int push(int push_this);
};

stack_class::stack_class(void){stack_ptr = -1;}

int stack_class::pop(int& pop_to)
{
    if(stack_ptr == -1)      // Stack is empty -- return error
        return 0;
    else                     // Else return data
        pop_to = data_buffer[stack_ptr--];
        return 1;
}

int stack_class::push(int push_this)
{
    if(stack_ptr >= 99)      // Stack is full -- return error
        return 0;
    else                     // Else store data
        data_buffer[++stack_ptr] = push_this;
        return 1;
}

main()
{
    int loop_index, popped_value;
    stack_class stack();

    cout << "Pushing values now...\n";
    for(loop_index = 0; loop_index < 10; loop_index++){
        stack.push(loop_index);
        cout << "Pushed value--> " << loop_index << "\n";
    }

    cout << "Popping values now...\n";
    for(loop_index = 0; loop_index < 10; loop_index++){
        stack.pop(popped_value);
```

Listing 3-3. *(continued)*

```
        cout << "Popped value--> " << popped_value << "\n";
    }
    return 0;
}
```

We need to know about reference calling because we'll use that method when we define the << operator function in our string class example. We'll learn more about this process in Chapter 5, when we cover C++'s I/O library, but we can get a head start now. To begin, the << operator works on a stream named *ostream*, the output stream from our program, so the prototype for the function operator<<( ) actually looks like this:

```
ostream &operator<<(ostream &stream, string a_string);
```

Here, we're passed a reference to ostream (which we name stream) and a string object (i.e., the string object we want to send to the screen with <<). The string data we want to display is a member of the string object (a_string) that's passed to us.

> **TIP** In general, when you set up a function that changes the variable(s) passed to it, it can often be less confusing to pass by pointer, not by reference. The reason is that using pointer notation makes it explicit that we're changing the passed argument, while when we pass by reference, there is no such indication.

Therefore, inside operator<<( ), we can send the string data to the screen like this: cout << a_string.the_string;. After we do, we have to return a reference to the same stream we got as a parameter, because << can be chained; in other words, expressions like this are legal:

```
cout << a_string << a_second_string;
```

That means that the operator function for << looks like this:

```
ostream &operator<<(ostream &stream, string a_string)
{
    cout << a_string.the_string;
    return stream;
}
```

And we're done. Now we've overloaded +, =, and <<, so it's possible to use statements like this in our program:

```
main()
{
→      string data_string("\0"), string1("Hello "), string2("world.\n");

→      data_string = string1 + string2;

→      cout << data_string;

       return 0;
}
```

At this point, then, we've been able to overload operators to work on our string objects. In this way, we've added a whole new ability to our programs — the ability to handle strings as objects, making statements like data_string = string1 + string2 possible. The entire program appears in Listing 3-4.

Listing 3-4. Operator Overloading Example

```
#include <iostream.h>
#include <string.h>
#include <ctype.h>

/* Operator overloading example */

class string {
public:
    char the_string[100];
    string(char *init_string);
    string operator+(string second_string);
    string operator=(string second_string);
};

string::string(char *init_string)
{
    strcpy(the_string, init_string);
}

string string::operator+(string second_string)
{
    string internal_string("\0");

    strcpy(internal_string.the_string, the_string);
```

Listing 3-4. *(continued)*

```
        strcat(internal_string.the_string, second_string.the_string);
        return internal_string;
}

string string::operator=(string second_string)
{
        strcpy(the_string, second_string.the_string);
        return *this;
}

ostream &operator<<(ostream &stream, string a_string)
{
        cout << a_string.the_string;
        return stream;
}

main()
{
        string data_string("\0"), string1("Hello "), string2("world.\n");

        data_string = string1 + string2;
        cout << data_string;

        return 0;
}
```

The Built-in Microsoft CString Class

It turns out that MS C++ already has a string class ready for us to use, and it's called CString. This class is part of the *Microsoft Foundation Class Libraries*, which we'll see a great deal about later, especially when we start working with Windows, but we can take a look at it here too.

The Microsoft Foundation Class (MFC) libraries are libraries of pre-written C++ classes, and they're found in the c:\c700\mfc\lib directory. The DOS versions are: safxcr.lib (small memory model — afx stands for Application Frameworks), mafxcr.lib (medium memory model), and lafxcr.lib (large memory model). Note that, by default, only mafxcr.lib is installed when you install MS C 7+, and to use it, you must specify that you're using the medium memory model. For example, if we wanted to use a program called cstring.cpp, we would use the /AM switch and link in the mafxcr.lib library like this:

```
C:\>cl /AM cstring.cpp mafxcr.lib
```

The code in cstring.cpp is just about the same as we've already developed above. All we have to do is to define an identifier named _DOS so that the compiler knows we want to create a DOS program, not a Windows program, and include afx.h like this:

```
→   #define _DOS

    #include <iostream.h>
→   #include <afx.h>

    /* Operator overloading example */

    main()
    {
        CString data_string(""), string1("Hello "), string2("world.\n");

        data_string = string1 + string2;

        cout << data_string;

        return 0;
    }
```

That's all there is to it; now the program functions as before. The CString class has a great deal of utility, and we'll run into it again later. Its member functions and data are shown in Table 3-1.

Now let's continue our discussion of functions, operators, and overloading by examining two very important C++ operators: new and delete.

The new and delete Operators

The functions malloc( ), calloc( ), realloc( ), and free( ) are all available in both C and C++; however, C++ adds two new operators named new and delete that perform many of the same tasks. In fact, that standard way of allocating and deallocating memory in C++ is to use new and delete. These operators are popular for two reasons — we can initialize objects with new (i.e., we can pass parameters to an object's constructors), and we can overload both of these

Member	Means
AnsiToOem	Convert string from Ansi to Oem char set
Collate	Compare country-dependent strings
Compare	Compares two strings, case sensitive
CompareNoCase	Compares two strings, case insensitive
CString	Constructor
Empty	Sets string length to 0
Find	Finds a character or substring in the string data
FindOneOf	Find first matching character
GetAt	Get character at a position
GetBuffer	Gets pointer to the chars in the CString
GetBufferSetLength	Get pointer to the chars, with truncation
GetLength	Get number of characters
IsEmpty	Is string empty?
Left	Get left part of a string
LoadString	Loads CString from Windows resource
MakeLower	Make characters lowercase
MakeReverse	Reverse characters
MakeUpper	Make characters uppercase
Mid	Get the middle part of a string
OemToAnsi	Convert from Oem chars to Ansi
operator +	Concatenates
operator +=	Concatenates and assigns
operator <<	Inserts to archive or dump
operator =	Assigns a new value
operator >>	Extracts from archive
operator ( )	Access char
operator [ ]	Get character at a given position
operators ==	Comparison operator ==
operators >	Comparison operator >
operators <	Comparison operator <
ReleaseBuffer	Yields control of buffer
ReverseFind	Find char starting from the end
Right	Get right part of a string
SetAt	Sets chars at a given position

Table 3-1. CString Member Functions and Data

Member	Means
SpanExcluding	Get substring containing char not in a set
SpanIncluding	Get substring containing chars in a set
~CString	Destructor

Table 3-1. (continued)

operators with respect to a certain class. The way these two operators work is like this:

```
pointer_to_class = new var_or_class_class;
delete pointer_to_class;
```

In other words, we don't need to use sizeof( ) to determine how many bytes to allocate; we can just indicate the data type (i.e., variable or class) that we want to allocate space for, and new does the rest. In fact, it even returns the correct pointer type, so we don't have to use a type cast (as we do with malloc( )). Also, if we have parameters to pass on to a constructor, we can do that like this with new:

```
pointer_to_class = new class_class(param1, param2,...);
```

A Memory-handling Object

Let's examine an example. If we took our class named counter_class:

```
#include <iostream.h>
#include <ctype.h>

/* Counter implemented as an object */

class counter_class {              // Declare counter_class class
public:
    char char_to_count;
    int number_of_char_seen;
    counter_class(char the_char);
    void add_one(void);
};
    :
```

then we could use new to allocate space for an object of this class — and send 'x' to the object's constructor — like this:

```
#include <iostream.h>
#include <ctype.h>

/* Counter implemented as an object */

class counter_class {                       // Declare counter_class class
public:
    char char_to_count;
    int number_of_char_seen;
    counter_class(char the_char);
    void add_one(void);
};

counter_class::counter_class(char the_char)
{
    char_to_count = the_char;
    number_of_char_seen = 0;
}

void counter_class::add_one(void){number_of_char_seen++;}

main()
{
    char in_char;
    counter_class *counter_ptr;

→   counter_ptr = new counter_class('x'); // Use new

    cout << "Type a few x's and q to quit: ";
    do{                                     // Read x's.
        cin >> in_char;
        if(in_char == counter_ptr->char_to_count)
            counter_ptr->add_one();
    } while (toupper(in_char) != 'Q');

    cout << "\nNumber of " << counter_ptr->char_to_count << "'s: " << \
        counter_ptr->counter;

    return 0;
}
```

The new operator returns a pointer to the new object in memory; if we want to delete that object, we just pass that pointer to delete. This kind of simple memory handling is very attractive to C++ programmers.

We can also use new and delete to allocate and release arrays. For example, to set up an array of 10 ints, we could use this statement:

```
#include <iostream.h>

main()
{
    int *the_ptr;

    the_ptr = new int[10];         // Allocate array

    the_ptr[2] = 1;
    cout << the_ptr[2];
        :
```

To delete this array, we do not pass the number of array elements; instead, we simply use the statement delete[ ] the_ptr; this way:

```
#include <iostream.h>

main()
{
    int *the_ptr;

    the_ptr = new int[10];         // Allocate array

    delete[] the_ptr;             // Delete array using C++ 2.1 syntax

    return 0;
}
```

We'll see new and delete very frequently in the rest of this book. Now that we've seen a little about how to use them, let's look at the process of overloading them.

Overloading new and delete

Overloading new and delete is much like overloading any operator. However, there are a few differences in the parameters passed here and the type of return value expected. In particular, new receives a parameter of type size_t, which is the type of the largest memory item that can be allocated (size_t is defined in stddef.h), and it returns a void pointer:

```
void *class_class::operator new(size_t size)
    :
```

In this example, we can overload this operator so that it lets us know when it is allocating memory, like this:

```
void *class_class::operator new(size_t size)
{
    cout << "allocating memory...";
    void *p = new char[size];
    return p;
}
```

On the other hand, we just pass the delete operator the pointer to the memory space to deallocate, like this:

```
void class_class::operator delete(void *p)
        :
```

That means that we can overload this operator to let us know when we're deallocating memory, like this:

```
void class_class::operator delete(void *p)
{
    cout << "deleting memory...";
    delete (void *) p;
}
```

We can put these new, overloaded versions of new and delete to work for us, as seen in Listing 3-5.

Listing 3-5. Overloading the new and delete Operators

```
#include <iostream.h>
#include <ctype.h>
#include <stddef.h>

/* Counter implemented as an object */

class counter_class {                  // Declare counter_class class
public:
    char char_to_count;
    int number_of_char_seen;
    counter_class(char the_char);
    void add_one(void);
    void *operator new(size_t size);
    void operator delete(void *p);
```

(continued)

Listing 3-5. *(continued)*

```cpp
};

counter_class::counter_class(char the_char)
{
    char_to_count = the_char;
    number_of_char_seen = 0;
}

void counter_class::add_one(void){number_of_char_seen++;}

void *counter_class::operator new(size_t size)
{
    cout << "allocating memory...";
    void *p = new char[size];
    return p;
}

void counter_class::operator delete(void *p)
{
    cout << "deleting memory...";
    delete (void *) p;
}

main()
{
    char in_char;
    counter_class *counter_ptr;

    cout << "Type a few x's and q to quit: ";
    counter_ptr = new counter_class('x'); // Use new

    do{                                    // Read x's.
        cin >> in_char;
        if(in_char == counter_ptr->char_to_count)
            counter_ptr->add_one();
    } while (toupper(in_char) != 'Q');

    cout << "\nNumber of " << counter_ptr->char_to_count << "'s: " << \
        counter_ptr->number_of_char_seen;

    return 0;
}
```

That's how to overload new and delete. Before leaving the topic of overloading altogether, however, we should take a look at the process of overloading the [ ] operator.

Overloading the [ ] Operator

Overloading the [ ], subscripting, operator is not difficult. Let's put together a small example that produces a vector class; that is, our objects will be one-dimensional arrays of, say, floating point numbers. In the Vector class' constructor, we can allocate space for the vector with new, like this:

```
Vector::Vector(int dimensions){internal_data_ptr = new float[dimensions];}
```

We can set up vector objects like this:

```
    main()
    {
→       Vector the_vector(10);        // Vector of 10 elements
            :
    }
```

If we overload the [ ] operator for this class, we can address elements of our array, like this:

```
    main()
    {
        Vector the_vector(10);        // Vector of 10 elements

→       the_vector[5] = 10.0;
→       cout << the_vector[5];

        return 0;
    }
```

To overload [ ], we need only need to fetch the array element out of the space we've set aside for the array. We can set up the operator[ ] function like this:

```
#include <iostream.h>

class Vector
```

```
    {
        float *internal_data_ptr;

    public:
        Vector(int dimensions);
→       float& operator[](int index) {return internal_data_ptr[index];}
    };

    Vector::Vector(int dimensions){internal_data_ptr = new float[dimensions];}

    main()
    {
        Vector the_vector(10);          // Vector of 10 elements

        the_vector[5] = 10.0;
        cout << the_vector[5];

        return 0;
    }
```

And that's it; we've overloaded the [ ] operator and created a vector class. This type of class is called a *container* class in C++; that is, it's a class that can contain other objects (in this case, floating point numbers).

Although Microsoft C++ does not fully support them yet, this is normally where we could use *templates* — to create container classes. Templates are not a built-in part of Microsoft C++ yet, but there is a source code implementation of templates that comes with MS C++ 7.0 in the directory c:\c700\mfc\samples\templdef. With templates, we can set up container classes without specifying the type of variables or objects that go into them. That makes it easy to create vectors of any object that we choose:

Vector Object the_vector

Obj1	Obj2	Obj3	Obj4	Obj5

If the class Vector was a template class, the elements of the vector are of an unspecified type, and we could fill it with any type of object we want — we don't need to specify the type of objects we'll store in it until we put it to use. Using templates, our previous example would look like this:

```
    #include <iostream.h>

    /* Class Template Example */
```

```
template <class T>
class Vector
{
    T *ptr_to_array;

public:
    Vector(int number_of_elements);
    T& operator[](int index) {return ptr_to_array[index];}
};

template <class T>
Vector<T>::Vector(int number_of_elements)
{
    ptr_to_array = new T[number_of_elements];
}

main()
{
    Vector<float> the_vector(10);     // Vector of 10 elements

    the_vector[5] = 10.0;

    cout << the_vector[5];

    return 0;
}
```

The designation "class T" stands for either a class or a variable type, and it becomes "float" when we specify that we want a vector of floating point numbers (i.e., Vector<float> the_vector(10);). If we wanted a vector of some other type or class of element, we would only have to declare it that way: Vector<other_type> the_vector(number_of_elements). This way, templates allow us to handle arguments of unspecified type, which is perfect for creating container classes which contain collections of objects.

There's one last topic that we should cover while still on the topic of functions, operators, and overloading. We've seen that we can pass and return objects to and from functions, but there's one case we didn't cover: What if the object we're passing has pointers or references in it?

Copy Constructors

Let's say that we passed an object to a function as we've done already in this chapter, except that now the object we pass has a pointer in it. The object is passed by value to the function, which means that an exact copy is made, including a copy of the pointer. That means that the copy of the object and the original object uninte. ionally share the same data space (i.e., the memory pointed to by the pointer). In addition, when we return from the function, the copy of the object is deleted, including the copy of the pointer, which means that the original object is left with a pointer that points to deleted memory.

Now consider what happens when we return an object from a function if that object has a pointer in it. When we return an object, we're really returning a temporary copy of the object. If the original object contained a pointer, the temporary copy will contain a copy of that pointer. If that pointer pointed to memory in the stack frame of the function, then when we leave the scope of the function, the copy of the pointer in the returned object will be left pointing to deleted stack space.

Both of these problems appear when copies are made of objects that contain pointers or references. If you simply duplicate an object with pointers in it, you'll duplicate the pointers also. That means that the pointers in the copy of the object will point to the same memory space as the pointers in the original object. The solution to this problem is to set up a *copy constructor* for that class.

Copy constructors are called when copies of an object are created. They allocate new memory space for the object they're constructing instead of copying over old pointers to already allocated memory. For example, let's say that our string example went from character arrays like this:

```
class string {
public:
    char the_string[100];
    string(char *init_string);
    string operator+(string second_string);
    string operator=(string second_string);
};
```

to pointers like this:

```
class string {
public:
    char *the_string;                          // Use pointers
    string(char *init_string);
    string operator+(string second_string);
    string operator=(string second_string);
};
```

Originally, there was no problem, because when a new object is created that has an array in it (the_string[100]), a new array is also created. Now, however, we're using a pointer to point to our string data (the memory for the string data will be allocated in the class' constructor), and when our object is copied, so is that pointer.

Say that we wanted to return string1 of class string from a function. To do that, C++ will create a temporary copy of string1, which we can name temp. The default procedure is simply to copy the_object over into temp, which would cause a problem now because of the internal pointer. However, if there is a copy constructor, C++ will use that instead because it knows that we want to override the default copying procedure. In particular, C++ will initialize temp from string1 like this, using the copy constructor:

```
string temp(string1);
```

Now, when temp gets returned, there will be no problem, because the string class' copy constructor allocated new space for it in memory. A copy constructor actually takes a constant reference to the original object, not the object itself, like this:

```
class string {
public:
    char *the_string;                      // Use pointer
    string(char *init_string);
    string operator+(string second_string);
    string operator=(string second_string);
};

string::string(char *init_string)
{
    the_string = new char[100];            // 100 chars
    strcpy(the_string, init_string);
}

string::string(const string &other_string)
{

}
```

In the copy constructor, then, we just use new to create a new character array, and we're set:

```
class string {
public:
    char *the_string;                       // Use pointer
    string(char *init_string);
    string operator+(string second_string);
    string operator=(string second_string);
};

string::string(char *init_string)
{
    the_string = new char[100];             // 100 chars
    strcpy(the_string, init_string);
}

string::string(const string &other_string)
{
→   the_string = new char[100];             // 100 chars
→   strcpy(the_string, other_string.the_string);
}
```

That's how a copy constructor looks; now we can perform all types of operations without error, including passing and returning objects of this class. Note
that we can also initialize one object with another (because this explicitly calls
the copy constructor):

```
main()
{
    string string1("Hello World");
→   string string2(string1);       // Possible problem w/ copied ptrs

    cout << string2;

    return 0;
}
```

When we initialize string2 from string1, the two will be separate in memory. In
addition, when C++ creates copies of our string objects, they will also be
separate in memory from the originals. In this way, copy constructors can
solve the problems that occur when we're passing or returning objects that
have pointers or references in them. Instead of copying over old pointers and
references (so the two objects unintentionally share the same data spaces), an
entirely new object is created. The entire program is in Listing 3-6.

TIP Keep in mind that if your objects require a copy constructor you might also have to overload other operators like the assignment operator, =, for the same reason (i.e., you want to allocate new memory space rather than copying over old pointers or references).

Listing 3-6. Copy Constructor Example

```
#include <iostream.h>
#include <string.h>

/* Copy Constructor example: Uses pointer, not array, to store chars*/

class string {
public:
    char *the_string;                    // Use pointer
    string(char *init_string);
    string operator+(string second_string);
    string operator=(string second_string);
};

string::string(char *init_string)
{
    the_string = new char[100];          // 100 chars
    strcpy(the_string, init_string);
}

string::string(const string &other_string)
{
    the_string = new char[100];          // 100 chars
    strcpy(the_string, other_string.the_string);
}

string string::operator+(string second_string)
{
    string internal_string("\0");

    strcpy(internal_string.the_string, the_string);
    strcat(internal_string.the_string, second_string.the_string);
    return internal_string;
}
```

(continued)

Listing 3-6. *(continued)*

```
string string::operator=(string second_string)
{
    strcpy(the_string, second_string.the_string);
    return *this;
}

ostream &operator<<(ostream &stream, string a_string)
{
    cout << a_string.the_string;
    return stream;
}

main()
{
    string string1("Hello World");
    string string2(string1);    // Possible problem w/ copied ptrs

    cout << string2;

    return 0;
}
```

We've progressed far in this chapter; we've seen function overloading, default function parameters, inline functions, friend functions, as well as how to overload both unary and binary operators in C++. Now that we have a good start in C++, we can start exploring another important part of object-oriented programming: How to derive one type of class from another. That will take place in the next chapter, where we examine C++ inheritance and polymorphism.

C++ Inheritance and Polymorphism

In this chapter, we'll see a great deal more about how inheritance works between objects in C++. We've already seen a little about inheritance in Chapter 2, but there are many questions that are still unanswered. For example: When should you use inheritance? How do constructors and destructors work with inherited objects? Is it possible to have multiple inheritance? Are the members of a base class public or private in a derived class?

Besides these questions, we'll also see some powerful new aspects of C++ here. In particular, we'll see virtual functions, pure virtual functions, and abstract classes — and how they relate to *run-time polymorphism*. In C++, polymorphism refers to the ability of one function name to stand for a variety of function implementations. We saw *compile time* polymorphism when we discussed function and operator overloading. In this chapter, we'll expand that concept to run-time overloading, which is called *overriding*. Let's get started at once.

Why to Use Inheritance

Inheritance is very popular in C++ because it allows you to take pre-existing code and classes and extend them. We already know something about inheritance; we've seen this example before:

```
#include <iostream.h>

class animal {
public:
    void eat(void);
    void sleep(void);
    void breathe(void);
};

class elephant : public animal {
public:
    void trumpet(void);
    void stampede(void);
} jumbo;

void animal::eat(void){cout << "Eating...\n";}
void animal::sleep(void){cout << "Sleeping...\n";}
void animal::breathe(void){cout << "Breathing...\n";}
void elephant::trumpet(void){cout << "Trumpeting...\n";}
void elephant::stampede(void){cout << "Stampeding...\n";}

main()
{
    jumbo.breathe();
    jumbo.trumpet();
    jumbo.breathe();

    return 0;
}
```

Here, we're declaring a *base class* named animal:

```
class animal {
public:
    void eat(void);
    void sleep(void);
    void breathe(void);
};
```

This class holds generic functions for all animals. We make use of those functions in the derived class, which we call elephant:

```
class animal {
public:
    void eat(void);
    void sleep(void);
    void breathe(void);
};
```

→
```
      class elephant : public animal {
      public:
           void trumpet(void);
           void stampede(void);
      } jumbo;
```

In this case, we are inheriting all the member functions of animal in the derived class named elephant, and we're setting up an object named jumbo. Following this, we define all the member functions like this:

```
      #include <iostream.h>

      class animal {
      public:
           void eat(void);
           void sleep(void);
           void breathe(void);
      };

      class elephant : public animal {
      public:
           void trumpet(void);
           void stampede(void);
      } jumbo;
```

→
→
→
→
→
```
      void animal::eat(void){cout << "Eating...\n";}
      void animal::sleep(void){cout << "Sleeping...\n";}
      void animal::breathe(void){cout << "Breathing...\n";}
      void elephant::trumpet(void){cout << "Trumpeting...\n";}
      void elephant::stampede(void){cout << "Stampeding...\n";}
           :
```

From now on, jumbo has access to all public members of animal( ); for example, these are now legal statements:

```
      #include <iostream.h>

      class animal {
      public:
           void eat(void);
           void sleep(void);
           void breathe(void);
      };

      class elephant : public animal {
      public:
           void trumpet(void);
```

```
     void stampede(void);
} jumbo;

void animal::eat(void){cout << "Eating...\n";}
void animal::sleep(void){cout << "Sleeping...\n";}
void animal::breathe(void){cout << "Breathing...\n";}
void elephant::trumpet(void){cout << "Trumpeting...\n";}
void elephant::stampede(void){cout << "Stampeding...\n";}

main()
{
     jumbo.breathe();
     jumbo.trumpet();
     jumbo.breathe();

     return 0;
}
```

Using animal as a base class, we have all the basic functions (eat( ), sleep( ), breathe( )) necessary as the base for all types of new classes like tiger, zebra, monkey, and so on. Since they all can use animal as a common base, we can save ourselves a great deal of programming.

A DOS Graphics Window Example

Inheritance is very important when working with a complex programming platform like Windows, as we'll see. There are dozens of pre-defined base classes in the Microsoft Foundation Class libraries that we will start with in Windows, but in order to use them, we'll have to tailor them to the program we have in mind. That's the way C++ for Windows works — inheritance may be the most important aspect of C++ as far as programming there goes. Even though we haven't reached our Windows chapters yet, we can see this with a small example that runs in DOS graphics modes. For example, we might want to place this window on the screen, using DOS graphics:

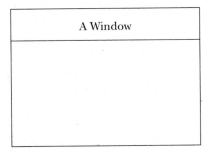
A Window

However, the window class that's available might look like this, where there is no provision made for a title (the title is "A Window" above):

```
class wnd {
public:
    void show_window(int l, int t, int r, int b);
};
```

This function, wnd::show_window( ) might only place a blank window on the screen like this:

Even so, we can use wnd as a base class, deriving our own window class, titled_wnd. That might look like this, where the new function, show_titled_window( ), will call wnd::show_window( ) to display the basic window and then add to that itself, placing the title we pass to it in that window:

```
class wnd {
public:
    void show_window(int l, int t, int r, int b);
};

class titled_wnd : public wnd {
public:
    void show_titled_window(int l, int t, int r, int b, char* wtitle);
};
```

In this way, we've started with a basic window class and augmented it into a titled window class. Here's how the whole program, doswin.cpp, would look (to create doswin.exe, use this command: cl doswin.cpp graphics.lib):

```
#include <graph.h>

/* DOS Graphics Window Example */

class wnd {
public:
```

```
        void show_window(int l, int t, int r, int b);
};

class titled_wnd : public wnd {
public:
        void show_titled_window(int l, int t, int r, int b, char* wtitle);
};

void wnd::show_window(int l, int t, int r, int b){
        _rectangle(_GBORDER, l*8, t*8, r*8, b*8);
}

void titled_wnd::show_titled_window(int l, int t, int r, int b,
        char* wtitle)
{
        _rectangle(_GBORDER, l*8, t*8, r*8, t*8+8);  // Title box
        _settextposition(t+1, l+11);
        _outtext(wtitle);                            // Title
        show_window(l, t, r, b);                     // Window itself
}

main()
{
        titled_wnd DOSWindow;
        _setvideomode(_HRES16COLOR);

        DOSWindow.show_titled_window(10, 5, 40, 16, "A Window");

        return 0;
}
```

Let's look into inheritance more closely now. There are three keywords we can use to give a program access to members of a class: public, private, and protected. If members are public, the rest of the program has access to them. If they're private, they do not. If, on the other hand, some members of a base class are *protected*, then access is the same as private for all parts of the program — except for derived classes.

How to Protect Members of Objects

If you declare a member of a base class protected, like this:

```
    class animal {
→   protected:
        void eat(void);
```

```
    void sleep(void);
    void breathe(void);
};
```

then those members are private to the rest of the program, expect for classes derived from this one:

```
class animal {
protected:
    void eat(void);
    void sleep(void);
    void breathe(void);
};
```

→
```
class elephant : public animal {
public:
    void trumpet(void);
    void stampede(void);
};
```

Here, the protected members of animal become protected members of elephant — inaccessible to all parts of the program, except member functions of elephant and classes derived from it. In other words, you use the keyword protected when you want to keep members of a class private in a base class and in all classes derived from it; that is, protected lets certain members stay hidden from the rest of the program, even in derived classes.

So far, we've been assuming public inheritance; that is, we've used the keyword public in this line:

→
```
class elephant : public animal {
public:
    void trumpet(void);
    void stampede(void);
};
```

If we use public here, then all public and protected parts of animal become public and protected parts of elephant (private parts of animal are not accessible to class elephant to begin with). The other option is private:

→
```
class elephant : private animal {
public:
    void trumpet(void);
    void stampede(void);
};
```

In this case, all public and protected members of animal become private members of elephant; that is, using private inheritance specifies that the public and protected members of a base class can only be inherited one level.

Let's see another, more useful example of inheritance now. Our stack provides us with a useful base class, since many computational operations can use a stack. For example, we may have a program in which we read a decimal integer, convert it to hex, and print it out:

```c
#include <iostream.h>

/* Convert decimal to hex. */

main()
{
    unsigned int i = 0, index = 0, hexdig = 0;
    char out_string[10];

    cout << "Type a positive integer please: ";
    cin >> i;
    do{
        out_string[index++] = (i%16 > 9 ? i%16 - 10 + 'a' : i%16 + '0');
    }while(i /= 16);

    cout << "That number in hexadecimal is ";
    while(index) cout << out_string[--index];
}
```

In this case, we set up an array named out_string[ ] in which we placed the successive digits:

```c
do{
    out_string[index++] = (i%16 > 9 ? i%16 - 10 + 'a' : i%16 + '0');
}while(i /= 16);
```

However, since we stripped them off (by successively dividing by 16) and stored them in reverse order, we have to take them out of the array backwards:

```c
    do{
        out_string[index++] = (i%16 > 9 ? i%16 - 10 + 'a' : i%16 + '0');
    }while(i /= 16);

    cout << "That number in hexadecimal is ";
→   while(index) cout << out_string[--index];
}
```

This would be easier — and make more sense logically — if we just used a stack, pushing the characters on until there were no more to push, and then popping and printing them. Let's use our class stack_class as a base class to provide stack support. From it, we can derive a new class, say number_print-ing_class, which might include the function print_in_hex( ). In other words, we can use stack_class as the base class for number_printing_class like this:

```
→   class number_printing_class : public stack_class {
    public:
        void print_in_hex(int i);
    };
```

Now the function print_in_hex( ) will have access to a stack. If we created an object of number_printing_class named, say, printem, then we could print numbers out in hex like this:

```
printem.print_in_hex(number);
```

Because of inheritance, the print_in_hex( ) function has access to both the push( ) and pop( ) functions, and it can use them freely. That means that print_in_hex( ) might look like this:

```
void number_printing_class::print_in_hex(int i)
{
    char the_char;

    do{
→       push((char) (i%16 > 9 ? i%16-10+'a' : i%16+'0'));
    }while(i /= 16);

    cout << "That number in hexadecimal is: ";

→   while(pop(&the_char)) cout << the_char;
}
```

We should note two things here. First, push( ) and pop( ) are now members of the object we've defined, printem, so we can just use them like this: push( ) and pop( ). Second, we want to push a char here, so we should define our stack as a char stack; we can do that like this in the class definition:

```
#include <iosteam.h>

/* Example showing inheritance   */
```

```
   class stack_class {
→      char char_data_buffer[50];
→      int char_stack_ptr;    // char_stack_ptr = -1 → stack is empty
   public:
       stack_class(void);
→      int pop(char *pop_to);
→      int push(char push_this);
   };
   :
```

Our class stack_class can now handle chars. Let's write the rest of the program now. After setting up our stack class, we set up the class number_printing_class to inherit stack_class like this:

```
#include <iosteam.h>

/* Example showing inheritance  */

class stack_class {
    char char_data_buffer[50];
    int char_stack_ptr;    // char_stack_ptr = -1 → stack is empty
public:
    stack_class(void);
    int pop(char *pop_to);
    int push(char push_this);
};

→ class number_printing_class : public stack_class {
  public:
      void print_in_hex(int i);
  };
      :
```

Following this are the definitions of all the member functions, including number_printing_class::print_in_hex( ):

```
#include <iostream.h>

/* Example showing inheritance  */

class stack_class {
    char char_data_buffer[50];
    int char_stack_ptr;    // char_stack_ptr = -1 → stack is empty
public:
    stack_class(void);
    int pop(char *pop_to);
```

```
        int push(char push_this);
    };

    class number_printing_class : public stack_class {
    public:
    void print_in_hex(int i);
    };

→   stack_class::stack_class(void){char_stack_ptr = -1;}

    int stack_class::pop(char *pop_to)
    {
        if(char_stack_ptr == -1)      // Stack is empty -- return error
            return 0;
        else                          // Else return data
            *pop_to = char_data_buffer[char_stack_ptr--];
            return 1;
    }

    int stack_class::push(char push_this)
    {
        if(char_stack_ptr >= 49)      // Stack is full -- return error
            return 0;
        else                          // Else store data
            char_data_buffer[++char_stack_ptr] = push_this;
            return 1;
    }

    void number_printing_class::print_in_hex(int i)
    {
        char the_char;

        do{
            push((char) (i%16 > 9 ? i%16-10+'a' : i%16+'0'));
        }while(i /= 16);
        cout << "That number in hexadecimal is: ";
        while(pop(&the_char)) cout << the_char;
    }
    :
```

Now we can declare and use printem in main( ) like this:

```
    main()
    {
        unsigned int number = 0;
→       number_printing_class printem;

        cout << "Type a positive integer please: ";
```

```
        cin >> number;

→       printem.print_in_hex(number);

        return 0;
}
```

Here we just ask for a positive integer and store it in the variable named number. We can then print it out in hex by using the print_in_hex( ) function as shown above. And that's all there is to it — we've seen how we can make our stack class an internal part of another class. The entire program appears in Listing 4-1.

Listing 4-1. C++ Inheritance Example

```
#include <iostream.h>

/* Example showing inheritance  */

class stack_class {
    char char_data_buffer[50];
    int char_stack_ptr;    // char_stack_ptr = -1 → stack is empty
public:
    stack_class(void);
    int pop(char *pop_to);
    int push(char push_this);
};

class number_printing_class : public stack_class {
public:
    void print_in_hex(int i);
} printem;

stack_class::stack_class(void){char_stack_ptr = -1;}

int stack_class::pop(char *pop_to)
{
    if(char_stack_ptr == -1)    // Stack is empty -- return error
        return 0;
    else                        // Else return data
        *pop_to = char_data_buffer[char_stack_ptr--];
        return 1;
}

int stack_class::push(char push_this)
{
    if(char_stack_ptr >= 49)    // Stack is full -- return error
```

Listing 4-1. *(continued)*

```
            return 0;
    else                        // Else store data
            char_data_buffer[++char_stack_ptr] = push_this;
            return 1;
}

void number_printing_class::print_in_hex(int i)
{
    char the_char;

    do{
        push((char) (i%16 > 9 ? i%16-10+'a' : i%16+'0'));
    }while(i /= 16);
    cout << "That number in hexadecimal is ";
    while(pop(&the_char)) cout << the_char;
}

main()
{
    unsigned int number = 0;

    cout << "Type a positive integer please: ";
    cin >> number;

    printem.print_in_hex(number);

    return 0;
}
```

Nested Classes

Before moving on, we might note that the stack was only used by the printem, so actually using a separate stack_class class wasn't really necessary:

```
#include <iostream.h>

/* Example showing inheritance  */

class stack_class {
    char char_data_buffer[50];
    int char_stack_ptr;     // char_stack_ptr = -1 → stack is empty
public:
    stack_class(void);
    int pop(char *pop_to);
```

```
        int push(char push_this);
    };
```

→
```
    class number_printing_class : public stack_class {
    public:
        void print_in_hex(int i);
    } printem;
```

It turns out that we can actually *nest* class definitions, and doing so can provide an alternative to inheritance. By nesting stack_class, we can keep it entirely internal to the number_printing_class like this:

```
    #include <iostream.h>

    /* Example showing nested classes  */

    class number_printing_class {
```
→ `        class stack_class {              // Nested class`
→ `            char char_data_buffer[50];`
→ `            int char_stack_ptr;`
→ `        public:`
→ `            stack_class(void);`
→ `            int pop(char *pop_to);`
→ `            int push(char push_this);`
→ `            };`
```
    public:
    void print_in_hex(int i);
    } printem;
        :
```

The only difference now between this program and Listing 4-1 is that when we define the stack's own internal functions, we preface them with number_printing_class:: like this:

→ `    number_printing_class::stack_class::stack_class(void){char_stack_ptr = -1;}`

→
```
    int number_printing_class::stack_class::pop(char *pop_to)
    {
    if(char_stack_ptr == -1)      // Stack is empty -- return error
        return 0;
    else                          // Else return data
        *pop_to = char_data_buffer[char_stack_ptr--];
        return 1;
    }
```

→ `    int number_printing_class::stack_class::push(char push_this)`

```
{
if(char_stack_ptr >= 49)      // Stack is full -- return error
    return 0;
else                          // Else store data
    char_data_buffer[++char_stack_ptr] = push_this;
    return 1;
}
```

And that's it; the program works as it did before.

Using Inherited Constructors

One thing we might note about the code in Listing 4-1 is that our stack class
has a constructor:

```
stack_class::stack_class(void){char_stack_ptr = -1;}
```

However, that raises a question about inherited classes: What if both the base
class and the derived class have constructors? Are they both executed? And, if
so, in what order? We'll look into that next. Let's give both our stack and the
derived class number_printing_class constructors, like this:

```
#include <iostream.h>

/* Example showing inheritance  */

class stack_class {
    char char_data_buffer[50];
    int char_stack_ptr;      // char_stack_ptr = -1 → stack is empty
public:
→       stack_class(void);
    int pop(char *pop_to);
    int push(char push_this);
};

class number_printing_class : public stack_class {
public:
→       number_printing_class(void);
    void print_in_hex(int i);
};

→ stack_class::stack_class(void)
    {
    cout << "Initializing stack...\n";
    char_stack_ptr = -1;
    }
```

```
        :
→  number_printing_class::number_printing_class(void)
   {
        cout << "Initializing derived object...\n";
   }
        :
```

In this case, neither constructor takes an argument, and the base class's constructor is run before the derived class's constructor. That's all there is to it. The entire program is in Listing 4-2; there, the stack's constructor prints out "Initializing stack...\n", and the derived object's constructor prints out "Initializing derived object...\n." When we run this program, we see this:

```
   Initializing stack...
   Initializing derived object...
```

Listing 4-2. C++ Inheritance Example

```
#include <iostream.h>

/* Example showing inheritance  */

class stack_class {
    char char_data_buffer[50];
    int char_stack_ptr;     // char_stack_ptr = -1 → stack is empty
public:
    stack_class(void);
    int pop(char *pop_to);
    int push(char push_this);
};

class number_printing_class : public stack_class {
public:
    number_printing_class(void);
    void print_in_hex(int i);
};

stack_class::stack_class(void)
{
    cout << "Initializing stack...\n";
    char_stack_ptr = -1;
}

int stack_class::pop(char *pop_to)
{
```

Listing 4-2. *(continued)*

```
    if(char_stack_ptr == -1)      // Stack is empty -- return error
        return 0;
    else                          // Else return data
        *pop_to = char_data_buffer[char_stack_ptr--];
        return 1;
}

int stack_class::push(char push_this)
{
    if(char_stack_ptr >= 49)      // Stack is full -- return error
        return 0;
    else                          // Else store data
        char_data_buffer[++char_stack_ptr] = push_this;
        return 1;
}

number_printing_class::number_printing_class(void)
{
    cout << "Initializing derived object...\n";
}

void number_printing_class::print_in_hex(int i)
{
    char the_char;

    do{
        push((char) (i%16 > 9 ? i%16-10+'a' : i%16+'0'));
    }while(i /= 16);

    cout << "That number in hexadecimal is ";

    while(pop(&the_char)) cout << the_char;
}

main()
{
    unsigned int number = 0;
    number_printing_class printem;

    cout << "Type a positive integer please: ";
    cin >> number;

    printem.print_in_hex(number);

    return 0;
}
```

Note the stack's constructor is invoked first, followed by the derived object's constructor. This is the general rule: Constructors are executed in order, running from the base class all the way up through the successively derived classes. Let's say we have a class named base, a class derived from it named derived1, and a class derived from *that* named derived 2:

```
base
  ↓
derived1
  ↓
derived2
```

Then, when we ran the program, base's constructor would be executed, followed by derived1's constructor, followed by derived2's constructor. Logically, this makes a good deal of sense: Since derived1 and derived2 are derived from base, base can have no knowledge of what goes on in those classes — its constructor must be logically separate from them. On the other hand, derived1's constructor may depend on what's happened with base's constructor, and so on up the line. For that reason, constructors are executed from the base class up — and destructors are executed in reverse order, from the last class derived down to the base class.

NOTE Keep in mind that none of our constructors took parameters here; we'll see how to pass parameters to constructors when dealing with derived objects in the following section.

Let's elaborate our techniques a little here; sometimes, we will need to inherit members from more than one base class. For example, we might need other classes besides just our stack class in a certain derived class. This is called multiple inheritance, and we'll look at it next.

The Next Step: Inheriting Multiple Classes

Let's say that we wanted to derive a class, named derived, from *two* base classes, which we might call base1 and base2. The derived class would have access to the members of both base classes. In other words, our base classes might look like this:

```
#include <iostream.h>

class base1 {
public:
    void a(void);
};

class base2 {
public:
    void b(void);
};
    :
```

And we can set up the derived class like this, where we use a base class list separated by commas, like this:

```
#include <iostream.h>

class base1 {
public:
    void a(void);
};

class base2 {
public:
    void b(void);
};

class derived : public base1, base2 {
public:
    void c(void);
};
      :
```

→

Now the class named derived has inherited all the public and protected members of base1 and base2. For example, if base1 and base2 had member functions named a( ) and b( ), and if derived itself defined c( ), then we could do this in main( ), where we set up an object named derived_object of class derived like this:

```
#include <iostream.h>

class base1 {
```

```
public:
    void a(void);
};

class base2 {
public:
    void b(void);
};

class derived : public base1, base2 {
public:
    void c(void);
};

void base1::a(void){cout << 'a';}
void base2::b(void){cout << 'b';}
void derived::c(void){cout << 'c';}

main()
{
→       derived derived_object;

→       derived_object.a();
→       derived_object.b();
→       derived_object.c();

        return 0;
}
```

On the other hand, what if these base classes had constructors? It turns out that, if base1, base2, and derived all had constructors like this:

```
#include <iostream.h>

class base1 {
public:
    base1(void);
};

class base2 {
public:
    base2(void);
};

class derived : public base1, base2 {
public:
    derived(void);
```

```
    } derived_object;
```
→
→
→
```
    base1::base1(void){cout << 'a';}
    base2::base2(void){cout << 'b';}
    derived::derived(void){cout << 'c';}

    main()
    {
        return 0;
    }
```

and if base1's constructor printed out 'a', base2's printed out 'b', and derived's printed out 'c', then the above program would print this on the screen:

```
    abc
```

In other words, base class' constructors are always executed first, working from the first base class up through the derived classes. Furthermore, since we declared the derived class like this:

→
```
    class derived : public base1, base2 {
    public:
        derived(void);
    };
```

then base1's constructor is executed before base2's. That's the way constructors work in multiple inheritance; they are executed from left to right in the base class list.

Let's explore a slightly more realistic constructor example now; often, constructors will have parameters of some kind (so far in this chapter, none of our constructors took parameters). However, this leaves us with a problem. When we set up a derived object, we'll want to specify parameters to its constructor on the spot:

```
    main()
    {
        int i = 5;
        float f = 3.14;
```
→
```
        derived derived_object('a', 'b', 'c');
            :
```

Passing parameters to derived_object's constructor seems easy — but how can we pass parameters to the constructors of derived_objects's base classes? In other words, what if we needed to pass parameters to the constructors of base1 and base2? We will examine this process now.

Passing Parameters to Multiple Constructors

It turns out that some or all of the parameters we pass to a derived object's constructor may be passed to the base class(es) constructors. For that reason, if any class's constructor has one or more parameters, all classes derived from it must also have constructors. For example, let's add a constructor to our class named derived like this:

```
#include <iostream.h>

class base1 {
public:
    base1(char the_char);
};

class base2 {
public:
    base2(char the_char);
};

class derived : public base1, base2 {
public:
    derived(char c1, char c2, char c3);
};

main()
{
    derived derived_object('c', 'a', 'b');

    return 0;
}
```

Here, we've given derived's constructor three parameters, and, when we declared the object named derived_object, we passed arguments of 'c', 'a', and 'b.' What happens to those parameters?

As mentioned, we can pass them along to earlier (i.e., base class) constructors if we wish. This will be very useful (in fact, required) in Windows when we derive modal dialog box objects — we'll have to pass parameters back to the base class' constructor (in that case, the base class will be CModalDialog and its constructor will be CModalDialog( )). Here's how we might define derived's constructor:

```
#include <iostream.h>

class base1 {
public:
    base1(char the_char);
};

class base2 {
public:
    base2(char the_char);
};

class derived : public base1, base2 {
public:
    derived(char c1, char c2, char c3);
};

base1::base1(char the_char){cout << the_char;}
base2::base2(char the_char){cout << the_char;}

derived::derived(char c1, char c2, char c3) : base1(c2), base2(c3)
{
    cout << c1;
}

main()
{
    derived derived_object('c', 'a', 'b');
    return 0;
}
```

In this case, we're actually passing the second two parameters, which we've named c2 and c3, to the constructors of the two base classes. That process looks like this:

```
derived::derived(char c1, char c2, char c3) : base1(c2), base2(c3)
```

Notice in particular the colon preceding base1( ) and base2( ), as well as the comma separating them. In general, we can pass parameters back to base class' constructors like this:

```
derived::derived(param list) : base1(param list), base2(param list)...
```

In this case, the parameter lists of the base classes constructors may contain any expression that has global scope (e.g., global constants, global variables, dynamically initialized global variables), as well as parameters that were passed to derived's construtor. In our example, we've passed the parameters c2 and c3 to the constructors of base1 and base2. In our program, then, we pass 'c', 'a', and 'b' to the constructors of derived, base1, and base2, respectively; since these execute in this order (i.e., base1, base2, and then derived), we see this on the screen:

```
abc
```

In this way, C++ lets us set up the constructor functions of derived classes in a manner that makes it easy to pass parameters back to the constructors of base classes. That's it for our coverage of constructors under inheritance. However, there is much more to inheritance. Let's move on now to a new topic that's a very important part of inheritance — virtual functions.

NOTE Multiple inheritance can be quite a complicated topic; for example, using private base classes can produce unanticipated results in derived classes, or you might end up duplicating member names from parent classes and so on. In general, you should exercise care here; the Programmer's Work-Bench has a tool (actually a PWB extension) that is helpful here — its source browser.

What Is a C++ Virtual Function?

In many ways, using virtual functions is similiar to using function overloading. In particular, we can replace the definition of a virtual function in some base class with a new version in a derived class. Let's see how this works. To start, we set up a virtual function in a base class by declaring it as virtual in the class declaration. For example, we can make the breathe( ) function in our class animal into a virtual function:

```
#include <iostream.h>

class animal {
public:
        void eat(void);
        void sleep(void);
→       virtual void breathe(void);
};
    :
```

Now let's say that we wanted to set up a new class named fish. Fish do not breathe in the same way as other animals, so we might want to redeclare the breathe( ) function in the derived class fish like this:

```
#include <iostream.h>

class animal {
public:
    void eat(void);
    void sleep(void);
    virtual void breathe(void);
};

class fish : public animal {
public:
    void breathe(void);
};
    :
```

(Note that we did not have to declare breathe( ) virtual here, only in the class declaration.) However, in the derived class named fish, the function fish::breathe( ) does more than overload animal::breathe( ) — it overwrites it entirely. In other words, animal::breathe( ) is not a member function of any object of the fish class. This process, more drastic than overloading, is called *function overriding*. For example, in the following program, animal::breathe( ) prints "Breathing..." on the screen, while fish::breathe( ) prints "Bubbling...."

```
#include <iostream.h>

class animal {
public:
    void eat(void);
    void sleep(void);
    virtual void breathe(void);
};

class fish : public animal {
public:
    void breathe(void);
};

void animal::eat(void){cout << "Eating...\n";}
void animal::sleep(void){cout << "Sleeping...\n";}
void animal::breathe(void){cout << "Breathing...\n";}
void fish::breathe(void){cout << "Bubbling...\n";}

main()
```

```
    {
        fish the_fish;
        the_fish.breathe();

        return 0;
    }
```

When we run the program, we see "Bubbling...." The virtual function in the base class, animal::breathe( ), has been overridden with the new version in the derived class.

To override a virtual function this way, all versions of the function must have the same prototype; that is, they must take the same parameters and return the same type. If they do not, C++ will merely consider the function overloaded. It is worth noting that while destructors may be virtual, constructors may not. In addition, virtual functions must be members of a class, not friends of that class.

The reason that overriding a function like this is useful is that it provides us with a consistent interface; in other words, we still use the breathe( ) function in the same way as before, although it has been redefined for this new, derived class. If a function has been overloaded, the parameters we pass to the various versions will be different, so C++ knows which version of the function to use. If a function has been overridden, on the other hand, the only way C++ knows what version of the function to use is by the type of the object we're using; in this case, we used an object of the type fish, so C++ knew that we should use the version of breathe( ) defined in fish. In other words, C++ selects the correct version of an overridden function depending on the type of the object it's a member of.

NOTE   Static member functions cannot be declared virtual.

This idea can take some interesting turns. To see that, we might note that in C++, a pointer to some base class can also point to classes derived from that base class. For example, if we had a pointer to an objects of type animal named obj_ptr:

```
    main()
    {
→       animal *obj_ptr;
            :
```

then we could point to two types of objects with obj_ptr: objects of the (base) class animal and the (derived) class fish:

```
main()
{
    animal *obj_ptr;

→       obj_ptr = &the_animal;        // Run-time polymorphism
        obj_ptr->breathe();

→       obj_ptr = &the_fish;
        obj_ptr->breathe();
            :
```

And, using that pointer, we could invoke the two versions of breathe( ):

```
main()
{
    animal *obj_ptr;

        obj_ptr = &the_animal;        // Run-time polymorphism
→       obj_ptr->breathe();

        obj_ptr = &the_fish;
→       obj_ptr->breathe();
            :
```

As before, C++ will have to determine which version of breathe( ) to invoke by the type of object pointed to — and that's the problem. The compiler has no idea what obj_ptr will be pointing at, because that's set at run-time. In other words, all the compiler sees is a statement like this:

```
obj_ptr->breathe();
```

At compile time, this statement is ambiguous, since the compiler would have to know how the whole program is going to run to know which type of object obj_ptr will be pointing at. In fact, this same statement may be executed twice, once when obj_ptr is pointing at the_animal, and once when it's pointing at the_fish:

```
main()
{
    animal *obj_ptr;

→       obj_ptr = &the_animal;
```

```
     for(int i = 0; i < 2; i++){
→        obj_ptr->bre the();
→        obj_ptr = &the_fish;
     }
     :
```

This means that the compiler cannot determine which version of breathe( ) to use — animal::breathe( ) or fish::breathe( ) — at compile time. Instead, that determination can only be made at run-time, and the appropriate version must be selected then. This is called *run-time polymorphism*.

What Is Run-Time Polymorphism?

Just as function and operator overloading gave us compile time polymorphism (i.e., one function name with many different versions), so virtual functions give us run-time polymorphism. And, as we've just seen, run-time polymorphism is necessary with virtual functions because an overriding function has the same return value and parameter list (i.e., there's no way of determining the correct version of the function except by the object it's a member of). In other words, run-time polymorphism is a necessary part of the consistent interface idea behind virtual functions.

Let's develop the example we've been discussing to see how this works. First, we set up our two classes:

```
#include <iostream.h>

/* Run-time polymorphism */

class animal {
public:
    void eat(void);
    void sleep(void);
    virtual void breathe(void);
} the_animal;

class fish : public animal {
public:
    void breathe(void);
};
    :
```

Note again that breathe( ) is declared virtual in the base class, animal. Next, we spell out the member functions (note that the keyword virtual is only used in the class declaration, not in front of the definition of animal::breathe( )):

```
#include <iostream.h>

/* Run-time polymorphism */

class animal {
public:
    void eat(void);
    void sleep(void);
    virtual void breathe(void);
};

class fish : public animal {
public:
    void breathe(void);
};

void animal::breathe(void){cout << "Breathing...\n";}
void animal::eat(void){cout << "Eating...\n";}
void animal::sleep(void){cout << "Sleeping...\n";}
void fish::breathe(void){cout << "Bubbling...\n";}
    :
```

Finally, we're ready for the body of the program. Let's use the for loop we saw earlier where we load obj_ptr first with a pointer to the_animal and then with a pointer to the_fish:

```
#include <iostream.h>

/* Run-time polymorphism */

class animal {
public:
    void eat(void);
    void sleep(void);
    virtual void breathe(void);
};

class fish : public animal {
public:
    void breathe(void);
};
```

```
void animal::breathe(void){cout << "Breathing...\n";}
void animal::eat(void){cout << "Eating...\n";}
void animal::sleep(void){cout << "Sleeping...\n";}
void fish::breathe(void){cout << "Bubbling...\n";}

main()
{
    animal the_animal;
    fish the_fish;
    animal *obj_ptr;

→    obj_ptr = &the_animal;

    for(int i = 0; i < 2; i++){
→        obj_ptr->breathe();
→        obj_ptr = &the_fish;
    }

    return 0;
}
```

This is what's happening here: First, obj_ptr is loaded with a pointer to the_animal, we enter the for loop, and invoke obj_ptr->breathe(). Since obj_ptr points to the_animal, the program determines — on the fly — that we want to use animal::breathe( ), so "Breathing..." is printed on the screen. Next, we reload obj_ptr with a pointer to the_fish and loop back up to the top, invoking obj_ptr->breathe( ) again:

```
main()
{
    animal the_animal;
    fish the_fish;
    animal *obj_ptr;

    obj_ptr = &the_animal;

    for(int i = 0; i < 2; i++){
→        obj_ptr->breathe();
         obj_ptr = &the_fish;
    }
    :
```

In this case, the program determines that we want to use fish::breathe( ), so "Bubbling..." appears on the screen. That's how run-time polymorphism works — to take advantage of it, you must use pointers to objects and override virtual functions. Since you can now select which function is executed by the same code, it's a powerful technique. For example, the object(s) you use — and the associated functions — can be determined by user input; the program code itself doesn't have to be rewritten to handle different objects in a different way. Note that by making our code object-independent in this fashion, C++ makes it more modular.

The difference between compile time and run-time polymorphism is called *early* vs. *late binding*. In early (compile time) binding, C++ selects which overloaded function to use when it's creating the .obj file. In late (run-time) binding, C++ selects which overridden function to use when it examines the contents of an object pointer.

Now let's dig into the use of object pointers a little deeper. We know that a pointer to a base class can point to derived classes as well. For example, we've just seen that obj_ptr can point to the_animal and the_fish. And, we can pick members out of those objects with the arrow operator like this: obj_ptr->breathe( ). However, that presents us with another problem. We know that obj_ptr was declared as a pointer to class animal:

```
main()
{
    animal the_animal;
    fish the_fish;
    animal *obj_ptr;
        :
```

→

but we can still reach members in the derived class fish, like fish::breathe( ), with it. However, what if we wanted to point to members of fish that were *not* members of the base class animal? For example, what if we wanted to point to fish::swim( ), which is not defined in class animal? Could we just use an expression like this: obj_ptr->swim( )?

It turns out that we cannot. Even so, the solution is very easy; all we need to do is to use a type cast, temporarily casting obj_ptr into a pointer that points at type fish instead. For example, that would look like this in the case of swim( ):

```
class fish : public animal {
public:
    void breathe(void);
    void swim(void);
};

main()
```

```
    {
        animal the_animal;
        fish the_fish;
        animal *obj_ptr;

        obj_ptr = &the_animal;        // Run-time polymorphism
        obj_ptr->breathe();

        obj_ptr = &the_fish;
        obj_ptr->breathe();

→       obj_ptr = &the_animal;
→       ((fish *)obj_ptr)->swim();    // Use pointer type override

        return 0;
    }
```

| TIP | It's interesting to note that not only can pointers to a base class reach members of derived classes, but also that sizeof(object) returns the size of the object's *base* class, not neccesarily the class in which the object was defined. |

The new version of this program is in Listing 4-3.

Listing 4-3. Type Casting an Object Pointer

```
#include <iostream.h>

/* Type Casting an Object Pointer Example */

class animal {
public:
    void eat(void);
    void sleep(void);
    virtual void breathe(void);
} the_animal;

class fish : public animal {
public:
    void breathe(void);
    void swim(void);
} the_fish;

void animal::breathe(void){cout << "Breathing...\n";}
void animal::eat(void){cout << "Eating...\n";}
```

Listing 4-3. *(continued)*

```
void animal::sleep(void){cout << "Sleeping...\n";}
void fish::breathe(void){cout << "Bubbling...\n";}
void fish::swim(void){cout << "Swimming...\n";}

main()
{
    animal *obj_ptr;

    obj_ptr = &the_animal;        // Run-time polymorphism
    obj_ptr->breathe();

    obj_ptr = &the_fish;
    obj_ptr->breathe();

    obj_ptr = &the_animal;
    ((fish *)obj_ptr)->swim();    // Use pointer type override

    return 0;
}
```

In some cases, you even put some virtual functions into a base class with no definitions at all. That is, although you include a prototype for them, you don't do anything more. The reason you might do this is to make sure that the classes derived from your class define those functions for themselves. For example, you might include a virtual function named looks_like( ) in the base class animal, but it would be no use defining the function there — animal is a generic class: putting in specifics about individual animals would be useless. The reason you would put that virtual function in is to make sure that all derived classes define a looks_like( ) function themselves. This might be the case if you're setting up a *class library* for use by others; in Chapter 5, we'll see that Microsoft C++ already has a few class libraries that come with it. Virtual functions which are not defined — and so have no body — are called *pure virtual functions.*

All About Pure Virtual Functions and Abstract Classes

Let's make the function animal::breathe( ) into a pure virtual function. In other words, we'll declare it in the class declaration but we won't define a body for it. However, we cannot just declare the class (and breathe( )) like this:

```
#include <iostream.h>

/* Abstract class example */

class animal {                          // An abstract class
public:
    void eat(void);
    void sleep(void);
    virtual void breathe(void);         // A virtual function
};
    :
```

and then omit the body of breathe( ); C++ counts that as an error. Instead, we have to indicate that we want breathe( ) to be a pure virtual function like this:

```
#include <iostream.h>

/* Abstract class example */

class animal {                          // An abstract class
public:
    void eat(void);
    void sleep(void);
    virtual void breathe(void) = 0;     // Pure virtual function
};
    :
```

Adding "= 0" to the end of a virtual function's prototype makes it pure virtual. Next, when we declare the class fish, we have to override the pure virtual function breathe( ) like this:

```
#include <iostream.h>

/* Abstract class example */

class animal {                          // An abstract class
public:
    void eat(void);
    void sleep(void);
    virtual void breathe(void) = 0;     // Pure virtual function
};

class fish : public animal {
public:
    void breathe(void);
};
```

C++ considers it an error not to override a pure virtual function when we start declaring objects (because the intention of using pure virtual functions is to make sure that derived classes define those functions themselves). In other words, if a class has one or more pure virtual functions (i.e., function proto-types without code), then we cannot create objects of that class directly. In fact, if a class contains one or more pure virtual functions, then it is called an *abstract class*, and there cannot be any objects of that class. Instead, we have to derive classes from that class, overriding the pure virtual function(s).

TIP   On the other hand, you can have *pointers* to an abstract class, because abstract classes usually serve as base classes, and the base class is important for pointers.

Note how useful this can be when you design a library of classes: You can make sure that functions you consider essential — but cannot be defined in the base class (e.g., looks_like( )) — get defined before objects are actually created and used. For example, you might want to make sure that all classes derived from yours define their own error handler and recovery routines, although such code might be very different for each such class.

Next in our program, we have to define all the member functions, including fish::breathe( ):

```cpp
#include <iostream.h>

/* Abstract class example */

class animal {                           // An abstract class
public:
    void eat(void);
    void sleep(void);
    virtual void breathe(void) = 0;      // Pure virtual function
};

class fish : public animal {
public:
    void breathe(void);
};

void animal::eat(void){cout << "Eating...\n";}
void animal::sleep(void){cout << "Sleeping...\n";}
void fish::breathe(void){cout << "Bubbling...\n";}
    :
```

After we do so, we're free to use these member functions in our code. The whole program appears in Listing 4-4.

Listing 4-4. Example of an Abstract Class

```
#include <iostream.h>

/* Abstract class example */

class animal {                            // An abstract class
public:
    void eat(void);
    void sleep(void);
    virtual void breathe(void) = 0;    // Pure virtual function
};

class fish : public animal {
public:
    void breathe(void);
};

void animal::eat(void){cout << "Eating...\n";}
void animal::sleep(void){cout << "Sleeping...\n";}
void fish::breathe(void){cout << "Bubbling...\n";}

main()
{
    fish the_fish;

    the_fish.breathe();
    return 0;
}
```

That's it for our coverage of inheritance; as we've seen, it provides some very powerful techniques. In this chapter, we've seen how the private, public, and protected keywords all work, as well as how inherited constructors work, how multiple inheritance works, and how virtual functions, pure virtual functions, and even abstract classes all work. We're on our way to becoming C++ experts. Now that we have a good idea how to derive classes, we can explore those base classes that Microsoft C++ has already set up for us — the C++ I/O class library — and we'll do that next.

C++ I/O Class Libraries

At this point in the book, we have a good idea of what classes are all about, and a good idea of how to create objects from them. In the last chapter, we started looking at virtual functions, which let us plan ahead in case other programmers want to use the classes we create — that is, we started exploring the possibility of creating class *libraries*. A class library is just a C++ extension of the normal C function libraries; here, however, we will be able to include classes, not just functions.

One can make class libraries in C++ by creating header files which contain both the class declarations and the definitions of the appropriate member functions. That header file can then be included in a program, and the classes in it become available. C++ automatically compiles the functions it finds in header files.

In fact, this method is so powerful that Microsoft has done just that in C++; they've created a number of class libraries, ready for us to use and declare objects with. In this chapter, we'll put that potential to work for us as we explore the C++ I/O class library, which holds classes that will make object I/O (to devices or files) easy to handle. As we'll see, the I/O class library makes this interface flexible as well as powerful. We're already familiar with some parts of the C++ I/O system (e.g., << and >>), but there is much more to see. For example, C++ has a whole I/O system to work with files, and we'll see that later in this chapter. To start, however, let's get an overview of the C++ I/O system itself.

How to Use the C++ I/O System

As you know, C++ is a superset of C, which means that whatever is available to us in C is also available in C++. For that reason, we can use scanf( ) to read from the keyboard, and printf( ) to print on the screen. However, as you also know, we've been using the more flexible << and >> overloaded operators in C++. These two operators are favorites in C++ for two reasons: The first is that they are more flexible and easy to use, and the second is that they may be overloaded to work with objects. The philosophy of C++ is to keep our objects as self-contained as possible. When it is time to print out results, it would be inconsistent to suddenly find ourselves with code like this throughout our program:

```
printf("%s's sock size is %d\n", clothing.name, clothing.socksize);
printf("%s's shoe size is %d\n", clothing.name, clothing.shoesize);
printf("%s's slipper size is %d\n", clothing.name, clothing.slippersize);
printf("%s's shirt size is %d\n", clothing.name, clothing.shirtsize);
```

Instead, and much more in the spirit of C++, we display the data in the object named clothing this way:

```
cout << clothing;
```

That's the reason that C++ needs its own I/O system — to be able to handle objects like this, keeping the details hidden and out of the way. One of the primary ways we've been using that I/O system is by using << and >>, and we'll see how to customize those C++ I/O operators for our own use soon.

The C++ I/O class library is made up of predefined streams; each of these streams corresponds to a class, and each has member functions. The lowest class is *streambuf*, which is set up in iostream.h and provides I/O at the lowest (unbuffered) level. The next class up, the *ios* class, is derived from streambuf. The ios class provides some support for buffered and formatted I/O as we'll see later. Three new classes are derived from ios; they are *istream, ostream,* and *iostream.* As their names suggest, we can create input streams from the istream class, output streams from the ostream class, and both from iostream. The >> and << operators are overloaded (in the file iostream.h) with respect to istream and ostream, respectively.

Besides these streams, C++ sets up some pre-defined streams that are already connected to physical devices. Those are: cin (connected to the standard input device), cout (connected to the standard output device), cerr (also connected to the standard output device), and clog (which is the same as cerr, except that it is buffered). Of these four, we're already familiar with cin and cout.

As we'll see later in this chapter, we can also associate streams with physical files and devices ourselves. For example, we'll see that the member functions of streams defined in fstream.h let us open files, and opening a file associates the stream with the physical file. That is, we'll take the ifstream and ofstream *classes* in fstream.h, define objects of those types, and then use their member functions (like open( )) to open files and so associate them with those streams.

First, however, let's start our discussion of C++ object-oriented I/O by working through the process of overloading << and >>. We saw this process briefly in Chapter 3, but let's dig into more detail now.

Overloading C++ Output Operators

The << operator is called an insertor because it inserts data into a stream. It is overloaded with respect to the output stream ostream, which handles the output that our programs generate (istream handles the input). For example, let's say that we had a class that looked like this:

```
#include <string.h>
#include <iostream.h>

/* Insertor overloading example */

class our_class {
public:
    char string1[100];
    char string2[100];
    char string3[100];
    our_class(char *s1, char *s2, char *s3);
};

our_class::our_class(char *s1, char *s2, char *s3)
{
    strcpy(string1, s1);
    strcpy(string2, s2);
```

```
        strcpy(string3, s3);
    }
    :
    main()
    {
→       our_class our_object("Hello", "there", "world.");

        return 0;
    }
```

We've defined an object named our_object such that:

```
    our_object.string1 = "Hello"
    our_object.string2 = "there"
    our_object.string3 = "world."
```

Now let's say that we want to customize the screen output process for our object so that cout << our_object produces this on the display:

```
    Hello
    there
    world.
```

In standard C, of course, this is impossible. We cannot simply send our_object to printf( ) and expect the correctly formatted I/O we want. In C++, however, we can overload the insertion operator <<, so let's get started. To do that, we need to set up an operator function, which is the standard way of overloading operators in C++. As we've seen, the prototype of an operator function looks like this:

```
    type operatorX(stream-parameter, object-parameter);
```

where X stands for the operator in question (i.e., +, -, &, etc.). In other words, we can begin our overloading function for << this way:

```
    #include <string.h>
    #include <iostream.h>

    /* Insertor overloading example */

    class our_class {
    public:
        char string1[100];
        char string2[100];
        char string3[100];
```

```
        our_class(char *s1, char *s2, char *s3);
    };

    our_class::our_class(char *s1, char *s2, char *s3)
    {
        strcpy(string1, s1);
        strcpy(string2, s2);
        strcpy(string3, s3);
    }

→   ostream &operator<<(ostream &stream, our_class the_object)
    {
    :
```

This might make a little more sense here than it did in Chapter 3. We already know that the stream that handles formatted output from our C++ programs is called ostream, and now we can see that we're defining a function that returns a reference to that stream (i.e., ostream &operator<<( )). Next, we notice that the first parameter is a reference to the current output stream, which we call stream (i.e., we'll send our output to stream), and the second parameter is an object of the type that we're overloading << to handle.

We might also notice here that these are not the typical parameters for a binary operator function. That kind of function usually gets only one parameter: a copy of the right hand object. In addition, a this pointer is passed implicitly which points to the left hand object, the object that invoked the binary operator. Here, however, the story is different; we're working on objects and streams, not just objects. In fact, because << and >> operator functions require different operands from other binary operators, they cannot be member functions of classes.

All we have to do is to take what we want from the object that was passed to us (the_object) and send it to the output stream (stream). Since the fields we want to display are just strings, and since << is already overloaded with respect to strings, we can just do this:

```
#include <string.h>
#include <iostream.h>

/* Insertor overloading example */

class our_class {
public:
    char string1[100];
```

```
        char string2[100];
        char string3[100];
        our_class(char *s1, char *s2, char *s3);
    };

    our_class::our_class(char *s1, char *s2, char *s3)
    {
        strcpy(string1, s1);
        strcpy(string2, s2);
        strcpy(string3, s3);
    }

    ostream &operator<<(ostream &stream, our_class the_object)
    {
→       stream << the_object.string1 << "\n";
→       stream << the_object.string2 << "\n";
→       stream << the_object.string3 << "\n";
→       return stream;
    }

    main()
    {
        our_class our_object("Hello", "there", "world.");

→       cout << our_object;

        return 0;
    }
```

Note that at the end of the operator function we returned the stream; this is necessary because the use of << can be chained like this:

```
    cout << "Here it comes: " << our_object << "The end.\n";
```

In other words, we need to return stream this way so that it may be passed to other << operators. We should also note that we did not send output directly to cout like this:

```
    #include <string.h>
    #include <iostream.h>

    /* Insertor overloading example */

    class our_class {
    public:
        char string1[100];
```

```
        char string2[100];
        char string3[100];
        our_class(char *s1, char *s2, char *s3);
    };

    ostream &operator<<(ostream &stream, our_class the_object)
    {
→       cout << the_object.string1 << "\n";
→       cout << the_object.string2 << "\n";
→       cout << the_object.string3 << "\n";
        return stream;
    }

    our_class::our_class(char *s1, char *s2, char *s3)
    {
        strcpy(string1, s1);
        strcpy(string2, s2);
        strcpy(string3, s3);
    }

    main()
    {
        our_class our_object("Hello", "there", "world.");

        cout << our_object;

        return 0;
    }
```

The reason for this is that the output stream may be redirected, so we should not tie our output to a stream that is in turn tied to the screen. Instead, it's better to send our output to the common output stream. That's it for this example; we've been able to produce the output we wanted:

```
    Hello
    there
    world.
```

However, the fact that << and >> operator functions cannot be members of a class presents us with a problem: What if we want to display some data that is usually kept private? For example, what if our object was declared like this, where the data strings are private:

```
    class our_class {
→       char string1[100];
```

```
→          char string2[100];
→          char string3[100];
    public:
        our_class(char *s1, char *s2, char *s3);
    } our_object("Hello", "there", "world.");
```

The answer to this problem, as you might expect, is that even though << and >> cannot be member functions of a class, they can be friend functions.

Friend Operator Functions

As we've seen, friend functions have access to a class' private members — this is exactly the kind of case that friend functions were designed for. To declare operator<<( ) as a friend function, we just have to put its prototype in the class declaration, preceded by "friend", like this:

```
#include <string.h>
#include <iostream.h>

/* Insertor overloading example */

class our_class {
    char string1[100];
    char string2[100];
    char string3[100];
public:
→       friend ostream &operator<<(ostream &stream, our_class the_object);
        our_class(char *s1, char *s2, char *s3);
};
        :
```

Now the program will work once again, even though the data strings are private:

```
#include <string.h>
#include <iostream.h>

/* Insertor overloading example */

class our_class {
    char string1[100];
    char string2[100];
    char string3[100];
public:
```

```
    friend ostream &operator<<(ostream &stream, our_class the_object);
    our_class(char *s1, char *s2, char *s3);
};

ostream &operator<<(ostream &stream, our_class the_object)
{
    stream << the_object.string1 << "\n";
    stream << the_object.string2 << "\n";
    stream << the_object.string3 << "\n";
    return stream;
}

our_class::our_class(char *s1, char *s2, char *s3)
{
    strcpy(string1, s1);
    strcpy(string2, s2);
    strcpy(string3, s3);
}

main()
{
    our_class our_object("Hello", "there", "world.");

→   cout << our_object;

    return 0;
}
```

That's it for overloading insertors; let's move on now to overloading extractors, >>.

Overloading C++ Input Operators

The >> operator is also called an extractor in C++, because it extracts data from a stream. In particular, >> extracts data from the C++ input stream, istream, which handles input for our program. Let's change our example program above so that instead of using three predefined words (i.e., "Hello there world."), it lets you type three words of your own in, which will be stored in string1, string2, and string3. After they're read in, the program will display them as before, using <<. If we overload the extractor operator >> as well, we'll be able to read those words in like this:

```
  cin >> our_object;
```

We can begin by declaring both << and >> as friend functions of our class:

```
#include <string.h>
#include <iostream.h>

/* Extractor overloading example */

class our_class {
    char string1[100];
    char string2[100];
    char string3[100];
public:
    friend istream &operator>>(istream &stream, our_class &the_object);
    friend ostream &operator<<(ostream &stream, our_class the_object);
};
    :
```

Next, we can set up the extractor overloading function, operator>>( ). In fact, that looks just as it did when we overloaded <<, with a few predictable differences. First, we have to operate with respect to istream, the input stream, not ostream. Next, we need a reference to the object we're working on, not just a copy of it. The reason for that is clear: We need to be able to place the data we get in that object (i.e., the same reason you need to pass pointers to scanf( )). Put together, these considerations mean that our operator>>( ) function looks like this:

```
#include <string.h>
#include <iostream.h>

/* Extractor overloading example */

class our_class {
    char string1[100];
    char string2[100];
    char string3[100];
public:
    friend istream &operator>>(istream &stream, our_class &the_object);
    friend ostream &operator<<(ostream &stream, our_class the_object);
};

istream &operator>>(istream &stream, our_class &the_object)
{
    :
}
    :
```

Next, we just read the keyboard input and we're done:

```
#include <string.h>
#include <iostream.h>

/* Extractor overloading example */

class our_class {
    char string1[100];
    char string2[100];
    char string3[100];
public:
    friend istream &operator>>(istream &stream, our_class &the_object);
    friend ostream &operator<<(ostream &stream, our_class the_object);
};

istream &operator>>(istream &stream, our_class &the_object)
{
    cout << "Please type three words: ";
    cin >> the_object.string1 >> the_object.string2 >> the_object.string3;
    return stream;
}
    :
```

Note that once again we returned stream to be able to handle other, similar operations down the line. The rest of the program goes as you might expect:

```
#include <string.h>
#include <iostream.h>

/* Extractor overloading example */

class our_class {
    char string1[100];
    char string2[100];
    char string3[100];
public:
    friend istream &operator>>(istream &stream, our_class &the_object);
    friend ostream &operator<<(ostream &stream, our_class the_object);
};

istream &operator>>(istream &stream, our_class &the_object)
{
    cout << "Please type three words: ";
    cin >> the_object.string1 >> the_object.string2 >> the_object.string3;
    return stream;
}
```

```
ostream &operator<<(ostream &stream, our_class the_object)
{
    cout << the_object.string1 << "\n";
    cout << the_object.string2 << "\n";
    cout << the_object.string3 << "\n";
    return stream;
}

main()
{
    our_class our_object;

→   cin >> our_object;
→   cout << our_object;

    getche();
    return 0;
}
```

And that's it; we've overloaded both << and >> with respect to our class our_class. Although we saw some of this earlier in the book, we now have a good handle on it. This is a good example of the flexibility that the Microsoft C++ I/O class libraries allow us — the ability to overload << and >>, two fundamental parts of those libraries.

Let's proceed now by exploring some of the *formatted* I/O options that the C++ I/O class library allows us. That is, up to this point, we've only been sending output and receiving input like this:

```
cout << our_int;
cin >> our_int;
```

However, we can actually format our character input and output, just as we could with printf( ) and scanf( ) (although it is not necessary to format our I/O, as it was with printf( ) and scanf( )).

How to Format I/O in C++

To begin our discussion of formatted I/O, we can note that there are a number of I/O *manipulators* defined in the file iomanip.h. Manipulators are special keywords and functions that we can use with the << and >> operators to format input and output, and a list of the available manipulators appears in Table 5-1.

Manipulator	Input and/or Output	Means
dec	I/O	Format numbers in base 10
endl	O	Send a newline, "\n", character
ends	O	Send a null, "\0"
flush	O	Flush a stream's buffer
hex	I/O	Format numbers in base 16
oct	I/O	Format numbers in base 8
resetiosflags(long fl)	I/O	Reset ios bits indicated in long fl
setbase(int i)	O	Format numbers in base i
setfill(char c)	I/O	Set fill character to c
setiosflags(long fl)	I/O	Set ios bits indicated in long fl
setprecision(int pr)	I/O	Set float precision to pr places
setw(int w)	I/O	Set field width to w places
ws	I	Skip over whitespace characters

Table 5-1. I/O Manipulators

Using these manipulators is actually very easy. For example, let's say that we had a program like this:

```
#include <iostream.h>
#include <iomanip.h>

/* Manipulator example. */

main()
{
    float pi = 3.14159;

    cout  << pi;

    return 0;
}
```

This program places our value of pi on the screen:

```
3.14159
```

If we printed out pi a second time:

```
#include <iostream.h>
#include <iomanip.h>

/* Manipulator example. */

main()
{
    float pi = 3.14159;

    cout  << pi;
    cout  << pi;

    return 0;
}
```

then it would appear right after the first one on the screen:

```
3.141593.14159
```

This doesn't look very good. Instead, let's print out the second value of pi by defining a field width of 12 spaces; the floating point numbers we display will then be right justified in that field. We can do this with the setw(12) manipulator (note also that we use the endl manipulator, which is just like sending a newline character, "\n"):

```
#include <iostream.h>
#include <iomanip.h>

/* Manipulator example. */

main()
{
    float pi = 3.14159;

    cout  << pi << setw(12) << pi << endl;

    return 0;
}
```

Now the output looks like this:

```
3.14159     3.14159
```

In addition, we might decide that we don't want five decimal places. We could specify four places like this instead, using the setprecision(4) manipulator:

```
#include <iostream.h>
#include <iomanip.h>

/* Manipulator example. */

main()
{
    float pi = 3.14159;

    cout  << pi << setw(12) << pi << endl;
    cout  << setprecision(4) << pi << endl;

    return 0;
}
```

Now the output looks like this:

```
3.14159     3.14159
3.1415
```

In fact, we can go even farther than this. Since we already know how to work with functions that take and return references to istream and ostream, we can even make our own custom manipulators.

Creating Custom Manipulators to Format I/O

For example, let's make a simple manipulator that simply inserts a space into the output stream. Since manipulators are used in a chain like this:

```
cout << "Hello" << our_manipulator << "world.\n";
```

we are passed a reference to ostream, and we should return the same thing. We start like this:

```
#include <iostream.h>
#include <iomanip.h>

/* Custom manipulator */

ostream &our_manipulator(ostream &stream)
{
:
```

All that remains is to insert our space into the stream and return stream like this:

```
#include <iostream.h>
#include <iomanip.h>

/* Custom manipulator */

ostream &our_manipulator(ostream &stream)
{
    stream << " ";
    return stream;
}

main()
{
    cout << "Hello" << our_manipulator << "world.\n";

    return 0;
}
```

And that's it; we've made our own custom manipulator. You can also create manipulators that work with >>. In that case, the manipulator is defined with respect to istream, not ostream.

Before you create your own manipulators for every contingency, however, we should note that there is a second way of formatting I/O in the I/O class library. In particular, the ios class (which is the base class of istream, ostream, and iostream) has a number of member functions that we can use for this purpose, so let's look into that next.

Formatted I/O and the ios Member Functions

It turns out that there are a number of *flags* defined in the ios class which determine the way I/O will be formatted. These flags can set the numeric base for I/O, right- or left-justify values, and perform a number of other operations. When a flag is set, that particular formatting operation (such as skipping whitespace characters or using scientific notation) is in effect. A list of these flags appears in Table 5-2.

We can reach those flags (and therefore the formatting options they represent) through three member functions of the ios class:

```
ios::setf(long f);
ios::unsetf(long f);
ios::flags(long f);
```

The setf( ) function sets flags (and we've seen this function briefly in Chapter 3). For example, let's say that we had a program like this:

```
#include <iostream.h>

/* Example of ios member flags */

main()
{
    float big_number = 1234.5;

    cout << big_number << "\n";

    return 0;
}
```

ios Flag	Numeric Value	Means
ios::skipws	0x0001	Skip over whitespace (input only)
ios::left	0x0002	Left-align output
ios::right	0x0004	Right-align output
ios::internal	0x0008	Pad numbers with spaces after signs or base indicators
ios::dec	0x0010	Format in base 10
ios::oct	0x0020	Format in base 8
ios::hex	0x0040	Format in base 16
ios::showbase	0x0080	Show base indicator (output only)
ios::showpoint	0x0100	Show decimal point (float output)
ios::uppercase	0x0200	Use uppercase for base 16 output
ios::showpos	0x0400	Show '+' for integers > 0
ios::scientific	0x0800	Use scientific notation: 1.2345E3
ios::fixed	0x1000	Used fixed point notation: 1234.5
ios::unitbuf	0x2000	Flush streams after insertion
ios::stdio	0x4000	Flush stdout, stderr after insertion

Table 5-2. The ios Formatting Flags

That produces an output like this:

```
1234.5
```

Now let's say that we wanted to use scientific notation, so the result would look like this: 1.2345e+03. We can do that by setting the ios::scientific flag with setf( ):

```
#include <iostream.h>

/* Example of ios member flags */

main()
{
    float big_number = 1234.5;

    cout << big_number << "\n";

    cout.setf(ios::scientific);

    cout << big_number << "\n";

    return 0;
}
```

→

Now the output looks like this:

```
1234.5
1.234500e+003
```

Note that, because setf( ) is a member function of ios, and because cout is derived from ios, we could use setf( ) like this: cout.setf( ) (i.e., we're making direct use of a member function of the I/O class library). We could even make the e in 1.234500e+003 into uppercase with setf(ios::uppercase):

```
#include <iostream.h>

/* Example of ios member flags */

main()
{
    float big_number = 1234.5;

    cout << big_number << "\n";

    cout.setf(ios::scientific);
```

```
        cout << big_number << "\n";

→       cout.setf(ios::uppercase);

        cout << big_number << "\n";

        return 0;
    }
```

This program displays this data:

```
1234.5
1.234500e+003
1.234500E+003
```

Now let's say that we wanted to turn these formatting options off. To do that, we can use unsetf( ). We can also unset (or set, using setf( )) a number of options at the same time by ORing them together:

```
#include <iostream.h>

/* Example of ios member flags */

main()
{
    float big_number = 1234.5;

    cout << big_number << "\n";
    cout.setf(ios::scientific);
    cout << big_number << "\n";
    cout.setf(ios::uppercase);
    cout << big_number << "\n";

→   cout.unsetf(ios::uppercase | ios::scientific);

    cout << big_number << "\n";
    return 0;
}
```

The result of this program is:

```
1234.5
1.234500e+003
1.234500E+003
1234.5
```

The third ios formatting member function is flags( ), which returns a long value that indicates how the flags are set (i.e., the bits set in the return value will match the numeric values in Table 5-2). That's it for formatted screen I/O in this chapter; let's move on now to the next major section of the specialized C++ I/O class library, files.

File Objects

Since we've been able to display objects on the screen and read data for them from the keyboard, it makes sense that C++ would extend its object I/O to files as well. The classes that handle files are in the header file fstream.h. Note that because many member functions in fstream.h build on the streams in iostream.h, we'll have to include iostream.h in our programs before including fstream.h.

The fundamental idea behind C++ file I/O (using stream classes) isn't very different from using file I/O in standard C. Here, we have to do things this way: We take a stream class, create an object of that class (i.e., the actual, physical stream), and then use member functions of that object (i.e., that stream) to open a file. When we open a file using the stream's member function open( ), we automatically associate the file with that stream. Let's see how this works in code.

Writing the File Hello.Dat in ASCII

We use the ifstream class when we open a file for input, the ofstream class for output, and fstream for both. To start, let's create a small file named hello.dat that simply contains the words "Hello world\n." To do that, we'll need a stream of class ofstream for output:

```
#include <iostream.h>
#include <fstream.h>

/* A file example */

main()
{
     ofstream our_file;
       :
```

We've named this stream our_file, which will make sense when we start performing operations on the file itself. Now let's create the actual file (which is named hello.dat) on disk. The ofstream class has a member function called open( ) for just this purpose:

```
#include <iostream.h>
#include <fstream.h>

/* A file example */

main()
{
    ofstream our_file;

    our_file.open("hello.dat", ios::out, 0);
        :
```

→

This associates the stream our_file with the file on disk. Now we can just send data to this stream as we've done before with the predefined streams cin and cout. In general, this is what the member function open( ) looks like for the file streams:

```
void open(char *name, int mode, int file_attrb);
```

Here, mode is one of these values (from fstream.h):

ios::app	Append to the file
ios::ate	Go to end of file
ios::in	Open file for input
ios::nocreate	Do not create if file does not exist
ios::out	Open file for output
ios::trunc	Truncate file to zero length, then open

In addition, file_attrb is the file's attribute, indicating what kind of file we want as defined in DOS:

0	Plain file
1	Read-only
2	Hidden
4	System
8	Set archive bit

In this example, we've opened a plain file (file_attrb = 0) for output (ios::out). Now we're ready to send data to the file's stream. For instance, this is the way we send "Hello world.\n" to our file:

```
#include <iostream.h>
#include <fstream.h>

/* A file example */

main()
{
    ofstream our_file;

    our_file.open("hello.dat", ios::out, 0);

    our_file << "Hello world.\n";
        :
```

→

That's it; now all that remains is to close the file, and we can do that with the ofstream member function close():

```
#include <iostream.h>
#include <fstream.h>

/* A file example */

main()
{
    ofstream our_file;

    our_file.open("hello.dat", ios::out, 0);

    our_file << "Hello world.\n";

    our_file.close();

    return 0;
}
```

→

And we're done; the file is on the disk. Typing it out reveals our message, "Hello world.\n." There is one point to note here; we opened the file with the ofstream member function open() like this:

```
our_file.open("hello.dat", ios::out, 0);
```

However, it turns out that open( ) has a number of default parameters, and they are exactly that mode = ios::out and file_attrb = 0, so we can actually open the file this way:

```
#include <iostream.h>
#include <fstream.h>

/* A file example */

main()
{
    ofstream our_file;

    our_file.open("hello.dat");

    our_file << "Hello world.\n";

    our_file.close();

    return 0;
}
```

In fact, we can go farther. Because we associate a file with a stream when we open it, and because ifstream, ofstream, and fstream are supposed to be used with files, our first action will usually be to use the member function open( ) (note, incidentally, that fstream::open( ) does not have any default parameters, while both ifstream::open( ) and ofstream::open( ) do). Knowing that, the designers of the file I/O classes have collapsed those two steps into one, allowing us to pass to the stream's constructor the same parameters we might pass to open. That means that our final version of this example looks like this:

```
#include <iostream.h>
#include <fstream.h>

/* A file writing example */

main()
{
    ofstream our_file("hello.dat");

    our_file << "Hello world.\n";

    our_file.close();

    return 0;
}
```

In other words, we're able to declare the object our_file and associate it with the disk file hello.data at the same time. The next logical step, now that we've produced a file on disk, is to read it back in. We can do that with the ifstream (i.e., file input) class next.

Reading a File as ASCII

We already have the file named hello.dat on the disk. We've written it as a string, using the overloaded << operator, so the file is an ASCII file containing the characters "Hello world.\n." However, when we read from it using the overloaded operator >>, the space between the words will be regarded as a whitespace character, so we'll have to read from the file twice to get both words. We can start by declaring two buffer strings and by opening hello.dat using the ifstream member function open( ):

```
#include <iostream.h>
#include <fstream.h>

/* A file reading example */

main()
{
    char string1[20], string2[20];
    ifstream our_file("hello.dat");
        :
```

Now all we have to do is to read from the file input stream which we've named our_file this way:

```
#include <iostream.h>
#include <fstream.h>

/* A file reading example */

main()
{
    char string1[20], string2[20];
    ifstream our_file("hello.dat");

→       our_file >> string1;
→       our_file >> string2;
        :
```

To print the results out, we print out both words, separated by a space, and then close the file:

```
#include <iostream.h>
#include <fstream.h>

/* A file reading example */

main()
{
    char string1[20], string2[20];
    ifstream our_file("hello.dat");

    our_file >> string1;
    our_file >> string2;
    cout << string1 << " " << string2 << "\n";

    our_file.close();

    return 0;
}
```

That's it. Notice that we had to be careful what we were doing here — because we were dealing with ASCII files, C++ interpreted the data as two strings. That would not have happened if we had treated the data as purely binary (i.e., neither C nor C++ perform any translation or interpretation on binary file data). For that reason, we'll look into binary file I/O next.

Writing Hello.Dat in Binary

Two of the most important file stream member functions for binary file I/O are get( ) and put( ):

```
istream &get(char &c);
ostream &put(char &c);
```

Both of these functions operate byte by byte, without interpreting what bytes they're working on. Let's start our binary file example by opening a file for output:

```
#include <iostream.h>
#include <fstream.h>

/* A binary file example */
```

```
main()
{
    ofstream the_out_file("test.dat");
        :
```

Now we can write out a string that contains "Hello world.\n" character by character, using put( ). After we're done, we can close hello.dat; the whole thing looks like this:

```
#include <iostream.h>
#include <fstream.h>

/* A binary file example */

main()
{
    char our_char, string[] = "Hello world.";
    int i = 0;

    ofstream the_out_file("hello.dat");
    while(string[i]) the_out_file.put(string[i++]);
    the_out_file.close();
        :
```

That's it; hello.dat is on the disk. Now let's read it back in with get( ).

Reading a File in Binary

First, we reopen hello.dat for input:

```
#include <iostream.h>
#include <fstream.h>

/* A binary file example */

main()
{
    char our_char, string[] = "Hello world.";
    int i = 0, j = 0;

    ofstream the_out_file("hello.dat");
    while(string[i]) the_out_file.put(string[i++]);
    the_out_file.close();

    ifstream the_in_file("hello.dat");
        :
```

Now we've set up the stream the_in_file, and associated it with the data in hello.dat. We can read byte by byte from hello.dat using get( ) until we've read it all in. When we reach the end of hello.dat, the stream *itself* returns 0, so we can read bytes like this:

```
#include <iostream.h>
#include <fstream.h>

/* A binary file example */

main()
{
    char our_char, string[] = "Hello world.";
    int i = 0, j = 0;

    ofstream the_out_file("hello.dat");
    while(string[i]) the_out_file.put(string[i++]);
    the_out_file.close();

    ifstream the_in_file("hello.dat");
    while(the_in_file){
        the_in_file.get(our_char);
        cout << our_char;
    }
    the_in_file.close();

    return 0;
}
```

In fact, because get( ) returns the stream it is working on, we can actually do that like this (which is the normal way you'll see it):

```
#include <iostream.h>
#include <fstream.h>

/* A binary file example */

main()
{
    char our_char, string[] = "Hello world.";
    int i = 0, j = 0;

    ofstream the_out_file("hello.dat");
    while(string[i]) the_out_file.put(string[i++]);
    the_out_file.close();

    ifstream the_in_file("hello.dat");
```

→
```
        while(the_in_file.get(our_char)) cout << our_char;
        the_in_file.close();

        return 0;
}
```

TIP   Another way of keeping track when we reach the end of the file is with the member function int eof( ), which returns a True (nonzero) value when we're at the end of the file, and False (zero) otherwise.

Although get( ) and put( ) function quite well, it's usually a little easier to use two different member functions (especially when reading and writing objects); those functions are read( ) and write( ). These two allow us to read and write blocks of data, not just individual bytes.

Using the Functions read( ) and write( )

Let's convert our get( ) and put( ) program to use read( ) and write( ) instead. The prototypes for these two functions are:

```
istream &read(unsigned char *char_buffer, int number_bytes);
ostream &write(const unsigned char *char_buffer, int number_bytes);
```

We start this way, by opening a file for output:

```
#include <string.h>
#include <iostream.h>
#include <fstream.h>

/* A binary file writing example */

main()
{

        ofstream our_file("hello.dat");
        :
```

→

Next, we can set up a string:

```
#include <string.h>
#include <iostream.h>
#include <fstream.h>

/* A binary file writing example */
```

```
    main()
    {
→       char hello_buf[] = "Hello world.\n";

        ofstream our_file("hello.dat");
             :
```

If we were using put( ), we'd have to put each character of this string into hello.dat individually. Using write( ), however, we can do that all at once by passing a pointer to the string (i.e., the name of the character array, string_buf), and the number of bytes to write (i.e., sizeof(hello_buf)). After we write the data out, we just close the file and we're done:

```
    #include <string.h>
    #include <iostream.h>
    #include <fstream.h>

    /* A binary file writing example */

    main()
    {
        char hello_buf[] = "Hello world.\n";

        ofstream our_file("hello.dat");

→       our_file.write(hello_buf, sizeof(hello_buf));

        our_file.close();

        return 0;
    }
```

In other words, the advantage of write( ) over put( ) is that we can write a block of data at one time. Now the file hello.dat is on the disk, and we can expand our program to read it back in using read( ). To start, we open the file and associate an input stream named the_in_file with it like this:

```
    #include <string.h>
    #include <iostream.h>
    #include <fstream.h>

    /* A binary file reading example */

    main()
    {
        char hello_buf[] = "Hello world.\n";
```

```
        ofstream the_out_file("hello.dat");
        the_out_file.write(hello_buf, sizeof hello_buf);
        the_out_file.close();

→       ifstream the_in_file("hello.dat");
          :
```

That is, we just declare the object the_in_file( ) at this point in the program, which is where we need it. Following that, we have to read the same number of bytes that we just finished writing, close the file, and display the resulting string on the screen:

```
#include <string.h>
#include <iostream.h>
#include <fstream.h>

/* A binary file reading example */

main()
{
    char hello_buf[] = "Hello world.\n";

    ofstream the_out_file("hello.dat");
    the_out_file.write(hello_buf, sizeof hello_buf);
    the_out_file.close();

    ifstream the_in_file("hello.dat");
→   the_in_file.read(hello_buf, sizeof hello_buf);
    the_in_file.close();

    cout << hello_buf;

    return 0;
}
```

That's how read( ) and write( ) work; they're useful because they can perform block reads and writes. For that reason, we can also use them to read and write objects to and from disk as well. We'll examine that process next.

Reading and Writing Objects

Let's say that we had an object like this:

```
class entry{
public:
```

```
        char name[20];
        float owes;
    };
```

In it, you can store a person's name and, say, the amount of money they owe you. In this example, we'll store 15 of these objects on disk. We might start this way, by opening the file for output:

```
    #include <iostream.h>
    #include <fstream.h>
    #define INDEX 15

    class entry{
    public:
        char name[20];
        float owes;
    };

    main()
    {
        entry our_data[INDEX];
        ofstream our_file("file.dat");
            :
```

Before placing these objects on disk, let's put some data in them like this:

```
    #include <string.h>
    #include <iostream.h>
    #include <fstream.h>
    #define INDEX 15

    class entry{
    public:
        char name[20];
        float owes;
    };

    main()
    {
        entry our_data[INDEX];
        ofstream our_file("file.dat");

→       strcpy(our_data[0].name,"Ebeneezer Scrooge");
        our_data[0].owes = 0.01;

→       strcpy(our_data[1].name,"Bob Crachit");
        our_data[1].owes = 312.59;
            :
```

Now we're free to write the whole array of objects out to disk with write( ) this way:

```
#include <string.h>
#include <iostream.h>
#include <fstream.h>
#define INDEX 15

class entry{
public:
    char name[20];
    float owes;
};

main()
{
    entry our_data[INDEX];
    ofstream our_file("file.dat");

    strcpy(our_data[0].name,"Ebeneezer Scrooge");
    our_data[0].owes = 0.01;

    strcpy(our_data[1].name,"Bob Crachit");
    our_data[1].owes = 312.59;

    our_file.write((char *) our_data, INDEX * sizeof(entry));

    our_file.close();

    return 0;
}
```

At this point, we've created a file on disk named file.dat. Let's read that array back in next with a new program. We start by opening the file for input and associating it with a stream named our_file:

```
#include <iostream.h>
#include <fstream.h>
#define INDEX 15

class entry{
public:
    char name[20];
    float owes;
};
```

```
      main()
      {
          entry our_data[INDEX];
→         ifstream our_file("file.dat");
              :
```

Next, we can read the entire array back into memory with one read( ) statement:

```
      #include <iostream.h>
      #include <fstream.h>
      #define INDEX 15

      class entry{
      public:
          char name[20];
          float owes;
      };

      main()
      {
          entry our_data[INDEX];
          ifstream our_file("file.dat");

→         our_file.read((char *) our_data, INDEX * sizeof(entry));
              :
```

This fills the array our_data[ ] once again. Finally, we can just print out the results and close the file like this:

```
      #include <string.h>
      #include <iostream.h>
      #include <fstream.h>
      #define INDEX 15

      class entry{
      public:
          char name[20];
          float owes;
      };

      main()
      {
          entry our_data[INDEX];
          ifstream our_file("file.dat");
```

```
          our_file.read((char *) our_data, INDEX * sizeof(entry));
```

→
```
          cout << our_data[0].name << "owes $" << our_data[0].owes;
```
→
```
          cout << our_data[1].name << "owes $" << our_data[1].owes;

          our_file.close();

          return 0;
     }
```

That works well if we don't mind reading the entire array into memory. However, we might have a huge database file thousands of objects long. In that case, it would be easier to simply specify which object we want to read and just read that one in. In fact, we can do that with the seekg( ) and seekp( ) member functions, coming up next.

Positioning Ourselves in a File

Let's say that we filled the file file.dat with 15 objects:

	Object 0
	Object 1
	Object 2
	Object 3
	Object 4
	Object 5
	Object 6
	Object 7
	Object 8
	Object 9
	Object 10
	Object 11
	Object 12
	Object 13
	Object 14

and, that we had filled the data members in object 9 like this:

```
strcpy(our_data[9].name,"George Orwell");
our_data[9].owes = 19.84;
```

Now, let's say that we wanted to retrieve that data, but we didn't want to read in the whole array of objects just to get object number 9. It turns out that the I/O file stream classes define two pointers for use inside a file, the *get pointer* and the *put pointer*. The location of the get pointer indicates where we'll get our data from the next time we read from the file, and the location of the put pointer indicates where we'll write data next. Since we're interested in object number 9, we position the get pointer there and then use read( ):

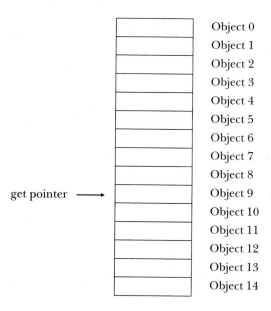

	Object 0
	Object 1
	Object 2
	Object 3
	Object 4
	Object 5
	Object 6
	Object 7
	Object 8
get pointer ⟶	Object 9
	Object 10
	Object 11
	Object 12
	Object 13
	Object 14

Let's see how that would look in a program. To position the get and put pointers, we can use two member functions, seekg( ) and seekp( ):

```
istream &seekg(streamoff file_offset, seek_dir org);
ostream &seekp(streamoff file_offset, seek_dir org);
```

The streamoff type (from iostream.h) can hold the largest legal value of file_offset, which is the location in the file at which we want to place the get or put pointer. The seek_dir type can hold one of these values:

ios::beg	Beginning of the file
ios::end	End of the file
ios::cur	Current position in the file

To set the location of the get or put pointer, we first select an origin value for the parameter org, the origin, which can be at the beginning of the file, at the end, or at the pointer's current location. Then we set file_offset, the offset in bytes of the new location for the pointer with respect to the origin we've chosen.

In a program, we start by opening file.dat, the file that holds the array of objects:

```
#include <iostream.h>
#include <fstream.h>
#define INDEX 15

/* Read object 9 from a file */

class entry{
public:
    char name[20];
    float owes;
};

main()
{
    entry our_data[INDEX], our_record;
    ifstream our_file("file.dat");
        :
```

Next, we can use seekg( ) to position the get pointer where we want it, at the beginning of object 9:

```
#include <string.h>
#include <iostream.h>
#include <fstream.h>
#define INDEX 15

/* Read object 9 from a file */

class entry{
public:
    char name[20];
    float owes;
};

main()
{
    entry our_data[INDEX], our_record;
```

```
         ifstream our_file("file.dat");

→        our_file.seekg(9 * sizeof(entry) + 1, ios::beg);
           :
```

The next time we read from the file, we'll be reading from this position —
that is, we'll be reading in object 9. We can do that with read( ), print out the
results, and close the file like this:

```
#include <string.h>
#include <iostream.h>
#include <fstream.h>
#define INDEX 15

/* Read object 9 from a file */

class entry{
public:
    char name[20];
    float owes;
};

main()
{
    entry our_data[INDEX], our_record;
    ifstream our_file("file.dat");

    our_file.seekg(9 * sizeof(entry) + 1, ios::beg);
→   our_file.read((char *) &our_record, sizeof(entry));

→   cout << our_record.name << " owes $" << our_record.owes;

    our_file.close();

    return 0;
}
```

And that's all there is to it; we've successfully read an individual object from
the file. In general, we can read one object or record from a file of many such
objects or records in two different ways — with *sequential* or *random access*.
Sequential access means successively reading from a file until you get to the
object or record you want (like listening to an audio tape); in random access,
we can use seekg( ) and seekp( ) to read any object or record we want (like
reading from a book, where we can open the book to any page).

Random access to files is supported in the file class library with four functions: seekg( ), seekp( ), tellg( ), and tellp( ). The tellg( ) and tellp( ) functions return the present location of the get and put pointers, respectively, and we can use them like this:

```
streampos tellg(void);
streampos tellp(void);
```

The streampos type, defined in iostream.h, is a type that can hold the largest possible return value from these two functions. Finally, there are two more member functions we should know about: ios::fail( ) and ios::bad( ). If the last I/O operation failed, or was invalid, or if the stream is in an irrecoverable error state, then ios::fail( ) returns true (nonzero). The ios::bad( ) function is the same, except that it only returns true in the last two cases: if the I/O operation was invalid, or if the stream is in an irrecoverable error state (in commercial applications, you should always check the state of a stream rather than assuming the requested operation went well).

That's it for the file stream classes, then, and that's it for the C++ I/O class libraries. As we've seen, these libraries provide a powerful, yet flexible, I/O system for C++, capable of customization — just as we would expect of C++.

The Microsoft Foundation Class libraries which come with MS C++ have an additional set of classes that can work in much the same way — especially when it comes to files. That will be our final topic in this chapter.

Microsoft Foundation Classes File Handling

Most of the classes in the Microsoft Foundation Classes (MFC) libraries are designed to be with Windows, and we'll see a great deal about them starting in the next chapter. However, some of them can be used under DOS (called the non-Windows MFC classes). For example, we've already seen the CString object in Chapter 3. Other classes that can be used in DOS include: CArray (object array), CObList (object list), CMap (object maps), CFile (MFC binary file handling object), and CArchive (like cin, cout, but works in binary).

TIP   Although you normally define what type of objects you place into a CArray object array, some pre-defined array types are already available, including: CByteArray, CDWordArray, CObArray, CPtrArray, CStringArray, and CWordArray.

One big advantage of using MFC objects is that they can *serialize* themselves —
that is, write themselves out to disk. Before leaving the topic of files in this
chapter, let's take a look at that process by creating, say, a short database as an
example. We might use this database to keep track of some friends. Let's say
that we had a class named Friend_Class and that objects of that class kept track
of the CStrings FirstName and LastName, and that we had two such objects
like this:

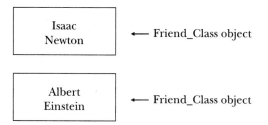

We could place them in an object list, that is, a CObList-based class we might
call Friend_ClassList. Such a list is really a collection of pointers like this:

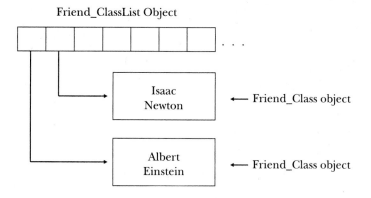

After we set up a list like this, we can automatically send it out to disk and read
it back in later. Objects that we can "serialize" (i.e., automatically write out to
disk) in this fashion need to be derived from the base class CObject, so we can
set up the class that holds the friends' names, Friend_Class, like this (we
include the new include file, afxcoll.h, to implement MFC collection classes
like CObList):

```
#define _DOS
#include <iostream.h>
#include <afx.h>
#include <afxcoll.h>
```

```
class Friend_Class : public CObject      ←
{

};
```

Notice that we defined the identifier _DOS at the beginning, as we did in our CString examples earlier to indicate that we are creating a DOS .exe file, not a Windows one. Also note that we derive Friend_Class (the class that will hold the names "Issac Newton" and "Albert Einstein" in two of its objects) from the MFC class CObject so that we will be able to serialize our list. CObject's member functions and data appear in Table 5-3.

TIP Another reason to use CObject-based objects is that they allow you to determine which class you're dealing with at run-time. This information usually doesn't exist in .exe files, but can be implemented in CObject-based objects with the DECLARE_DYNAMIC and IMPLEMENT_DYNAMIC macros.

Member	Means	
AssertValid	Is object valid?	
CObject	Copy constructor	
CObject	Default constructor	
Dump	Create diagnostic dump	
GetRuntimeClass	Get CRuntimeClass structure	
IsKindOf	Tests relationship to given class	
IsSerializable	Tests if can be serialized	
operator =	Assignment	
operator delete	Delete operator	
operator new	New operator	
Serialize	Loads or stores to or from archive	
~CObject	Destructor	
DECLARE_DYNAMIC	Macro	Gives access to run-time class information
DECLARE_SERIAL	Macro	Allows serialization
IMPLEMENT_DYNAMIC	Macro	Implements access to run-time class information
IMPLEMENT_SERIAL	Macro	Implements serialization
RUNTIME_CLASS	Macro	Gets CRuntimeClass structure

Table 5-3. CObject's Member Functions and Data

Next, we declare two constructors for Friend_Class: Friend_Class( ) and Friend_Class(CString First, CString Last). The first one, without arguments, is necessary for classes that you want to serialize, simply so that CObject's constructor will be called. We'll use the other one, which takes two CString arguments, to initialize the FirstName and LastName member strings. For example, this declaration: Friend_Class Friend1("Issac", "Newton") will give us an object like this:

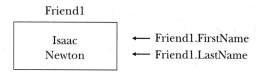

Here's how those prototypes appear in our class' definition:

```
        #define _DOS
        #include <iostream.h>
        #include <afx.h>
        #include <afxcoll.h>

        class Friend_Class : public CObject
        {
→           Friend_Class(){};
                 :
        public:
→           Friend_Class(CString First, CString Last);
            CString        FirstName;
            CString        LastName;
                 :
        };
```

In addition, we do two more things to support initialization: we include the macro DECLARE_SERIAL in our class definition, and we indicate that we will override the (virtual) function Serialize( ):

```
        #define _DOS
        #include <iostream.h>
        #include <afx.h>
        #include <afxcoll.h>

        class Friend_Class : public CObject
        {
            Friend_Class(){};
→           DECLARE_SERIAL(Friend_Class);
        public:
```

```
        Friend_Class(CString First, CString Last);
        CString         FirstName;
        CString         LastName;
→       void Serialize(CArchive& archive);
  };
```

C++ itself will expand the DECLARE_SERIAL macro into the prototypes it needs for serialization, and in the function Serialize( ), we will indicate which class data we wish to send out to disk, and in what order.

Next comes the list class Friend_ClassList, which will make up the list of our objects of class Friend_Class:

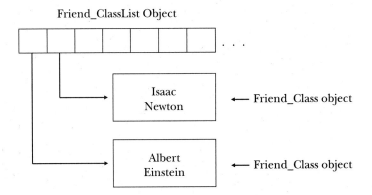

Friend_ClassList Object

We declare that in a similar fashion, with a constructor that takes no arguments (necessary for all classes that can be serialized), and with the DECLARE_SERIAL macro. This class is a list, so instead of deriving it from CObject, we derive it from COblist, a class whose member functions and data appear in Table 5-4:

```
#define _DOS
#include <iostream.h>
#include <afx.h>
#include <afxcoll.h>

class Friend_Class : public CObject
{
    Friend_Class(){};
    DECLARE_SERIAL(Friend_Class);
public:
    Friend_Class(CString First, CString Last);
    CString         FirstName;
```

```
    CString        LastName;
    void Serialize(CArchive& archive);
};


class Friend_ClassList : public CObList     ←
{
public:
    Friend_ClassList(){};
→   DECLARE_SERIAL(Friend_ClassList)
};
```

Member	Means
AddHead	Add element to head of the list
AddTail	Add element to the tail of the list
CObList	Constructor (makes an empty list)
Find	Gets position of an element
FindIndex	Gets position of an element specified by index
GetAt	Gets element at specified position
GetCount	Get number of elements in list
GetHead	Gets the head element of the list
GetHeadPosition	Gets the position of the head element
GetNext	Gets the next element
GetPrev	Gets the previous element
GetTail	Gets the tail element
GetTailPosition	Gets the position of the tail
InsertAfter	Inserts new element after specified position
InsertBefore	Inserts new element before specified position
IsEmpty	Tests for the empty list
RemoveAll	Removes all the elements from the list
RemoveAt	Removes an element at specified position
RemoveHead	Removes element from the head of list
RemoveTail	Removes element from the tail of list
SetAt	Sets the element at specified position
~CObList	Destructor

Table 5-4. CObList's Member Functions and Data

Now that our class declarations are complete, we can write the code in Friend_Class's constructor, which will load two CString objects into the Friend_Class::FirstName and Friend_Class::LastName CStrings like this:

```
#define _DOS
#include <iostream.h>
#include <afx.h>
#include <afxcoll.h>

class Friend_Class : public CObject
{
    Friend_Class(){};
    DECLARE_SERIAL(Friend_Class);
public:
    Friend_Class(CString First, CString Last);
    CString         FirstName;
    CString         LastName;
    void Serialize(CArchive& archive);
};

class Friend_ClassList : public CObList
{
public:
    Friend_ClassList(){};
    DECLARE_SERIAL(Friend_ClassList)
};

Friend_Class::Friend_Class(CString First, CString Last)
{
    FirstName = First;
    LastName = Last;
}
```

We can also define the Friend_Class::Serialize( ) function, which handles the process of sending our data out to disk. This function is defined for the individual objects in our list, not for the list as a whole. That's the way it works in general: If you want to serialize a collection of objects, you define the function Serialize( ) for those objects. We've sent and received data to and from streams like cin and cout, but here we'll be using a new stream class, CArchive, which handles serialization of data in a binary fashion:

```
Archive ← data ← Serialize()
```

Archive streams are specially created to handle this serialization process, and we send data to them (which sends data to the disk) like this: Archive <<

Member	Means
CArchive	Constructor
Close	Flushes data and disconnects from CFile
Flush	Flushes data
GetFile	Gets the CFile pointer
IsLoading	Is the archive loading?
IsStoring	Is the archive storing?
operator <<	Loads objects
operator >>	Stores objects
Read	Reads bytes
ReadObject	Calls Serialize function for loading
Write	Writes bytes
WriteObject	Calls Serialize function for storing
~CArchive	Destructor

Table 5-5. CArchive's Member Functions and Data

Friend1.FirstName << Friend1.Lastname. The CArchive member functions and data appear in Table 5-5; in particular, we'll check the IsStoring data member to see if we're writing data out to the disk or reading it back in. In addition, we have to first serialize the base class CObject, and we do that by calling the base class' Serialize( ) function. The whole thing looks like this:

```
#define _DOS
#include <iostream.h>
#include <afx.h>
#include <afxcoll.h>

class Friend_Class : public CObject
{
    Friend_Class(){};
    DECLARE_SERIAL(Friend_Class);
public:
    Friend_Class(CString First, CString Last);
    CString         FirstName;
    CString         LastName;
    void Serialize(CArchive& archive);
};
```

```
class Friend_ClassList : public CObList
{
public:
    Friend_ClassList(){};
    DECLARE_SERIAL(Friend_ClassList)
};

Friend_Class::Friend_Class(CString First, CString Last)
{
    FirstName = First;
    LastName = Last;
}

void Friend_Class::Serialize(CArchive& archive)
{
    CObject::Serialize(archive);
    if (archive.IsStoring()) archive << FirstName << LastName;
    else archive >> FirstName >> LastName;
}

IMPLEMENT_SERIAL(Friend_Class, CObject, 0)
IMPLEMENT_SERIAL(Friend_ClassList, CObList, 0)
```

At the end, you might notice that we used the macro IMPLEMENT_SERIAL, which is where C++ adds the functions actually needed for serialization. We use IMPLEMENT_SERIAL for both the list Friend_ClassList and the elements of that list, which are of type Friend_Class. Notice also that we indicate the base classes that each of them are derived from (the last parameter in the macro, 0, is a placeholder in Microsoft's implementation for future expansion).

Now we're ready to write main( ). We want to create two objects and put them into a list, like this:

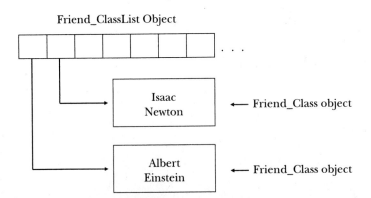

Friend_ClassList Object

To do that, we only need to use new to allocate two objects of class Friend_Class and a list of class Friend_ClassList. We'll get pointers to the two objects, which we can call friend_ptr_1 and friend_ptr_2, and a pointer to the list, which we can call data_list_ptr. We fill our friend objects with data when we construct them, and we can add them to the list with the AddHead( ) function (a member function of CObList) like this:

```
main()
{
    Friend_Class* friend_ptr_1 = new Friend_Class("Issac", "Newton");
    Friend_Class* friend_ptr_2 = new Friend_Class("Albert", "Einstein");
    Friend_ClassList* data_list_ptr = new Friend_ClassList;

→   data_list_ptr->AddHead(friend_ptr_1);
→   data_list_ptr->AddHead(friend_ptr_2);
            :
```

AddHead( ) simply adds an element to the list at the position called the *head*. In general, the head of a list is the position at which new items are added. After adding two items, the head of our list will be in the third position:

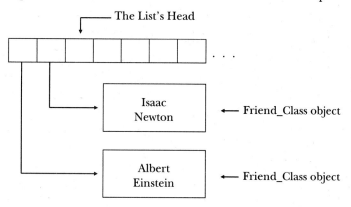

At this point, our list is complete and we're ready to send it out to disk. We can call our disk file friends.dat, and we can open that file as a CFile object. This class is specially used to handle CObject objects, and its member data and functions appear in Table 5-6. Next, we associate an archive object with this file by passing a pointer to the file object to CArchive's constructor and indicating that this archive is for storing data like this:

```
main()
{
    CFile the_file;
    CFileException exc;
```

```
char* pfilename = "friends.dat";
Friend_ClassList* data_list_ptr = new Friend_ClassList;
Friend_Class* friend_ptr_1 = new Friend_Class("Issac", "Newton");
Friend_Class* friend_ptr_2 = new Friend_Class("Albert", "Einstein");

data_list_ptr->AddHead(friend_ptr_1);
data_list_ptr->AddHead(friend_ptr_2);
```

→   `the_file.Open(pfilename, CFile::modeCreate | CFile::modeWrite, &exc);`
→   `CArchive the_out_Archive(&the_file, CArchive::store);`
        :

Like cin and cout, an archive object can only be associated with storing or loading data, not both (i.e., we'll have to create a new archive object to read

Member	Means
CFile	Constructor
Close	Closes file, deletes object
Duplicate	Duplicate object
Flush	Flushes data
GetLength	Get length of the file
GetPosition	Gets file pointer
GetStatus	Get status of the specified file
LockRange	Lock range of file bytes
Open	Opens a file (with error-testing option)
Read	Reads data from file
Remove	Deletes specified file
Rename	Renames specified file
Seek	Moves file pointer
SeekToBegin	Moves file pointer to beginning of file
SeekToEnd	Moves file pointer to end of file
SetLength	Change length of file
SetStatus	Sets status of specified file
UnlockRange	Unlock range of file bytes
Write	Writes to current file position
~CFile	Destructor

Table 5-6. CFile's Member Functions and Data

our data back in). Now we're ready to send our list to the archive stream, which sends it to the disk file friends.dat:

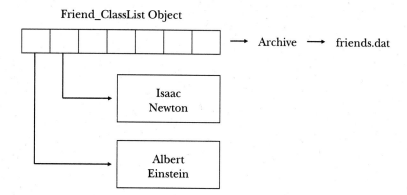

To serialize our list of objects (i.e., write it out to disk), we send it the output archive by passing it the pointer to the list like this: the_out_Archive << data_list_ptr;. Then we close both the archive and the file:

```
main()
{
    CFile the_file;
    CFileException exc;
    char* pfilename = "friends.dat";
    Friend_ClassList* data_list_ptr = new Friend_ClassList;
    Friend_Class* friend_ptr_1 = new Friend_Class("Issac", "Newton");
    Friend_Class* friend_ptr_2 = new Friend_Class("Albert", "Einstein");

    data_list_ptr->AddHead(friend_ptr_1);
    data_list_ptr->AddHead(friend_ptr_2);

    the_file.Open(pfilename, CFile::modeCreate | CFile::modeWrite, &exc);
    CArchive the_out_Archive(&the_file, CArchive::store);
    the_out_Archive << data_list_ptr;
    the_out_Archive.Close();
    the_file.Close();
        :
```

At this point, the list of objects is stored in the file friends.dat. We've successfully stored it on disk. To read it back in, we reverse the process, creating a new input archive called the_in_archive, and reading our list back like this:

```
main()
{
    CFile the_file;
    CFileException exc;
    char* pfilename = "friends.dat";
    Friend_ClassList* data_list_ptr = new Friend_ClassList;
    Friend_Class* friend_ptr_1 = new Friend_Class("Issac", "Newton");
    Friend_Class* friend_ptr_2 = new Friend_Class("Albert", "Einstein");

    data_list_ptr->AddHead(friend_ptr_1);
    data_list_ptr->AddHead(friend_ptr_2);

    the_file.Open(pfilename, CFile::modeCreate | CFile::modeWrite, &exc);
    CArchive the_out_Archive(&the_file, CArchive::store);
    the_out_Archive << data_list_ptr;
    the_out_Archive.Close();
    the_file.Close();

    the_file.Open(pfilename, CFile::modeRead, &exc);
    CArchive the_in_Archive(&the_file, CArchive::load);
    the_in_Archive >> data_list_ptr;
    the_in_Archive.Close();
    the_file.Close();
        :
```

Now that the list is read back in, the head position will be set back to the first element. We can get pointers to the objects in the list with GetHeadPosition( ) (which returns a value of type POSITION) and GetNext( ) (which takes a value of type POSITION and allows us to increment through the list). Finally, we print the data members FirstName and LastName of the objects we retrieved out on the screen like this:

```
main()
{
    CFile the_file;
    CFileException exc;
    char* pfilename = "friends.dat";
    Friend_ClassList* data_list_ptr = new Friend_ClassList;
    Friend_Class* friend_ptr_1 = new Friend_Class("Issac", "Newton");
    Friend_Class* friend_ptr_2 = new Friend_Class("Albert", "Einstein");

    data_list_ptr->AddHead(friend_ptr_1);
    data_list_ptr->AddHead(friend_ptr_2);

    the_file.Open(pfilename, CFile::modeCreate | CFile::modeWrite, &exc);
    CArchive the_out_Archive(&the_file, CArchive::store);
```

```
        the_out_Archive << data_list_ptr;
        the_out_Archive.Close();
        the_file.Close();

        the_file.Open(pfilename, CFile::modeRead, &exc);
        CArchive the_in_Archive(&the_file, CArchive::load);
        the_in_Archive >> data_list_ptr;
        the_in_Archive.Close();
        the_file.Close();

→       POSITION pos = data_list_ptr->GetHeadPosition();
→       friend_ptr_1 = (Friend_Class*)data_list_ptr->GetNext(pos);
→       friend_ptr_2 = (Friend_Class*)data_list_ptr->GetNext(pos);

→       cout << friend_ptr_1->FirstName << " ";
→       cout << friend_ptr_1->LastName << "\n";
→       cout << friend_ptr_2->FirstName << " ";
→       cout << friend_ptr_2->LastName << "\n";

        return 0;
}
```

And that's it. We've created a list of MFC objects, serialized it, and examined the objects in it. The program is a success; the code appears in Listing 5-1. If you name this program, say, serial.cpp, then to create serial.exe, make sure that you link in one of the MFC libraries (safxcr.lib, mafxcr.lib, or lafxcr.lib depending on your memory model) like this: cl /AM serial.cpp mafxcr.lib.

Listing 5-1. Serialization Example Using MFC Libraries

```
#define _DOS
#include <iostream.h>
#include <afx.h>
#include <afxcoll.h>

class Friend_Class : public CObject
{
    Friend_Class(){};
    DECLARE_SERIAL(Friend_Class);
public:
    Friend_Class(CString First, CString Last);
    CString         FirstName;
    CString         LastName;
    void Serialize(CArchive& archive);
};
```

(continued)

Listing 5-1. *(continued)*

```
class Friend_ClassList : public CObList
{
public:
    Friend_ClassList(){};
    DECLARE_SERIAL(Friend_ClassList)
};

Friend_Class::Friend_Class(CString First, CString Last)
{
    FirstName = First;
    LastName = Last;
}

void Friend_Class::Serialize(CArchive& archive)
{
    CObject::Serialize(archive);
    if (archive.IsStoring()) archive << FirstName << LastName;
    else archive >> FirstName >> LastName;
}

IMPLEMENT_SERIAL(Friend_Class, CObject, 0)
IMPLEMENT_SERIAL(Friend_ClassList, CObList, 0)

main()
{
    CFile the_file;
    CFileException exc;
    char* pfilename = "friends.dat";
    Friend_ClassList* data_list_ptr = new Friend_ClassList;
    Friend_Class* friend_ptr_1 = new Friend_Class("Issac", "Newton");
    Friend_Class* friend_ptr_2 = new Friend_Class("Albert", "Einstein");

    data_list_ptr->AddHead(friend_ptr_1);
    data_list_ptr->AddHead(friend_ptr_2);

    the_file.Open(pfilename, CFile::modeCreate | CFile::modeWrite, &exc);
    CArchive the_out_Archive(&the_file, CArchive::store);
    the_out_Archive << data_list_ptr;
    the_out_Archive.Close();
    the_file.Close();

    the_file.Open(pfilename, CFile::modeRead, &exc);
    CArchive the_in_Archive(&the_file, CArchive::load);
    the_in_Archive >> data_list_ptr;
    the_in_Archive.Close();
    the_file.Close();
```

Listing 5-1. *(continued)*

```
POSITION pos = data_list_ptr->GetHeadPosition();
friend_ptr_1 = (Friend_Class*)data_list_ptr->GetNext(pos);
friend_ptr_2 = (Friend_Class*)data_list_ptr->GetNext(pos);

cout << friend_ptr_1->FirstName << " ";
cout << friend_ptr_1->LastName << "\n";
cout << friend_ptr_2->FirstName << " ";
cout << friend_ptr_2->LastName << "\n";

return 0;
}
```

That's it for the DOS versions of the class libraries (both the I/O classes and the non-Windows MFC classes) that come with Microsoft C++. Now, however, it's time to turn to Windows programming and *really* put C++ to work. We'll start that immediately in Chapter 6.

Welcome to C++ for Windows

If you've done any programming for Windows in C, then you'll find that this is where C++ really shines. The Windows programming interface is extensive and complicated; much of it has to do with the enormous number of options programmers have in terms of window styles, ways of running the program, window dimensions, memory allocation, and so on. The great majority of Windows programs, however, do not need such great ranges of choices, which is why C++ is perfect here. All the option selections can be wrapped up into standard classes, and we can derive our own classes from them. Then, when we want to do something unusual, we can override a previous virtual function. In this way, the details become hidden from view, and the "surface area" of the Windows programming interface shrinks rapidly, back to a manageable size. Here, we'll not only learn about programming Windows, but about using C++ for large scale applications in general.

In this chapter, we'll start with an overview of Windows to get our terms right, then we'll get an overview of event-driven Windows programming, and how well it fits into the object-oriented programming method. Following that, we'll put together our first Windows program in C++, which will simply display the text "Hello, World." in a window (and we'll also see the corresponding C code for comparison). Let's get started.

All About Windows

Many people believe that Graphical User Interfaces — GUIs — are the wave of the future in microcomputing, and they could be right. Certainly Windows 3.0 was the quickest selling software package in history (500,000 copies in its first six weeks; 3,000,000 in its first nine months). In most significant ways, Windows is a full operating environment by itself.

Windows is very different from DOS; one of the most fundamental differences is that Windows is a GUI, which introduces many new concepts. One of the primary ideas here is that most of the available options are presented to the user at once, in the form of objects on the screen, much like tools ready to be used. The utility of this simple approach is surprising — rather than remembering complex techniques and keywords, a user can simply select the correct tool for the task at hand and begin work. In this way, graphical interfaces fulfill much of the promise of computers as endlessly adaptable tools. Let's take a look at some of the background of this operating environment.

Historical Windows

Microsoft actually started working on Windows in 1983, only two years after the PC had appeared. However, the original version, Windows 1.01, didn't actually ship until 1985. This version was supposed to run on the standard machine of that time: an IBM PC with two 360K diskette drives, 256K, and an 8088. The display was automatically tiled; that is, the windows were arranged to cover the whole screen. It looked very two dimensional — and far from impressive.

The next major version, Windows 2, came out two years later. For the first time, windows could overlap on the screen. However, Windows 2 could only run in 80x86 real mode, which meant that it was limited to a total of one megabyte of memory. For a while, Windows even split into Windows 286 and Windows 386 to take advantage of the capabilities of the (then new) 80386 chip. Progress had been made, but it was clear that much more was still needed.

In May of 1990, Microsoft introduced Windows 3.0. The look and feel of Windows 3.0 was a great improvement over its ancestors, and it featured proportional fonts, which made displays look more refined. Version 3.0 also had better support for DOS programs. Version 3.1, introduced in April 1992, improved on Version 3.0, especially when it came to managing files. Many users are now using Windows as their primary operating environment for the PC.

The MS-DOS Executive of earlier versions was replaced by a trinity of windows that manage Windows: The *Program Manager,* the *Task List,* and the *File Manager.* From a programming point of view, one of the most important features of Windows 3+ is that they can support extended memory: up to 16 megabytes of RAM. And, in its 386-enhanced mode, Windows uses the built-in virtual memory capabilities of the 80/3/4/586 (that is, it can store sections of memory temporarily on disk) to give programmers access to up to four times the amount of actual installed memory. In a machine that has 16 megabytes, then, Windows can actually provide 64 megabytes. The removal of memory restrictions has always been one of the advantages of OS/2, but now more and more programmers are coming back to Windows. With Windows 3+, Windows had at last arrived.

Dissecting a Window

A typical Windows 3+ window appears in Figure 6-1, and you should be familiar with its parts and the names given to them before we going on. As you probably know, it's important to know what the user expects from a Windows application before writing one. Let's spend a little time reviewing Windows terminology ourselves; this will help us later in the book. At the upper left of the window in Figure 6-1 is a system menu box, which, when selected, displays a menu that typically allows the user to move the window, close it, or minimize it. At the top center is the title or caption bar, and this provides an easy way of labeling an application.

To the right of the title bar are the Minimize and Maximize boxes, which allow the user to reduce the window to an icon (called an application's *iconic* state), or expand it fully, usually to the whole screen. Under the title bar is usually a

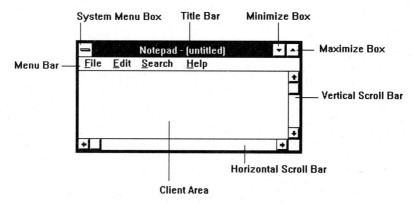

Figure 6-1. A Windows 3+ Window

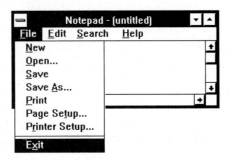

Figure 6-2. A Windows 3+ Window with Menu

menu bar offering the currently available menu options for the application. In almost every stand-alone application, there will be a menu bar with at least one menu item in it: the File menu. This is the menu that usually offers the Exit item at the bottom, as shown in Figure 6-2.

TIP   The Exit item is the usual way for users to leave an application, so if your application supports file handling, you should include the Exit item at the bottom of your File menu. (In fact, Windows applications often have a File menu to provide an Exit item even if they don't use files.)

Under the menu bar is the *client area*; in fact, the client area makes up the whole of a window under the menu bar except for the borders and scroll bars (it's the area that the window is designed to display). This is our drawing area, the area we will work with directly in Microsoft C++; that is, this is the part of the window on which we'll place buttons, list boxes, text boxes, and the other parts of our programs. In Windows, these visual objects are called *controls*.

To the right of the client area is a vertical scroll bar, which is a common part of a window that displays text. If there is too much text to fit in the window at once, scroll bars let you look at some subsection of the whole, moving around in the document. (As you may know, the small square that moves up and down which you use to manipulate your position in the scroll bar is called a *thumb*.)

On the bottom of the window is another scroll bar, a horizontal one which scrolls the text in the client area horizontally. Everything in the window but the client area is called the non-client area. Even the border is part of the non-client area. Windows will be responsible for maintaining the non-client area of the window, and we'll be responsible for the client area.

Program Design in Windows

Let's take a moment to discuss the design of windows and Windows programs. When the program starts, the first thing the user sees is almost invariably a window:

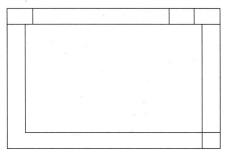

Just a blank window — where nothing is happening — can be a little confusing. If your program edit files, for example, you might want to pop up a dialog box first (we'll see how to do this soon) asking for the filename the user wants to edit:

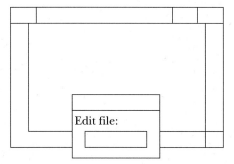

In addition, you might want to place a few buttons on your main window to indicate what operations the user can select from (e.g., cut and paste text), but this temptation might better be resisted. Usually, controls like buttons, listboxes, and combo boxes are used in dialog boxes, not in the main window. Instead, the choices in the main window are usually presented in the form of menus:

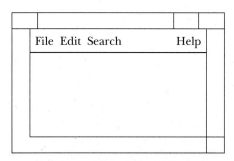

When the user positions the mouse cursor on a menu name and holds the mouse button down, the menu opens:

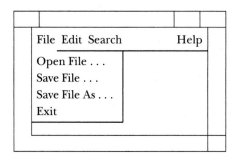

(Note that the last menu item in the File menu is usually Exit, and File is usually the first menu.) The dots after the menu items indicate that selecting them opens a dialog box. Your application can have as many dialog boxes as you want, and they can be very helpful to the user; some programmers use the rule of thumb that any control that is not a text box or menu should go in a dialog box (dialog boxes cannot have menus).

In addition, we'll see how to "grey out" (that is, make inactive) menu items that do not present valid options at some point (e.g., using Save File As... before there is any text to save). However, you should do this with care — there are few things more frustrating than to be presented with a huge menu in which almost all items are greyed out. A better option is to remove the inactive menu items from the menu if there are too many of them (we'll see how to do this too).

Contrary to main windows, dialog boxes can have as many controls as you like (note the single border for a dialog box, as opposed to the double border for a main window):

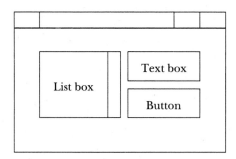

One option you should always provide the user with in a dialog box is a Cancel button so he can back out of an operation gracefully. Another customary button to use here is an OK button (indicating that a user has made his choices and wants to put them into effect).

Both main windows and dialog boxes have title bars; the name in the main window's title bar should be the name of the application (so the user can pick it out among other windows), and the name in the title bar of a dialog box is usually the name of the menu item it represents (e.g., Save File As...). Although some applications need to maintain multiple windows on the screen, it's much more common — and less confusing — to have a main window and use dialog boxes (that vanish after they've fulfilled their purpose) for additional input.

Besides the visual design of the program, there is more to program design in Windows. As you become more and more of an accomplished Windows programmer, you'll probably start using more and more resources — files, additional memory, serial ports, and so on. If you want your program to be popular among Windows users, you should adhere to the Windows programming philosophy: A program should have as little impact on other programs and on the programming environment (Windows itself) as possible.

The reason this is crucial is that many applications can run at once in Windows, and if they try to take one or more resources for themselves, there might be a conflict. For example, maintaining exclusive control of a file prevents other programs from using it. For that reason, most programming resources — like memory, files, and so on — can be allocated to your program in a way that allows them be shared with other programs. For example, you can allocate memory in Windows that is locked in a specific physical location in actual memory, but doing so means that the memory available to other programs will be fragmented around the block you own. When you get the option, it is always better to make your program flexible when handling resources. In this case, you can let Windows know that it can move the memory you're using around as it needs to.

This is most important when it comes to the most precious resource of all — CPU time. One of the worst things a Windows program can do is to grab and hold control, looping endlessly while waiting for input. This denies CPU time to all other windows and is very strongly against the Windows philosophy.

Instead of long, linear DOS programs, we'll be writing short chunks of code in our programs, and tying the code to specific Windows controls. This is very important — code is usually tied to Windows controls so that the user can direct program flow (e.g., by clicking buttons in the order she wants). In this way, she'll also be able to switch to other applications, and our program will have to give up control graciously, not hog CPU time. For this reason, our code is going to be very modular; each section of code will be separate, and each will (usually) be connected to some Windows control. We'll see more about this very soon.

Preserving the Feel of Windows

As mentioned, when programming in C++ for Windows, you should be very familiar with the way the user expects Windows programs to work and feel. In particular, you should be at home with the language of mouse clicks and double clicks, and anticipating what the user might expect from your application.

For example, the fact that the File menu usually has an Exit item, and that item, if present, is always last, is part of the Windows interface you'll be programming in. There are many other aspects of the way users expect Windows applications to work that you should be familiar with before producing applications yourself; in other words, there is a large number of Windows conventions that you should adhere to. Although we'll discuss these conventions as we reach the appropriate topics, there's no substitute for working with existing Windows applications to get the correct feel for the Windows interface.

After a while, these conventions become quite automatic. For instance, in file list boxes (where the program is showing you which files are available to be opened), one click of the mouse should highlight a filename (called *selecting*), and two clicks should open the file (called *choosing*). On the other hand, it is also supposed to be possible to use Windows without a mouse at all — just with the keyboard — so you should provide keyboard support at the same time (in this case, the user would use the <Tab> key to move to the correct box, the arrow keys to highlight a filename, and the <Enter> key to choose it).

NOTE   For the purposes of program design in this book, we are assuming that you have a mouse to go along with C++. Although it is possible to use Windows *applications* without a mouse, Windows *programmers* (or even experienced Windows users) are hampered without one, seriously crippling their productivity.

There are other conventions that Windows users expect. If there's some object that can be moved around the screen, users expect to be able to drag it with the mouse. They expect accelerator keys in menus, system menus that let them close a window, and windows that can be moved, resized, or minimized. As mentioned, the best way to know what will be expected of your program is to work with existing Windows applications.

All About Windows Programming

Now let's take a look at how one programs applications for Windows, and what makes it different from programming under DOS. To start, DOS programs are written sequentially; that is, one statement follows another. In a DOS program, control goes down the list of statements, more or less in the order that the programmer designed. For example, this is the way an introductory program from a DOS C++ book might look:

```
#include <iostream.h>

main()
{
    cout << "Hello ";
    cout << "World.\n";

    return 0;
}
```

Control goes sequentially from line to line, and the message "Hello World.\n" appears on the screen. If there were more statements, control would continue on with them, looping and progressing in the way that the programmer designed it to work. However, Windows is different.

Under Windows, an application typically presents all possible options (in the form of visual objects) on the screen for the user to select. In this way, it represents an entirely new kind of programming — *event-driven* programming. That is to say, the programmer is no longer completely responsible for the flow of the program — the user is. The user selects among all the options presented to them, and it is up to the program to respond correctly. For example, there may be three buttons on a window, as shown in Figure 6-3. Clearly, we can't just write our program assuming that the user is going to push them in some sequence.

Instead, we'll have to write separate code for each button. That's going to be the case in general, and it has significant consequences for us in this book.

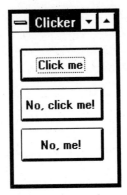

Figure 6-3. Our Clicker Window

Instead of monolithic programs that you can read from beginning to end, our code will necessarily be divided up into smaller sections, one such section for one kind of event. For example, we may want to display the string "Hello, World". In that case, our program might look like this:

```
void CMainWindow::OnPaint()
{
    CString hello_string = "Hello, World";
    CPaintDC dc(this);

    dc.TextOut(0, 0, hello_string, hello_string.GetLength() );
}
```

This code is specifically designed to handle one type of event: when the window is "painted" — that is, refreshed (i.e., when the window is first drawn or uncovered when another window moves). Our Windows C++ programs will typically be collections of code sections like this, one after the other. That's how event-driven programming works: We'll largely be designing our code around the I/O interface. Our programs won't have "modes," like an editor can have modes (e.g., insert mode, marking mode, and so on); instead, all the options available at one time will be represented on the screen, ready to be used. We'll see how this works soon.

Besides being event driven, Windows programming is also naturally object oriented. That is easy enough to see on the screen: Just pick up an object such as an icon or paintbrush and move it around. This corresponds closely to object oriented programming, as we'll see. Here, we'll be able to break up a program into discrete objects in a natural way, each of which has its own code and data associated with it. Each of the objects can be independent from the others.

Using object-oriented programming is perfect for event-driven software, because it breaks the program up into discrete, modular objects. And this is the way we'll be treating our windows and all the buttons, text boxes, and so on that we put in them: as objects.

Hungarian Notation

We should also know the naming convention of Windows variables. There is a Windows convention called Hungarian notation (named for the nationality of its inventor, Charles Simonyi, a Microsoft programmer). Because Windows programs can be so long, it's easy to lose track of what all the variables mean. To help, Hungarian notation provides letters that can be used as prefixes, and they appear in Table 6-1 for reference (which you might refer to frequently

Prefix	Means
a	array
b	bool (int)
by	unsigned char (byte)
c	char
cb	count of bytes
cr	color reference value
cx, cy	short (count of x, y length)
dw	unsigned long (dword)
fn	function
h	handle
i	integer
n	short or int
np	near pointer
p	pointer
l	long
lp	long pointer
s	string
sz	string terminated with a zero
tm	text metric
w	unsigned int (word)
x, y	short (x or y coordinate)

Table 6-1. Hungarian Notation

throughout this book). They can also be combined; for example, lpszMyString means: a long pointer to a zero-terminated string named MyString. And, as far as C++ goes, if lpszMyString is a member of some class, it would be named m_lpszMyString in the Microsoft Foundation Class libraries (and this chapter is largely an exploration of those libraries).

Now that we have the background, let's look at a typical C program for Windows. This will get new Windows programmers up to speed, and will give experienced Windows programmers a point of reference.

WinMain( ) and WindowProc( )

The goal of the program we're going to develop in this chapter is to put the string "Hello World." into a window and display it. First we'll design that program in broad strokes using C (this is useful because it will show us much about how to program in Windows), and then we'll do it in detail in C++. There are two major functions in a standard C for Windows program: WinMain( ) and WindowProc( ), like this:

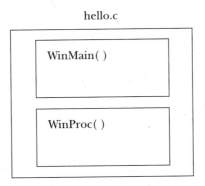

hello.c

WinMain( )

WinProc( )

NOTE   You can give WindowProc( ) almost any name you like, but WinMain( ) must be called WinMain( ).

The WinMain( ) function sets up the window by allowing us to design and register a window class, and then displays it. From then on, WindowProc( ) takes over. In standard Windows applications, it is WindowProc( ) that handles responses from the user, such as button pushes or menu selections. It does that by receiving *Windows messages*.

This is a crucial point; every time an event occurs in Windows, a message is sent to the currently active program, letting it know what's happening. For example, if a key is pressed, a special message is sent to our function WindowProc( ). That's how our program interfaces to Windows — through messages. In a C program, the prototype of WindowProc( ) looks like this:

```
LONG FAR PASCAL WindowProc(HWND hWnd, WORD Message, WORD wParam, LONG lParam)
```

The first parameter, hWnd, is a *window handle,* which tells us which window the message is for. Handles are used because one window procedure like WindowProc( ) can handle messages for many windows, and each of these windows are identified by their own handles.

The next parameter is the message itself, one word long. This parameter holds values that are defined in the file windows.h. For example, depending on what occurred, these are the kinds of messages that will be passed to us by Windows (there are actually about 150 such messages):

WM_CREATE	The window is being created
WM_KEYDOWN	A key was pressed
WM_SIZE	Window was sized or resized
WM_MOVE	Window was moved
WM_PAINT	Window needs to be (re)drawn

The prefix WM stands for Window Message. The usual procedure in a C window procedure like WindowProc( ) is to set up a switch statement, and to take the appropriate action depending on which message was sent:

```
LONG FAR PASCAL WindowProc(HWND hWnd, WORD Message, WORD wParam, LONG lParam)
{
 switch (Message)
   {
   case WM_CREATE:
        :
        break;       /*  End of WM_CREATE                         */

   case WM_MOVE:     /*  code for moving the window               */
        :
        break;

   case WM_SIZE:     /*  code for sizing client area              */
        :
        break;       /*  End of WM_SIZE                           */
```

```
    case WM_PAINT:      /* code for the window's client area           */
         :
         break;         /*  End of WM_PAINT                            */

    case WM_CLOSE:   /* close the window                               */
         :
         break;

    default:
    }
}
```

The next two parameters, wParam and lParam, hold data that is important for this message; wParam is one word long, and lParam is two words long. For example, if a window is moved, these parameters hold its new location.

Since a Windows program is *event-driven* — i.e., we wait for events like button pushes or menu selections — we have to wait for Windows to send us the appropriate messages that match the events which have occurred. These messages stack up in a *message queue* (internal to Windows), and we read them one at a time, handling them in order. For example, if the user moved our window and then pressed a key, Windows would call WindowProc( ) with a WM_MOVE message, followed by a WM_KEYDOWN message.

It turns out that one of the primary jobs of WinMain( ) is to set up this message queue for us, informing Windows that we want our program messages sent to WindowProc( ). In addition, it sets up the window(s) we want in the first place, and displays it (or them) on the screen. In fact, when our program is first loaded, WinMain( ) is called first by Windows — this is how our program gets started.

Messages are handled in Windows by filling the fields of a MSG structure. That structure is defined this way (in windows.h):

```
/* Message structure */
typedef struct tagMSG
  {
     HWND     hwnd;
     WORD     message;
     WORD     wParam;
     LONG     lParam;
     DWORD    time;
     POINT    pt;
  } MSG;
```

The first field of this structure holds the handle of the window that this message is targeted for (each message can go to only one window). The next field holds the message itself, encoded in pre-defined constants like WM_SIZE, WM_PAINT, or WM_MOUSEMOVE. The following two fields hold the two data items associated with each message, wParam and lParam. After that, the time the event occurred is encoded in a field called time, and the field named pt holds the coordinates of the mouse cursor at the time the message was generated. We might note that pt is itself a structure of the POINT type, which, in Windows, looks like this:

```
typedef struct tagPOINT
   {
     int    x;
     int    y;
   } POINT;
```

To make sure we get all the messages that come to us, we now enter the message loop in WinMain( ). To get a message in the first place, we call the Windows function GetMessage( ). This function fills a message structure and returns a value. The return value is nonzero (i.e., logically true) if the message we just got was anything but WM_QUIT, which is the final message Windows applications receive. If we get a WM_QUIT message, we want to leave the message loop and finish up with WinMain( ) (i.e., there will not be any more messages to receive), so we can set up our message loop like this (recall that WM_QUIT makes GetMessage( ) return a 0 value, which terminates the loop):

```
int PASCAL WinMain(HANDLE hInstance, HANDLE hPrevInstance, \
        LPSTR lpszCmdLine, int nCmdShow)
           :
 // Begin message loop!
   while(GetMessage(&msg, NULL, 0, 0))          /* Until WM_QUIT message */
    {

    }
}
```

We've already seen that when a key is pressed, a WM_KEYDOWN message is generated. However, it's a little difficult to extract information — such as what letter was actually typed, and whether or not it's a capital or small letter — from a WM_KEYDOWN message. Instead, we can call TranslateMessage( ) to translate the information in a WM_KEYDOWN message, and to generate a

WM_CHAR message, which passes the ASCII code of the struck key on to us directly (in the parameter wParam). We use TranslateMessage( ) like this in the message loop:

```
int PASCAL WinMain(HANDLE hInstance, HANDLE hPrevInstance, \
       LPSTR lpszCmdLine, int nCmdShow)
           :
 // Begin message loop!
 while(GetMessage(&msg, NULL, 0, 0))              /* Until WM_QUIT message */
   {
     TranslateMessage(&msg);
           :
   }
}
```

At this point in our C code, we're ready to pass the message on to our window procedure, WindowProc( ), and we do that simply with DispatchMessage( ), like this (WinMain( ) has previously indicated to Windows that dispatched messages should be sent to WindowProc( )):

```
int PASCAL WinMain(HANDLE hInstance, HANDLE hPrevInstance, \
       LPSTR lpszCmdLine, int nCmdShow)
           :
 // Begin message loop!
 while(GetMessage(&msg, NULL, 0, 0))              /* Until WM_QUIT message */
   {
     TranslateMessage(&msg);
     DispatchMessage(&msg);
   }
}
```

In this way, we keep looping over messages in the message loop, continually receiving them and forwarding them to WindowProc( ) until we receive a WM_QUIT message, at which time we leave the message loop and exit WinMain( ), ending the program. In other words, the flow of control looks something like this, where we send all messages except WM_QUIT to WindowProc( ):

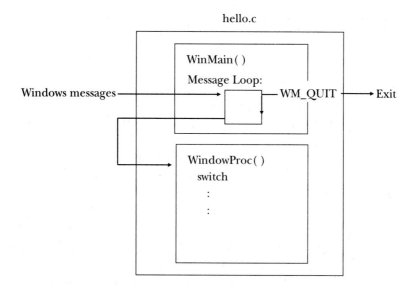

The system messages which are directed towards Windows also come in through this message loop, and we have to pass them on to WindowProc( ) so that they can be handled by the default window procedure, DefWindowProc( ), at the end:

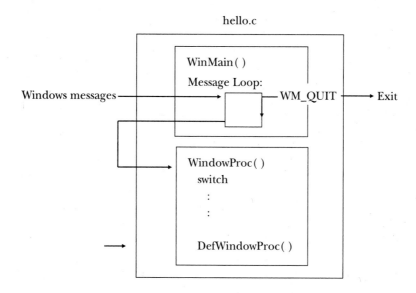

This is pretty much the standard form for message loops to take. The important WindowProc( ) event for us here, in our first program, is the WM_PAINT event. This is a request from Windows for us to draw the client area of our window. A WM_PAINT message is issued when our window is first displayed, and every time thereafter when it needs to be redrawn. For example, another window may be moved over ours on the screen; when ours is uncovered again, Windows will send our WindowProc( ) function a WM_PAINT message, telling us to redraw — and therefore restore — our window. This is when we'll print our "Hello, world." string.

Professional Windows applications almost always have some code in the WM_PAINT case. We get a WM_PAINT message whenever we have to redraw some or all of our window; that is, if some part of our window has been covered and is now uncovered, or if the window is being drawn the first time.

If some portion of our window needs to be redrawn, that portion, which may be the whole window, is called *invalid.* In Windows, these portions are rectangles. For example, let's say that another window was covering the lower right corner of ours. When the user removes that window, the newly uncovered part of our window is called invalid by Windows:

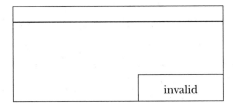

In this case, Windows would send us a WM_PAINT message telling us where the invalid rectangle was in our window, and ask us to redraw it. The way it tells us what the dimensions of the invalid rectangle are is by passing that information to us in a specialized structure called a *paint structure.*

TIP   One easy way of fixing a window without worrying about exactly which part of it is invalid is to redraw the whole thing (if that doesn't take too much time). Windows will restrict all drawing attempts to the invalid rectangle, and drawing outside it will simply have no effect.

In WindowProc( ), the WM_PAINT case starts by clearing the fields of a paint structure we've defined as ps:

```
LONG FAR PASCAL WindowProc(HWND hWnd, WORD Message, WORD wParam, LONG lParam)
→     PAINTSTRUCT ps;                     /* holds PAINT information        */
{
 switch (Message)
    {
    case WM_CREATE:
         :
         break;        /*  End of WM_CREATE                                 */

    case WM_MOVE:      /*  code for moving the window                       */
         :
         break;

    case WM_SIZE:      /*  code for sizing client area                      */
         :
         break;        /*  End of WM_SIZE                                   */

    case WM_PAINT:     /* code for the window's client area                 */
→        memset(&ps, 0x00, sizeof(PAINTSTRUCT));
         :
         break;        /*  End of WM_PAINT                                  */

    case WM_CLOSE:     /* close the window                                  */
         :
         break;

    default:
    }
}
```

Next, we fill that paint structure with a call to the Windows function BeginPaint( ). Note that we pass it the handle of our window so that Windows will know which window's invalid rectangle we're requesting information about, and the address of our paint structure:

```
    case WM_PAINT: /* code for the window's client area                    */
        memset(&ps, 0x00, sizeof(PAINTSTRUCT));
→       hDC = BeginPaint(hWnd, &ps);
         :
```

This way, the BeginPaint( ) function fills the paint structure. The fields of that structure look like this:

```
typedef struct tagPAINTSTRUCT
  {
    HDC      hdc;
    BOOL     fErase;
    RECT     rcPaint;
    BOOL     fRestore;
    BOOL     fIncUpdate;
    BYTE     rgbReserved[16];
  } PAINTSTRUCT;
```

Note in particular the third field, which is of type RECT. This is how Windows passes the dimensions of the invalid rectangle to us, in a structure of type RECT, which stands for rectangle. That structure is defined this way:

```
typedef struct tagRECT
  {
    int      left;
    int      top;
    int      right;
    int      bottom;
  } RECT;
```

The top left corner of our invalid rectangle has the coordinates (left, top) and the bottom left corner has the coordinates (right, bottom). These coordinates are measured in pixels from the top left of our window, which is the origin, (0,0), like this:

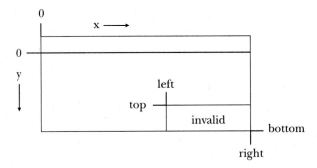

Note also that BeginPaint( ) has a return value, hDC:

```
case WM_PAINT:  /* code for the window's client area          */
    memset(&ps, 0x00, sizeof(PAINTSTRUCT));
→   hDC = BeginPaint(hWnd, &ps);
        :
```

This is a *handle* to the invalid rectangle, and allows us to draw in it. It might seem strange to have a second handle like this — after all, we already have a handle to our window — but this is a handle to the invalid rectangle, and all drawing operations must be performed with this handle, hDC, not hWnd (we'll see why soon).

The first time a window is displayed, a WM_PAINT message is generated and the whole client area (the area we can draw on) is declared invalid. We can use that WM_PAINT message to place our message at the upper left of the window — that is, at location (0,0) as measured in pixel coordinates — and this is how we do it with the Windows function named TextOut( ):

```
case WM_PAINT:  /* code for the window's client area          */
    memset(&ps, 0x00, sizeof(PAINTSTRUCT));
    hDC = BeginPaint(hWnd, &ps);

→   /* USER-ADDED CODE                                         */
→   TextOut (hDC, 0, 0, (LPSTR) "Hello, world.", strlen("Hello, world."));

    EndPaint(hWnd, &ps);
    break;       /* End of WM_PAINT                            */
```

TextOut( ) takes five parameters: the handle of the rectangle we're drawing in, hDC; the x (horizontal) and y (vertical) coordinates of our message, which will be (0, 0) in our case; a far pointer to our message itself, which we pass this way: (LPSTR) "Hello, world."; and, finally, the length of the string to print, which we find with strlen( ). (The LPSTR type override converts a near pointer to a string into a far one, and is defined in windows.h.)

As an overview, then, that's really all there is to the C program, although there are some additional support files that we'll need (as we'll see later). The actual

C code for hello.c (as created with Microsoft QuickC for Windows'
QuickCASE:W tool) is in Listing 6-1; you can see that it is very long, even for
this simple program in which we only put one line of text into a window.

Listing 6-1. Hello.c

```
/* QuickCase:W KNB Version 1.00 */
#include "HELLO.h"

/*************************************************************************/
/*                                                                     */
/* Windows Main Program Body                                           */
/*                                                                     */
/* The following routine is the Windows Main Program.  The Main Program */
/* is executed when a program is selected from the Windows Control      */
/* Panel or File Manager.  The WinMain routine registers and creates    */
/* the program's main window and initializes global objects.  The       */
/* WinMain routine also includes the applications message dispatch      */
/* loop.  Every window message destined for the main window or any      */
/* subordinate windows is obtained, possibly translated, and            */
/* dispatched to a window or dialog processing function. The dispatch   */
/* loop is exited when a WM_QUIT message is obtained.  Before exiting    */
/* the WinMain routine should destroy any objects created and free      */
/* memory and other resources.                                          */
/*                                                                     */
/*************************************************************************/

int PASCAL WinMain(HANDLE hInstance, HANDLE hPrevInstance,
        LPSTR lpszCmdLine, int nCmdShow)
{
  /*************************************************************************/
  /* HANDLE hInstance;       handle for this instance                   */
  /* HANDLE hPrevInstance;   handle for possible previous instances     */
  /* LPSTR  lpszCmdLine;     long pointer to exec command line           */
  /* int    nCmdShow;        Show code for main window display           */
  /*************************************************************************/

  MSG        msg;            /* MSG structure to store your messages
  */
  int        nRc;            /* return value from Register Classes
  */

  strcpy(szAppName, "HELLO");
  hInst = hInstance;
  if(!hPrevInstance)
    {
    /* register window classes if first instance of application      */
    if ((nRc = nCwRegisterClasses()) == -1)
```

Listing 6-1. *(continued)*

```c
    {
    /* registering one of the windows failed                      */

    LoadString(hInst, IDS_ERR_REGISTER_CLASS, szString, sizeof(szString));
    MessageBox(NULL, szString, NULL, MB_ICONEXCLAMATION);
    return nRc;
    }
  }

/* create application's Main window                               */
hWndMain = CreateWindow(
                szAppName,              /* Window class name      */
                NULL,                 /* no title                 */
                WS_CAPTION      |       /* Title and Min/Max      */
                WS_SYSMENU      |       /* Add system menu box     */
                WS_MINIMIZEBOX  |       /* Add minimize box        */
                WS_MAXIMIZEBOX  |       /* Add maximize box        */
                WS_THICKFRAME   |       /* thick sizeable frame    */
                WS_CLIPCHILDREN |       /* don't draw in child windows */
                WS_OVERLAPPED,
                CW_USEDEFAULT, 0,       /* Use default X, Y        */
                CW_USEDEFAULT, 0,       /* Use default X, Y        */
                NULL,                  /* Parent window's handle  */
                NULL,                  /* Default to Class Menu    */
                hInst,                 /* Instance of window      */
                NULL);                 /* Create struct for WM_CREATE */


if(hWndMain == NULL)
  {
  LoadString(hInst, IDS_ERR_CREATE_WINDOW, szString, sizeof(szString));
  MessageBox(NULL, szString, NULL, MB_ICONEXCLAMATION);
  return IDS_ERR_CREATE_WINDOW;
  }

ShowWindow(hWndMain, nCmdShow);                /* display main window      */

while(GetMessage(&msg, NULL, 0, 0))            /* Until WM_QUIT message    */
  {
  TranslateMessage(&msg);
  DispatchMessage(&msg);
  }

/* Do clean up before exiting from the application               */
CwUnRegisterClasses();
```

(continued)

Listing 6-1. *(continued)*

```
return msg.wParam;
} /*  End of WinMain                                                     */
/***********************************************************************/
/*                                                                     */
/* Main Window Procedure                                               */
/*                                                                     */
/* This procedure provides service routines for the Windows events     */
/* (messages) that Windows sends to the window, as well as the user    */
/* initiated events (messages) that are generated when the user selects*/
/* the action bar and pulldown menu controls or the corresponding      */
/* keyboard accelerators.                                              */
/*                                                                     */
/* The SWITCH statement shown below distributes the window messages to */
/* the respective message service routines, which are set apart by the */
/* CASE statements. The window procedures must provide an appropriate  */
/* service routine for its end user initiated messages, as well as the */
/* general Windows messages (i.e., WM_CLOSE message). If a message is  */
/* sent to this procedure for which there is no programmed CASE clause  */
/* (i.e., no service routine), the message is defaulted to the         */
/* DefWindowProc function, where it is handled by Windows              */
/*                                                                     */
/* For the end-user initiated messages, this procedure is concerned    */
/* principally with the WM_COMMAND message. The menu control ID (or the */
/* corresponding accelerator ID) is communicated to this procedure in  */
/* the first message parameter (wParam). The window procedure provides  */
/* a major CASE statement for the WM_COMMAND message and a subordinate  */
/* SWITCH statement to provide CASE clauses for the message service    */
/* routines for the various menu item's, identified by their ID values. */
/*                                                                     */
/* The message service routines for the individual menu items are the  */
/* main work points in the program. These service routines contain the */
/* units of work performed when the end user select one of the menu    */
/* controls. The required application response to a menu control is    */
/* programmed in its associated CASE clause. The service routines may  */
/* contain subroutine calls to separately compiled and libraried       */
/* routines, in-line calls to subroutines to be embodied in this source */
/* code module, or program statements entered directly in the CASE     */
/* clauses. Program control is switched to the appropriate service     */
/* routine when Windows recognizes the end user event and sends a WM_COMMAND */
/* message to the window procedure. The service routine provides the   */
/* appropriate application-specific response to the end user initiated  */
/* event, then breaks to return control to the WinMain() routine which  */
/* continues to service the message queue of the window(s).            */
/*                                                                     */
/***********************************************************************/
```

Listing 6-1. *(continued)*

```
LONG FAR PASCAL WindowProc(HWND hWnd, WORD Message, WORD wParam, LONG
lParam)
{
HMENU        hMenu=0;              /* handle for the menu                */
HBITMAP      hBitmap=0;            /* handle for bitmaps                 */
HDC          hDC;                  /* handle for the display device      */
PAINTSTRUCT  ps;                   /* holds PAINT information            */
int          nRc=0;                /* return code                        */

switch (Message)
   {
   case WM_CREATE:
        /* The WM_CREATE message is sent once to a window when the     */
        /* window is created.  The window procedure for the new window */
        /* receives this message after the window is created, but      */
        /* before the window becomes visible.                          */
        /*                                                             */
        /* Parameters:                                                 */
        /*                                                             */
        /*     lParam  -  Points to a CREATESTRUCT structure with      */
        /*                the following form:                          */
        /*                                                             */
        /*     typedef struct                                          */
        /*              {                                              */
        /*              LPSTR     lpCreateParams;                      */
        /*              HANDLE    hInst;                               */
        /*              HANDLE    hMenu;                               */
        /*              HWND      hwndParent;                          */
        /*              int       cy;                                 */
        /*              int       cx;                                 */
        /*              int       y;                                  */
        /*              int       x;                                  */
        /*              LONG      style;                              */
        /*              LPSTR     lpszName;                           */
        /*              LPSTR     lpszClass;                          */
        /*              DWORD     dwExStyle;                          */
        /*              }  CREATESTRUCT;                              */

        break;       /*  End of WM_CREATE                              */

   case WM_MOVE:     /*  code for moving the window                   */
        break;

   case WM_SIZE:     /*  code for sizing client area                  */
```

(continued)

Listing 6-1. *(continued)*

```
                /* wParam contains a code indicating the requested sizing     */
                /* lParam contains the new height and width of the client area */
                break;        /* End of WM_SIZE                                */

        case WM_PAINT:    /* code for the window's client area              */
                /* Obtain a handle to the device context                      */
                /* BeginPaint will sends WM_ERASEBKGND if appropriate          */
                memset(&ps, 0x00, sizeof(PAINTSTRUCT));
                hDC = BeginPaint(hWnd, &ps);

                /* Included in case the background is not a pure color         */
                SetBkMode(hDC, TRANSPARENT);

                /* Application should draw on the client window using          */
                /* the GDI graphics and text functions.  'ps' the PAINTSTRUCT  */
                /* returned by BeginPaint contains a rectangle to the          */
                /* area that must be repainted.                                */

                /* USER-ADDED MESSAGE                                          */
                TextOut (hDC, 0, 0, (LPSTR) "Hello, world.", strlen("Hello, world."));

                /* Inform Windows painting is complete                         */
                EndPaint(hWnd, &ps);
                break;        /*  End of WM_PAINT                              */

        case WM_CLOSE:  /* close the window                                    */
                /* Destroy child windows, modeless dialogs, then, this window  */
                DestroyWindow(hWnd);
                if (hWnd == hWndMain)
                  PostQuitMessage(0);  /* Quit the application                 */
                break;

        default:
                /* For any message for which you don't specifically provide a  */
                /* service routine, you should return the message to Windows   */
                /* for default message processing.                             */
                return DefWindowProc(hWnd, Message, wParam, lParam);
    }
 return 0L;
}      /* End of WindowProc                                                    */

/****************************************************************************/
/*                                                                          */
/* nCwRegisterClasses Function                                              */
/*                                                                          */
/* The following function registers all the classes of all the windows      */
/* associated with this application. The function returns an error code      */
```

Listing 6-1. *(continued)*

```c
/* if unsuccessful, otherwise it returns 0.                             */
/*                                                                      */
/**********************************************************************/

int nCwRegisterClasses(void)
{
 WNDCLASS   wndclass;    /* struct to define a window class             */
 memset(&wndclass, 0x00, sizeof(WNDCLASS));


 /* load WNDCLASS with window's characteristics                         */
 wndclass.style = CS_HREDRAW | CS_VREDRAW | CS_BYTEALIGNWINDOW;
 wndclass.lpfnWindowProc = WindowProc;
 /* Extra storage for Class and Window objects                          */
 wndclass.cbClsExtra = 0;
 wndclass.cbWndExtra = 0;
 wndclass.hInstance = hInst;
 wndclass.hIcon = LoadIcon(NULL, IDI_APPLICATION);
 wndclass.hCursor = LoadCursor(NULL, IDC_ARROW);
 /* Create brush for erasing background                                 */
 wndclass.hbrBackground = (HBRUSH)(COLOR_WINDOW+1);
 wndclass.lpszMenuName = szAppName;   /* Menu Name is App Name */
 wndclass.lpszClassName = szAppName;  /* Class Name is App Name */
 if(!RegisterClass(&wndclass))
   return -1;


 return(0);
} /* End of nCwRegisterClasses                                          */

/**********************************************************************/
/*   CwUnRegisterClasses Function                                      */
/*                                                                      */
/*   Deletes any refrences to windows resources created for this        */
/*   application, frees memory, deletes instance, and handles           */
/*   clean up before exiting the window                                 */
/*                                                                      */
/**********************************************************************/

void CwUnRegisterClasses(void)
{
 WNDCLASS   wndclass;    /* struct to define a window class             */
 memset(&wndclass, 0x00, sizeof(WNDCLASS));

 UnregisterClass(szAppName, hInst);
}    /* End of CwUnRegisterClasses                                      */
```

Introducing C++ Windows Programming

We've seen a little about how to create hello.c, and we've seen that even a Windows program that does something simple is pretty complex when written in C. However, C++ does things a little differently, and it's going to make our job much easier.

Now that we've seen hello.c, let's look into the process of creating hello.cpp. To begin, we don't have two functions named WinMain( ) and WindowProc( ); instead, we have two objects, one derived from the Microsoft Foundation Class CWinApp and one derived from the MFC class CFrameWnd:

hello.cpp

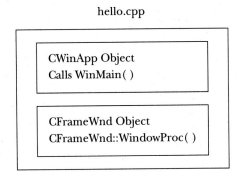

Almost all the code in Listing 6-1 is hidden in these objects. We'll be able to use both CWinApp and CFrameWnd as base classes and tailor them for our own uses by deriving our own objects from them. Our actual program will be quite short.

You might be wondering what happened to WinMain( ) and WindowProc( ). In fact, they are still there, but now those details are hidden from view. The CWinApp object takes over for WinMain( ), setting up WinMain( ) and the message loop by itself. And WindowProc( ) has become a member function of CFrameWnd, which we can override if we want to:

hello.cpp

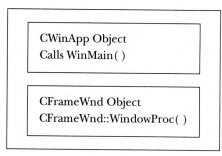

You might recall that we handled Windows messages with a switch statement in WindowProc( ) before:

```
LONG FAR PASCAL WindowProc(HWND hWnd, WORD Message, WORD wParam, LONG lParam)
{
switch (Message)
    {
    case WM_CREATE:

        break;       /*  End of WM_CREATE                                  */

    case WM_MOVE:    /*  code for moving the window                        */

        break;

    case WM_SIZE:    /*  code for sizing client area                       */

        break;       /* End of WM_SIZE                                     */

    case WM_PAINT:   /* code for the window's client area                  */

        break;       /*  End of WM_PAINT                                   */

    case WM_CLOSE:   /* close the window                                   */

        break;

    default:
        return DefWindowProc(hWnd, Message, wParam, lParam);
    }
}
```

Now, however, there is even a better way — a way that helps keep our program very modular. The CFrameWnd object will call functions we set up, one for each type of Windows message. For example, let's say we want to handle the WM_PAINT message (our window needs to be redrawn), WM_SIZE message (our window's size was changed), and WM_CLOSE message (our window was closed). In that case, we'll only need to set up three functions: OnPaint( ), OnSize( ), and OnClose( ). They will be member functions of our CFrameWnd object, and will be called when our window receives the corresponding message:

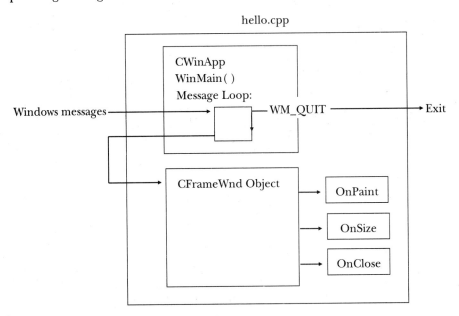

Breaking our code up in this way will make it much easier to write — one function to handle one Windows message (that is, one type of Windows event). Let's start writing our C++ program now to see how this works.

Writing the Example Program Hello.cpp

We can start our C++ program by setting up our main window, whose base class will be the MFC class CFrameWnd. Some of the members of CFrameWnd appear in Table 6-2 (a full list would go on for many pages). In our case (as in almost all C++ Windows programs) we'll derive a class, named CMainWindow here, from the base class CFrameWnd. The reason for this is that CFrameWnd simply creates a default window, but nothing more happens. We want to specify what type of window we want (many types are available), and we want to print "Hello World." when the window gets a WM_PAINT message. To do that, we must derive our own class, so we derive CMainWindow from CFrameWnd like this:

```
#include <afxwin.h>

class CMainWindow : public CFrameWnd      ←
{
public:
    CMainWindow();
    afx_msg void OnPaint();

    DECLARE_MESSAGE_MAP()
};
```

BeginPaint	Fills a PAINTSTRUCT data structure
BringWindowToTop	Bring CWnd to top of stack of windows
CFrameWnd	Constructor
CloseWindow	Closes window
Create	Create Windows frame window
CreateCaret	Creates system caret
CreateSolidCaret	Creates a solid block caret
CWnd	Constructor for CWnd (CFrameWnd base class)
DrawMenuBar	Redraw menu bar
EnableWindow	Enables/disables mouse and kbd input
EndPaint	Marks end of paint operation
FindWindow	Get handle of window
GetActiveWindow	Get active window
GetCapture	Get CWnd that has mouse captured
GetClientRect	Get dimensions of CWnd client area
GetDC	Get display context for client area
GetDlgItem	Get handle of a control in dialog box
GetDlgItemInt	Get integer value from text in a dialog control
GetDlgItemText	Get text associated with dialog box control
GetFocus	Get CWnd with input focus
GetFont	Get current font

Table 6-2. Some of CFrameWnd (and Base Class CWnd) Members

GetMenu	Gets a pointer to menu
GetParent	Get parent window
GetSystemMenu	Give application access to Control menu
GetUpdateRect	Get coordinates of update region
GetWindowDC	Get display context for the whole window
GetWindowRect	Get screen coordinates of CWnd
GetWindowText	Gets CWnd caption title
HideCaret	Hides caret
Invalidate	Invalidates client area
InvalidateRect	Invalidates given rectangle
IsIconic	Is CWnd iconic?
IsWindowEnabled	Is window is enabled for mouse and kbd input?
IsWindowVisible	Is window visible?
IsZoomed	Is CWnd maximized?
LoadAccelTable	Loads an accelerator table
MoveWindow	Moves CWnd
m_hAccelTable	Command accelerator table
OpenIcon	Activates and restores iconic CWnd
rectDefault	Default size and location for window
ReleaseDC	Releases device contexts
SetActiveWindow	Activates window
SetCapture	Capture the mouse
SetCaretPos	Move caret to a specified location
SetFocus	Set input focus
SetFont	Sets current font
SetMenu	Sets menu to specified menu
SetParent	Changes parent window
SetWindowText	Sets CWnd caption title
ShowCaret	Show caret
ShowWindow	Shows/hides CWnd
UpdateWindow	Update client area
ValidateRect	Validates given rectangle
~CFrameWnd	Destructor
~CWnd	Destructor for CWnd (CFrameWnd base class)

Table 6-2. (continued)

To use the MFC Windows libraries (which hold the definitions of the classes like CWinApp and CFrameWnd), we have to include the file afxwin.h (afx stands for application frameworks). You might notice that above, we've supplied a constructor for CMainWindow:

```
#include <afxwin.h>

class CMainWindow : public CFrameWnd
{
public:
    CMainWindow();
    afx_msg void OnPaint();

    DECLARE_MESSAGE_MAP()
};
```

That's because when the window is being constructed in CMainWindow( ), we'll have the chance to indicate what kind of window it should be, and to put text into the title bar.

We also indicate that we want to intercept the WM_PAINT message when it's sent by declaring a function named OnPaint( ) in our window's class:

```
#include <afxwin.h>

class CMainWindow : public CFrameWnd
{
public:
    CMainWindow();
    afx_msg void OnPaint();

    DECLARE_MESSAGE_MAP()
};
```

The identifier afx_msg that precedes the declaration of OnPaint( ) is simply an empty string in MS C Version 7.0, but is reserved for future use. It must precede all prototypes for Windows-handling functions like OnPaint( ). The name OnPaint( ) is only one of many predefined names for message-handling functions; this one is designed to be called when the window gets a WM_PAINT message from Windows. The names of some of the other "OnMessage( )" functions appear in Table 6-3, one for each type of Windows message.

OnActivate	OnInitMenuPopup	OnPaintClipboard
OnActivateApp	OnKeyDown	OnPaintIcon
OnAskCbFormatName	OnKeyUp	OnPaletteChanged
OnCancel	OnKillFocus	OnParentNotify
OnCancelMode	OnLButtonDblClk	OnQueryDragIcon
OnChangeCbChain	OnLButtonDown	OnQueryEndSession
OnChar	OnLButtonUp	OnQueryNewPalette
OnCharToItem	OnMButtonDblClk	OnQueryOpen
OnChildActivate	OnMButtonDown	OnRButtonDblClk
OnClose	OnMButtonUp	OnRButtonDown
OnCommand	OnMDIActivate	OnRButtonUp
OnCompacting	OnMeasureItem	OnRenderAllFormats
OnCompareItem	OnMenuChar	OnRenderFormat
OnCreate	OnMenuSelect	OnSetCursor
OnCtlColor	OnMouseActivate	OnSetFocus
OnDeadChar	OnMouseMove	OnSetFont
OnDeleteItem	OnMove	OnShowWindow
OnDestroy	OnNcActivate	OnSize
OnDestroyClipboard	OnNcCalcSize	OnSizeClipboard
OnDevModeChange	OnNcCreate	OnSpoolerStatus
OnDrawClipboard	OnNcDestroy	OnSysChar
OnDrawItem	OnNcHitTest	OnSysColorChange
OnEnable	OnNcLButtonDblClk	OnSysCommand
OnEndSession	OnNcLButtonDown	OnSysDeadChar
OnEnterIdle	OnNcLButtonUp	OnSysKeyDown
OnEraseBkgnd	OnNcMButtonDblClk	OnSysKeyUp
OnFontChange	OnNcMButtonDown	OnTimeChange
OnGetDlgCode	OnNcMButtonUp	OnTimer
OnGetMinMaxInfo	OnNcMouseMove	OnVKeyToItem
OnHScroll	OnNcPaint	OnVScroll
OnHScrollClipboard	OnNcRButtonDblClk	OnVScrollClipboard
OnIconEraseBkgnd	OnNcRButtonDown	OnWinIniChange
OnIdle	OnNcRButtonUp	
OnInitDialog	OnOK	
OnInitMenu	OnPaint	

Table 6-3. Available OnMessage Functions

Next, we place a macro, DECLARE_MESSAGE_MAP( ), in our class declaration (much as we placed the DECLARE_SERIAL macro in our serializing example in the last chapter):

```
#include <afxwin.h>

class CMainWindow : public CFrameWnd
{
public:
    CMainWindow();
    afx_msg void OnPaint();

    DECLARE_MESSAGE_MAP()
};
```

→

C++ will expand this macro into the prototypes of the function(s) it needs to make sure that OnPaint( ) — and any other Windows message-handling functions like OnSize( ) — get called properly. This macro is necessary for window classes that want to handle windows messages, as we do here.

At this stage, we're ready to write the constructor for our window, CMainWindow::CMainWindow( ). Here, we'll be able to specify the *window style* that we want, and we'll specify what is probably the most common: an overlapped window (when windows that overlap ours are removed, we'll get a WM_PAINT message). We do this with CFrameWnd's member function Create( ), which creates windows. This function takes a window class name (a Windows window class is not the same as a C++ class) which must be a type of window that was previously registered with Windows. Since we don't have such a class that we want to use, we use NULL here. Next, we pass the preferred window style, which will be WS_OVERLAPPEDWINDOW for us (the prefix WS_ stands for window style). The available window styles appear in Table 6-4.

Then we get a chance to specify where the window will appear on the screen when we display it by passing its screen coordinates in a Windows rect structure. The default here is called rectDefault, and we can use that (our window will cover the upper portion of the screen). Finally, we indicate that this window has no parent window by passing a NULL for the next parameter, and that we don't want to set up our own menu system in this window with another NULL list like this:

```
#include <afxwin.h>

class CMainWindow : public CFrameWnd
```

```
    {
    public:
        CMainWindow();
        afx_msg void OnPaint();

        DECLARE_MESSAGE_MAP()
    };

    CMainWindow::CMainWindow()
    {
        Create(NULL, "Hello World Example", WS_OVERLAPPEDWINDOW,
            rectDefault, NULL, NULL);
    }
```

Now that we've designed our window, we can write the function named OnPaint( ). This member function will be called when our window receives a WM_PAINT message, so that means that we can place our string "Hello, World." in the window at that time. You might recall that in C we did this by getting a handle to a *device context* using the Windows function BeginPaint( ) and then we used the Windows function TextOut( ). At the end of our code, the EndPaint( ) function released the device context handle:

```
case WM_PAINT:   /* code for the window's client area            */
    memset(&ps, 0x00, sizeof(PAINTSTRUCT));
    hDC = BeginPaint(hWnd, &ps);

    /* USER-ADDED CODE                                            */
    TextOut (hDC, 0, 0, (LPSTR) "Hello, world.", strlen("Hello, world."));

    EndPaint(hWnd, &ps);
    break;       /*  End of WM_PAINT                              */
```

All drawing or graphics manipulation in Windows is done in device contexts. These device contexts can correspond to various things: a window (or part of one), the whole screen, a printer, and so on. By unifying those varying environments into the idea of a device context (which has Windows-defined standard tools and functions available in it), Windows lets us operate in a device-independent way.

In C++, we get a device context *object* of class CPaintDC, instead of a handle. All the functions that one could use with a device context before (like TextOut( )) have become member functions of device context objects. In

Window Style	Means
WS_OVERLAPPED	Overlapped window with caption and border
WS_POPUP	Pop-up window (do not use with WS_CHILD)
WS_CHILD	A child window
WS_MINIMIZE	Window of minimum size
WS_VISIBLE	Makes window initially visible
WS_DISABLED	Makes window initially disabled
WS_CLIPSIBLINGS	Clip children relative to each other
WS_CLIPCHILDREN	Do not redraw children
WS_MAXIMIZE	Winodw of maximum size
WS_CAPTION	WS_BORDER ¦ WS_DLGFRAME
WS_BORDER	Add a border
WS_DLGFRAME	Use dialog box border, no title
WS_VSCROLL	Add vertical scroll bar
WS_HSCROLL	Add horizontal scroll bar
WS_SYSMENU	Add a system menu
WS_THICKFRAME	Use thick border
WS_GROUP	Member of a group of controls
WS_TABSTOP	Can receive the input focus
WS_MINIMIZEBOX	Add a minimize box
WS_MAXIMIZEBOX	Add a maximize box
WS_TILED	WS_OVERLAPPED
WS_ICONIC	WS_MINIMIZE
WS_SIZEBOX	WS_THICKFRAME
WS_OVERLAPPEDWINDOW	WS_OVERLAPPED ¦ WS_CAPTION ¦ WS_SYSMENU ¦ WS_THICKFRAME ¦ WS_MINIMIZEBOX ¦ WS_MAXIMIZEBOX
WS_POPUPWINDOW	WS_POPUP ¦ WS_BORDER ¦ WS_SYSMENU
WS_CHILDWINDOW	WS_CHILD
WS_TILEDWINDOW	WS_OVERLAPPEDWINDOW
WS_EX_DLGMODALFRAME	Dialog box can have title and system menu

Table 6-4. Window Styles for Use with CWnd::Create( )

CPaintDC	Constructs CPaintDC object
m_ps	Contains PAINTSTRUCT used to paint
m_hWnd	HWND for this CPaintDC object
~CPaintDC	Destructor

Table 6-5. CPaintDC Members

particular, the members of the CPaintDC class appear in Table 6-5. To get a device context object for our window, we just pass a pointer to our window object to CPaintDC's constructor — and that pointer is simply a this pointer (since OnPaint( ) is a member function of our class CMainWindow).

We can call our device context object dc; then we can use the member function TextOut( ) to place text in our window. TextOut( ) takes four parameters: the x and y position in the window we want to display the text at (we'll use (0, 0), which is the upper left of the window), the string "Hello, world." itself (in a CString object), and the length of the string (which we can find with the CString member function CString::GetLength( )). That looks like this in code:

```
#include <afxwin.h>

class CMainWindow : public CFrameWnd
{
public:
    CMainWindow();
    afx_msg void OnPaint();

    DECLARE_MESSAGE_MAP()
};

CMainWindow::CMainWindow()
{
    Create(NULL, "Hello World Example", WS_OVERLAPPEDWINDOW,
        rectDefault, NULL, NULL);
}

void CMainWindow::OnPaint()
{
    CPaintDC dc(this);
    CString hello_string = "Hello, World";

    dc.TextOut(0, 0, hello_string, hello_string.GetLength() );
}
```

That's all there is to it; now, when our window is (re)painted, our string will appear in it. The next step is to implement the message-handling functions which we declared with the macro DECLARE_MESSAGE_MAP( ), and we do that with a pair of macros: BEGIN_MESSAGE_MAP( ) and END_MES-SAGE_MAP( ). We indicate what Windows messages we want to intercept using these two macros like this:

```
#include <afxwin.h>

class CMainWindow : public CFrameWnd
{
public:
    CMainWindow();
    afx_msg void OnPaint();

    DECLARE_MESSAGE_MAP()
};

CMainWindow::CMainWindow()
{
    Create(NULL, "Hello World Example", WS_OVERLAPPEDWINDOW,
        rectDefault, NULL, NULL);
}

void CMainWindow::OnPaint()
{
    CPaintDC dc(this);
    CString hello_string = "Hello, World";

    dc.TextOut(0, 0, hello_string, hello_string.GetLength() );
}

BEGIN_MESSAGE_MAP( CMainWindow, CFrameWnd )
    ON_WM_PAINT()
END_MESSAGE_MAP()
```

Here, Microsoft C++ will set up the functions which will make sure that OnPaint( ) is called when our window gets a WM_PAINT message. As we'll see, if we had more messages to read, like WM_SIZE when our window is (re)sized, we could add them like this (insuring that the function OnSize( ) is called):

```
BEGIN_MESSAGE_MAP( CMainWindow, CFrameWnd )
    ON_WM_PAINT()
    ON_WM_SIZE()
END_MESSAGE_MAP()
```

Some of the Windows messages that a program like ours might see appear in Table 6-6.

TIP It is common for C++ programmers to place class declarations into a .h include file, separate from the code (which we're not doing here in the interests of clarity and to keep the number of neeeded files to a minimum). If you do so, you should include the DECLARE_MESSAGE_MAP( ) macros in the class declaration and the BEGIN_MESSAGE_MAP...END_MES-SAGE_MAP macros in the .cpp file.

Now that our window is designed, we can write the rest of the program — the part that will put it on the screen and set up a message loop so that we'll get Windows messages. All we've done so far is to create a class named CMainWindow, which is a type of window, but we haven't done anything about displaying it yet, or connecting it to Windows. That's done with an object of class CWinApp:

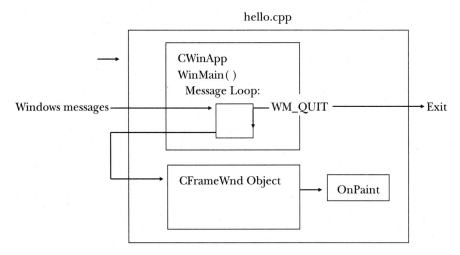

In fact, we'll derive a class from CWinApp, which we might name CtheApp. We'll do that so that we can override the function CWinApp::InitInstance( ), which is run when our program first starts. Many copies of a Windows program can run at the same time, and each one of them is referred to as an *instance*; that means that InitInstance( ) is the function that is used when our program is first loaded. In InitInstance( ), we can set up our window, which will be of class CMainWindow.

WM_ACTIVATE	Windows becoming active or inactive
WM_ACTIVATEAPP	Window being activated belongs to a different app
WM_CANCELMODE	Cancels system mode
WM_CHILDACTIVATE	Child window moved
WM_CLOSE	Window was closed
WM_CREATE	CreateWindow function was called
WM_CTLCOLOR	Control or message box about to be drawn
WM_DESTROY	DestroyWindow function was called
WM_ENABLE	window was enabled or disabled
WM_ENDSESSION	Session is ending
WM_ENTERIDLE	Waiting for user action
WM_ERASEBKGND	Window background needs to be erased
WM_GETDLGCODE	Query to control's input procedure
WM_GETMINMAXINFO	Get size info about the window
WM_GETTEXT	Copies text corresponding to window
WM_GETTEXTLENGTH	Gets length of text associated with window
WM_ICONERASEBKGND	Iconic window background needs to be erased
WM_KILLFOCUS	Window losing the input focus
WM_MENUCHAR	User pressed char not in current menu
WM_MENUSELECT	User has selected a menu item
WM_MOVE	Window was moved
WM_PAINT	Request to repaint a portion of window
WM_PAINTICON	Request to repaint a portion of icon
WM_PARENTNOTIFY	Child window is created or destroyed
WM_QUERYDRAGICON	User about to drag an iconic window
WM_QUERYENDSESSION	User chose End Session command
WM_QUERYNEWPALETTE	Window about to realize its color palette
WM_QUERYOPEN	User requests icon be opened
WM_QUIT	Terminate application
WM_SETFOCUS	Window received input focus
WM_SETFONT	Font changed
WM_SETREDRAW	Sets or clears redraw flag
WM_SETTEXT	Sets title text of window
WM_SHOWWINDOW	Window is to be hidden or shown
WM_SIZE	Size of window changed

Table 6-6. Windows Messages

In addition, Windows programs don't have to start by placing their full windows on the screen — they can start in an iconic state, or even without any window at all. We will indicate that we want to place our full window on the screen when we overload InitInstance( ). In other words, the purpose of deriving CtheApp from CWinApp is so that we can override InitInstance( ), create a window of class CMainWindow, and put it on the screen. That means that our definition of CtheApp looks like this:

```
#include <afxwin.h>

class CMainWindow : public CFrameWnd
{
public:
    CMainWindow();
    afx_msg void OnPaint();

    DECLARE_MESSAGE_MAP()
};

CMainWindow::CMainWindow()
{
    Create(NULL, "Hello World Example", WS_OVERLAPPEDWINDOW,
        rectDefault, NULL, NULL);
}

void CMainWindow::OnPaint()
{
    CPaintDC dc(this);
    CString hello_string = "Hello, World";

    dc.TextOut(0, 0, hello_string, hello_string.GetLength() );
}

BEGIN_MESSAGE_MAP( CMainWindow, CFrameWnd )
    ON_WM_PAINT()
END_MESSAGE_MAP()

class CTheApp : public CWinApp     ←
{                                  ←
public:                            ←
    BOOL InitInstance();           ←
};                                 ←
```

TIP C++ Windows programs almost always override InitInstance( ) so that they can create the window of the class they desire, and display it.

In InitInstance( ), we create a new window of class CMainWindow simply by using new. Next, we connect it to the CtheApp object (i.e., our program itself) by placing the pointer that we got from new into the CWinApp member pointer m_pMainWindow. This is exactly what InitInstance( ) does; it creates a new window object and connects it into the rest of the program by placing a pointer to it in the CWinApp data member m_pMainWindow. Next, we show the window on the screen with the CFrameWnd member function ShowWindow( ) and cause a WM_PAINT message to be sent to it by calling the CFrameWnd member function UpdateWindow( ). That looks like this:

```cpp
#include <afxwin.h>

class CMainWindow : public CFrameWnd
{
public:
    CMainWindow();
    afx_msg void OnPaint();

    DECLARE_MESSAGE_MAP()
};

CMainWindow::CMainWindow()
{
    Create(NULL, "Hello World Example", WS_OVERLAPPEDWINDOW,
        rectDefault, NULL, NULL);
}

void CMainWindow::OnPaint()
{
    CPaintDC dc(this);
    CString hello_string = "Hello, World";

    dc.TextOut(0, 0, hello_string, hello_string.GetLength() );
}

BEGIN_MESSAGE_MAP( CMainWindow, CFrameWnd )
    ON_WM_PAINT()
END_MESSAGE_MAP()

class CTheApp : public CWinApp
{
public:
    BOOL InitInstance();
};

BOOL CTheApp::InitInstance()
```

```
     {
→        m_pMainWnd = new CMainWindow();
→        m_pMainWnd->ShowWindow(m_nCmdShow);
→        m_pMainWnd->UpdateWindow();

         return TRUE;
     }
```

Note that the CFrameWnd member function ShowWindow( ) takes a parameter, m_nCmdShow. This parameter indicates how we are supposed to open the window (as determined by Windows) — that is, as a full window or iconic — and was originally passed as the parameter nCmdShow to our WinMain( ) function. Here we just pass it on to ShowWindow( ).

TIP By passing m_nCmdShow to ShowWindow( ), we indicate how Windows has instructed us to open the window. If you simply want to open the window to a full window no matter what, set m_nCmdShow to True before passing it to ShowWindow( ).

You might wonder how we're actually going to get the program started. We do that simply with CtheApp's constructor, which launches the whole thing. That means, believe it or not, now that we've set up our two classes, CMainWindow and CtheApp, our entire program is run when we simply declare an object of class CtheApp (and therefore execute its constructor):

```
#include <afxwin.h>

class CMainWindow : public CFrameWnd
{
public:
    CMainWindow();
    afx_msg void OnPaint();

    DECLARE_MESSAGE_MAP()
};

CMainWindow::CMainWindow()
{
    Create(NULL, "Hello World Example", WS_OVERLAPPEDWINDOW,
        rectDefault, NULL, NULL );
}

void CMainWindow::OnPaint()
```

```
    {
        CString hello_string = "Hello, World";
        CPaintDC dc( this );
        CRect rect;

        dc.TextOut(0, 0, hello_string, hello_string.GetLength() );
    }

BEGIN_MESSAGE_MAP( CMainWindow, CFrameWnd )
    ON_WM_PAINT()
END_MESSAGE_MAP()

class CTheApp : public CWinApp
{
public:
    BOOL InitInstance();
};

BOOL CTheApp::InitInstance()
{
    m_pMainWnd = new CMainWindow();
    m_pMainWnd->ShowWindow(m_nCmdShow);
    m_pMainWnd->UpdateWindow();

    return TRUE;
}

CTheApp theApp;                    ←
```

TIP If you've programmed in Windows before, you might wonder what happened to window handles, which we used to send to functions like ShowWindow( ). As you might expect, our main window's handle (which we won't need) is now a data member of CFrameWindow; actually, it's a member of CFrameWnd's base class, CWnd (it's CWnd::m_hWnd). Since everything is wrapped up into objects in C++, we won't have to deal with handles any more — we only need to call an object's associated member function instead of passing a handle to a general Windows function. That's one of the reasons that programming for Windows in C++ is much more natural than programming for Windows in C.

And that's it; running the constructor starts the program (internally, control is eventually passed to WinMain( ), the message loop is set up, and everything is up and running). That's it for our entire C++ program; compare the code above to Listing 6-1. As you can see, wrapping the functions and data into objects works extremely well here, and it's cut the size of our program down tremendously. In the beginning of the next chapter, we'll see what additional support files (non-code files) we have to add, and then we'll create (and run) hello.exe.

CHAPTER 7

Keyboard and Mouse Input

In this chapter, we're going to put C++ to work in Windows by seeing how to create Windows executable files and running them. Our first executable program will be the one we wrote in the previous chapter: hello.cpp, which will become hello.exe. Our next step will be to start accepting user input; which, in Windows, means accepting both keyboard and mouse input.

We'll start by learning the various methods of reading keyboard input; since this is Windows, that input will come to us through Windows messages. It turns out that there are two different types of keyboard messages — those generated by the action of a key (like WM_KEYDOWN and WM_KEYUP), and those generated after Windows translates such messages into ASCII for us (WM_CHAR messages). We'll see both in this chapter, and then we'll see an example program that reads input from the keyboard and displays it in a window.

Next, we'll work with the mouse, examining the variety of mouse-specific Windows messages that we might receive (such as WM_MOUSEMOVE or WM_LBUTTONDOWN), and we'll put them to work in an example program of their own. Note that since we'll be displaying the results of our programs as well as accepting input in this chapter, we'll learn a little more about text output as well. In particular, we'll learn that using a variable width font (the Windows default) can create some interesting problems for us when we want to display and change strings in a window.

Let's begin, then, by creating and running our first program, hello.exe.

Creating a Windows Executable File

In the last chapter, we developed the C++ code for our first program: hello.cpp. Now we're going to create hello.exe from it. We can do that using either the NMAKE utility that comes with Microsoft C++ or the Programmer's WorkBench (PWB), which runs NMAKE for us. If we use NMAKE, we'll have to put together a file called *makefile* that indicates what compiler and linker options we want; if we use Programmer's WorkBench, we'll have to create a file named hello.mak to make hello into a PWB *project.*

Either way, we'll have to create an additional file, hello.def, which will indicate to the linker that we are creating a Windows executable file. This file is necessary when you create a C++ Windows executable file (technically, all that's necessary are the files hello.cpp and hello.def). In this file, we'll specify information that's necessary to create hello.exe as a Windows program. We can start by giving the executable a name and a description:

```
NAME         Hello
DESCRIPTION  'Hello World Example'
   :
```

Next, we indicate that we want to create a Windows-type executable file with the line EXETYPE WINDOWS. After that, we also indicate that we want a *stub* module named winstub.exe added to our .exe file. After it becomes part of our program, this stub module prints out "This program requires Microsoft Windows." if someone tries to run our program under DOS:

```
NAME         Hello
DESCRIPTION  'Hello World Example'

EXETYPE      WINDOWS
STUB         'WINSTUB.EXE'
   :
```

After that, we also specify that Windows can move our code and data segments around in memory (which it does to optimize performance), and give the heap and stack sizes we want. Because this program is so short, we use just about the minimum you can use in Windows, which is a heap of 1024 bytes and a stack of 4096 bytes:

```
NAME          Hello
DESCRIPTION   'Hello World Example'

EXETYPE       WINDOWS
STUB          'WINSTUB.EXE'

CODE          PRELOAD MOVEABLE DISCARDABLE
DATA          PRELOAD MOVEABLE MULTIPLE

HEAPSIZE      1024
STACKSIZE     4096
```

And that's it for hello.def; the whole file appears in Listing 7-1. When we link, we'll pass this file to the linker so that we will end with a Windows .exe file.

Listing 7-1. Hello.def

```
NAME          Hello
DESCRIPTION   'Hello World Example'

EXETYPE       WINDOWS
STUB          'WINSTUB.EXE'

CODE          PRELOAD MOVEABLE DISCARDABLE
DATA          PRELOAD MOVEABLE MULTIPLE

HEAPSIZE      1024
STACKSIZE     4096
```

The next step is to actually compile and link hello.cpp into hello.exe. Let's use the NMAKE utility first, since it's easier to create the associated file, makefile.

Using NMAKE

The NMAKE utility that comes with Microsoft C++ is more useful than the cl DOS-level command because of the large number of arguments we have to supply to the linker. When you type NMAKE, it searches the current directory for a file named makefile. In that file, we start by giving the usual compiler flags used to create a Windows executable:

```
CPPFLAGS= /AS /W3 /Zp /GA /GEs /G2
    :
```

Next, we indicate that we want to create hello.exe, the *target* file, using the files hello.obj (created by compiling hello.cpp) and hello.def — these are called the *dependents* like this:

```
CPPFLAGS= /AS /W3 /Zp /GA /GEs /G2
hello.exe:     hello.obj hello.def
    :
```

Now we specify that we want to link in the Windows libraries safxcr.lib (small model Microsoft Foundation Class library), libw.lib (called the Windows *import* library), and slibcew.lib (small model general Windows routines), all coordinated by hello.def like this:

```
CPPFLAGS= /AS /W3 /Zp /GA /GEs /G2
hello.exe:     hello.obj hello.def
 link /NOD /ONERROR:NOEXE hello, hello, NUL, safxcw libw slibcew, hello.def;
```

This line is called a *command* line. Note that the target line must be flush left in the file (i.e., it cannot have any spaces or tabs in front of it), and the command lines must have spaces or tabs in front of them (that's how NMAKE tells them apart). And that's it for makefile, which appears in Listing 7-2. Now we have the three files we need: hello.cpp, which appears in Listing 7-3 for reference, hello.def, and makefile. All we have to do now is to type NMAKE at DOS level, and that utility will invoke the cl compiler as well as the linker, creating hello.exe for us.

TIP   Occasionally, you have a number of projects going, which makes it awkward that NMAKE can only read one file named makefile. It turns out that you can name a makefile anything if you use the /f switch. For example, if you store the makefile for hello.exe in hello.nmk, you can create it with the command NMAKE /f hello.nmk.

Listing 7-2. Hello.exe's Makefile

```
CPPFLAGS= /AS /W3 /Zp /GA /GEs /G2
hello.exe:      hello.obj hello.def
 link /NOD /ONERROR:NOEXE hello, hello, NUL, safxcw libw
 slibcew,hello.def;
```

Listing 7-3. Hello.cpp

```cpp
#include <afxwin.h>

class CMainWindow : public CFrameWnd
{
public:
    CMainWindow();
    afx_msg void OnPaint();

    DECLARE_MESSAGE_MAP()
};

CMainWindow::CMainWindow()
{
    Create(NULL, "Hello World Example", WS_OVERLAPPEDWINDOW,
        rectDefault, NULL, NULL );
}

void CMainWindow::OnPaint()
{
    CString hello_string = "Hello, World";
    CPaintDC dc( this );
    CRect rect;

    dc.TextOut(0, 0, hello_string, hello_string.GetLength() );
}

BEGIN_MESSAGE_MAP( CMainWindow, CFrameWnd )
    ON_WM_PAINT()
END_MESSAGE_MAP()

class CTheApp : public CWinApp
{
public:
    BOOL InitInstance();
};
```

(continued)

Listing 7-3. *(continued)*

```
BOOL CTheApp::InitInstance()
{
    m_pMainWnd = new CMainWindow();
    m_pMainWnd->ShowWindow( m_nCmdShow );
    m_pMainWnd->UpdateWindow();

    return TRUE;
}

CTheApp theApp;
```

Now that hello.exe has been created, you can run it under Windows in two ways: You can type this at the DOS prompt:

```
C:\>win hello.exe
```

or you can run hello.exe with the Run... item in the Windows File Manager's File menu. When you do, you'll see our first window, as shown in Figure 7-1. Note that our window already has built-in (and functional) minimizing and maximizing buttons, as well as a system menu (which you can use to close the application). Our hello.exe program is a success.

Using Programmer's WorkBench

The second method of creating hello.exe is with the Programmer's Work-Bench, which also comes with Microsoft C++. Programmer's WorkBench is actually a DOS utility, so it's a little clumsy to run under Windows.

One way of doing that is simply by clicking the Programmer's WorkBench icon that Microsoft C++ installs in the Windows Program Manager. Doing that, however, opens a full-screen PWB session; that is, Programmer's Work-Bench takes over the full screen (as it does under DOS). Windows program-mers prefer to run their utilities in windows, not as full screen programs. To create a windowed version of PWB, copy the file pwb.pif (.pif means program information file) from c:\c700\bin to c:\windows. Next, add a PWB icon in the Program Manager with the New... item in Windows' Program Manager's File menu. It will ask you if you want to add a new program item or a program group; select item. A window named Program Item Properties will open with two text boxes in it, labeled Description and Command Line. Type PWB for the description and pwb.exe for the command line. A new icon labeled PWB

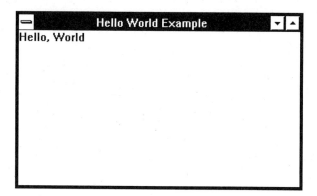

Figure 7-1. Hello.exe at Work

will appear in the Program Manager. When you click it, a windowed version of PWB will open, as shown in Figure 7-2.

TIP If you want to expand the windowed version of PWB to the full screen (or back to a window again), type <Alt><Enter>. This expands any DOS program running in a window to full screen (or switches back to the windowed version).

```
=                              PWB                          ▼ ▲
  File   Edit   Search   Project   Run   Options   Browse   Window
=[   2]===========================c:\c7win\hello.cpp ==========
#include <afxwin.h>

class CMainWindow : public CFrameWnd
{
public:
    CMainWindow();
    afx_msg void OnPaint();

    DECLARE_MESSAGE_MAP()
};

CMainWindow::CMainWindow()

-[   1]————————————————————— Build Results —————





<F1=Help> <Alt=Menu> <F6=Window>
◄                                                            ►
```

Figure 7-2. Windowed Programmers' WorkBench

To load hello.cpp, you can use the Open... item in PWB's File menu. One drawback, however, is that you can't use the mouse while running PWB in a window (because it's reserved for Windows). To reach a menu item, just type <Alt> and the first letter of the menu. For example, to exit, type <Alt>F to open the file menu (<Esc> closes a menu if you don't want to make a selection after all). You'll see that the 'x' in Exit is highlighted, making it the shortcut key here; type x next, and you'll leave PWB.

TIP You can make working with PWB in Windows a little easier with the WXServer Windows program, which comes with Microsoft C++. Since PWB is a DOS program, you wouldn't be able to run programs you create using the Execute item in PWB's Run menu (since they would run under DOS). However, if you start WXServer (simply by double clicking its icon), any program you run from PWB Windows session will start under Windows — meaning that you can run your .exe files without having to leave PWB and return to Windows.

Programmers' WorkBench manages everything in *projects*, and each project has a .mak file. We'll store all the support files we need for creating hello.exe in the project file hello.mak, which appears in Listing 7-4. When you want to work on a project, open the corresponding .mak file from the Project menu using the Open Project... menu item.

Listing 7-4. Hello.mak

```
ORIGIN = PWB
PROJ = hello
PROJFILE = hello.mak
DEBUG = 0

CC   = cl
CFLAGS_G   = /W2 /GA /GEf /Zp /BATCH
CFLAGS_D   = /f /Zi /Od /Gs
CFLAGS_R   = /f- /Oe /Og /Os /Gs
CXX   = cl
CXXFLAGS_G   = /W3 /G2 /GA /GEs /Zp /BATCH
CXXFLAGS_D   = /f /Od /Zi /D_DEBUG
CXXFLAGS_R   = /f- /Os /Ol /Og /Oe /Gs
MAPFILE_D   = NUL
MAPFILE_R   = NUL
LFLAGS_G   = /NOD /BATCH /ONERROR:NOEXE
LFLAGS_D   = /CO /NOF
```

Listing 7-4. *(continued)*

```
LFLAGS_R  = /NOF
LLIBS_G  = LIBW.LIB
LINKER  = link
ILINK  = ilink
LRF  = echo > NUL
ILFLAGS  = /a /e
LLIBS_R  = SAFXCW /NOD:SLIBCE SLIBCEW
LLIBS_D  = SAFXCWD /NOD:SLIBCE SLIBCEW

FILES  = HELLO.CPP HELLO.DEF
DEF_FILE  = HELLO.DEF
OBJS  = HELLO.obj

all: $(PROJ).exe

.SUFFIXES:
.SUFFIXES:
.SUFFIXES: .obj .cpp

HELLO.obj : HELLO.CPP
!IF $(DEBUG)
        $(CXX) /c $(CXXFLAGS_G) $(CXXFLAGS_D) /FoHELLO.obj
HELLO.CPP
!ELSE
        $(CXX) /c $(CXXFLAGS_G) $(CXXFLAGS_R) /FoHELLO.obj
HELLO.CPP
!ENDIF

$(PROJ).exe : $(DEF_FILE) $(OBJS)
!IF $(DEBUG)
        $(LRF) @<<$(PROJ).lrf
$(RT_OBJS: = +^
) $(OBJS: = +^
)
$@
$(MAPFILE_D)
$(LIBS: = +^
) +
$(LLIBS_G: = +^
) +
$(LLIBS_D: = +^
)
$(DEF_FILE) $(LFLAGS_G) $(LFLAGS_D);
```

(continued)

Listing 7-4. *(continued)*

```
<<
!ELSE
        $(LRF) @<<$(PROJ).lrf
$(RT_OBJS: = +^
) $(OBJS: = +^
)
$@
$(MAPFILE_R)
$(LIBS: = +^
) +
$(LLIBS_G: = +^
) +
$(LLIBS_R: = +^
)
$(DEF_FILE) $(LFLAGS_G) $(LFLAGS_R);
<<
!ENDIF
        $(LINKER) @$(PROJ).lrf
        $@

.cpp.obj :
!IF $(DEBUG)
        $(CXX) /c $(CXXFLAGS_G) $(CXXFLAGS_D) /Fo$@ $<
!ELSE
        $(CXX) /c $(CXXFLAGS_G) $(CXXFLAGS_R) /Fo$@ $<
!ENDI

run: $(PROJ).exe
        WX $(WXFLAGS) $(PROJ).exe $(RUNFLAGS)

debug: $(PROJ).exe
        WX $(WXFLAGS) CVW $(CVFLAGS) $(PROJ).exe $(RUNFLAGS)
```

You can find many sample makefiles and PWB .mak files, ready to be modified in the directory c:\c700\mfc\samples. If you wish, you can also create new .mak files in PWB with the Project menu's New Project... item. Specify the name of the new .mak file in the New Project dialog box that appears, and click the <Set Project Template...> button. In the Set Project Template dialog box, select the Windows 3.1 EXE choice. Close both dialog boxes by selecting <OK> in each, and a last dialog box appears: the Edit Project dialog box. Click the names of the files you want to associate with this project (e.g., hello.cpp and hello.def here). Then click <OK> and PWB will create the new .mak file automatically.

To create hello.exe, just load hello.mak in as our project file with the Open Project... item in PWB's Project menu. Next, select the Build item in the Project menu to create hello.exe, or the Execute item in the Run menu to create and run it. PWB invokes NMAKE to compile and link our program, creating hello.exe. When you run hello.exe, you'll see the same result as before, as shown in Figure 7-1.

TIP   Microsoft C 7+ is targeted for Windows 3.1 or later versions; to build Windows 3.0 projects (which will run in Windows 3.0 and 3.1) with PWB, choose the Windows 3.0 EXE item in the Set Project Template dialog box. To compile Windows 3.0 executables at the command-line level, you must either add the line: #define WINVER 0x0300 to your source file (before the line including the file windows.h), or use the /DWINVER=0x0300 cl option when compiling. In addition, we'll be using the resource compiler, rc.exe, later. Use the /30 rc option when combining the .exe and .res files (as explained in the next chapter) where we use the rc /t option, but do not use the /30 option in lines where we use the /r option.

Note that so far, we've only been able to display our string starting at location (0, 0). We can change that using a few device context member functions; for example, we might want to display our string in the center of the window. We can do that by getting the dimensions of our window, and by using the device context SetTextAlign( ) member function. All text strings can be thought of as appearing in a bounding rectangle. When you specify the point, say (px, py), to print text at with TextOut( ), the text rectangle is set up using that point as its upper left corner:

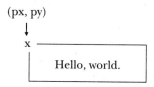

Using SetTextAlign( ), you can align the text rectangle so that the point is in many different positions. For example, we can display text so that the top of the box is centered on the point we pass to TextOut( ), (px, py):

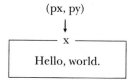

In this way, Windows can automatically center text for you. These are the values that SetTextAlign( ) can take (note that they can be ORed together):

TA_BASELINE   Center vertically on text baseline
TA_BOTTOM   Center vertically on text rectangle bottom
TA_CENTER   Center text rectangle
TA_LEFT   Use left side of text rectangle (default)
TA_RIGHT   Use right side of text rectangle
TA_TOP   Center vertically on text rectangle top (default)

That means that we can center our text on the point we pass to TextOut( ) like this:

```
void CMainWindow::OnPaint()
{
    CString hello_string = "Hello, World";
    CPaintDC dc( this );

    dc.SetTextAlign(TA_CENTER);
}
```

→

But now we need to pass the point that corresponds to the exact center of the window. To do that, we can use the very handy device context function GetClientRect( ). This function returns an object of class CRect, which is declared like this:

```
class CRect : public tagRECT
{
public:
    CRect();
    CRect(int l, int t, int r, int b);
    CRect(const RECT& srcRect);
    CRect(LPRECT lpSrcRect);
    CRect(POINT point, SIZE size);
    int Width() const;
    int Height() const;
    CSize Size() const;
    CPoint& TopLeft();
    CPoint& BottomRight();
    operator LPRECT();
    BOOL IsRectEmpty() const;
    BOOL IsRectNull() const;
    BOOL PtInRect(POINT point) const;
    void SetRect(int x1, int y1, int x2, int y2);
    void SetRectEmpty();
```

```
      void CopyRect(LPRECT lpSrcRect);
      BOOL EqualRect(LPRECT lpRect) const;
      void InflateRect(int x, int y);
      void InflateRect(SIZE size);
      void OffsetRect(int x, int y);
      void OffsetRect(SIZE size);
      void OffsetRect(POINT point);
      int IntersectRect(LPRECT lpRect1, LPRECT lpRect2);
      int UnionRect(LPRECT lpRect1, LPRECT lpRect2);
      void operator=(const RECT& srcRect);
      BOOL operator==(const RECT& rect) const;
      BOOL operator!=(const RECT& rect) const;
      void operator+=(POINT point);
      void operator-=(POINT point);
      void operator&=(const RECT& rect);
      void operator|=(const RECT& rect);
      CRect operator+(POINT point) const;
      CRect operator-(POINT point) const;
      CRect operator&(const RECT& rect2) const;
      CRect operator|(const RECT& rect2) const;
  };
```

The CRect class is derived from the Windows structure Rect:

```
typedef struct tagRECT
  {
    int     left;
    int     top;
    int     right;
    int     bottom;
  } RECT;
```

That means that we can find the dimensions of our client area rectangle (in pixels) like this:

```
    void CMainWindow::OnPaint()
    {
        CString hello_string = "Hello, World";
        CPaintDC dc( this );
→       CRect rect;

        dc.SetTextAlign(TA_CENTER);
→       GetClientRect(rect);
            :
    }
```

TIP Besides GetClientRect( ), a useful function to use in an OnPaint( ) function is GetUpdateRect( ) which returns the rectangle that has been declared invalid (i.e., the rectangle that has to be repainted — and which may not be the whole client area). Also, if you want to convert between client area coordinates and screen coordinates (where the top left pixel of the screen is (0, 0)), you can use CWnd::ScreenToClient( ) and CWnd::ClientToScreen( ) (note that CWnd is the base class of CFrameWindow, which in turn is the base class of our class CMainWindow).

Now we know that our client area rectangle (the area that excludes the title bar and any scroll bars that might be on the right and bottom) looks like this:

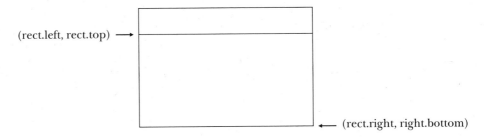

(rect.left, rect.top) ⟶

⟵ (rect.right, right.bottom)

That means that we can set place the text in the middle of our window like this:

```
void CMainWindow::OnPaint()
{
    CString hello_string = "Hello, World";
    CPaintDC dc( this );
    CRect rect;

    dc.SetTextAlign(TA_CENTER);
    GetClientRect(rect);
    dc.TextOut(rect.right/2, rect.bottom/2,
            hello_string, hello_string.GetLength());
}
```

→

The result appears in Figure 7-3 — our new program works as expected. Here's the new code for hello.cpp:

```
#include <afxwin.h>

class CMainWindow : public CFrameWnd
{
```

```
public:
    CMainWindow();
    afx_msg void OnPaint();

    DECLARE_MESSAGE_MAP()
};

CMainWindow::CMainWindow()
{
    Create(NULL, "Hello World Example", WS_OVERLAPPEDWINDOW,
        rectDefault, NULL, NULL );
}

void CMainWindow::OnPaint()
{
    CString hello_string = "Hello, World";
    CPaintDC dc( this );
    CRect rect;

    GetClientRect(rect);
    dc.SetTextAlign(TA_BASELINE | TA_CENTER);
    dc.TextOut(rect.right/2, rect.bottom/2,
                hello_string, hello_string.GetLength());
}

BEGIN_MESSAGE_MAP( CMainWindow, CFrameWnd )
    ON_WM_PAINT()
END_MESSAGE_MAP()

class CTheApp : public CWinApp
{
public:
    BOOL InitInstance();
};

BOOL CTheApp::InitInstance()
{
    m_pMainWnd = new CMainWindow();
    m_pMainWnd->ShowWindow( m_nCmdShow );
    m_pMainWnd->UpdateWindow();

    return TRUE;
}

CTheApp theApp;
```

Now that we know something about displaying data in a window, let's see if we can't get some user input from the keyboard.

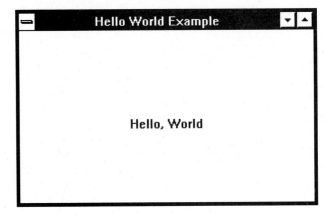

Figure 7-3. Centering Our Text in a Window

Using the Keyboard in Windows

Even in a multitasking windowing environment, we still only have one keyboard. That means that even though we might have a dozen windows displayed on the screen at once, only *one* can actively be accepting keyboard input. In Windows, we say that that window has the current *focus*, and the window that has the focus is the currently *active window*. It's easy to tell which window is currently active in a Windows session; if the window has a caption bar at the top, Windows highlights it. If the window does not have a caption bar, Windows highlights the window's frame. In fact, even an icon can be the active window, and if it is, Windows highlights the caption text underneath it. When you type using the keyboard, a stream of keyboard messages is sent to the window with the focus.

Windows Keyboard Input Conventions

In Windows, there is usually a flashing cursor to indicate where text is going to go when you type it (often either a vertical bar or an I beam shape). We should note that, in Windows, the mouse cursor is usually referred to as the cursor, while what we call the cursor in DOS is called the *insertion point* or *caret* in Windows. That is, text appears as the insertion point or caret after you type it, and when you move the mouse, you're moving the cursor (not the insertion point or caret).

Also, when there are a number of buttons, listboxes, or text boxes in a window — what Windows calls *controls* — the user is usually able to select which control has the focus by clicking it with the mouse. For example, if a button has the current focus, Windows highlights its border (which also means that the user can choose this button by pressing the Enter key). The user might then click a text box instead, and a flashing insertion point appears there (and the button's border returns to normal as it loses the focus).

Furthermore, under Windows, the user expects to be able to press the tab key to move the focus between controls in a window. That is, if the text box we just mentioned follows the button in the window's *tab order*, then the user can move from the button to the text box simply by pressing the tab key. In general, the user is supposed to be able to circulate around a window's controls simply by pressing the tab button. You might also note that when a dialog box first appears, one of the buttons is often highlighted already (often the button marked OK); in that case, we say that that button has the *default focus*.

TIP Two functions that are useful here are GetFocus( ) and SetFocus( ), which allow us to see who has the focus and set it ourselves. Also, when our window gets the focus, it will receive a WM_SETFOCUS message, and when it loses it, it will see a WM_KILLFOCUS message.

In addition, certain keys usually do certain things. For example, the F1 key is usually reserved for Help. F2 is supposed to correspond to the New item in your menus if you have one (as in New Game, New File... or New Spreadsheet...). Alt+X is supposed to mean the same as Exit if the File menu is open, and so on. (It's easy to see what key conventions are standard — just use Windows applications.)

One final point about using the keyboard from the user's point of view is that, under Windows, the user is supposed to be able to use the keyboard to replace the mouse for input operations. In some cases, this is more theoretically true than actually true (as in a graphics paint program), but in most applications, the keyboard should be able to duplicate the mouse's actions. When designing Windows applications, we should keep that in mind.

Reading Keystroke Messages

There are only five keystroke messages, and they are sent to the window with the current focus:

WM_KEYDOWN	Key was pressed
WM_SYSKEYDOWN	System key was pressed

WM_KEYUP	Key was released
WM_SYSKEYUP	System key was released
WM_CHAR	Translated key

As you might expect, WM_KEYDOWN is generated when a key is struck, WM_KEYUP when the key is released. In addition, Windows makes a distinction for system keystrokes (the keystrokes that are commands to Windows, usually in combination with the <Alt> key, including <Alt><Esc>, which switches the active window). Those messages are: WM_SYSKEYDOWN and WM_SYSKEYUP, but we won't work very much with the system keyboard messages here.

The WM_KEYDOWN and WM_KEYUP messages are handled by the functions OnKeyDown( ) and OnKeyUp( ) in Microsoft C++ like this:

```
afx_msg void OnKeyDown(UINT nChar, UINT nRepCnt, UINT nFlags);
afx_msg void OnKeyUp(UINT nChar, UINT nRepCnt, UINT nFlags);
```

TIP If you ever need to find a protype for a message-handling function (like OnKeyDown( ) or OnKeyUp( )), you'll find them all in the file c:\c700\mfc\include\afxwin.h.

In particular, for these messages, the parameter nFlags is coded this way, bit by bit:

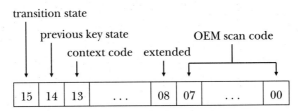

The transition state is 0 if the key was just pressed (i.e., for **WM_KEYDOWN** messages), and 1 if just released (WM_KEYUP messages). The previous key state is 0 if the key was previously up and 1 if previously down. The context code is 1 if the Alt key is pressed; usually this is 0 for **WM_KEYDOWN** and **WM_KEYUP**, and 1 for system messages. Also, the extended flag is 1 if the keystroke is the result of pressing or releasing one of the additional keys on the IBM enhanced keyboard (as used with the PS/2) — note that programs usually do not use this field.

TIP   If you keep a key pressed and generate "typematic" keystrokes, the previous state key will be set to 1.

The OEM (OEM stands for Original Equipment Manufacturer) scan code holds the scan code for the key as generated by the keyboard itself. For each keystroke or valid combination of keystrokes (such as Shift-a), the keyboard generates a unique *scan code*. This is the raw, untranslated information from the keyboard port (port 60h) on the I/O bus, and we won't use this information ourselves until it's been translated (into ASCII) by Windows.

The repeat count is an indication of typematic action. If you hold a key down and generate automatic repetitions of that key, this field will hold the number of repetitions. Usually, Windows does not produce a separate WM_KEY-DOWN or WM_SYSKEYDOWN message for typematic action (which would flood the message queue); instead, it bunches them together and places a nonzero value in the repeat count parameter nRepCnt.

You might notice that we still don't really know what key was pressed. The nChar parameter contains a *virtual key code*, which does tell us what key was pressed. A constant is defined for each keystroke, as indicated in Table 7-1.

TIP   Windows also includes three mouse virtual "key" codes in its list of virtual keys: VK_LBUTTON, VK_MBUTTON, and VK_RBUTTON, matching the left, middle, and right keys of a mouse. However, these virtual key codes will never be sent to us in with a WM_KEYUP or WM_KEYDOWN message, because the mouse communicates with its own set of Windows messages, not WM_KEYDOWN or WM_KEYUP. These constants are actually designed to be passed to functions like GetKeyState( ) (which is coming up) to find the current state of the mouse buttons — i.e., pressed or not pressed.

Note that Table 7-1 contains codes for keys that do not normally generate a printable character, such as the function keys, VK_F1 to VK_F16, or the keyboard arrow keys like VK_UP and VK_LEFT. And, in fact, this is the usual way for Windows programs to read such keys. In fact, you might think that we can read all keys this way, since even the letters (VK_A to VK_Z) are defined. However, there is a problem. Although we can now figure out what key was pressed, including the keys from VK_A to VK_Z, we can't actually tell the difference between capital and small letters like "A" and "a." That is, if you

VK_LBUTTON	VK_NEXT	VK_NUMPAD2	VK_F3
VK_RBUTTON	VK_END	VK_NUMPAD3	VK_F4
VK_CANCEL	VK_HOME	VK_NUMPAD4	VK_F5
VK_MBUTTON	VK_LEFT	VK_NUMPAD5	VK_F6
VK_BACK	VK_UP	VK_NUMPAD6	VK_F7
VK_TAB	VK_RIGHT	VK_NUMPAD7	VK_F8
VK_CLEAR	VK_DOWN	VK_NUMPAD8	VK_F9
VK_RETURN	VK_SELECT	VK_NUMPAD9	VK_F10
VK_SHIFT	VK_PRINT	VK_MULTIPLY	VK_F11
VK_CONTROL	VK_EXECUTE	VK_ADD	VK_F12
VK_MENU	VK_SNAPSHOT	VK_SEPARATOR	VK_F13
VK_PAUSE	VK_INSERT	VK_SUBTRACT	VK_F14
VK_CAPITAL	VK_DELETE	VK_DECIMAL	VK_F15
VK_ESCAPE	VK_HELP	VK_DIVIDE	VK_F16
VK_SPACE	VK_NUMPAD0	VK_F1	VK_NUMLOCK
VK_PRIOR	VK_NUMPAD1	VK_F2	VK_A-VK_Z, VK_0-VK_9

Table 7-1. Virtual Key Codes

press "A", wParam will hold the value VK_A — and if you press "a", wParam will also hold the value VK_A.

One way to resolve this difficulty is with the Windows function GetKeyState( ), which can indicate the state of the Shift key (or any other key, including the mouse buttons). We use it like this: GetKeyState(VK_SHIFT); if this value is negative, the shift key was down when the keystroke we're currently processing was generated.

NOTE   It's important to realize that GetKeyState( ) does not return the real-time state of a key, but rather the state of the key at the time that the keyboard message we're currently analyzing was generated.

However, this method is a very clumsy way of reading keyboard input if we're looking for characters like those in the string "Hello World.". A better way is to use the WM_CHAR message, whose message-handling function is OnChar( ):

```
afx_msg void OnChar(UINT wChar, UINT nRepCnt, UINT wFlags);
```

Here the first parameter, wChar, is the ASCII code of the key that was typed, and that's what we want. For example, let's write a sample program called char.cpp which reads keystrokes and echoes them in a window.

TIP   Keep in mind that WM_KEYDOWN and WM_KEYUP messages will allow us to process non-printing keys like function keys and keys like the right or left arrow keys.

A Keyboard Input Example

Here, our goal will be to read the keys that the user types. As they type keys, we can echo them in our window, starting at the upper left location, coordinates (0, 0). That is, if we type the letter 'T', we'd see this:

The location (0, 0) is the top left of the client area; y increases going down and x increases to the right:

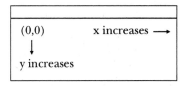

Now we can keep going, typing other characters like this:

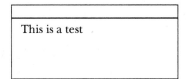

If the user pressed <Enter>, we can move to the next line and accept more input like this:

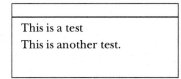

We want to use the OnChar( ) function here, so we declare it in our class CMainWindow and create the function like this:

```
#include <afxwin.h>

class CMainWindow : public CFrameWnd
{
public:
    CMainWindow();
    afx_msg void OnChar(UINT wChar, UINT nRepCnt, UINT wFlags);

    DECLARE_MESSAGE_MAP()
};

CMainWindow::CMainWindow()
{
    Create(NULL, "Character Input Example", WS_OVERLAPPEDWINDOW,
        rectDefault, NULL, NULL);
}

void CMainWindow::OnChar(UINT wChar, UINT nRepCnt, UINT wFlags)
{

}
```

In OnChar, we'll need to check if the incoming character, as passed to us in wChar, is a carriage return ('\r'). If it is, then we'll move to the next line down. In code, we might start like this:

```
void CMainWindow::OnChar(UINT wChar, UINT nRepCnt, UINT wFlags)
{
    if(wChar == (UINT) '\r'){

    }
    else{

    }
}
```

Let's assume that the character typed was not a carriage return, which means that we should print it on the screen. In that case, we can use TextOut( ), as before. You might recall that we used a device context object of class CPaintDC to display text with before. However, a paint-type device context is only used if a part of our window has been declared invalid, and even then we can only work with the invalid rectangle. Another way of getting a device context object, one that we can be sure includes our window's entire client area, is by using CClientDC( ). (Together, CPaintDC and CClientDC are the two most common classes of device context in Windows.) Using our CClientDC object, we'll be able to refer to the entire client area of our window. (At the end of our OnChar( ) function, the object's destructor will destroy it automatically.) We create the device context object by passing a pointer to our window object (i.e., this), and then we print our character on the screen using TextOut( ):

```
       void CMainWindow::OnChar(UINT wChar, UINT nRepCnt, UINT wFlags)
       {
           CString in_char = wChar;
→          CClientDC dc(this);

           if(wChar == (UINT) '\r'){

           }
           else{
→              dc.TextOut(0, 0, in_char, 1);
           }
       }
```

Since TextOut( ) takes a CString object, we placed the incoming character, wChar, in a CString object named in_char and then passed it to TextOut( ):

```
       void CMainWindow::OnChar(UINT wChar, UINT nRepCnt, UINT wFlags)
       {
→          CString in_char = wChar;
           CClientDC dc(this);

           if(wChar == (UINT) '\r'){

           }
           else{
→              dc.TextOut(0, 0, in_char, 1);
           }
       }
```

This prints the first character we receive at location (0, 0). Note that if we made the CString object in_char into a static object or class member named, say, in_string, we could simply add characters to this string as they're typed, and print out the whole string starting at location (0, 0) every time OnChar( ) was called with this statement:

```
        in_string += wChar;
            :
→       dc.TextOut(0, 0, in_string, in_string.GetLength());
```

However, to gain more experience with graphic control in Windows, let's print out the typed characters as they come in, one by one. That is, we'll store them one at a time in in_char, and then add them to the other characters already on the screen. Although we can print our first character at location (0, 0), we'll have to place succeeding characters to the right of it. That means that we'll have to specify the window coordinates at which we want to print each character, rather than simply printing the whole string starting at (0, 0). To do that, we'll have to keep track of the location at which the next character is to be printed, and we can do so by introducing two new members of CMainWindow, caret_x and caret_y:

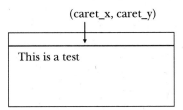

That is, (caret_x, caret_y) is the position of an invisible cursor or caret in our program. The units of screen measurements like these are, by default, in pixels. We can set them to zero in CMainWindow's constructor:

```
    #include <afxwin.h>

    class CMainWindow : public CFrameWnd
    {
    private:
→       int caret_x;
→       int caret_y;
    public:
        CMainWindow();
        afx_msg void OnChar(UINT wChar, UINT nRepCnt, UINT wFlags);

        DECLARE_MESSAGE_MAP()
    };

    CMainWindow::CMainWindow()
    {
→       caret_x = caret_y = 0;
```

```
    Create(NULL, "Character Input Example", WS_OVERLAPPEDWINDOW,
        rectDefault, NULL, NULL);
}

void CMainWindow::OnChar(UINT wChar, UINT nRepCnt, UINT wFlags)
{
    CClientDC dc(this);
    CString in_char = wChar;

    if(wChar == (UINT) '\r'){
    }
    else{
        dc.TextOut(0, 0, in_char, 1);

    }
}
```

Now in OnChar( ), we can place the character on the screen like this:

```
    void CMainWindow::OnChar(UINT wChar, UINT nRepCnt, UINT wFlags)
    {
        CClientDC dc(this);
        CString in_char = wChar;

        if(wChar == (UINT) '\r'){

        }
        else{
→           dc.TextOut(caret_x, caret_y, in_char, 1);

        }
    }
```

The next step is to update caret_x and caret_y to hold the location at which we should place the next character. Since we're printing on the same line, caret_y won't change. But what about caret_x? Since Windows uses a variable-width font, we're not sure just how wide the character we just printed out was. The solution is to use the function GetTextExtent( ), which is a member function of CMainWindow. This function returns an object of class CSize, which is declared like this:

```
    class CSize : public tagSIZE
    {
    public:
      CSize();
```

```
    CSize(int initCX, int initCY);
    CSize(SIZE initSize);
    CSize(POINT initPt);
    CSize(DWORD dwSize);
    BOOL operator==(SIZE size) const;
    BOOL operator!=(SIZE size) const;
    void operator+=(SIZE size);
    void operator-=(SIZE size);
    CSize operator+(SIZE size) const;
    CSize operator-(SIZE size) const;
};
```

Note in particular that CSize inherits the struct tagSize, which is a Windows struct that looks like this:

```
typedef struct tagSIZE
{
    int    cx;
    int    cy;
} SIZE;
```

Let's use GetTextExtent( ) like this to get an object of class CSize which we can name char_size:

```
    void CMainWindow::OnChar(UINT wChar, UINT nRepCnt, UINT wFlags)
    {
        CClientDC dc(this);
        CString in_char = wChar;
→       CSize char_size;

        if(wChar == (UINT) '\r'){

        }
        else{
            dc.TextOut(caret_x, caret_y, in_char, 1);
→           char_size = dc.GetTextExtent(in_char, 1);
                :
        }
    }
```

The member elements char_size.cx and char_size.cy (i.e., cx and cy come from the SIZE struct inside the CSIZE object char_size) hold the width and height of the string in_char, respectively. That means that we can update caret_x like this to hold the position at which we'll place the next character:

```
void CMainWindow::OnChar(UINT wChar, UINT nRepCnt, UINT wFlags)
{
    CClientDC dc(this);
    CString in_char = wChar;
    CSize char_size;

    if(wChar == (UINT) '\r'){

    }
    else{
        dc.TextOut(caret_x, caret_y, in_char, 1);
        char_size = dc.GetTextExtent(in_char, 1);
        caret_x += char_size.cx;
    }
}
```

Now let's examine the next case, where the typed key was a carriage return. In that case, we want to skip to the next line, which means setting caret_x to 0 and adding the height of a line to caret_y. To find the height of a line of screen text, we can send some dummy string to GetTextExtent( ) and then examine the cy member of the resulting CSize object. However, there's a better way to do this. We can use the device context function GetTextMetrics( ) instead. This function fills structure of type TEXTMETRIC (a Windows structure), which holds information about the current font in these fields:

```
typedef struct tagTEXTMETRIC
   {
    int      tmHeight;
    int      tmAscent;
    int      tmDescent;
    int      tmInternalLeading;
    int      tmExternalLeading;
    int      tmAveCharWidth;
    int      tmMaxCharWidth;
    int      tmWeight;
    BYTE     tmItalic;
    BYTE     tmUnderlined;
    BYTE     tmStruckOut;
    BYTE     tmFirstChar;
    BYTE     tmLastChar;
    BYTE     tmDefaultChar;
    BYTE     tmBreakChar;
    BYTE     tmPitchAndFamily;
    BYTE     tmCharSet;
    int      tmOverhang;
    int      tmDigitizedAspectX;
```

```
    int      tmDigitizedAspectY;
} TEXTMETRIC;
```

The one we're interested in here is tmHeight, the height of the current font.
We can use it like this to update caret_y:

```
void CMainWindow::OnChar(UINT wChar, UINT nRepCnt, UINT wFlags)
{
    TEXTMETRIC tm;
    CClientDC dc(this);
    CString in_char = wChar;
    CSize char_size;

    if(wChar == (UINT) '\r'){
        dc.GetTextMetrics(&tm);
        caret_y += tm.tmHeight;
        caret_x = 0;
    }
    else{
        dc.TextOut(caret_x, caret_y, in_char, 1);
        char_size = dc.GetTextExtent(in_char, 1);
        caret_x += char_size.cx;
    }
}
```

Now CMainWindow::OnChar( ) is complete. We just need to add the other
functions and macros, all of which we've seen before. That is, we need to use
BEGIN_MESSAGE_MAP( ) and END_MESSAGE_MAP( ), as well as overriding CtheAPP::InitInstance( ). We can use the same code as we did with
hello.cpp — except that now we indicate that we want to intercept the
WM_CHAR message, not WM_PAINT:

```
void CMainWindow::OnChar(UINT wChar, UINT nRepCnt, UINT wFlags)
{
    TEXTMETRIC tm;
    CClientDC dc(this);
    CString in_char = wChar;
    CSize char_size;

    if(wChar == (UINT) '\r'){
        dc.GetTextMetrics(&tm);
        caret_y += tm.tmHeight;
        caret_x = 0;
    }
    else{
        dc.TextOut(caret_x, caret_y, in_char, 1);
```

```
            char_size = dc.GetTextExtent(in_char, 1);
            caret_x += char_size.cx;
        }
    }

    BEGIN_MESSAGE_MAP(CMainWindow, CFrameWnd)
        ON_WM_CHAR()
    END_MESSAGE_MAP()

    class CTheApp : public CWinApp
    {
    public:
        BOOL InitInstance();
    };

    BOOL CTheApp::InitInstance()
    {
        m_pMainWnd = new CMainWindow();
        m_pMainWnd->ShowWindow(m_nCmdShow);
        m_pMainWnd->UpdateWindow();

        return TRUE;
    }

    CTheApp theApp;
```

All the code appears in Listing 7-5, char.def appears in Listing 7-6, and the associated makefile in Listing 7-7. Note that we also included the file windows.h in char.cpp for the definition of TEXTMETRIC. In passing, we might note that another popular way of determining graphic dimensions besides GetTextMetrics( ) is with the Windows function GetSystemMetrics(nIndex), where nIndex corresponds to one of the Windows.h constants as shown in Table 7-2. Simply pass the constant you're interested in learning about — such as SM_CXICON (SM stands for System Metrics) to learn the horizontal width of an icon — and GetSystemMetrics( ) will return that value in its integer return value.

TIP Note that a quick way to determine if there is a mouse present in the computer you're working with is by using the return value of GetSystemMetrics(SM_MOUSEPRESENT). If nonzero, a mouse is present.

Note that we have not included any provision for backspace ('\b'), tab ('\t'), or other control characters.

SM Constant	Means
SM_CXSCREEN	Width of screen
SM_CYSCREEN	Height of screen
SM_CXVSCROLL	Width of scroll bar
SM_CYHSCROLL	Height of scroll bar
SM_CYCAPTION	Height of caption
SM_CXBORDER	Width of borders
SM_CYBORDER	Height of borders
SM_CXDLGFRAME	Width of dialog box frames
SM_CYDLGFRAME	Height of dialog box frames
SM_CXHTHUMB	Width of scroll bar thumbs
SM_CYVTHUMB	Height of scroll bar thumbs
SM_CXICON	Width of icon
SM_CYICON	Height of icon
SM_CXCURSOR	Width of cursor
SM_CYCURSOR	Height of cursor
SM_CYMENU	Height of menu bar
SM_CXFULLSCREEN	Width of full screen
SM_CYFULLSCREEN	Height of full screen
SM_CYKANJIWINDOW	Width of Kanji window
SM_MOUSEPRESENT	Nonzero if there is a mouse
SM_CYVSCROLL	Height of scroll bar
SM_CXHSCROLL	Width of scroll bar
SM_DEBUG	Nonzero if in Windows debugging version
SM_SWAPBUTTON	Nonzero if left and right buttons swapped
SM_RESERVED1	Reserved
SM_RESERVED2	Reserved
SM_RESERVED3	Reserved
SM_RESERVED4	Reserved
SM_CXMIN	Minimum width of window
SM_CYMIN	Minimum height of window
SM_CXSIZE	Width of bitmaps in title bar
SM_CYSIZE	Height of bitmaps in title bar
SM_CXMINTRACK	Minimum tracking width of window
SM_CYMINTRACK	Minimum tracking height of window

Table 7-2. System Metrics Constants

TIP Note that our window is redrawn when it is resized, so if you resize this window, the words will disappear. The way to fix that is to draw the same string again when we get a WM_PAINT message.

Listing 7-5. Char.cpp Reads Characters

```cpp
#include <afxwin.h>
#include <windows.h>

class CMainWindow : public CFrameWnd
{
private:
    int caret_x;
    int caret_y;
public:
    CMainWindow();
    afx_msg void OnChar(UINT wChar, UINT nRepCnt, UINT wFlags);

    DECLARE_MESSAGE_MAP()
};

CMainWindow::CMainWindow()
{
    caret_x = caret_y = 0;
    Create(NULL, "Character Input Example", WS_OVERLAPPEDWINDOW,
        rectDefault, NULL, NULL);
}

void CMainWindow::OnChar(UINT wChar, UINT nRepCnt, UINT wFlags)
{
    TEXTMETRIC tm;
    CClientDC dc(this);
    CString in_char = wChar;
    CSize char_size;

    if(wChar == (UINT) '\r'){
        dc.GetTextMetrics(&tm);
        caret_y += tm.tmHeight;
        caret_x = 0;
    }
    else{
        dc.TextOut(caret_x, caret_y, in_char, 1);
        char_size = dc.GetTextExtent(in_char, 1);
        caret_x += char_size.cx;
    }
}
```

(continued)

Listing 7-5. *(continued)*

```
BEGIN_MESSAGE_MAP(CMainWindow, CFrameWnd)
    ON_WM_CHAR()
END_MESSAGE_MAP()

class CTheApp : public CWinApp
{
public:
    BOOL InitInstance();
};

BOOL CTheApp::InitInstance()
{
    m_pMainWnd = new CMainWindow();
    m_pMainWnd->ShowWindow( m_nCmdShow );
    m_pMainWnd->UpdateWindow();

    return TRUE;
}

CTheApp theApp;
```

Listing 7-6. Char.def

```
NAME          Char
DESCRIPTION   'Character Reading Example'

EXETYPE       WINDOWS
STUB          'WINSTUB.EXE'

CODE          PRELOAD MOVEABLE DISCARDABLE
DATA          PRELOAD MOVEABLE MULTIPLE

HEAPSIZE      1024
STACKSIZE     4096
```

Listing 7-7. Char's Makefile

```
CPPFLAGS= /AS /W3 /Zp /GA /GEs /G2
char.exe:    char.obj char.def
 link /NOD /ONERROR:NOEXE char, char, NUL, safxcw libw
 slibcew,char.def;
```

TIP One easy way to add tabs to our output is to use the device context function TabbedTextOut( ) function instead of TextOut( ). This way, you specify the tab positions you want at the same time you send the string to be printed. We'll see how to delete characters later.

Adding a Character Caret

For all of char.cpp's deficiencies, one stands out: There is no blinking insertion point or caret that indicates where the text will go. Usually in Windows, we have some indication of where the characters we type are going to be put. As mentioned in the beginning of the chapter, that location is called the insertion point or caret. It turns out that the caret is controlled by five CMainWindow functions:

```
CreateCaret( )
SetCaretPos( )
ShowCaret( )
HideCaret( )
DestroyCaret( )
```

To add a caret, we will start it at position (0, 0):

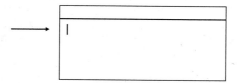

Then, as we type, we will advance it, showing where the next character will go:

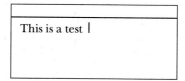

Let's put all of the caret functions to work. A caret is associated with our window, not with a device context, so one place to create a caret is when our window is being created with CMainWindow::Create( ), that is, in our window's constructor (but after the call to Create( )). Another place is when we receive a WM_CREATE Windows message (i.e., during the call to Create( )). Let's see how that works. We can declare a prototype (copied from afxwin.h) for OnCreate( ) like this:

```
#include <afxwin.h>
#include <windows.h>

class CMainWindow : public CFrameWnd
{
private:
    int caret_x;
    int caret_y;
public:
    CMainWindow();
    afx_msg void OnChar(UINT wChar, UINT nRepCnt, UINT wFlags);
    afx_msg int OnCreate(LPCREATESTRUCT lpCreateStruct);

    DECLARE_MESSAGE_MAP()
};
```

OnCreate( ) takes a long pointer to a **CREATESTRUCT** structure, which is declared like this:

```
typedef struct tagCREATESTRUCT
  {
    LPSTR    lpCreateParams;
    HANDLE   hInstance;
    HANDLE   hMenu;
    HWND     hwndParent;
    int      cy;
    int      cx;
    int      y;
    int      x;
    LONG     style;
    LPSTR    lpszName;
    LPSTR    lpszClass;
    DWORD    dwExStyle;
  } CREATESTRUCT;
typedef CREATESTRUCT FAR    *LPCREATESTRUCT;
```

Now, in OnCreate( ), we can create the caret with the function CMainWindow::CreateSolidCaret( ). This function takes two arguments, the caret's width and height. We can tie our caret to the current font by making it, say, the height of one character and one-eighth its width. We can find those properties with GetTextMetrics( ) like this:

```
#include <afxwin.h>
#include <windows.h>

class CMainWindow : public CFrameWnd
{
private:
    int caret_x;
    int caret_y;
public:
    CMainWindow();
    afx_msg void OnChar(UINT wChar, UINT nRepCnt, UINT wFlags);
    afx_msg int OnCreate(LPCREATESTRUCT lpCreateStruct);

    DECLARE_MESSAGE_MAP()
};

CMainWindow::CMainWindow()
{
    Create(NULL, "Character Input Example", WS_OVERLAPPEDWINDOW,
        rectDefault, NULL, NULL);
}

int CMainWindow::OnCreate(LPCREATESTRUCT lpCreateStruct)
{
    CClientDC dc(this);
    TEXTMETRIC tm;

    dc.GetTextMetrics(&tm);
    CreateSolidCaret(tm.tmAveCharWidth/8, tm.tmHeight);

}
```

The next step is to position the caret and to show it. To do that, we can use the functions CMainWindow::SetCaretPos( ) and ShowCaret( ). SetCaretPos( ) takes an argument of type POINT, which is defined like this in Windows:

```
typedef struct tagPOINT
  {
    int     x;
    int     y;
  } POINT;
```

That means that our completed OnCreate( ) function looks like this:

```
#include <afxwin.h>
#include <windows.h>
```

```
class CMainWindow : public CFrameWnd
{
private:
    int caret_x;
    int caret_y;
public:
    CMainWindow();
    afx_msg void OnChar(UINT wChar, UINT nRepCnt, UINT wFlags);
    afx_msg int OnCreate(LPCREATESTRUCT lpCreateStruct);

    DECLARE_MESSAGE_MAP()
};

CMainWindow::CMainWindow()
{
    Create(NULL, "Character Input Example", WS_OVERLAPPEDWINDOW,
        rectDefault, NULL, NULL);
}

int CMainWindow::OnCreate(LPCREATESTRUCT lpCreateStruct)
{
    POINT pt;
    CClientDC dc(this);
    TEXTMETRIC tm;

    dc.GetTextMetrics(&tm);
    CreateSolidCaret(tm.tmAveCharWidth/8, tm.tmHeight);
    pt.x = pt.y = 0;
    SetCaretPos(pt);
    ShowCaret();
    return 0;
}
```

Note that at the end we had to return a value of 0; this is necessary to indicate that what we did in OnCreate( ) was a success. If we wanted to stop creation of the window, we could return any other value (e.g., 1). All that's left to do in our program now is to make sure that we update the position of the caret to match caret_x and caret_y when those values are updated, and we do that in OnChar( ):

```
void CMainWindow::OnChar(UINT wChar, UINT nRepCnt, UINT wFlags)
{
    TEXTMETRIC tm;
    CClientDC dc(this);
    CString in_char = wChar;
    CSize char_size;
```

```
        POINT pt;

→       HideCaret();

        if(wChar == (UINT) '\r'){
            dc.GetTextMetrics(&tm);
            caret_y += tm.tmHeight;
            caret_x = 0;
        }
        else{
            dc.TextOut(caret_x, caret_y, in_char, 1);
            char_size = dc.GetTextExtent(in_char, 1);
            caret_x += char_size.cx;
        }
→       pt.x = caret_x;
→       pt.y = caret_y;
→       SetCaretPos(pt);
→       ShowCaret();
    }
```

TIP Note that before moving the caret, we hide it first with HideCaret( ) and later restore it with ShowCaret( ). If we had moved the caret abruptly, while it happened to be on the screen, it would have left its image behind.

The whole program, caret.cpp, is in Listing 7-8. The support files caret.def and the associated makefile are in Listings 7-9 and 7-10.

Listing 7-8. Caret.cpp

```cpp
#include <afxwin.h>
#include <windows.h>

class CMainWindow : public CFrameWnd
{
private:
    int caret_x;
    int caret_y;
public:
    CMainWindow();
    afx_msg void OnChar(UINT wChar, UINT nRepCnt, UINT wFlags);
    afx_msg int OnCreate(LPCREATESTRUCT lpCreateStruct);

    DECLARE_MESSAGE_MAP()
};
```

(continued)

Listing 7-8. *(continued)*

```
CMainWindow::CMainWindow()
{
    Create(NULL, "Character Input Example", WS_OVERLAPPEDWINDOW,
        rectDefault, NULL, NULL);
}

int CMainWindow::OnCreate(LPCREATESTRUCT lpCreateStruct)
{
    POINT pt;
    CClientDC dc(this);
    TEXTMETRIC tm;

    dc.GetTextMetrics(&tm);
    CreateSolidCaret(tm.tmAveCharWidth/8, tm.tmHeight);
    pt.x = pt.y = 0;
    SetCaretPos(pt);
    ShowCaret();
    return 0;
}

void CMainWindow::OnChar(UINT wChar, UINT nRepCnt, UINT wFlags)
{
    TEXTMETRIC tm;
    CClientDC dc(this);
    CString in_char = wChar;
    CSize char_size;
    POINT pt;

    HideCaret();

    if(wChar == (UINT) '\r'){
        dc.GetTextMetrics(&tm);
        caret_y += tm.tmHeight;
        caret_x = 0;
    }
    else{
        dc.TextOut(caret_x, caret_y, in_char, 1);
        char_size = dc.GetTextExtent(in_char, 1);
        caret_x += char_size.cx;
    }
    pt.x = caret_x;
    pt.y = caret_y;
    SetCaretPos(pt);
    ShowCaret();
}
```

Listing 7-8. *(continued)*

```
BEGIN_MESSAGE_MAP(CMainWindow, CFrameWnd)
    ON_WM_CHAR()
    ON_WM_CREATE()
END_MESSAGE_MAP()

class CTheApp : public CWinApp
{
public:
    BOOL InitInstance();
};

BOOL CTheApp::InitInstance()
{
    m_pMainWnd = new CMainWindow();
    m_pMainWnd->ShowWindow( m_nCmdShow );
    m_pMainWnd->UpdateWindow();

    return TRUE;
}

CTheApp theApp;
```

Listing 7-9. Caret.def

```
NAME          Caret
DESCRIPTION   'Caret Example'

EXETYPE       WINDOWS
STUB          'WINSTUB.EXE'

CODE          PRELOAD MOVEABLE DISCARDABLE
DATA          PRELOAD MOVEABLE MULTIPLE

HEAPSIZE      1024
STACKSIZE     4096
```

Listing 7-10. Caret's Makefile

```
CPPFLAGS= /AS /W3 /Zp /GA /GEs /G2
caret.exe:    caret.obj caret.def
 link /NOD /ONERROR:NOEXE caret, caret, NUL, safxcw libw
 slibcew,caret.def;
```

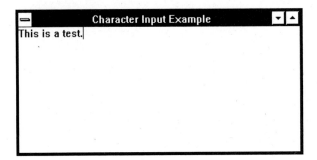

Figure 7-4. The Caret Program at Work

The result of all this work appears in Figure 7-4; our program is a success.

TIP   In general, it's more appropriate to show the cursor when your application gets the input focus, and to hide it again when you lose it. You can tell when you're getting the input focus by adding an OnSetFocus( ) function, and when you're losing it in an OnKillFocus( ) function.

However, there are still many faults to caret.cpp. For example, we have no choice but to display our character string starting at (0, 0). We can fix that by using, say, the mouse to indicate where we want the caret to appear in our window. After moving the caret, we're free to continue typing, and we should see our words appear at the new location. Let's look into this next, which brings us to the topic of interpreting mouse movements.

The Mouse and Mouse Events

As you might expect, mouse events such as clicking, double clicking, or moving are all communicated to us through Windows messages like these:

WM_MOUSEMOVE	Mouse was moved
WM_LBUTTONUP	Left button up
WM_LBUTTONDBLCLK	Left button double click
WM_LBUTTONDOWN	Left button down
WM_RBUTTONUP	Right button up
WM_RBUTTONDBLCLK	Right button double click
WM_RBUTTONDOWN	Right button down
WM_MBUTTONUP	Middle button up
WM_MBUTTONDBLCLK	Middle button double click
WM_MBUTTONDOWN	Middle button down

We should also note that Windows does not generate a WM_MOUSEMOVE message for every pixel location over which the mouse cursor travels. Instead, as the mouse moves, it sends only so many messages a second, as we'll see when we construct our paint application.

> **TIP** It's also important to know that if the user moves the mouse out of our window, we may get a WM_LBUTTONDOWN message without ever getting a WM_LBUTTONUP message (or the reverse), so beware of programming these in pairs.

The above mouse messages all refer to the client area of our window, that is, the area under our control. But since all messages for our window pass through WindowProc( ), our program also sees non-client area messages (i.e., for the menu bar, the system menu if there is one, and so on). Using these messages, Windows knows when to move, resize, or close our window. Although Windows applications very rarely use such messages, here they are for reference (note that NC stands for non-client area):

WM_NCMOUSEMOVE	Non-client mouse move
WM_NCLBUTTONDOWN	Non-client left button down
WM_NCLBUTTONUP	Non-client left button up
WM_NCLBUTTONDBLCLK	Non-client left button double click
WM_NCRBUTTONDOWN	Non-client right button down
WM_NCRBUTTONUP	Non-client right button up
WM_NCRBUTTONDBLCLK	Non-client right button double click
WM_NCMBUTTONDOWN	Non-client middle button down
WM_NCMBUTTONUP	Non-client middle button up
WM_NCMBUTTONDBLCLK	Non-client middle button double click

Note that since these messages refer to non-client areas, they can't use client area coordinates (unless they use negative values). Instead, they use *screen area coordinates* like this (starting in the upper left corner of the screen):

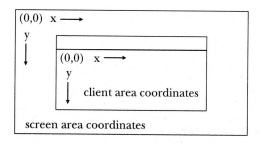

The most important messages for our use will involve the right or left buttons: WM_LBUTTONDOWN, WM_LBUTTONUP, WM_RBUTTONDOWN, and WM_RBUTTONUP. Using these messages and decoding the data sent to us in the associated OnXXX( ) functions, we'll be able to determine where the mouse cursor is when some action was taken with the buttons.

Using the Mouse in Code

Using direct mouse information is made very easy through the use of mouse messages. In our case, we just want to move the text insertion point to a new location on the screen. We start at (0,0):

When the caret is there, we can type our messages:

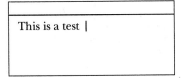

Next, we might move the mouse cursor somewhere else and click it. The caret should then move to that location:

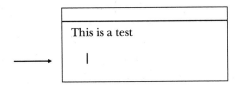

And we should be able to type again:

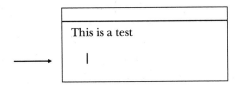

We start by adding support for the WM_LBUTTONDOWN message like this:

```cpp
#include <afxwin.h>
#include <windows.h>

class CMainWindow : public CFrameWnd
{
private:
    int caret_x;
    int caret_y;
public:
    CMainWindow();
    afx_msg void OnChar(UINT wChar, UINT nRepCnt, UINT wFlags);
    afx_msg int OnCreate(LPCREATESTRUCT lpCreateStruct);
    afx_msg void OnLButtonDown(UINT nFlags, CPoint point);

    DECLARE_MESSAGE_MAP()
};

CMainWindow::CMainWindow()
{
    Create(NULL, "Mouse Input Example", WS_OVERLAPPEDWINDOW,
        rectDefault, NULL, NULL);
}

void CMainWindow::OnLButtonDown(UINT nFlags, CPoint point)   ←
{

}
```

The nFlags parameter is an unsigned integer that can take these values, which indicate the state of the mouse buttons (and associated keyboard keys):

MK_CONTROL	Control key was down
MK_LBUTTON	Left mouse button down
MK_MBUTTON	Middle mouse button down
MK_RBUTTON	Right mouse button down
MK_SHIFT	Shift key was down

The point parameter is an object of class CPoint, which is declared like this:

```cpp
class CPoint : public tagPOINT
{
public:
  CPoint();
```

```
      CPoint(int initX, int initY);
      CPoint(POINT initPt);
      CPoint(SIZE initSize);
      CPoint(DWORD dwPoint);
      void Offset(int xOffset, int yOffset);
      void Offset(POINT point);
      void Offset(SIZE size);
      BOOL operator==(POINT point) const;
      BOOL operator!=(POINT point) const;
      void operator+=(SIZE size);
      void operator-=(SIZE size);
      CPoint operator+(SIZE size) const;
      CPoint operator-(SIZE size) const;
      CSize operator-(POINT point) const;
   };
```

Note that it is derived from the base structure POINT, which we've already seen, and which looks like this:

```
   typedef struct tagPOINT
     {
       int     x;
       int     y;
     } POINT;
```

That means that when our function OnLButtonDown() is called:

```
   void CMainWindow::OnLButtonDown(UINT nFlags, CPoint point)    ←
   {

   }
```

that the mouse button was pressed when the mouse cursor was at location (point.x, point.y). Since the mouse button was pressed, we can assume that the user wants to establish a new location in the window for the caret. Because this location is the new point at which we'll start printing characters, we can call it our new origin point, and refer to it in terms of coordinates like this: (origin_x, origin_y):

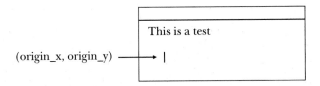

We can store (origin_x, origin_y) in our class declaration like this:

```
#include <afxwin.h>
#include <windows.h>

class CMainWindow : public CFrameWnd
{
private:
    int caret_x;
    int caret_y;
    int origin_x;
    int origin_y;
public:
    CMainWindow();
    afx_msg void OnChar(UINT wChar, UINT nRepCnt, UINT wFlags);
    afx_msg int OnCreate(LPCREATESTRUCT lpCreateStruct);
    afx_msg void OnLButtonDown(UINT nFlags, CPoint point);

    DECLARE_MESSAGE_MAP()
};
```

And we can place data in origin_x and origin_y in the OnLButtonDown( ) function like this (i.e., when you click the mouse button, you're establishing a new origin):

```
void CMainWindow::OnLButtonDown(UINT nFlags, CPoint point)
{
    origin_x = point.x;
    origin_y = point.y;
        :
}
```

Since our text string is defined with respect to the origin, we should also set caret_x and caret_y to 0:

```
void CMainWindow::OnLButtonDown(UINT nFlags, CPoint point)
{
    origin_x = point.x;
    origin_y = point.y;
    caret_x = caret_y = 0;
        :
}
```

Now we can move the caret to the new location this way:

```
void CMainWindow::OnLButtonDown(UINT nFlags, CPoint point)
{
    origin_x = point.x;
    origin_y = point.y;
    caret_x = caret_y = 0;
    HideCaret();
    SetCaretPos(point);
    ShowCaret();
}
```

The only remaining step in our program is to make sure that when we type, the characters appear not at (caret_x, caret_y), but at (origin_x + caret_x, origin_y + caret_y), because we want to print characters with respect to the origin. That looks like this in our character-handling function OnChar( ):

```
void CMainWindow::OnChar(UINT wChar, UINT nRepCnt, UINT wFlags)
{
    TEXTMETRIC tm;
    CClientDC dc(this);
    CString in_char = wChar;
    CSize char_size;
    POINT pt;

    HideCaret();

    if(wChar == (UINT) '\r'){
        dc.GetTextMetrics(&tm);
        caret_y += tm.tmHeight;
        caret_x = 0;
    }
    else{
        dc.TextOut(origin_x+caret_x, origin_y+caret_y, in_char, 1);
        char_size = dc.GetTextExtent(in_char, 1);
        caret_x += char_size.cx;
    }
    pt.x = caret_x+origin_x;
    pt.y = caret_y+origin_y;
    SetCaretPos(pt);
    ShowCaret();
}
```

That's it; the full code of our keyboard and mouse input program, which we might call moucaret.cpp, appears in Listing 7-11. The associated .def and

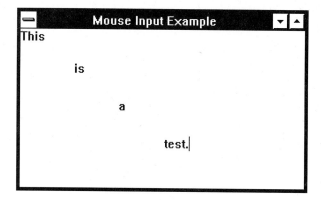

Figure 7-5. Using Both Mouse and Keyboard Input

makefiles appear in Listings 7-12 and 7-13. Now we can type wherever we want to in our window, as shown in Figure 7-5.

Listing 7-11. Moucaret.cpp

```
#include <afxwin.h>
#include <windows.h>

class CMainWindow : public CFrameWnd
{
private:
    int caret_x;
    int caret_y;
    int origin_x;
    int origin_y;
public:
    CMainWindow();
    afx_msg void OnChar(UINT wChar, UINT nRepCnt, UINT wFlags);
    afx_msg int OnCreate(LPCREATESTRUCT lpCreateStruct);
    afx_msg void OnLButtonDown(UINT nFlags, CPoint point);

    DECLARE_MESSAGE_MAP()
};

CMainWindow::CMainWindow()
{
    Create(NULL, "Mouse Input Example", WS_OVERLAPPEDWINDOW,
        rectDefault, NULL, NULL);
}

void CMainWindow::OnLButtonDown(UINT nFlags, CPoint point)
```

(continued)

Listing 7-11. (continued)

```
{
    origin_x = point.x;
    origin_y = point.y;
    HideCaret();
    SetCaretPos(point);
    ShowCaret();
}

int CMainWindow::OnCreate(LPCREATESTRUCT lpCreateStruct)
{
    POINT pt;
    CClientDC dc(this);
    TEXTMETRIC tm;

    dc.GetTextMetrics(&tm);
    CreateSolidCaret(tm.tmAveCharWidth/8, tm.tmHeight);
    pt.x = pt.y = 0;
    SetCaretPos(pt);
    ShowCaret();
    return 0;
}

void CMainWindow::OnChar(UINT wChar, UINT nRepCnt, UINT wFlags)
{
    TEXTMETRIC tm;
    CClientDC dc(this);
    CString in_char = wChar;
    CSize char_size;
    POINT pt;

    HideCaret();

    if(wChar == (UINT) '\r'){
        dc.GetTextMetrics(&tm);
        caret_y += tm.tmHeight;
        caret_x = 0;
    }
    else{
        dc.TextOut(origin_x+caret_x, origin_y+caret_y, in_char, 1);
        char_size = dc.GetTextExtent(in_char, 1);
        caret_x += char_size.cx;
    }
    pt.x = caret_x+origin_x;
    pt.y = caret_y+origin_y;
    SetCaretPos(pt);
    ShowCaret();
}
```

Listing 7-11. *(continued)*

```
BEGIN_MESSAGE_MAP(CMainWindow, CFrameWnd)
    ON_WM_CHAR()
    ON_WM_CREATE()
    ON_WM_LBUTTONDOWN()
END_MESSAGE_MAP()

class CTheApp : public CWinApp
{
public:
    BOOL InitInstance();
};

BOOL CTheApp::InitInstance()
{
    m_pMainWnd = new CMainWindow();
    m_pMainWnd->ShowWindow( m_nCmdShow );
    m_pMainWnd->UpdateWindow();

    return TRUE;
}

CTheApp theApp;
```

Listing 7-12. Moucaret.def

```
NAME         Moucaret
DESCRIPTION  'Moucaret Example'

EXETYPE      WINDOWS
STUB         'WINSTUB.EXE'

CODE         PRELOAD MOVEABLE DISCARDABLE
DATA         PRELOAD MOVEABLE MULTIPLE

HEAPSIZE     1024
STACKSIZE    4096
```

Listing 7-13. Moucaret's Makefile

```
CPPFLAGS= /AS /W3 /Zp /GA /GEs /G2
moucaret.exe:     moucaret.obj moucaret.def
 link /NOD /ONERROR:NOEXE moucaret, moucaret, NUL,
       safxcw libw slibcew,moucaret.def;
```

That's how to put the mouse to work — through the use of the mouse messages. We'll see more about how to use the mouse later, when we put together our paint program. In the meantime, let's turn to another very popular Windows topic — creating and using menus.

Menus

We're all familiar with menus under Windows; menus are the (extraordinarily popular) way of letting users select from among a variety of program options. We'll see all the techniques necessary to handle menus in this chapter: How to interface a menu to our program in the first place, how to add accelerator keys, how to gray menu items out, or how to add check marks to menu items. We'll even see how to add menu items at run time when we write a phone book program that will let us add people's names to our File menu at run time. Let's see how to work with menus in our programs.

Menu Conventions

The type of menu we'll be adding to our programs are called popup menus, also called dropdown menus or submenus, and they appear on command. At the top of the window is the title bar, and directly underneath that is the program's menu bar, also called the main menu or top-level menu:

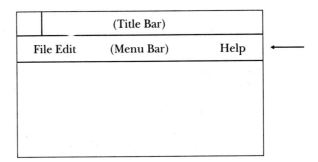

Here, three of the most common menus are indicated — File, Edit, and Help (note that Help is flush right). When the user selects one of these, like the File menu (using either the mouse or keyboard), the corresponding popup menu appears:

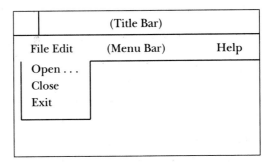

It's standard for Windows applications to have a File menu (often even if they don't handle files), because the user has come to expect it; the final menu item in the File menu is almost always the Exit item, allowing the user to quit the program. You might note that the Open... item has an ellipsis, three dots, after it, which indicates to the user that selecting this item opens a dialog box. Other standard ways of working with menu items include graying out menu items that are inappropriate and adding check marks in front of items to indicate that a certain option is (and will remain) selected. We'll adhere to these user expectations in our programs as well.

Adding Menus to Our Programs

We can modify our hello.cpp example by adding a File menu with one item in it: Hello, like this:

```
┌──┬──────────────────────────────┐
│  │        Menu Example          │
├──┴──────────────────────────────┤
│ File                            │
├──┬──────────────┬───────────────┤
│ Hello           │               │
│  └──────────────┘               │
│                                 │
│                                 │
│                                 │
└─────────────────────────────────┘
```

When the user selects that item, we can print Hello, world in the center of our window:

```
┌──┬──────────────────────────────┐
│  │        Menu Example          │
├──┴──────────────────────────────┤
│ File                            │
├─────────────────────────────────┤
│                                 │
│          Hello, world.          │
│                                 │
│                                 │
└─────────────────────────────────┘
```

In Windows, we usually design menus, icons, and dialog boxes before adding them to our program, and they're known as *resources*. For example, we'll be able to design the shape, location, type, and size of dialog boxes before writing any C++ code (using the Dialog Editor, as we'll see in the next chapter), and we will place that specification into a *resource file*, which has the extension .rc. We can do the same for menus.

This means that to design our File menu here, we will create a new file, menu.rc. When we're done, we'll use the *resources compiler* (rc.exe) to compile this file, then we'll link it into menu.exe. We start menu.rc by including a few include files common to .rc files:

```
#include <windows.h>
#include <afxres.h>
    :
```

Next, we can start designing our main menu system with a MENU statement. Here, we'll call the menu resource that we're designing "MainMenu" so that we'll be able to refer to it easily in our code, menu.cpp:

```
#include <windows.h>
#include <afxres.h>

MainMenu MENU    ←
{

}
```

This resource, MainMenu, will hold the declaration of all menus visible at once in the menu bar. In our case, that's only one menu, our File menu. It's a popup menu, so we indicate that like this:

```
#include <windows.h>
#include <afxres.h>

MainMenu MENU
{
  POPUP        "File"   ←
  {

  }
}
```

> **TIP** If you prefer, you can use the keyword BEGIN instead of a left brace ("{") in .rc files, and the keyword END instead of a right brace ("}"). They are interchangeable.

Designing our menu resource like this means that we'll get one popup menu, named File, at run time:

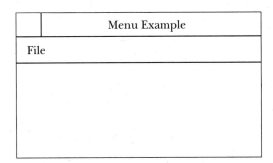

Before adding the menu's one item (i.e., "Hello"), we can add a little more functionality here. You may have noticed that most menu names and menu

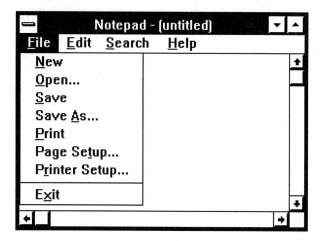

Figure 8-1. Using ALT Keys in Windows Menus

choices have one underlined character, as shown in Figure 8-1. These are Alt keys. For example, if the F in File is underlined, you can open that menu by pressing <Alt>F. Once the menu is open, you can access the Alt keys in that menu (but not before). For example, if the last item in the File menu is Exit, and the x is underlined, pressing <Alt>x will exit the program.

We can make the F in our File menu into an Alt key simply by placing an ampersand (&) in front of the F like this:

```
#include <windows.h>
#include <afxres.h>

MainMenu MENU
{
  POPUP         "&File"   ←
  {

  }
}
```

Now the F in File will be underlined when our program runs. We are ready to add the File menu's single item, Hello. When our program runs and the Hello item is selected, we'll get the Windows message WM_COMMAND, which indicates that a menu choice was made. However, there can be many menu choices in a menu — and for that matter, many menus (e.g., File, Edit, Help) in a program — so simply getting a WM_COMMAND message isn't enough. Instead, we have to associate a value with each menu item while designing the menu. When we do, that value will be passed to us along with the WM_COM-MAND message. For example, we can define a new constant, IDM_HELLO, whose value is, say, 100 (its value is arbitrary but unique):

```
#include <windows.h>
#include <afxres.h>
#define IDM_HELLO 100      ←

MainMenu MENU
{
  POPUP         "&File"
  {

  }
}
```

The IDM in IDM_HELLO is the standard prefix for such constants, and it stands for menu ID. Using IDM_HELLO, we can add our menu item Hello like this:

```
#include <windows.h>
#include <afxres.h>
#define IDM_HELLO 100

MainMenu MENU
{
  POPUP         "&File"
  {
→       MENUITEM "Hello", IDM_HELLO
  }
}
```

Now our File menu will have one item in it, Hello:

When the user selects that item, we'll get both a WM_COMMAND message and a passed value of IDM_HELLO (we'll see how this works in a minute). Before finishing our menu.rc file, let's add an ALT key to our Hello menu choice like this:

```
#include <windows.h>
#include <afxres.h>
#define IDM_HELLO 100

MainMenu MENU
{
  POPUP        "&File"
  {
      MENUITEM "&Hello", IDM_HELLO
  }
}
```

Now menu.rc is complete; let's turn to menu.cpp. We start by defining IDM_HELLO there, too, so we can refer to it in code (note that if we had many such constants we should place them into a separate include file, menu.h):

```
#include <afxwin.h>
#define IDM_HELLO   100
      :
```

Next, we can declare a function to handle the case in which the user selects our Hello menu item. Since we can call our menu items anything, there are no predefined Onxxx( ) functions here. Instead, we can define our own function, which we'll call OnHello( ):

```
#include <afxwin.h>
#define IDM_HELLO   100

class CMainWindow : public CFrameWnd
{
public:
  CMainWindow();
  afx_msg void OnHello();       ←

  DECLARE_MESSAGE_MAP()
};
```

Next, we indicate to Windows which menu system to use from our resource file when we create the window by making "MainMenu" the last parameter in Create( ) (before, when we didn't have a menu, this parameter was NULL):

```
#include <afxwin.h>
#define IDM_HELLO    100

class CMainWindow : public CFrameWnd
{
public:
  CMainWindow();
  afx_msg void OnHello();

  DECLARE_MESSAGE_MAP()
};

CMainWindow::CMainWindow()
{
 Create(NULL, "Menu Application",
   WS_OVERLAPPEDWINDOW, rectDefault, NULL, "MainMenu");     ←
}
```

We'll also associate OnHello( ) with WM_COMMAND (which we get when a menu selection was made) and with IDM_HELLO (the value we receive when that menu selection was the Hello menu item) like this:

```
#include <afxwin.h>
#define IDM_HELLO    100

class CMainWindow : public CFrameWnd
{
public:
  CMainWindow();
  afx_msg void OnHello();

  DECLARE_MESSAGE_MAP()
};

CMainWindow::CMainWindow()
{
 Create(NULL, "Menu Application",
   WS_OVERLAPPEDWINDOW, rectDefault, NULL, "MainMenu");
}

BEGIN_MESSAGE_MAP( CMainWindow, CFrameWnd )
```

```
      ON_COMMAND(IDM_HELLO, OnHello)                    ←
    END_MESSAGE_MAP()
```

Now when a menu selection is corresponding to our constant **IDM_HELLO**, our function **OnHello( )** is called. We will write OnHello( ) next. In that function, we place "Hello, world." into our window, centered in the middle, as we've done before. That looks like this:

```
    #include <afxwin.h>
    #define IDM_HELLO    100

    class CMainWindow : public CFrameWnd
    {
    public:
      CMainWindow();
      afx_msg void OnHello();

      DECLARE_MESSAGE_MAP()
    };

    CMainWindow::CMainWindow()
    {
     Create(NULL, "Menu Application",
       WS_OVERLAPPEDWINDOW, rectDefault, NULL, "MainMenu");
    }

    void CMainWindow::OnHello()                          ←
    {
     CString out_string = "Hello, world.";
     CClientDC dc(this);
     CRect rect;

     GetClientRect(rect);
     dc.SetTextAlign(TA_CENTER);
     dc.TextOut((rect.right / 2), (rect.bottom / 2), out_string,
          out_string.GetLength() );
    }

    BEGIN_MESSAGE_MAP( CMainWindow, CFrameWnd )
     ON_COMMAND(IDM_HELLO, OnHello)
    END_MESSAGE_MAP()
```

And that's it; the full program, menu.cpp, appears in Listing 8-1. Menu.def looks just as it did for our previous programs, and it appears in Listing 8-2. Menu.rc, which we developed above, appears in Listing 8-3. The last file we'll need is the makefile.

Listing 8-1. Menu.cpp

```cpp
#include <afxwin.h>
#define IDM_HELLO   100

class CMainWindow : public CFrameWnd
{
public:
  CMainWindow();
  afx_msg void OnHello();

  DECLARE_MESSAGE_MAP()
};

CMainWindow::CMainWindow()
{
 Create(NULL, "Menu Application",
    WS_OVERLAPPEDWINDOW, rectDefault, NULL, "MainMenu");
}

void CMainWindow::OnHello()
{
 CString out_string = "Hello, world.";
 CClientDC dc(this);
 CRect rect;

 GetClientRect(rect);
 dc.SetTextAlign(TA_CENTER);
 dc.TextOut((rect.right / 2), (rect.bottom / 2), out_string,
        out_string.GetLength() );
}

BEGIN_MESSAGE_MAP( CMainWindow, CFrameWnd )
 ON_COMMAND(IDM_HELLO, OnHello)
END_MESSAGE_MAP()

class CTheApp : public CWinApp
{
public:
  BOOL InitInstance();
};

BOOL CTheApp::InitInstance()
{
 m_pMainWnd = new CMainWindow();
 m_pMainWnd->ShowWindow( m_nCmdShow );
 m_pMainWnd->UpdateWindow();

 return TRUE;
}

CTheApp theApp;
```

Listing 8-2. Menu.def

```
NAME            Menu
DESCRIPTION     'Menu Example'

EXETYPE         WINDOWS
STUB            'WINSTUB.EXE'

CODE            PRELOAD MOVEABLE DISCARDABLE
DATA            PRELOAD MOVEABLE MULTIPLE

HEAPSIZE        1024
STACKSIZE       4096
```

Listing 8-3. Menu.rc

```
#include <windows.h>
#include <afxres.h>
#define IDM_HELLO 100

MainMenu MENU
{
  POPUP         "&File"
  {
      MENUITEM "&Hello", IDM_HELLO
  }
}
```

Creating the makefile is easy; all we have to do is to indicate that we want to include the resources in menu.rc as well. When we compile a resource file using the resource compiler, we generate a file with the extension .res, so we'll include that in the list of files we need:

```
CPPFLAGS= /AS /W3 /Zp /GA /GEs /G2

menu.exe:      menu.obj menu.def menu.res      ←
   link /NOD /ONERROR:NOEXE menu, menu, NUL, safxcw libw slibcew,menu.def;
```

In addition, we can indicate that we want a protected mode-only version of the executable file with the resource compiler /t switch like this:

```
CPPFLAGS= /AS /W3 /Zp /GA /GEs /G2

menu.exe:      menu.obj menu.def menu.res
   link /NOD /ONERROR:NOEXE menu, menu, NUL, safxcw libw slibcew,menu.def;
   rc /t menu.res      ←
```

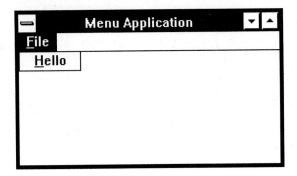

Figure 8-2. Our First Menu Program

We use rc.exe after linking our file menu.exe so that rc.exe will combine menu.res with menu.exe, creating the final executable program. For reference, this makefile also appears in Listing 8-4. And that's it; NMAKE is smart enough to know that it should create menu.res from a file named menu.rc. It does so by invoking the resource compiler, rc.exe, automatically. With this makefile, all you need to do is to type NMAKE and menu.exe will be created.

Now run menu.exe under Windows. When you do, you'll see a File menu has been added to our window. Opening that menu reveals our Hello menu item, as shown in Figure 8-2. Selecting that item makes the program display "Hello, world.", as shown in Figure 8-3. We've gotten a menu program up and running.

Listing 8-4. Menu's Makefile

```
CPPFLAGS= /AS /W3 /Zp /GA /GEs /G2

menu.exe:     menu.obj menu.def menu.res
  link /NOD /ONERROR:NOEXE menu, menu, NUL, safxcw libw
  slibcew,menu.def;
  rc /t menu.res
```

However, you might note that the only way to quit our program is with the system menu's Close item. We can fix that by adding an Exit item to our File menu, and doing so will also indicate how to add additional menu items to menus.

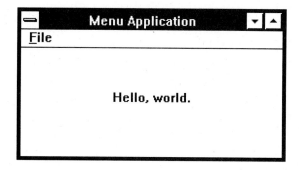

Figure 8-3. Our Menu Program at Work

Adding an Exit Menu Item to Our Example

The next step in developing our menu project is to add an Exit item like this:

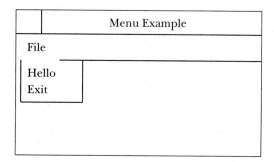

We can add another menu item in the resource file by defining a new constant, IDM_EXIT, which we can set to, say, 200, and by using it like this (note that we make the x in Exit the ALT key):

```
#include <windows.h>
#include <afxres.h>
#define IDM_HELLO 100
#define IDM_EXIT  200     ←

MainMenu MENU
{
  POPUP         "&File"
  {
```

```
        MENUITEM "&Hello", IDM_HELLO
        MENUITEM "E&xit", IDM_EXIT              ←
    }
  }
```

That's all we have to do here; however, you might have seen that in Windows menus, menu choices are frequently grouped according to function, and they're separated by a separator bar, as shown in Figure 8-4.

We can add a separator bar in our program between the Hello and Exit menu items with the special keyword SEPARATOR like this:

```
#include <windows.h>
#include <afxres.h>
#define IDM_HELLO 100
#define IDM_EXIT  200

MainMenu MENU
{
  POPUP        "&File"
  {
      MENUITEM "&Hello", IDM_HELLO
      MENUITEM SEPARATOR                    ←
      MENUITEM "E&xit", IDM_EXIT
  }
}
```

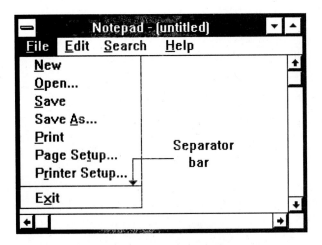

Figure 8-4. Menu Separator Bar

If you want a menu name to be flush right in the menu bar, such as the Help menu, place the characters "\a" before the menu's name in the resource file, like this: POPUP "\aHelp".

Now the new version of menu.rc is complete. All we have to do is to add the code to support our Exit item in menu.cpp. We do that by first defining the constant we'll see when the user selects Exit, IDM_EXIT:

```
#include <afxwin.h>
#define IDM_HELLO    100
#define IDM_EXIT     200  ←
        :
```

Next, we declare a new function to handle that item, which we can call OnExit( ):

```
#include <afxwin.h>
#define IDM_HELLO    100
#define IDM_EXIT     200

class CMainWindow : public CFrameWnd
{
public:
  CMainWindow();
  afx_msg void OnHello();
  afx_msg void OnExit();         ←

  DECLARE_MESSAGE_MAP()
};
```

Now we associate OnExit( ) with IDM_EXIT like this:

```
#include <afxwin.h>
#define IDM_HELLO    100
#define IDM_EXIT     200

class CMainWindow : public CFrameWnd
{
public:
  CMainWindow();
  afx_msg void OnHello();
  afx_msg void OnExit();

  DECLARE_MESSAGE_MAP()
};
```

```
CMainWindow::CMainWindow()
{
 Create(NULL, "Menu Application",
   WS_OVERLAPPEDWINDOW, rectDefault, NULL, "MainMenu");
}

void CMainWindow::OnHello()
{
 CString out_string = "Hello, world.";
 CClientDC dc(this);
 CRect rect;

 GetClientRect(rect);
 dc.SetTextAlign(TA_CENTER);
 dc.TextOut((rect.right / 2), (rect.bottom / 2), out_string,
       out_string.GetLength() );
}

BEGIN_MESSAGE_MAP( CMainWindow, CFrameWnd )
 ON_COMMAND(IDM_HELLO, OnHello)
 ON_COMMAND(IDM_EXIT, OnExit)                    ←
END_MESSAGE_MAP()
```

The final step is to write OnExit( ) itself. To do that, we use the CMainWindow member function DestroyWindow( ), which invokes the window's destructor and removes it from the screen:

```
#include <afxwin.h>
#define IDM_HELLO   100
#define IDM_EXIT    200

class CMainWindow : public CFrameWnd
{
public:
  CMainWindow();
  afx_msg void OnHello();
  afx_msg void OnExit();

  DECLARE_MESSAGE_MAP()
};

CMainWindow::CMainWindow()
{
 Create(NULL, "Menu Application",
   WS_OVERLAPPEDWINDOW, rectDefault, NULL, "MainMenu");
}
```

```
void CMainWindow::OnHello()
{
 CString out_string = "Hello, world.";
 CClientDC dc(this);
 CRect rect;

 GetClientRect(rect);
 dc.SetTextAlign(TA_CENTER);
 dc.TextOut((rect.right / 2), (rect.bottom / 2), out_string,
         out_string.GetLength() );
}

void CMainWindow::OnExit()
{
    DestroyWindow();
}

BEGIN_MESSAGE_MAP( CMainWindow, CFrameWnd )
 ON_COMMAND(IDM_HELLO, OnHello)
 ON_COMMAND(IDM_EXIT, OnExit)
END_MESSAGE_MAP()
```

And that's it for the new version of menu.cpp, which appears in Listing 8-5. The new resource file, menu.rc, appears in Listing 8-6. The files menu.def and the makefile are the same as before.

Listing 8-5. Menu.cpp with an Exit Item

```
#include <afxwin.h>
#define IDM_HELLO    100
#define IDM_EXIT     200

class CMainWindow : public CFrameWnd
{
public:
  CMainWindow();
  afx_msg void OnHello();
  afx_msg void OnExit();

  DECLARE_MESSAGE_MAP()
};

CMainWindow::CMainWindow()
{
 Create(NULL, "Menu Application",
   WS_OVERLAPPEDWINDOW, rectDefault, NULL, "MainMenu");
}
```

(continued)

Listing 8-5. *(continued)*

```
void CMainWindow::OnHello()
{
 CString out_string = "Hello, world.";
 CClientDC dc(this);
 CRect rect;

 GetClientRect(rect);
 dc.SetTextAlign(TA_CENTER);
 dc.TextOut((rect.right / 2), (rect.bottom / 2), out_string,
        out_string.GetLength() );
}

void CMainWindow::OnExit()
{
    DestroyWindow();
}

BEGIN_MESSAGE_MAP( CMainWindow, CFrameWnd )
 ON_COMMAND(IDM_HELLO, OnHello)
 ON_COMMAND(IDM_EXIT, OnExit)
END_MESSAGE_MAP()

class CTheApp : public CWinApp
{
public:
  BOOL InitInstance();
};

BOOL CTheApp::InitInstance()
{
 m_pMainWnd = new CMainWindow();
 m_pMainWnd->ShowWindow( m_nCmdShow );
 m_pMainWnd->UpdateWindow();

 return TRUE;
}

CTheApp theApp;
```

Listing 8-6. Menu.rc with Exit Item

```
#include <windows.h>
#include <afxres.h>
#define IDM_HELLO 100
```

Listing 8-6. *(continued)*

```
#define IDM_EXIT  200

MainMenu MENU
{
  POPUP         "&File"
  {
      MENUITEM "&Hello",  IDM_HELLO
      MENUITEM SEPARATOR
      MENUITEM "E&xit",   IDM_EXIT
  }
}
```

Running this new version of menu.exe gives us two menu items, Hello and Exit (separated with a separator bar), as shown in Figure 8-5. To leave the program, you only need to select the Exit item.

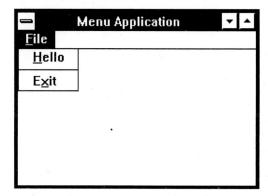

Figure 8-5. Our Menu Example with Exit Item

Adding Accelerator Keys to Menus

We've seen ALT keys already. These keys work in conjunction with the <Alt> key to open menus or to allow menu selections once the menu is open. In addition, some menu items have *menu accelerators* which function whether or not the menu is open. Such accelerator keys appear to the right of menu items, as shown in Figure 8-6. Here's a list of the allowed accelerators in Windows:

```
F1-F12
CTRL+A-Z
```

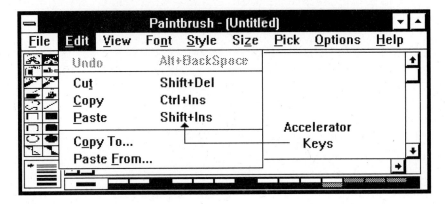

Figure 8-6. A Menu with Accelerator Keys

```
ALT+,SHIFT+,CTRL+F1-F12
ALT+,SHIFT+,CTRL+TAB
ALT+,SHIFT+,CTRL+HOME
ALT+,SHIFT+,CTRL+BACKSPACE
ALT+,SHIFT+,CTRL+END
ALT+,SHIFT+,CTRL+ESC
```

We can add such accelerators to our program. For example, let's say that we wanted to add the accelerator Ctrl+H to the Hello menu item and F10 to the Exit item like this:

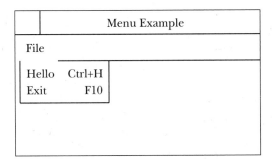

To do that, we have to make changes to menu.rc. We start by indicating what accelerators do what in the menu item descriptions like this:

```
#include <windows.h>
#include <afxres.h>
#define IDM_HELLO 100
#define IDM_EXIT  200
```

```
     MainMenu MENU
     {
       POPUP        "&File"
       {
→          MENUITEM "&Hello\tCtrl+H", IDM_HELLO
           MENUITEM SEPARATOR
→          MENUITEM "E&xit\tF10", IDM_EXIT
       }
     }
```

Adding \t here works as it does in C: as a format specifier meaning that a tab should be inserted. In this case, that means that our accelerator choices will appear on the right half of the menu, as they should. However, that does not make them active; all we've done is to print out Ctrl+H and F10 in our File menu. To make them active, we have to set up an *accelerator table*. We can call that table, say, MainAccelTable and we define it with the keyword ACCELER-ATORS like this:

```
     #include <windows.h>
     #include <afxres.h>
     #define IDM_HELLO 100
     #define IDM_EXIT  200

     MainMenu MENU
     {
       POPUP        "&File"
       {
           MENUITEM "&Hello\tCtrl+H", IDM_HELLO
           MENUITEM SEPARATOR
           MENUITEM "E&xit\tF10", IDM_EXIT
       }
     }


     MainAccelTable ACCELERATORS      ←
     {

     }
```

To create an accelerator table entry, we list the key or virtual key first, followed by the IDM constant we want to associate with that accelerator. If the key is a virtual key, we include the keyword VIRTKEY and also indicate what other controls keys will be down: SHIFT, ALT, or CONTROL. Table 8-1 shows some accelerator table examples.

Accelerator	*Acelerator Table Entry*
F2	VK_F2, IDM_ITEM1, VIRTKEY
ALT+F3	VK_F3, IDM_ITEM2, ALT, VIRTKEY
CTRL+X	"^X", IDM_ITEM3
SHIFT+F4	VK_F4, IDM_ITEM4, SHIFT, VIRTKEY
CTRL+F5	VK_F5, IDM_ITEM5, VIRTKEY, CONTROL
SHIFT+HOME	VK_HOME, IDM_ITEM6, SHIFT, VIRTKEY
SHIFT+END	VK_END, IDM_ITEM7, SHIFT, VIRTKEY
CONTROL+BACKSPACE	VK_BACK, IDM_ITEM8, VIRTKEY, CONTROL
SHIFT+DELETE	VK_DELETE, IDM_ITEM9, SHIFT, VIRTKEY

Table 8-1. Accelerator Table Examples

Note that we refer to virtual keys with the VK_ prefix, as defined in the last chapter (i.e., Table 7-1). In our example, we want to associate Ctrl+H with IDM_HELLO and F10 with IDM_EXIT, so that looks like this:

```
#include <windows.h>
#include <afxres.h>
#define IDM_HELLO 100
#define IDM_EXIT  200

MainMenu MENU
{
  POPUP        "&File"
  {
      MENUITEM "&Hello\tCtrl+H", IDM_HELLO
      MENUITEM SEPARATOR
      MENUITEM "E&xit\tF10", IDM_EXIT
  }
}

MainAccelTable ACCELERATORS
{
  "^H", IDM_HELLO                ←
  VK_F10, IDM_EXIT, VIRTKEY      ←
}
```

Our new version of the accelerator table is complete. To load it into our program, we only have to make one change to menu.cpp — we use the LoadAccelTable( ) function in CMainWindow( )'s constructor like this:

```
#include <afxwin.h>
#define IDM_HELLO    100
#define IDM_EXIT     200

class CMainWindow : public CFrameWnd
{
public:
  CMainWindow();
  afx_msg void OnHello();
  afx_msg void OnExit();

  DECLARE_MESSAGE_MAP()
};

CMainWindow::CMainWindow()
{
 LoadAccelTable("MainAccelTable");          ←
 Create(NULL, "Menu Application",
   WS_OVERLAPPEDWINDOW, rectDefault, NULL, "MainMenu");
}
```

You might wonder why we install the accelerator table here. It turns out that we have to modify the program's message loop if we want to use accelerator keys. The reason for this is that Windows messages are examined and translated by this loop before being dispatched to our window, and we have to change that translation process slightly when we add acclerators. For example, when the user press Ctrl+H, we should not pass that along as the keys <Ctrl> and H anymore. Instead, a WM_COMMAND message should be sent with the value IDM_HELLO, and the LoadAccelerator( ) function makes this kind of change to the message loop:

hello.cpp

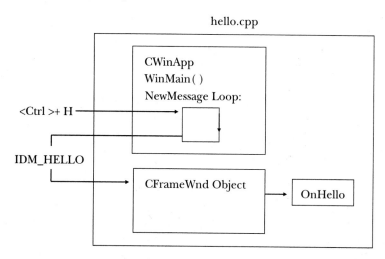

The new version of menu.cpp is in Listing 8-7, and the new version of **menu.rc** is in Listing 8-8.

Listing 8-7. Menu.cpp with Accelerator Keys

```cpp
#include <afxwin.h>
#define IDM_HELLO    100
#define IDM_EXIT     200

class CMainWindow : public CFrameWnd
{
public:
  CMainWindow();
  afx_msg void OnHello();
  afx_msg void OnExit();

  DECLARE_MESSAGE_MAP()
};

CMainWindow::CMainWindow()
{
 LoadAccelTable("MainAccelTable");
 Create(NULL, "Menu Application",
   WS_OVERLAPPEDWINDOW, rectDefault, NULL, "MainMenu");
}

void CMainWindow::OnHello()
{
 CString out_string = "Hello, world.";
 CClientDC dc(this);
 CRect rect;

 GetClientRect(rect);
 dc.SetTextAlign(TA_CENTER);
 dc.TextOut((rect.right / 2), (rect.bottom / 2), out_string,
        out_string.GetLength() );
}

void CMainWindow::OnExit()
{
    DestroyWindow();
}

BEGIN_MESSAGE_MAP( CMainWindow, CFrameWnd )
 ON_COMMAND(IDM_HELLO, OnHello)
 ON_COMMAND(IDM_EXIT, OnExit)
END_MESSAGE_MAP()
```

Listing 8-7. *(continued)*

```cpp
class CTheApp : public CWinApp
{
public:
  BOOL InitInstance();
};

BOOL CTheApp::InitInstance()
{
 m_pMainWnd = new CMainWindow();
 m_pMainWnd->ShowWindow( m_nCmdShow );
 m_pMainWnd->UpdateWindow();

 return TRUE;
}

CTheApp theApp;
```

Listing 8-8. Menu.rc

```cpp
#include <windows.h>
#include <afxres.h>
#define IDM_HELLO 100
#define IDM_EXIT  200

MainMenu MENU
{
  POPUP        "&File"
  {
      MENUITEM "&Hello\tCtrl+H", IDM_HELLO
      MENUITEM SEPARATOR
      MENUITEM "E&xit\tF10", IDM_EXIT
  }
}

MainAccelTable ACCELERATORS
{
  "^H", IDM_HELLO
  VK_F10, IDM_EXIT, VIRTKEY
}
```

Once you create the new menu.exe and run it, you'll see that the **File** menu now has acclerators in it, as shown in Figure 8-7.

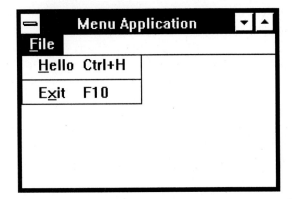

Figure 8-7. Our Menu Example with Accelerators

Graying Out Menu Items

After we print "Hello, world." in our window, not much else happens with our program. Selecting the Hello menu item results in the same display, so it appears that nothing has changed. In fact, we can disable Hello item to indicate that selecting it does nothing more. When you disable a menu item in Windows, it turns gray and the user can no longer select it.

As you might expect, we can gray menu items with the member functions of a menu object, but that raises a problem. How do we get a menu object in the first place? You may recall that we didn't create a menu object to load our main menu in; we simply defined it as "MainMenu" in our resource file:

```
MainMenu MENU    ←
{
  POPUP   "&File"
  {
        MENUITEM "&Hello\tCtrl+H", IDM_HELLO
        MENUITEM SEPARATOR
        MENUITEM "E&xit\tF10", IDM_EXIT
  }
}
```

And then loaded it in when we created our window:

```
CMainWindow::CMainWindow()
{
    Create(NULL, "Font Application",
      WS_OVERLAPPEDWINDOW, rectDefault, NULL, "MainMenu");    ←
}
```

It turns out that we can access a menu object with the CMainWindow member function GetMenu( ) (inherited from the CWnd class), and, using that object, we'll be able to gray our Hello menu item out in OnHello( ). GetMenu( ) will return a pointer to the window's menu object like this:

```
void CMainWindow::OnHello()
{
    CString out_string = "Hello, world.";
    CClientDC dc(this);
    CRect rect;

    GetClientRect(rect);
    dc.SetTextAlign(TA_CENTER);
    dc.TextOut((rect.right / 2), (rect.bottom / 2), out_string,
        out_string.GetLength() );
    CMenu* pMenu = GetMenu();
        :
}
CTheApp theApp;
```

Next, we can use the menu object's EnableMenuItem( ) member function, passing it the ID of the menu item we want to work with, and graying it out by passing the constant **MF_GRAYED**:

```
void CMainWindow::OnHello()
{
    CString out_string = "Hello, world.";
    CClientDC dc(this);
    CRect rect;

    GetClientRect(rect);
    dc.SetTextAlign(TA_CENTER);
    dc.TextOut((rect.right / 2), (rect.bottom / 2), out_string,
        out_string.GetLength() );
    CMenu* pMenu = GetMenu();
    pMenu->EnableMenuItem(IDM_HELLO, MF_GRAYED);
}
CTheApp theApp;
```

Here are the other MF (menu function) constants that we can OR together and use with EnableMenuItem():

MF_BYCOMMAND   We're indicating what menu item to work on by menu ID value (default)

MF_BYPOSITION	We're indicating what menu item to work on by passing the 0-based position of menu item
MF_DISABLED	Disables menu item so it cannot be selected but does not gray it
MF_ENABLED	Enables menu item
MF_GRAYED	Dims and disables menu item

Note that we can indicate what menu item we want to change either by menu ID value (the default, MF_BYCOMMAND) or by position (MF_BYPOSITION). If you select a menu item by position, the first item in a menu is item 0, the next is item 1, and so on. However, you might be surprised to learn that this code (where we use MF_BYPOSITION) grays the *File* item in the menu bar out, not Hello, the first item in that menu:

```
CMenu* pMenu = GetMenu();
pMenu->EnableMenuItem(0, MF_BYPOSITION | MF_GRAYED);
```

The reason for this is that pMenu is actually a pointer to the menu object for our whole menu system (i.e., for all menus that appear in the menu bar). When we refer to the first item in the menu system, that's File, not Hello:

	Menu Example	
File	Edit	
Hello	Ctrl+H	
Exit	F10	

The next menu (Edit above) is item 1 and so on. We didn't have to worry about this when we selected menu items with MF_BYCOMMAND (the default), because only one menu item in the whole menu system has the ID IDM_HELLO. Here, however, to indicate the menu item's correct position, we have to make an object out of the File popup menu before we can use pMenu->EnableMenuItem(0, MF_BYPOSITION | MF_GRAYED), and we can create that object with GetSubMenu( ). GetSubMenu(0) returns a pointer to the menu object which holds the first submenu, File:

```
      CMenu* pMenuBar = GetMenu();
  →   CMenu* pMenu = pMenuBar->GetSubMenu(0);
  →   pMenu->EnableMenuItem(0, MF_BYPOSITION | MF_GRAYED);
```

Now pMenu *is* a pointer to the File menu, and this code works as before, graying the first item in that menu (the Hello item). Note that to do it, we had to get two pointers to menu objects like this:

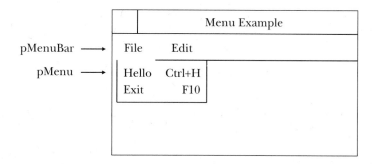

The result of our new program appears in Figure 8-8, where we've grayed the Hello item. We'll see more about GetSubMenu( ) soon, but first let's examine how to add check marks to our menus.

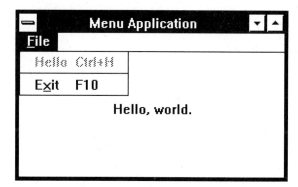

Figure 8-8. Graying Our Hello Menu Item

Adding Check Marks to Menu Items

Let's expand our menu example a little to include a second menu, a Font menu which will let us print out our message in an alternate font. When the alternate font is selected, we can mark it with a check mark. This will do two things: It will show us how to use check marks, and it will show us how to install more than one popup menu in our programs.

In fact, installing a second popup menu is very easy. As you might expect, we can do that inside the MainMenu block of our resource file like this (where we're defining a new constant, IDM_ALTERNATEFONT):

```
#include <windows.h>
#include <afxres.h>
#define IDM_HELLO 100
#define IDM_EXIT  200
#define IDM_ALTERNATEFONT 300    ←

MainMenu MENU
{
  POPUP  "&File"
  {
        MENUITEM "&Hello\tCtrl+H", IDM_HELLO
        MENUITEM SEPARATOR
        MENUITEM "E&xit\tF10", IDM_EXIT
  }
  POPUP  "F&ont"
  {
        MENUITEM "&Alternate Font\tCtrl+A", IDM_ALTERNATEFONT
  }
}

MainAccelTable ACCELERATORS
{
    "^H", IDM_HELLO
    VK_F10, IDM_EXIT, VIRTKEY
    "^A", IDM_ALTERNATEFONT
}
```

You might also note that we gave the Alternate Font menu item an accelerator key of Ctrl+A. Now we have to support this new menu in code. We do that by adding a new message-handling function, OnAlternateFont( ) like this:

```
#include <afxwin.h>
#define IDM_HELLO          100
#define IDM_EXIT           200
#define IDM_ALTERNATEFONT  300           ←

class CMainWindow : public CFrameWnd
```

```
  {
public:
  CMainWindow();
  afx_msg void OnHello();
  afx_msg void OnExit();
  afx_msg void OnAlternateFont();          ←

  DECLARE_MESSAGE_MAP()
};
  :
```

Now we can start writing OnAlternateFont( ). We do that by clearing the window by issuing a call to UpdateWindow( ) (which sends our program a WM_PAINT message):

```
void CMainWindow::OnAlternateFont()
{
    UpdateWindow();          //Clear window
              :
}
```

Next, we simply want to print out the usual "Hello, world." message, after switching to an alternate font. It turns out that fonts are associated with device context objects, and we'll be able to use the device context member function SelectStockObject( ) here. The Object in SelectStockObject( ) has nothing to do with C++ objects; this function allows us to install several stock Windows "objects" in our device context, and the objects available appear in Table 8-2. Here we'll use the alternate font, SYSTEM_FIXED_FONT, which is a fixed width font.

We can make SYSTEM_FIXED_FONT the font for our device context like this:

```
    void CMainWindow::OnAlternateFont()
    {
→       CClientDC dc(this);

        UpdateWindow();          //Clear window
→       dc.SelectStockObject(SYSTEM_FIXED_FONT);
                  :
    }
```

Now we print out "Hello, world." in that font using code that we've used before:

Stock Object	Means
BLACK_BRUSH	Black brush
DKGRAY_BRUSH	Dark gray brush
GRAY_BRUSH	Gray brush
HOLLOW_BRUSH	Hollow brush
LTGRAY_BRUSH	Light gray brush
NULL_BRUSH	Null brush
WHITE_BRUSH	White brush
BLACK_PEN	Black pen
NULL_PEN	Null pen
WHITE_PEN	White pen
ANSI_FIXED_FONT	ANSI fixed system font
ANSI_VAR_FONT	ANSI variable system font
DEVICE_DEFAULT_FONT	Device-dependent font
OEM_FIXED_FONT	OEM-dependent fixed font
SYSTEM_FONT	The default system font
SYSTEM_FIXED_FONT	Fixed-width system font
DEFAULT_PALETTE	Default color palette

Table 8-2. Windows Stock Objects

```
void CMainWindow::OnAlternateFont()
{
    CString out_string = "Hello, world.";
    CClientDC dc(this);
    CRect rect;

    UpdateWindow();          //Clear window
    dc.SelectStockObject(SYSTEM_FIXED_FONT);
    GetClientRect(rect);
    dc.SetTextAlign(TA_CENTER);
    dc.TextOut((rect.right / 2), (rect.bottom / 2), out_string,
            out_string.GetLength());
              :
}
```

Finally, we want to indicate that we're using the alternate font by adding a check mark in front of the Alternate Font menu item. We can do that with the menu object CheckMenuItem( ) function. That function takes these values:

MF_BYCOMMAND	We're indicating what menu item to work on by menu ID value (default)
MF_BYPOSITION	We're indicating what menu item to work on by passing the 0-based position of menu item
MF_CHECKED	Check the menu item
MF_UNCHECKED	Remove check mark

All we need to do is to create a menu object and use CheckMenuItem( ) like this (since the ID IDM_ALTERNATEFONT is unique among our menu items, we can use it to indicate which menu item we want to check):

```
void CMainWindow::OnAlternateFont()
{
    CString out_string = "Hello, world.";
    CClientDC dc(this);
    CRect rect;

    UpdateWindow();         //Clear window
    dc.SelectStockObject(SYSTEM_FIXED_FONT);
    GetClientRect(rect);
    dc.SetTextAlign(TA_CENTER);
    dc.TextOut((rect.right / 2), (rect.bottom / 2), out_string,
            out_string.GetLength() );
    CMenu* pMenu = GetMenu();
    pMenu->CheckMenuItem(IDM_ALTERNATEFONT, MF_CHECKED);
}
```

Here's the whole C++ program, including OnAlternateFont( ), which is connected to the **IDM_ALTERNATEFONT** message with the **BEGIN_MESSAGE_MAP** macro like this:

```
#include <afxwin.h>
#define IDM_HELLO           100
#define IDM_EXIT            200
#define IDM_ALTERNATEFONT   300

class CMainWindow : public CFrameWnd
{
public:
  CMainWindow();
  afx_msg void OnHello();
  afx_msg void OnExit();
  afx_msg void OnAlternateFont();
```

```
  DECLARE_MESSAGE_MAP()
};

CMainWindow::CMainWindow()
{
 LoadAccelTable("MainAccelTable");
 Create(NULL, "Font Application",
   WS_OVERLAPPEDWINDOW, rectDefault, NULL, "MainMenu");
}

void CMainWindow::OnHello()
{
 CString out_string = "Hello, world.";
 CClientDC dc(this);
 CRect rect;

 GetClientRect(rect);
 dc.SetTextAlign(TA_CENTER);
 dc.TextOut((rect.right / 2), (rect.bottom / 2), out_string,
        out_string.GetLength() );
}

void CMainWindow::OnExit()
{
    DestroyWindow();
}

void CMainWindow::OnAlternateFont()
{
 CString out_string = "Hello, world.";
 CClientDC dc(this);
 CRect rect;

 UpdateWindow();          //Clear window
 dc.SelectStockObject(SYSTEM_FIXED_FONT);
 GetClientRect(rect);
 dc.SetTextAlign(TA_CENTER);
 dc.TextOut((rect.right / 2), (rect.bottom / 2), out_string,
        out_string.GetLength() );
 CMenu* pMenu = GetMenu();
 pMenu->CheckMenuItem(IDM_ALTERNATEFONT, MF_CHECKED);
}

BEGIN_MESSAGE_MAP( CMainWindow, CFrameWnd )
 ON_COMMAND(IDM_HELLO, OnHello)
 ON_COMMAND(IDM_EXIT, OnExit)
 ON_COMMAND(IDM_ALTERNATEFONT, OnAlternateFont)          ←
END_MESSAGE_MAP()
```

```
class CTheApp : public CWinApp
{
public:
  BOOL InitInstance();
};

BOOL CTheApp::InitInstance()
{
 m_pMainWnd = new CMainWindow();
 m_pMainWnd->ShowWindow( m_nCmdShow );
 m_pMainWnd->UpdateWindow();

 return TRUE;
}


CTheApp theApp;
```

That's it; now we can use this C++ file together with the resource file we created earlier:

```
#include <windows.h>
#include <afxres.h>
#define IDM_HELLO 100
#define IDM_EXIT  200
#define IDM_ALTERNATEFONT 300

MainMenu MENU
{
  POPUP   "&File"
  {
        MENUITEM "&Hello\tCtrl+H", IDM_HELLO
        MENUITEM SEPARATOR
        MENUITEM "E&xit\tF10", IDM_EXIT
  }
  POPUP   "F&ont"
  {
        MENUITEM "&Alternate Font\tCtrl+A", IDM_ALTERNATEFONT
  }
}

MainAccelTable ACCELERATORS
{
    "^H", IDM_HELLO
    VK_F10, IDM_EXIT, VIRTKEY
    "^A", IDM_ALTERNATEFONT
}
```

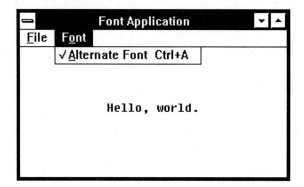

Figure 8-9. Our Menu Example with Two Menus

The new menu program has two menus in the menu bar, as shown in Figure 8-9. When you select the Alternate Font item, it will be checked, as shown in that figure. The program is a success — now we can handle check marks and multiple menus.

There's still more that we can do with menus. For example, we can add menu items to menus on the fly, as the program runs. Let's look into that by building a small database program that will allow us to keep track of phone numbers.

Adding Menu Items at Run-Time

As an example program showing how to add menu items at run-time, we might write a small phone book application. This example will also show us how to erase characters in a window. (Since we're mostly concerned with menus in this chapter, this program will not be a polished application, but it will serve us well as an example.) We can enter a person's name simply by typing it and watching it appear in our window as before:

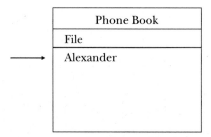

Then we could type a few spaces and type the person's phone number, like this:

```
┌──────────────────────────────┐
│         Phone Book           │
├──────────────────────────────┤
│ File                         │
├──────────────────────────────┤
│ Alexander   298-5595         │
│                              │
│                              │
│                              │
│                              │
└──────────────────────────────┘
```

To add this name to our phone book data base, we might have an Add Name menu item:

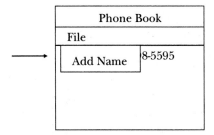

When selected, this item adds, say, the first 10 characters of what we've typed (here, that would be "Alexander" plus one space) to the file menu and clears the main window:

```
┌──────────────────────────────┐
│         Phone Book           │
├──────────────────────────────┤
│ File                         │
│ ┌────────────────┐           │
│ │ Add Name       │           │
│ │ Alexander      │           │
│ └────────────────┘           │
│                              │
└──────────────────────────────┘
```

We could then repeat the process, adding more names to the File menu like this:

```
┌──────────────────────────────┐
│         Phone Book           │
├──────────────────────────────┤
│ File                         │
│ ┌────────────────┐           │
│ │ Add Name       │           │
│ │ Alexander      │           │
│ │ George         │           │
│ │ Sam            │           │
│ └────────────────┘           │
```

If we then chose a name to look up from the menu, the corresponding name and number should appear on the screen:

Phone Book
File
Alexander   298-5595

To do this, we'll only need one menu item in our resource file — Add Name, with the menu ID value IDM_ADDNAME:

```
#include <windows.h>
#include <afxres.h>
#define IDM_ADDNAME 100                        ←

MainMenu MENU
{
  POPUP         "&File"
  {
      MENUITEM "Add Name", IDM_ADDNAME    ←
  }
}
```

We'll add the other menu items ourselves at run-time. Let's get started with the phone book's C++ file, which we can call, say, pbook.cpp. We start with our character handling routine, which we'll need to handle the input typed by the user:

```
#include <afxwin.h>
#define IDM_ADDNAME    100

class CMainWindow : public CFrameWnd
{
public:
    CMainWindow();
    afx_msg void OnChar(UINT wChar, UINT nRepCnt, UINT wFlags);

    DECLARE_MESSAGE_MAP()
};
```

```
CMainWindow::CMainWindow()
{
    nameindex = 0;
    Create(NULL, "Menu Application",
        WS_OVERLAPPEDWINDOW, rectDefault, NULL, "MainMenu");
}


void CMainWindow::OnChar(UINT wChar, UINT nRepCnt, UINT wFlags)    ←
{

}
```

All we really have to do here is to store the characters typed (so we can restore them to the screen when asked) and display them. To do that, we can declare a handy CString object named, say, out_string (note that we make it private):

```
#include <afxwin.h>
#define IDM_ADDNAME    100

class CMainWindow : public CFrameWnd
{
private:
    CString out_string;
public:
    CMainWindow();
    afx_msg void OnChar(UINT wChar, UINT nRepCnt, UINT wFlags);

    DECLARE_MESSAGE_MAP()
};

CMainWindow::CMainWindow()
{
    nameindex = 0;
    Create(NULL, "Menu Application",
        WS_OVERLAPPEDWINDOW, rectDefault, NULL, "MainMenu");
}

void CMainWindow::OnChar(UINT wChar, UINT nRepCnt, UINT wFlags)
{

}
```

→ (CString out_string; line marked)

Now we just accept characters, add them to out_string, and display out_string as we have before, starting at (0, 0):

```
#include <afxwin.h>
#define IDM_ADDNAME    100

class CMainWindow : public CFrameWnd
{
private:
    int nameindex;
    CString out_string;
    CString Names[10];
public:
    CMainWindow();
    afx_msg void OnChar(UINT wChar, UINT nRepCnt, UINT wFlags);

    DECLARE_MESSAGE_MAP()
};

CMainWindow::CMainWindow()
{
    nameindex = 0;
    Create(NULL, "Menu Application",
        WS_OVERLAPPEDWINDOW, rectDefault, NULL, "MainMenu");
}

void CMainWindow::OnChar(UINT wChar, UINT nRepCnt, UINT wFlags)
{
    CClientDC dc(this);
    CString in_char = wChar;

    out_string += in_char;
    dc.TextOut(0, 0, out_string, out_string.GetLength());
}
```

And that's it for character input. The more important part of our program occurs when we receive menu input, specifically, when the user selects the Add Name menu item. In that case, we want to add the first ten characters of the string on the screen (i.e., the first ten characters of out_string) to the File menu. And we can get the first ten characters of out_string, like this: out_string.Left(10).

TIP   Besides using out_string.Left( ) to get characters from the left side of the CString object out_string, we can also get characters from the right side of out_string with out_string.Right( ) and characters from the middle with out_string.Mid( ).

You might think that to handle the Add Name menu item, we should put together a CMainWindow member function named OnAddname( ) like this:

```
class CMainWindow : public CFrameWnd
{
private:
    int nameindex;
    CString out_string;
public:
    CMainWindow();
    afx_msg void OnChar(UINT wChar, UINT nRepCnt, UINT wFlags);
    afx_msg void OnAddname();          ←
```

Then we would connect it to the Add Name menu item like this:

```
BEGIN_MESSAGE_MAP( CMainWindow, CFrameWnd )
 ON_COMMAND(IDM_ADDNAME, OnAddName)    ←
END_MESSAGE_MAP()
```

This is fine as far as it goes, however, we run into a problem when we want to handle the other menu items (i.e., the ones we add at run time). For example, say the first name we add to our File list is Alexander:

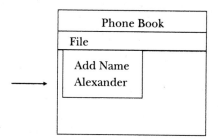

At run time, it's clear that we can't suddenly add a function to our code named, say, OnAlexander( ), which handles the constant **IDM_ALEXANDER**. The code that handles all menu items has to be in place at compile time. One way to handle this is to create as many functions as we have space in our menu for names. That might look something like this, where we're preparing to handle up to 10 names, Name0 - Name9:

```
class CMainWindow : public CFrameWnd
{
private:
    int nameindex;
    CString out_string;
```

```
public:
    CMainWindow();
    afx_msg void OnChar(UINT wChar, UINT nRepCnt, UINT wFlags);
    afx_msg void OnAddname();            ←
    afx_msg void OnName0();              ←
    afx_msg void OnName1();              ←
    afx_msg void OnName2();              ←
    afx_msg void OnName3();              ←
    afx_msg void OnName4();              ←
    afx_msg void OnName5();              ←
    afx_msg void OnName6();              ←
    afx_msg void OnName7();              ←
    afx_msg void OnName8();              ←
    afx_msg void OnName9();              ←
```

And we could connect them to their various menu ID messages like this:

```
BEGIN_MESSAGE_MAP( CMainWindow, CFrameWnd )
  ON_COMMAND(IDM_ADDNAME, OnAddName)
  ON_COMMAND(IDM_NAME0, OnName0)        ←
  ON_COMMAND(IDM_NAME1, OnName1)        ←
  ON_COMMAND(IDM_NAME2, OnName2)        ←
  ON_COMMAND(IDM_NAME3, OnName3)        ←
  ON_COMMAND(IDM_NAME4, OnName4)        ←
  ON_COMMAND(IDM_NAME5, OnName5)        ←
  ON_COMMAND(IDM_NAME6, OnName6)        ←
  ON_COMMAND(IDM_NAME7, OnName7)        ←
  ON_COMMAND(IDM_NAME8, OnName8)        ←
  ON_COMMAND(IDM_NAME9, OnName9)        ←
END_MESSAGE_MAP()
```

Next, we'd have to write each of these functions. Although it's possible to write the program this way, there is an easier method. We can override the function that handles menu messages.

That function, OnCommand( ), is a member function of CMainWindow (actually, it's an inherited member from CWnd through CFrameWnd). When we get a menu message, that's the function that is called. If we use the ON_COMMAND( ) macro in the message map, as we have done before, then we're actually adding code to the OnCommand( ) function. For example, this macro:

```
BEGIN_MESSAGE_MAP( CMainWindow, CFrameWnd )
  ON_COMMAND(IDM_HELLO, OnHello)        ←
END_MESSAGE_MAP()
```

adds code to OnCommand( ) so that it calls OnHello( ) when we see a IDM_HELLO message. Simplistically, OnCommand( ) will look something like this (the Windows parameter wParam holds the menu item's ID number):

```
BOOL OnCommand(UINT wParam, LONG lParam);
{
    if(wParam == IDM_HELLO){
        OnHello()
        return TRUE;   //Return TRUE if we handle message
    }
    return FALSE;       //Return FALSE if we don't handle message
}
```

So far we've let the macro **ON_COMMAND** deal with the OnCommand( ) function in our programs, but it's a virtual function which Microsoft designed to be overridden in cases exactly like the one we face — calling the right code for menu items that don't even exist yet. To see why, note the two parameters passed to OnCommand( ), wParam and lParam. We saw these two parameters briefly in Chapter 6, and they're very well known to Windows programmers that use C. These two parameters are the usual ones that accompany Windows messages. In this case, the word-long parameter wParam will hold the menu item's ID, which could be, say, 0 for the first name we add to our File menu, 1 for the next, and so on. The long parameter lParam holds information about the menu message we're getting:

```
lParam          lParam
hi word         lo word         Command is from a
───────         ───────         ─────────────────
   0               0            menu
   1               0            accelerator key
```

Since the menu item's ID is passed to us in wParam, we know which string the user wants us to display, as indexed by wParam. For example, let's set up an array of CStrings named, say, Names[ ]. When we add a name to the File menu, we can set its ID value equal to its place in the array Names[ ]:

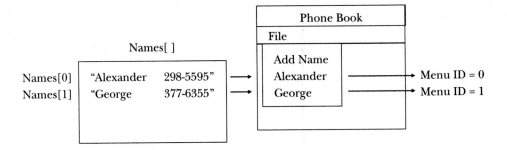

Then, when we get a menu message asking us to display a name, we know that the user wants Names[wParam]. When we override OnCommand( ), we can print out Names[wParam] on the spot, allowing us to handle all menu items in that function. In other words, since we have indexed the names — and that index is passed to us in OnCommand( ) — we don't have to call separate functions for each menu item. This is how the process of handling menu items added at run time usually works, by overriding OnCommand( ) and handling them there.

NOTE   Handling menu items or other Windows controls like buttons by giving them an index like this is sometimes called setting up a control array.

Let's write that function, OnCommand( ), now. Since we're going to override it from the base class CWnd, we have to place its prototype (from afxwin.h) in our class declaration like this:

```
#include <afxwin.h>
#define IDM_ADDNAME    100

class CMainWindow : public CFrameWnd
{
private:
    int nameindex;
    CString out_string;
    CString Names[10];
public:
    CMainWindow();
    afx_msg void OnChar(UINT wChar, UINT nRepCnt, UINT wFlags);
    BOOL OnCommand(UINT wParam, LONG lParam);

    DECLARE_MESSAGE_MAP()
};
```

Note that we return a value of type BOOL; this return value is TRUE if we've handled the menu message and FALSE otherwise. In this example, we'll only receive messages from our File menu, so we'll return TRUE (since we'll be able to handle all File menu messages here):

```
BOOL CMainWindow::OnCommand(UINT wParam, LONG lParam)
{
            :
        return TRUE;
}
```

Now we've got to check what message we received. If it's IDM_ADDNAME, then we should add the current name (i.e., out_string.Left(10)) to the File menu. We can check that by checking wParam:

```
BOOL CMainWindow::OnCommand(UINT wParam, LONG lParam)
{

    if(wParam == IDM_ADDNAME){

    }
    else{

    }
        return TRUE;
}
```

TIP In this case, we're handling all the menu messages in OnCommand( ). However, in a larger program, you might still want to use separate functions OnSaveFile( ), OnExit( ), OnHelp( ), and so on. In that case, you can either call them yourself from OnCommand( ), or you can handle only certain menu messages in OnCommand( ) (i.e., members of a control array) and then call the base function CFrameWnd::OnCommand( ) to handle the others. If you do, you should use the BEGIN_MESSAGE_MAP( ) and END_MESSAGE_MAP( ) macros as usual to connect the functions OnSaveFile( ), OnExit( ), OnHelp( ) and so on to their associated messages.

If we are being asked to add the current name to the File menu, the first step is to erase the text from the screen in preparation for other names. We can erase characters in a window in a number of ways: by erasing the window, by drawing over the characters with a borderless rectangle that is the same color as the window's background color, or by printing over them in the background color. Let's use the third method here. First, we get a device context object, then we set its printing color to the window's background color with the GetBkColor( ) and SetTextColor( ) functions. In Windows, a color is stored as a DWORD value. SetTextColor( ) returns the old text color, and we save that since we'll have to restore it soon:

```
BOOL CMainWindow::OnCommand(UINT wParam, LONG lParam)
{
    DWORD crOldTextColor;

    if(wParam == IDM_ADDNAME){
→       CClientDC dc(this);
→       crOldTextColor = dc.SetTextColor(dc.GetBkColor());
            :
    }
    else{

    }
        return TRUE;
}
```

Next, we erase out_string from the window simply by printing over it in the background color, and then we restore the text drawing color that the window originally had:

```
BOOL CMainWindow::OnCommand(UINT wParam, LONG lParam)
{
    DWORD crOldTextColor;

    if(wParam == IDM_ADDNAME){
        CClientDC dc(this);
        crOldTextColor = dc.SetTextColor(dc.GetBkColor());
→       dc.TextOut(0, 0, out_string, out_string.GetLength());
→       dc.SetTextColor(crOldTextColor);
            :
    }
    else{

    }
        return TRUE;
}
```

Now we can append out_string.Left(10) to the File menu. First, we need to get a pointer to that menu object. Since it's a submenu (i.e., a popup menu, not an item in the menubar), we have to do that as before, with GetSubMenu( ):

```
BOOL CMainWindow::OnCommand(UINT wParam, LONG lParam)
{
    DWORD crOldTextColor;

    if(wParam == IDM_ADDNAME){
        CClientDC dc(this);
        crOldTextColor = dc.SetTextColor(dc.GetBkColor());
        dc.TextOut(0, 0, out_string, out_string.GetLength());
        dc.SetTextColor(crOldTextColor);
        CMenu* pMenuBar = GetMenu();
        CMenu* pMenu = pMenuBar->GetSubMenu(0);
            :
    }
    else{

    }
        return TRUE;
}
```

We can use the CMenu member function AppendMenu( ) to append out_string.Left(10) to the File menu. This CMenu member function takes three parameters. The first is a constant indicating what kind of menu item we're adding, as shown in Table 8-3, and we'll use MF_STRING, indicating

MF Value	*Means*
MF_CHECKED	Place check mark next to item
MF_DISABLED	Disables menu item
MF_ENABLED	Enables menu item
MF_GRAYED	Disables menu item and dims it
MF_MENUBARBREAK	Places item on new column in pop-up menus
MF_MENUBREAK	Places item on new column in pop-up menus
MF_OWNERDRAW	Item is an owner-draw item like a bitmap
MF_POPUP	New menu item has pop-up menu associated with it
MF_SEPARATOR	Draws separator bar
MF_STRING	Menu item is a string
MF_UNCHECKED	Remove check next to item

Table 8-3. AppendMenu( ) Values

that the item we're adding is a string. The second parameter is the menu ID value, and the third item is a long pointer to the new menu item itself.

To specify the new menu item's ID value, we'll have to know how many items we've added already. That is, the first item can have an ID value of 0:

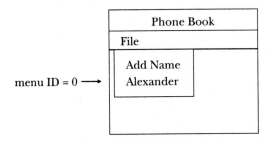

The next can have ID value 1:

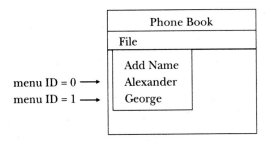

We can keep track of the current name's index with a private data member called, say, nameindex:

```
#include <afxwin.h>
#define IDM_ADDNAME    100

class CMainWindow : public CFrameWnd
{
private:
    int nameindex;                      ←
    CString out_string;
public:
    CMainWindow();
    afx_msg void OnChar(UINT wChar, UINT nRepCnt, UINT wFlags);
    BOOL OnCommand(UINT wParam, LONG lParam);

    DECLARE_MESSAGE_MAP()
};
```

This variable will start at 0 and we can increment it every time we add a name to the File menu. In other words, we can append the current name to the File menu like this:

```
BOOL CMainWindow::OnCommand(UINT wParam, LONG lParam)
{
    DWORD crOldTextColor;

    if(wParam == IDM_ADDNAME){
        CClientDC dc(this);
        crOldTextColor = dc.SetTextColor(dc.GetBkColor());
        dc.TextOut(0, 0, out_string, out_string.GetLength());
        dc.SetTextColor(crOldTextColor);
        CMenu* pMenuBar = GetMenu();
        CMenu* pMenu = pMenuBar->GetSubMenu(0);
→       pMenu->AppendMenu(MF_STRING, nameindex, out_string.Left(10));
→       DrawMenuBar();
            :
    }
    else{

    }
        return TRUE;
}
```

TIP You can add a whole new menu to the menubar if you use pMenuBar ->AppendMenu( ) instead of pMenu->AppendMenu( ).

Note that we call the function DrawMenuBar( ) after appending the name to the File menu. This is the recommended procedure after all changes to the menu system in Windows. The last thing to do here is to store the name and phone number in our array called Names[ ], to update nameindex for the next time, and, now that this name has been added to the menu, to reset out_string to an empty string (using the CString Empty( ) member function):

```
BOOL CMainWindow::OnCommand(UINT wParam, LONG lParam)
{
    DWORD crOldTextColor;

    if(wParam == IDM_ADDNAME){
        CClientDC dc(this);
        crOldTextColor = dc.SetTextColor(dc.GetBkColor());
        dc.TextOut(0, 0, out_string, out_string.GetLength());
```

```
        dc.SetTextColor(crOldTextColor);
        CMenu* pMenuBar = GetMenu();
        CMenu* pMenu = pMenuBar->GetSubMenu(0);
        pMenu->AppendMenu(MF_STRING, nameindex, out_string.Left(10));
        DrawMenuBar();
→       Names[nameindex] = out_string;
→       nameindex++;
→       out_string.Empty();
    }
    else{

    }
        return TRUE;
}
```

Now the only case that remains is when we're being asked to display a name from the File menu. Here, the menu item's ID number will be 0 for the first item, 1 for the next, and so on:

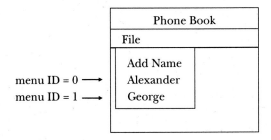

Our first step is to erase what's on the screen now in preparation for restoring an old name and number, and we do that by setting the text color to the window's background color and reprinting the text in that color, erasing what was on the screen:

```
BOOL CMainWindow::OnCommand(UINT wParam, LONG lParam)
{
    DWORD crOldTextColor;

    if(wParam == IDM_ADDNAME){
        CClientDC dc(this);
        crOldTextColor = dc.SetTextColor(dc.GetBkColor());
        dc.TextOut(0, 0, out_string, out_string.GetLength());
        dc.SetTextColor(crOldTextColor);
        CMenu* pMenuBar = GetMenu();
        CMenu* pMenu = pMenuBar->GetSubMenu(0);
        pMenu->AppendMenu(MF_STRING, nameindex, out_string.Left(10));
        DrawMenuBar();
```

```
            Names[nameindex] = out_string;
            nameindex++;
            out_string.Empty();
        }
        else{
            CClientDC dc(this);

→           crOldTextColor = dc.SetTextColor(dc.GetBkColor());
→           dc.TextOut(0, 0, out_string, out_string.GetLength());
→           dc.SetTextColor(crOldTextColor);
                     :
        }
            return TRUE;
    }
```

The index of the name we're being asked to restore is the same as its menu ID, which is passed to us in wParam, so all we have to do is to place Names[wParam] on the screen like this:

```
BOOL CMainWindow::OnCommand(UINT wParam, LONG lParam)
{
    DWORD crOldTextColor;

    if(wParam == IDM_ADDNAME){
        CClientDC dc(this);
        crOldTextColor = dc.SetTextColor(dc.GetBkColor());
        dc.TextOut(0, 0, out_string, out_string.GetLength());
        dc.SetTextColor(crOldTextColor);
        CMenu* pMenuBar = GetMenu();
        CMenu* pMenu = pMenuBar->GetSubMenu(0);
        pMenu->AppendMenu(MF_STRING, nameindex, out_string.Left(10));
        DrawMenuBar();
        Names[nameindex] = out_string;
        nameindex++;
        out_string.Empty();
    }
    else{
        CClientDC dc(this);

        crOldTextColor = dc.SetTextColor(dc.GetBkColor());
        dc.TextOut(0, 0, out_string, out_string.GetLength());
        dc.SetTextColor(crOldTextColor);
→       out_string = Names[wParam];
→       dc.TextOut(0, 0, out_string, out_string.GetLength());
    }
        return TRUE;
}
```

And that's it; the whole program, pbook.cpp, appears in Listing 8-9, pbook.rc appears in Listing 8-10, pbook.def appears in Listing 8-11, and the associated makefile in Listing 8-12.

Listing 8-9. Pbook.cpp

```cpp
#include <afxwin.h>
#define IDM_ADDNAME    100

class CMainWindow : public CFrameWnd
{
private:
    int nameindex;
    CString out_string;
    CString Names[10];
public:
    CMainWindow();
    afx_msg void OnChar(UINT wChar, UINT nRepCnt, UINT wFlags);
    BOOL OnCommand(UINT wParam, LONG lParam);

    DECLARE_MESSAGE_MAP()
};

CMainWindow::CMainWindow()
{
    nameindex = 0;
    Create(NULL, "Menu Application",
        WS_OVERLAPPEDWINDOW, rectDefault, NULL, "MainMenu");
}

BOOL CMainWindow::OnCommand(UINT wParam, LONG lParam)
{
    DWORD crOldTextColor;

    if(wParam == IDM_ADDNAME){
        CClientDC dc(this);
        crOldTextColor = dc.SetTextColor(dc.GetBkColor());
        dc.TextOut(0, 0, out_string, out_string.GetLength());
        dc.SetTextColor(crOldTextColor);
        CMenu* pMenuBar = GetMenu();
        CMenu* pMenu = pMenuBar->GetSubMenu(0);
        pMenu->AppendMenu(MF_STRING, nameindex, out_string.Left(10));
        DrawMenuBar();
        Names[nameindex] = out_string;
        nameindex++;
```

Listing 8-9. *(continued)*

```cpp
            out_string.Empty();
        }
    else{
        CClientDC dc(this);

        crOldTextColor = dc.SetTextColor(dc.GetBkColor());
        dc.TextOut(0, 0, out_string, out_string.GetLength());
        dc.SetTextColor(crOldTextColor);
        out_string = Names[wParam];
        dc.TextOut(0, 0, out_string, out_string.GetLength());
    }

        return TRUE;
}


void CMainWindow::OnChar(UINT wChar, UINT nRepCnt, UINT wFlags)
{
    CClientDC dc(this);
    CString in_char = wChar;

    out_string += in_char;
    dc.TextOut(0, 0, out_string, out_string.GetLength());
}


BEGIN_MESSAGE_MAP(CMainWindow, CFrameWnd)
    ON_WM_CHAR()
END_MESSAGE_MAP()

class CTheApp : public CWinApp
{
public:
    BOOL InitInstance();
};

BOOL CTheApp::InitInstance()
{
 m_pMainWnd = new CMainWindow();
 m_pMainWnd->ShowWindow( m_nCmdShow );
 m_pMainWnd->UpdateWindow();

 return TRUE;
}

CTheApp theApp;
```

Listing 8-10. Pbook.rc

```
#include <windows.h>
#include <afxres.h>
#define IDM_ADDNAME 100

MainMenu MENU
{
  POPUP       "&File"
  {
      MENUITEM "Add Name", IDM_ADDNAME
  }
}
```

Listing 8-11. Pbook.def

```
NAME          Menu
DESCRIPTION   'Menu Example'

EXETYPE       WINDOWS
STUB          'WINSTUB.EXE'

CODE          PRELOAD MOVEABLE DISCARDABLE
DATA          PRELOAD MOVEABLE MULTIPLE

HEAPSIZE      1024
STACKSIZE     4096
```

Listing 8-12. Pbook's Makefile

```
CPPFLAGS= /AS /W3 /Zp /GA /GEs /G2

pbook.exe:    pbook.obj pbook.def pbook.res
  link /NOD /ONERROR:NOEXE pbook, pbook, NUL, safxcw libw
  slibcew,pbook.def;
  rc /t pbook.res
```

When you run the result of all this, pbook.exe, you can type a name and it will appear in the main window, as shown in Figure 8-10. When you select the Add

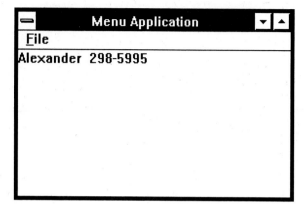

Figure 8-10. Our Phone Book Example

Name item in the File menu, you add (the first 10 characters of) that name to the menu. Adding name after name, you can fill the File menu, as shown in Figure 8-11. Then, when you select a name in that menu, that name and phone number will be displayed as shown in Figure 8-12. Our program is a success. Now we can modify our menus at run time by adding items to them.

That completes our survey of menus. As you can see, there is a great deal of utility here. We've created menus, grayed and disabled menu items, added check marks, accelerator keys, and Alt keys, and finally tailored our menus

Figure 8-11. Adding Menu Items at Run-Time

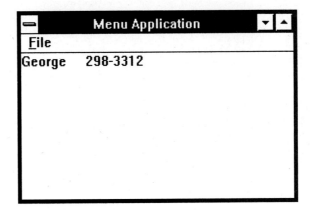

Figure 8-12. A Retrieved Name and Phone Number

directly at run-time. All this makes for a very powerful package. Of course, there's a great deal more to Windows; for example, now that we have menus under our belts, we can press on to the next chapter about dialog boxes.

CHAPTER 9

Dialog Boxes

We've all seen dialog boxes; in Windows, they represent the standard way of receiving control input from the user beyond the menu level. The Windows user uses dialog boxes to open files, rename files, customize windows or application parameters, select colors, or almost anything that a simple menu selection can't specify. Dialog boxes are so common that the user already knows that menu items with an ellipsis (three dots) after them, like Save As..., open dialog boxes.

In this chapter, we'll start putting together dialog boxes of our own, and we'll start seeing the kind of objects that the user can manipulate in dialog boxes, specifically, buttons and text boxes. These types of objects are called controls in Windows (controls include: Buttons, text boxes — which are also called edit controls — scroll bars, list boxes, and so on). Designing dialog boxes used to be difficult, but it's been made a lot easier with the Dialog Editor utility, which is included in Microsoft C++. Let's start immediately with a quick way to place dialog boxes on the screen.

Message Boxes

The quickest way to put a simple dialog box on the screen is with the Windows MessageBox( ) function:

```
int MessageBox(lpText, lpCaption, wType);
```

Here, lpText is a far pointer to the text we want in our message box, lpCaption is a far pointer to the caption text we want to appear in the message box's title bar (if this is NULL, the default caption is "Error", which gives you an idea of what Windows expects you to use message boxes for), and wType specifies the controls you can have in your message box, as we'll see.

This function lets you design a dialog box to a certain extent, and allows the user to communicate to your program through buttons: OK, Cancel, Abort, Retry, Ignore, Yes, or No. To see how MessageBox( ) works, we might create a small program that places a window on the screen with a menu item named Message Box... in the File menu. The resource file of this program, message.rc, will look like this:

```
#include <windows.h>
#include <afxres.h>
#define IDM_MESSAGE 100
#define IDM_EXIT    200

MainMenu MENU
{
  POPUP        "&File"
  {
    MENUITEM "&Message Box...\tF1", IDM_MESSAGE
    MENUITEM "E&xit", IDM_EXIT
  }
}

MainAccelTable ACCELERATORS
{
  VK_F1,       IDM_MESSAGE,  VIRTKEY
}
```

And the resulting menu is as shown in Figure 9-1 (note that we're including three dots after the name Message Box to indicate that a dialog box will appear).

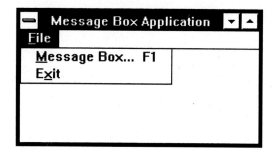

Figure 9-1. Message Box Example

The program to create this window might look something like this (adapted from our menu examples):

```
#include <afxwin.h>
#define IDM_MESSAGE    100
#define IDM_EXIT       200

class CMainWindow : public CFrameWnd
{
public:
    CMainWindow();
    afx_msg void OnMessage();
    afx_msg void OnExit();

    DECLARE_MESSAGE_MAP()
};

CMainWindow::CMainWindow()
{
    LoadAccelTable("MainAccelTable");
    Create(NULL, "Message Box Application",
        WS_OVERLAPPEDWINDOW, rectDefault, NULL, "MainMenu" );
}

void CMainWindow::OnMessage()
{

}

void CMainWindow::OnExit()
{
    DestroyWindow();
}
```

```
BEGIN_MESSAGE_MAP(CMainWindow, CFrameWnd)
    ON_COMMAND(IDM_MESSAGE, OnMessage)
    ON_COMMAND(IDM_EXIT, OnExit)
END_MESSAGE_MAP()

class CTheApp : public CWinApp
{
public:
    BOOL InitInstance();
};

BOOL CTheApp::InitInstance()
{
    m_pMainWnd = new CMainWindow();
    m_pMainWnd->ShowWindow( m_nCmdShow );
    m_pMainWnd->UpdateWindow();

 return TRUE;
}

CTheApp theApp;
```

When the user selects the Message Box... item, the program calls the OnMessage( ) member function, which we have yet to write:

```
void CMainWindow::OnMessage()
{

}
```

In that function, we can simply place this code:

```
void CMainWindow::OnMessage()
{
    MessageBox((LPSTR) "This is a message box.", (LPSTR) "Message Box",
        MB_OKCANCEL);
}
```

The Windows LPSTR casts turn the pointers to strings into far pointers. Note the MB (message box) constant that makes up the last parameter: MB_OKCANCEL. In general, this is how we specify what kinds of controls we want in our message box. MB_OKCANCEL indicates that we want an OK button and a Cancel button. The different message box types, which can be ORed together and then passed to MessageBox( ), appear in Table 9-1. A few

wType	*Means*
MB_ABORTRETRYIGNORE	Abort, Retry, Ignore buttons
MB_APPLMODAL	Modal on application level
MB_DEFBUTTON1	First button is default
MB_DEFBUTTON2	Second button is default
MB_DEFBUTTON3	Third button is default
MB_ICONASTERISK	Same as MB_ICONINFORMATION
MB_ICONEXCLAMATION	Include exclamation point icon
MB_ICONHAND	Same as MB_ICONSTOP
MB_ICONINFORMATION	Include circle i icon
MB_ICONQUESTION	Include question mark icon
MB_ICONSTOP	Include stop sign icon
MB_OK	OK button
MB_OKCANCEL	OK and Cancel buttons
MB_RETRYCANCEL	Retry and Cancel buttons
MB_SYSTEMMODAL	Modal on system level
MB_YESNO	Yes and No buttons
MB_YESNOCANCEL	Yes, No, Cancel buttons

Table 9-1. Message Box Types

of them deserve special attention: MB_DEFBUTTON1, for example, makes the first button in the message box the *default*. When a button is the default, it is surrounded by a black border, indicating that if the user presses <Enter>, that is the button that will be selected.

Two more important MB types are: MB_APPLMODAL and MB_SYS-TEMMODAL. We say a dialog box is *modal* when we expect the user to deal with it before continuing with the rest of the program (as opposed to non-modal dialog boxes, which can appear and operate side by side with other windows). An MB_APPLMODAL message box is one that is modal on the application level; that is, before the user can continue using the application, they have to finish with dialog box. Clicking any other windows belonging to the application results in a beep. MB_SYSTEMMODAL message boxes, on the other hand, don't even allow the user to switch to other applications before closing the message box.

TIP Almost every dialog box that has buttons should have a Cancel button in it, because Windows users expect them. Cancel buttons allow users to close the dialog box without making changes in the course of the rest of the program.

Our message box appears as in Figure 9-2. As you can see, we've set up the message box's caption, internal text, and buttons (OK and Cancel). It was that easy. When the user clicks one of the buttons or closes the message box, we get an integer return value corresponding to one of these constants (as defined in windows.h):

IDABORT	User clicked Abort Button
IDCANCEL	User clicked Cancel Button
IDIGNORE	User clicked Ignore Button
IDNO	User clicked No Button
IDOK	User clicked Ok Button
IDRETRY	User clicked Retry Button
IDYES	User clicked Yes Button

Checking the return value of MessageBox( ) against this list will allow you to determine what action the user took.

As helpful as MessageBox( ) is, we can go much farther when we design our own dialog boxes, as we'll see. For example, what if we wanted to add a text

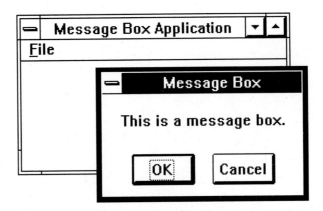

Figure 9-2. Our Message Box's Appearance

box to the message box in Figure 9-2? In that case, we'd have to design our own dialog box. Fortunately, the Dialog Editor makes that an easy job, so let's turn to that at once.

Designing Dialog Boxes

Let's say that our goal is simply to set up a dialog box much like the one in Figure 9-2, except that we want to add a text box and a button marked Push Me. When the user clicks this button, we can put the phrase "Hello, world." into the text box. We'll design our dialog box with the Dialog Editor and then integrate it into a program which we might name dialog.cpp.

Start by clicking the Dialog Editor icon (labeled Dialog Editor) in the Microsoft C Windows program group. The Dialog Editor appears, as in Figure 9-3. For us, the most important part of the Dialog Editor will be the toolbox, which appears in Figure 9-4. With the toolbox, we'll be able to create the controls that users have come to expect in dialog boxes; each of the tools in the toolbox is labeled in Figure 9-4, indicating what kind of control it is used to create.

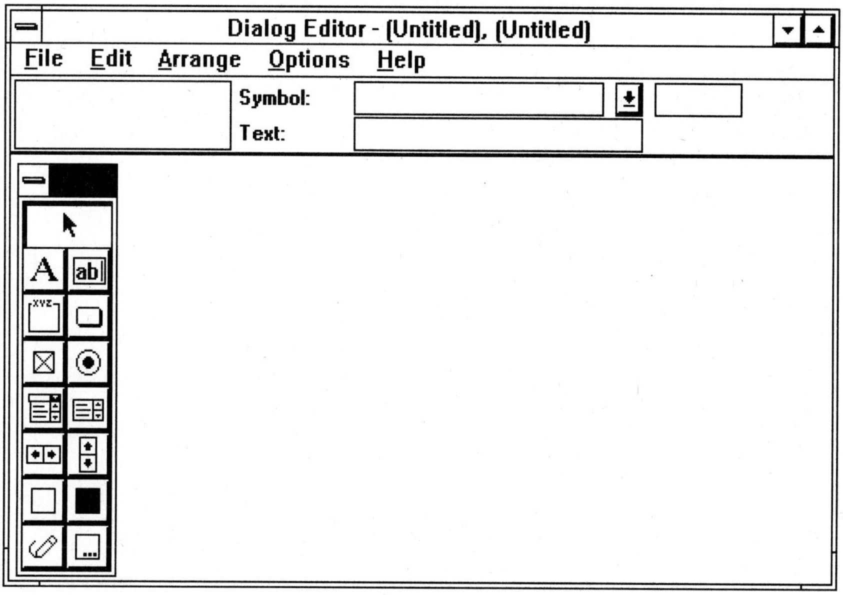

Figure 9-3. The Dialog Editor

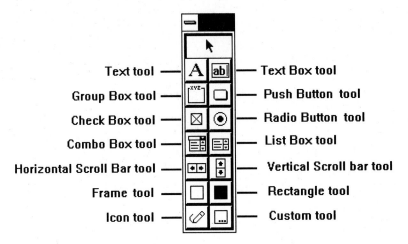

Text tool —— Text Box tool
Group Box tool —— Push Button tool
Check Box tool —— Radio Button tool
Combo Box tool —— List Box tool
Horizontal Scroll Bar tool —— Vertical Scroll bar tool
Frame tool —— Rectangle tool
Icon tool —— Custom tool

Figure 9-4. The Dialog Editor's Toolbox

Let's begin the design process by creating our own dialog box. To do that, select the New item in the Dialog Editor's File menu. A new dialog box template appears in the Dialog Box's window as shown in Figure 9-5.

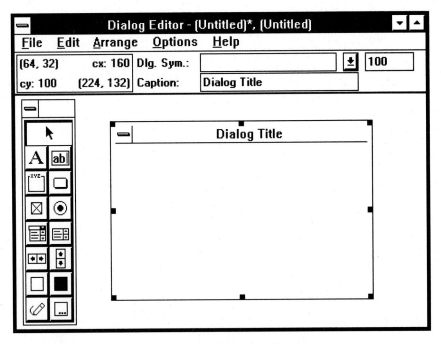

Figure 9-5. New Dialog Box Template

We can resize this new dialog box with the small black tabs you see around the perimeter of the new dialog box, called *sizing handles*. Using the sizing handles, you can stretch the dialog box into the shape you require. The first thing we can do is to give the dialog box a new title; currently, that's set to Dialog Title, both in the caption of the dialog box itself, and in the Caption box above it. To change that, edit the Caption box and change the title to, say, Dialog Box, since this is our first dialog box.

Now we're ready to start adding controls. First, click the push button tool in the toolbox (second tool down on the right), position the button outline that will follow the mouse cursor in the upper left of the new dialog box, and click. A new button appears, as in Figure 9-6.

Change the text in this button from its default, Push, to, say, Push Me simply by editing the Caption box above it (which is now renamed the Text box) and pressing <Enter>. The button's text now becomes "Push Me", as shown in Figure 9-7.

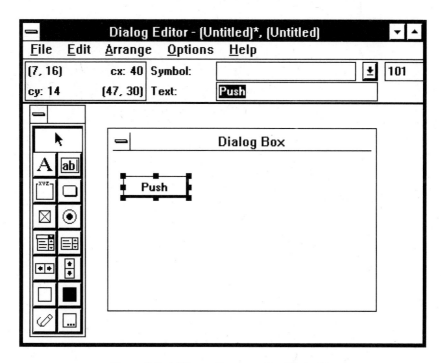

Figure 9-6. Adding a Button to Our Dialog Box

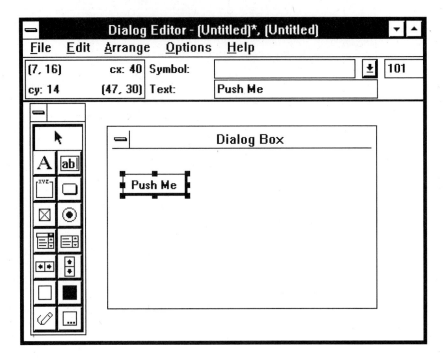

Figure 9-7. Changing a Button's Text

Note that there is now a number associated with this button, as you can see in the upper right hand corner of the Dialog Editor, and the number is 101. This is the button's ID number, and we'll see it later; when the button is clicked, for example, 101 will be passed to us in wParam so we know which control is sending us a message. Each control we add to our dialog box will have an ID like this (the dialog box itself is number 100). We can also associate a symbol (i.e., a text string) with controls like these instead of numbers like 101, and you can see the Symbol box above the Text text box in Figure 9-7.

In addition, we can customize any of the controls we add to a dialog box by double clicking the control itself when we design our dialog box. For example, double clicking the button Push Me now brings up the dialog box shown in Figure 9-8, showing the options available for buttons.

TIP   One of the button options is particularly worth noticing: the Default option. If set, this makes the button into the default control for the dialog box (i.e., it has the focus) when the dialog box appears. It's often customary to make an OK button the default so the user has only to press <Enter>.

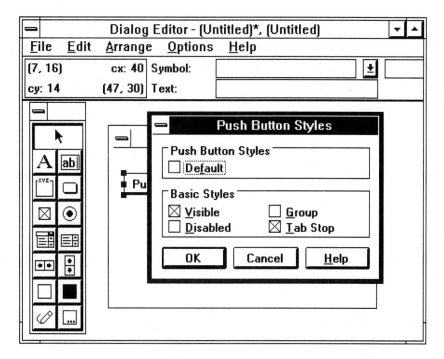

Figure 9-8. Button Customization Box

In fact, we can double click the new dialog box itself to see what other options are available for it, as shown in Figure 9-9. Here you can select what font is used, what the dialog box's border will be like, and many other options.

In our case, we want a few more controls: We need a text box to display the string "Hello, world.", and we should also add OK and Cancel buttons, since most dialog boxes have them. To add a text box, simply click the text box tool in the toolbox (the first tool down on the right), position the text box outline in the upper right-hand corner of the new dialog box, and click. Next, add two buttons, labeling them OK and Cancel (using the Text text box), as shown in Figure 9-10. The ID numbers for these new controls are: Text box: 102, OK button: 103, Cancel button: 104. We'll need to keep these numbers in mind for later use.

We can save some time by indicating to the Dialog Editor that the buttons we've just added are supposed to function as OK and Cancel buttons. The CModalDialog C++ class that we'll use soon *already* has OnOK( ) and OnCancel( ) functions in it, including much of the correct code for these

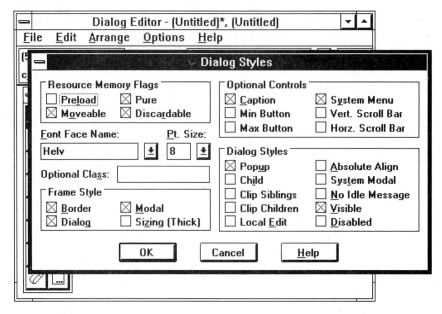

Figure 9-9. Dialog Box Options

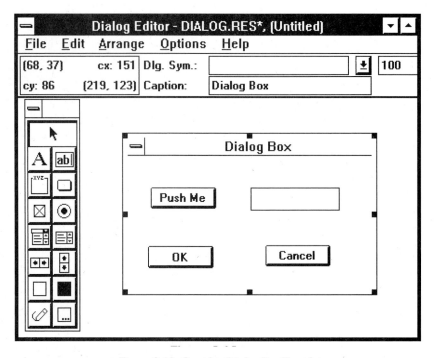

Figure 9-10. Complete Dialog Box Template

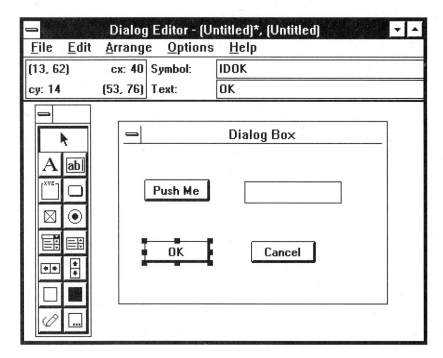

Figure 9-11. Configuring an OK button

buttons already. To indicate that a button is either an OK or Cancel button, use the symbol IDOK or IDCANCEL for it, as shown in Figure 9-11. Select the IDOK option for the OK button, and IDCANCEL for the Cancel button. This changes the ID number for the OK button to IDOK and the ID for the Cancel button to IDCANCEL. When our program sees these values later, it will know that we want it to use the OnOK( ) and OnCancel( ) functions to handle these particular buttons.

Now we're ready to generate the dialog box itself. The file that the Dialog Box editor produces is a .dlg file, which we'll add to our .rc file. We can call our .dlg file, say, dialog.dlg by selecting the Save As... item in the Dialog Editor's File menu and giving the name dialog.dlg. When we do, dialog.dlg is created. This file holds the complete specification for our dialog box, like this:

```
100 DIALOG 90, 39, 151, 86
STYLE DS_MODALFRAME | WS_POPUP | WS_VISIBLE | WS_CAPTION | WS_SYSMENU
CAPTION "Dialog Box"
FONT 8, "Helv"
BEGIN
```

```
        EDITTEXT        101, 76, 20, 55, 15, ES_AUTOHSCROLL
        PUSHBUTTON      "Push Me", 102, 15, 20, 40, 14
        PUSHBUTTON      "OK", IDOK, 13, 58, 40, 14
        PUSHBUTTON      "Cancel", IDCANCEL, 85, 57, 40, 14
END
```

That's all there is to it — you can see that all of our controls are here, along with their IDs, positions (as measured in screen pixels), and sizes. Now we can write dialog.cpp.

As mentioned, the CModalDialog that we're going to use as the base class for our dialog boxes already has two built-in functions that are very handy: OnOK( ) and OnCancel( ). If your dialog box only uses those two functions, i.e., the only controls (besides text) are an OK and/or a Cancel button (e.g., an "About" box), then you can use the CModalDialog box class directly. You create an object of that class and place it on the screen (as we'll see how to do in a minute). When the user clicks OK or Cancel, the box is removed. For all but the simplest applications, however, we'll want to derive our own class from CModalDialog. For example, in our case, we have a button marked Push Me, and when the user clicks it, we want to place text into our text box. To do that, we'll need a function to respond to button pushes, and we can call that OnPushMe( ). That means that we can derive our class called, say, CMainDialog class from CModalDialog like this (just as we derived CMainWindow from CFrameWnd):

```
#include <afxwin.h>

class CMainDialog : public CModalDialog         ←
{
public:
    CMainDialog(UINT resource_number, CWnd* parentWnd);
    afx_msg void OnPushMe();

    DECLARE_MESSAGE_MAP()
};
```

Note the similarities to our declaration of our main window, CMainWindow, which looks like this (including prototypes for the two menu items Dialog Box... and Exit):

```
class CMainWindow : public CFrameWnd
{
public:
```

```
    CMainWindow();
    afx_msg void OnDialog();
    afx_msg void OnExit();

    DECLARE_MESSAGE_MAP()
};
```

This is because our dialog box will be a window also. One significant difference, however, is that the CModalDialog constructor takes two arguments: The dialog template we just defined in dialog.dlg, and a pointer to the parent window object (here, that's our CMainWindow object). You can indicate which dialog template you want to use in two ways: As a name (e.g., "MainDialog") or as a number (e.g., 100, as in our .dlg file above). Let's do this now.

The Dialog Editor has given our dialog template a number, 100 (from dialog.dlg):

```
100 DIALOG 90, 39, 151, 86        ←
STYLE DS_MODALFRAME | WS_POPUP | WS_VISIBLE | WS_CAPTION | WS_SYSMENU
CAPTION "Dialog Box"
FONT 8, "Helv"
BEGIN
    EDITTEXT        101, 76, 20, 55, 15, ES_AUTOHSCROLL
    PUSHBUTTON      "Push Me", 102, 15, 20, 40, 14
    PUSHBUTTON      "OK", IDOK, 13, 58, 40, 14
    PUSHBUTTON      "Cancel", IDCANCEL, 85, 57, 40, 14
END
```

| TIP | The Dialog Editor gives the number 100 to each dialog box it creates. If you have a number of dialog boxes in the same program, you can edit the .dlg files, changing these values and making them unique. |

So when we add this dialog template to our .rc file, we'll be able to refer to our dialog box as resource 100, and this is the number we can pass to the CModalDialog constructor. To do that, we give the constructor of our derived class, CMainDialog, two arguments as well:

```
#include <afxwin.h>

class CMainDialog : public CModalDialog
{
```

```
        public:
  →         CMainDialog(UINT resource_number, CWnd* parentWnd);
            afx_msg void OnPushMe();

            DECLARE_MESSAGE_MAP()
        };
```

Here, resource_number is the resource number, and parentWnd will be a pointer to our main window's object. The only thing we need to do in our class' constructor is to pass those values on to CModalDialog's constructor, so we can write our constructor like this:

```
#include <afxwin.h>

class CMainDialog : public CModalDialog
{
public:
    CMainDialog(UINT resource_number, CWnd* parentWnd);
    afx_msg void OnPushMe();

    DECLARE_MESSAGE_MAP()
};

CMainDialog::CMainDialog(UINT resource_number, CWnd* parentWnd) :   ←
        CModalDialog(resource_number, parentWnd)                   ←
{

}
```

Now when we want to create a dialog box of class CMainDialog that uses our dialog box template, we can construct an object named, say, dialog_box, of that type like this:

```
  CMainDialog dialog_box(100, pMainWindow);
```

Here, pMainWindow is a pointer to our main window object (we'll use a this pointer). Next, we can define the function OnPushMe( ). When the user clicks the button marked Push Me, we want to place the string "Hello, world." into the text box using code in OnPushMe( ):

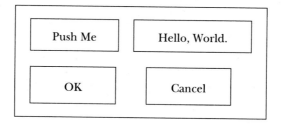

To do that in OnPushMe( ), we can use the CModalDialog member function SetDlgItemText( ). Our text box has the ID number 101 in the file that the Dialog Editor created (here the text box is called EDITTEXT):

```
100 DIALOG 90, 39, 151, 86
STYLE DS_MODALFRAME | WS_POPUP | WS_VISIBLE | WS_CAPTION | WS_SYSMENU
CAPTION "Dialog Box"
FONT 8, "Helv"
BEGIN
        EDITTEXT        101, 76, 20, 55, 15, ES_AUTOHSCROLL
        PUSHBUTTON      "Push Me", 102, 15, 20, 40, 14
        PUSHBUTTON      "OK", IDOK, 13, 58, 40, 14
        PUSHBUTTON      "Cancel", IDCANCEL, 85, 57, 40, 14
END
```

This means that in OnPushMe( ), we only have to execute this code:

```
#include <afxwin.h>
#define IDM_DIALOG    1000
#define IDM_EXIT      2000

class CMainDialog : public CModalDialog
{
public:
        CMainDialog(UINT resource_number, CWnd* parentWnd);
        afx_msg void OnPushMe();

        DECLARE_MESSAGE_MAP()
};

CMainDialog::CMainDialog(UINT resource_number, CWnd* parentWnd) :
        CModalDialog(resource_number, parentWnd)
{

}
```

```
       void CMainDialog::OnPushMe()
       {
→          SetDlgItemText(101, "Hello, world.");
       }
```

And that's it for OnPushMe( ). Note that if we had wanted to get the text now in the text box, we could have used the GetDlgItemText( ) function instead. All that remains in the design of our dialog box is to connect OnPushMe( ) to the correct dialog box message. That is, we get messages from our dialog boxes (just as we do from our windows) when the user clicks some control like button. These messages are called *notification messages,* and the noticiation that a button (e.g., Push Me) was pushed is BN_CLICKED. The Push Me button is control number 102 as defined by the dialog editor:

```
100 DIALOG 90, 39, 151, 86
STYLE DS_MODALFRAME | WS_POPUP | WS_VISIBLE | WS_CAPTION | WS_SYSMENU
CAPTION "Dialog Box"
FONT 8, "Helv"
BEGIN
       EDITTEXT        101, 76, 20, 55, 15, ES_AUTOHSCROLL
→      PUSHBUTTON      "Push Me", 102, 15, 20, 40, 14
       PUSHBUTTON      "OK", IDOK, 13, 58, 40, 14
       PUSHBUTTON      "Cancel", IDCANCEL, 85, 57, 40, 14
END
```

That means that we can connect the Push Me button to the function OnPushMe( ) with the BEGIN_MESSAGE_MAP macro like this:

```
#include <afxwin.h>

class CMainDialog : public CModalDialog
{
public:
       CMainDialog(UINT resource_number, CWnd* parentWnd);
       afx_msg void OnPushMe();

       DECLARE_MESSAGE_MAP()
};

CMainDialog::CMainDialog(UINT resource_number, CWnd* parentWnd) :
       CModalDialog(resource_number, parentWnd)
{

}
```

```
void CMainDialog::OnPushMe()
{
     SetDlgItemText(101, "Hello, world.");
}

BEGIN_MESSAGE_MAP(CMainDialog, CModalDialog)
     ON_BN_CLICKED(102, OnPushMe)
END_MESSAGE_MAP()
```

This is very similar to the way we used BEGIN_MESSAGE_MAP for our main window, except that here we're using it for the class CMainDialog, which was derived from CModalDialog:

```
  BEGIN_MESSAGE_MAP(CMainDialog, CModalDialog)  ←
       ON_BN_CLICKED(102, OnPushMe)
  END_MESSAGE_MAP()
```

Now the Push Me button is connected to the OnPushMe( ) function in code. There are many notification codes for the various Windows controls, and they appear in Table 9-2.

For each notification code, e.g., BN_CLICKED, you use a line like this in the BEGIN_MESSAGE_MAP macro: ON_BN_CLICKED(button_ID_number, button_handling_function). Then, when the program receives that code, your function is called. At this point, then, our program is almost ready to go. We have to set up our main window and add a menu to it with two items: Dialog Box... (handled by OnDialog( )) and Exit (handled by OnExit( )). We can do that as we've done before:

```
#include <afxwin.h>
#define IDM_DIALOG   1000
#define IDM_EXIT     2000

class CMainDialog : public CModalDialog
{
public:
     CMainDialog(UINT resource_number, CWnd* parentWnd);
     afx_msg void OnPushMe();

     DECLARE_MESSAGE_MAP()
};

CMainDialog::CMainDialog(UINT resource_number, CWnd* parentWnd) :
        CModalDialog(resource_number, parentWnd)
```

BN_CLICKED	Button has been clicked
BN_DOUBLECLICKED	Button has been double clicked
EN_CHANGE	Edit control (text box) contents changed
EN_ERRSPACE	Edit control is out of space
EN_HSCROLL	Edit control's horizontal scroll clicked
EN_KILLFOCUS	Edit control lost input focus
EN_MAXTEXT	Insertion exceeded specified number of chars
EN_SETFOCUS	Edit control got input focus
EN_UPDATE	Edit control to display altered text
EN_VSCROLL	Edit control's vertical scroll clicked
LBN_DBLCLK	List box string was double-clicked
LBN_ERRSPACE	System is out of memory
LBN_KILLFOCUS	List box lost input focus
LBN_SELCHANGE	List box selection has changed
LBN_SETFOCUS	List box got input focus
CBN_DBLCLK	Combo box string was double-clicked
CBN_DROPDOWN	Combo box's list box to be dropped down
CBN_EDITCHANGE	User has changed text in the edit control
CBN_EDITUPDATE	Edit control to display altered text
CBN_ERRSPACE	System is out of memory
CBN_KILLFOCUS	Combo box lost input focus
CBN_SELCHANGE	Combo box selection was changed
CBN_SETFOCUS	Combo box got input focus

Table 9-2. Windows Controls Notification Codes

```
{

}

void CMainDialog::OnPushMe()
{
     SetDlgItemText(101, "Hello, world.");
}

BEGIN_MESSAGE_MAP(CMainDialog, CModalDialog)
    ON_BN_CLICKED(102, OnPushMe)
END_MESSAGE_MAP()

class CMainWindow : public CFrameWnd            ←
```

```
{
public:
    CMainWindow();
    afx_msg void OnDialog();
    afx_msg void OnExit();

    DECLARE_MESSAGE_MAP()
};


CMainWindow::CMainWindow()                              ←
{
    LoadAccelTable("MainAccelTable");
    Create(NULL, "Dialog Box Application",
        WS_OVERLAPPEDWINDOW, rectDefault, NULL, "MainMenu" );
}
```

Now we can write the function OnDialog( ), which is called when the user clicks the Dialog Box... menu item:

```
void CMainWindow::OnDialog()
{


}
```

Here we want to create a dialog box of class CMainDialog and display it. To create it, we simply pass the dialog template's resource number, 100, and a pointer to the main window to the object's constructor. Since CMainWindow::OnDialog( ) is a member function of our CMainWindow class, the pointer to the main window is simply the this pointer, which lets us create the dialog box like this:

```
void CMainWindow::OnDialog()
{
    CMainDialog dialog_box(100, this);
        :
}
```

Now our dialog box object, dialog_box, has been created. To make it active, we use the CModalDialog member function DoModal( ):

```
void CMainWindow::OnDialog()
{
    CMainDialog dialog_box(100, this);
→   dialog_box.DoModal();
}
```

And that's it; when this selection is made, the dialog box is placed on the screen:

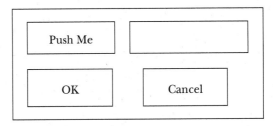

TIP If we only used an OK (ID = IDOK) and/or Cancel (ID = IDCANCEL) button in our dialog box, we could have used an object of class CModalDialog directly, because those functions (i.e., OnOK( ) and OnCancel( )) are already built in to that class. In code, it would look like this: CModalDialog dialog_box(100, this); dialog_box.DoModal( );.

To remove our dialog box, we use the DestroyWindow( ) member function, which is called in OnOK( ) and OnCancel( ) (i.e., when the user clicks OK or Cancel). Note that we did not have to provide any code for the functions OnOK( ) or OnCancel( ), because they're built into the CModalDialog class already. All they do is to call DestroyWindow( ):

```
void CModalDialog()
{
    DestroyWindow();
}
```

This function simply invokes the dialog box's destructor and removes it from the screen. If you want OnOK( ) or OnCancel( ) to do anything more, of course, you can override them. The remainder of the program is much like our previous programs:

```
#include <afxwin.h>
#define IDM_DIALOG    1000
#define IDM_EXIT      2000

class CMainDialog : public CModalDialog
{
public:
    CMainDialog(UINT resource_number, CWnd* parentWnd);
    afx_msg void OnPushMe();
```

```
        DECLARE_MESSAGE_MAP()
};

CMainDialog::CMainDialog(UINT resource_number, CWnd* parentWnd) :
        CModalDialog(resource_number, parentWnd)
{

}

void CMainDialog::OnPushMe()
{
    SetDlgItemText(101, "Hello, world.");
}

BEGIN_MESSAGE_MAP(CMainDialog, CModalDialog)
    ON_BN_CLICKED(102, OnPushMe)
END_MESSAGE_MAP()

class CMainWindow : public CFrameWnd
{
public:
    CMainWindow();
    afx_msg void OnDialog();
    afx_msg void OnExit();

    DECLARE_MESSAGE_MAP()
};

CMainWindow::CMainWindow()
{
    LoadAccelTable("MainAccelTable");
    Create(NULL, "Dialog Box Application",
        WS_OVERLAPPEDWINDOW, rectDefault, NULL, "MainMenu" );
}

void CMainWindow::OnDialog()
{
    CMainDialog dialog_box(100, this);
    dialog_box.DoModal();
}

void CMainWindow::OnExit()
{
    DestroyWindow();
}

BEGIN_MESSAGE_MAP(CMainWindow, CFrameWnd)
    ON_COMMAND(IDM_DIALOG, OnDialog)
```

```
        ON_COMMAND(IDM_EXIT, OnExit)
END_MESSAGE_MAP()

class CTheApp : public CWinApp                    ←
{
public:
    BOOL InitInstance();
};

BOOL CTheApp::InitInstance()                      ←
{
    m_pMainWnd = new CMainWindow();
    m_pMainWnd->ShowWindow( m_nCmdShow );
    m_pMainWnd->UpdateWindow();

 return TRUE;
}
```

That finishes the .cpp file. The final step is to design the file dialog.rc and incorporate dialog.dlg (the template of our dialog box) in it. Dialog.rc simply has the definition of the File menu in it, and looks like this:

```
#include <windows.h>
#include <afxres.h>
#define IDM_DIALOG 1000
#define IDM_EXIT   2000

MainMenu MENU
{
  POPUP        "&File"
  {
    MENUITEM "&Dialog Box...\tF1", IDM_DIALOG
    MENUITEM "E&xit", IDM_EXIT
  }
}

MainAccelTable ACCELERATORS
{
  VK_F1,       IDM_DIALOG,  VIRTKEY
}
```

To include our dialog box as an additional resource, we can either put the text of dialog.dlg into this file directly, or we can use the rcinclude command like this:

```
#include <windows.h>
#include <afxres.h>
#define IDM_DIALOG 1000
#define IDM_EXIT   2000

MainMenu MENU
{
  POPUP         "&File"
  {
    MENUITEM "&Dialog Box...\tF1", IDM_DIALOG
    MENUITEM "E&xit", IDM_EXIT
  }
}

MainAccelTable ACCELERATORS
{
  VK_F1,        IDM_DIALOG,   VIRTKEY
}

rcinclude pushme.dlg     ←
```

And that's it. The code for this program appears in Listing 9-1, the file dialog.rc in Listing 9-2, dialog.dlg in Listing 9-3, dialog.def in Listing 9-4, and the makefile in Listing 9-5.

Listing 9-1. Dialog.cpp

```
#include <afxwin.h>
#define IDM_DIALOG    1000
#define IDM_EXIT      2000

class CMainDialog : public CModalDialog
{
public:
    CMainDialog(UINT resource_number, CWnd* parentWnd);
    afx_msg void OnPushMe();

    DECLARE_MESSAGE_MAP()
};

CMainDialog::CMainDialog(UINT resource_number, CWnd* parentWnd) :
        CModalDialog(resource_number, parentWnd)
{

}
```

(continued)

Listing 9-1. *(continued)*

```
void CMainDialog::OnPushMe()
{
    SetDlgItemText(101, "Hello, world.");
}

BEGIN_MESSAGE_MAP(CMainDialog, CModalDialog)
    ON_BN_CLICKED(102, OnPushMe)
END_MESSAGE_MAP()

class CMainWindow : public CFrameWnd
{
public:
    CMainWindow();
    afx_msg void OnDialog();
    afx_msg void OnExit();

    DECLARE_MESSAGE_MAP()
};

CMainWindow::CMainWindow()
{
    LoadAccelTable("MainAccelTable");
    Create(NULL, "Dialog Box Application",
        WS_OVERLAPPEDWINDOW, rectDefault, NULL, "MainMenu" );
}

void CMainWindow::OnDialog()
{
    CMainDialog dialog_box(100, this);
    dialog_box.DoModal();
}

void CMainWindow::OnExit()
{
    DestroyWindow();
}

BEGIN_MESSAGE_MAP(CMainWindow, CFrameWnd)
    ON_COMMAND(IDM_DIALOG, OnDialog)
    ON_COMMAND(IDM_EXIT, OnExit)
END_MESSAGE_MAP()

class CTheApp : public CWinApp
{
public:
    BOOL InitInstance();
};
```

Listing 9-1. *(continued)*

```
BOOL CTheApp::InitInstance()
{
    m_pMainWnd = new CMainWindow();
    m_pMainWnd->ShowWindow( m_nCmdShow );
    m_pMainWnd->UpdateWindow();

 return TRUE;
}

CTheApp theApp;
```

Listing 9-2. Dialog.rc

```
#include "DIALOG.h"

DIALOG MENU
  BEGIN
    POPUP  "File"
      BEGIN
        MENUITEM "Dialog Box...", IDM_F_DIALOGBOX
        MENUITEM "Exit", IDM_F_EXIT
      END
  END


#include "DIALOG.DLG"

STRINGTABLE
BEGIN
  IDS_ERR_CREATE_WINDOW,     "Window creation failed!"
  IDS_ERR_REGISTER_CLASS,    "Error registering window class"
END
```

Listing 9-3. Dialog.dlg

```
100 DIALOG 90, 39, 151, 86
STYLE DS_MODALFRAME | WS_POPUP | WS_VISIBLE | WS_CAPTION |
    WS_SYSMENU
CAPTION "Dialog Box"
FONT 8, "Helv"
BEGIN
    EDITTEXT       101, 76, 20, 55, 15, ES_AUTOHSCROLL
    PUSHBUTTON     "Push Me", 102, 15, 20, 40, 14
    PUSHBUTTON     "OK", IDOK, 13, 58, 40, 14
    PUSHBUTTON     "Cancel", IDCANCEL, 85, 57, 40, 14
END
```

Listing 9-4. Dialog.def

```
NAME            Button
DESCRIPTION     'Push Button Example'

EXETYPE         WINDOWS
STUB            'WINSTUB.EXE'

CODE            PRELOAD MOVEABLE DISCARDABLE
DATA            PRELOAD MOVEABLE MULTIPLE

HEAPSIZE        1024
STACKSIZE       4096

CPPFLAGS= /AS /W3 /Zp /GA /GEs /G2
```

Listing 9-5. Dialog.exe's Makefile

```
dialog.exe:     dialog.obj dialog.def dialog.res
  link /NOD /ONERROR:NOEXE dialog, dialog, NUL, safxcw libw
  slibcew,dialog.def;
  rc /t dialog.res

dialog.res:  dialog.dlg
```

When you run this program, dialog.exe, and click the Dialog Box... item in the File menu, our dialog box appears. When you click the button marked Push Me, the string "Hello, world." appears in the text box, as shown in Figure 9-12. Our program is a success, and we've created our own dialog box.

A Calculator Example

Now that we know the details, we can work more quickly. Here are the general steps for adding a dialog box:

1. Design the dialog box with the Dialog Editor and save it, producing the .dlg file (one dialog box per .dlg file).

2. Add the dialog box to a program by placing the file into the program's .rc file or using rcinclude.

3. Edit the .cpp file, popping the dialog box on the screen when needed and adding the code to make the dialog box's controls active (e.g., add functions like OnPushMe( )).

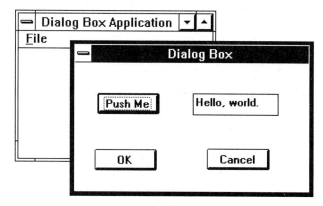

Figure 9-12. Our "Hello world" Dialog Box Example

Let's follow these steps and work with the controls we're familiar with so far, buttons and text boxes, to create a new example: a simple pop-up calculator that will let us add numbers. Start the Dialog Editor once again and give a new dialog box the caption Calculator. Next, add two text boxes as shown in Figure 9-13.

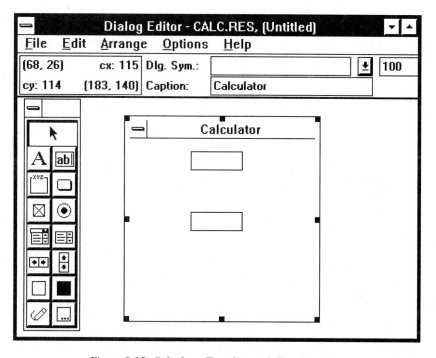

Figure 9-13. Calculator Template with Two Text Boxes

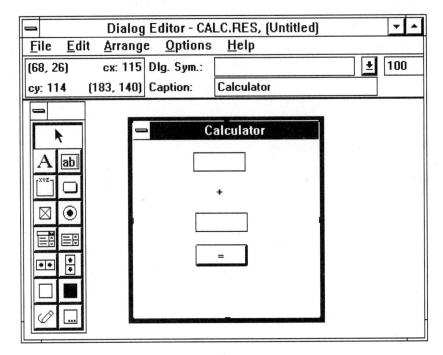

Figure 9-14. Nearly Complete Calculator Template

Now add a push button with the caption "=" under the text boxes, and, using the Text tool (first tool down on the left), place a plus sign, +, between the text boxes, as shown in Figure 9-14.

At this point, we've arranged our controls like this:

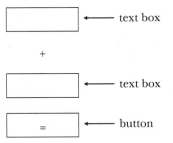

The user can place numbers in the two text boxes when the dialog box is active:

| 12 |

+

| 24 |

| = |

The next step is to display the answer when they click the = button:

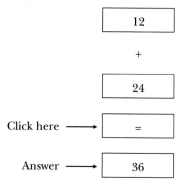

Note, however, that we don't want the answer to appear in a text box, because text boxes can be edited by the user; it would be more appropriate to display the answer as simple text, which we can change but which is not accessible to the user. To do that, first draw a rectangle using the Rectangle tool (sixth tool down on the left) so that the answer box looks like the text box controls above it. Next, click the Text tool, use the sizing handles that appear so that the text fills the rectangle, and place a 0 in it as shown in Figure 9-15. This text is actually a control, and we'll be able to change it from inside our program.

Now select the Save As... item in the File menu, and call this dialog box, say, calc.dlg. That file looks like this (note that all our controls are here, including the text fields):

```
100 DIALOG 68, 26, 115, 114
STYLE DS_MODALFRAME | WS_POPUP | WS_VISIBLE | WS_CAPTION | WS_SYSMENU
CAPTION "Calculator"
FONT 8, "Helv"
BEGIN
    EDITTEXT        101, 38, 8, 32, 12, ES_AUTOHSCROLL
    EDITTEXT        102, 38, 47, 32, 12, ES_AUTOHSCROLL
    PUSHBUTTON      "=", 103, 38, 67, 32, 14
    LTEXT           "+", 106, 51, 29, 9, 8
    CONTROL         "", 104, "Static", SS_BLACKFRAME, 40, 88, 30, 15
    LTEXT           "0", 105, 41, 90, 27, 11
END
```

Next we can start creating the code to make our calculator work. All the action occurs when the user clicks the button marked "="; when they do, we're supposed

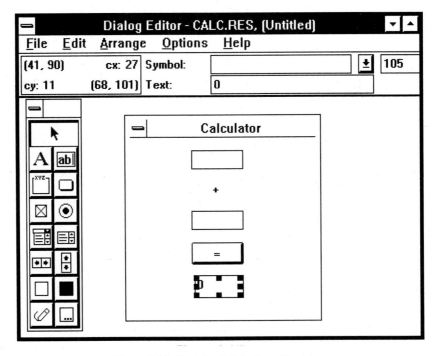

Figure 9-15. Completed Calculator Template

to take the numbers in the two text boxes, add them, and display them in the answer box. The controls we have, and their IDs, are set up like this:

12	101
+	
24	102
=	103
36	105

Therefore, we want to take action when the equals button, ID = 103, is pushed. First we set up our dialog box class and constructor like this:

```
#include <afxwin.h>
#define IDM_DIALOG    1000
#define IDM_EXIT      2000

class CMainDialog : public CModalDialog
{
public:
     CMainDialog(UINT resource_number, CWnd* parentWnd);

     DECLARE_MESSAGE_MAP()
};

CMainDialog::CMainDialog(UINT resource_number, CWnd* parentWnd) :
        CModalDialog(resource_number, parentWnd)
{

}
```

Next, we can write a function called OnEquals( ), which is invoked when the equals button, ID = 103, is pushed. We can connect OnEquals( ) to the = button with the BEGIN_MESSAGE_MAP macro like this:

```
#include <afxwin.h>
#define IDM_DIALOG    1000
#define IDM_EXIT      2000

class CMainDialog : public CModalDialog
{
public:
     CMainDialog(UINT resource_number, CWnd* parentWnd);
     afx_msg void OnEquals();        ←

     DECLARE_MESSAGE_MAP()
};

CMainDialog::CMainDialog(UINT resource_number, CWnd* parentWnd) :
        CModalDialog(resource_number, parentWnd)
{

}

void CMainDialog::OnEquals()            ←
{

}

BEGIN_MESSAGE_MAP(CMainDialog, CModalDialog)
    ON_BN_CLICKED(103, OnEquals)    ←
END_MESSAGE_MAP()
```

In OnEquals( ), we want to read the value in the top text box (ID = 101), add it to the value in the next text box (ID = 102), and display it in the result box (ID = 105):

`12`	101
+	
`24`	102
`=`	103
`36`	105

> **TIP** Because of their ascending ID numbers, the user can use our calculator's controls with the keyboard instead of the mouse. Because it has the lowest ID number, the top text box (ID = 101) has the focus when the dialog box appears. The users can type their number there and press the <Tab> key, which is the keyboard method of moving between controls in Windows. When they do, the focus moves to the next text box (ID = 102), so they can enter the next number. Pressing <Tab> again moves the focus to the equals button (ID = 103), and pressing <Enter> clicks that key, displaying the result in the Result box.

You may recall that we placed text into a text box earlier with the SetDlgItemText( ) function. That function is one of four we can use to read and set values in text boxes and labels:

GetDlgItemInt( )	Get int value as displayed in control
GetDlgItemText( )	Get text from dialog control
SetDlgItemInt( )	Display int value in control
SetDlgItemText( )	Display text in dialog control

Here, we'll restrict our calculator to use only integer values, so we can get the integer now stored in the top text box (ID = 101) with the GetDlgItemInt( ) function like this: GetDlgItemInt(101), and the int in the second text box like this: GetDlgItemInt(102). Then we can add those two values and place them in the result box with SetDlgItemInt( ) like this: SetDlgItemInt(105, Sum). In fact, we can put these statements together into one line like this:

```
#include <afxwin.h>
#define IDM_DIALOG   1000
#define IDM_EXIT     2000

class CMainDialog : public CModalDialog
{
public:
    CMainDialog(UINT resource_number, CWnd* parentWnd);
    afx_msg void OnEquals();

    DECLARE_MESSAGE_MAP()
};
```

```
CMainDialog::CMainDialog(UINT resource_number, CWnd* parentWnd) :
        CModalDialog(resource_number, parentWnd)
{

}

void CMainDialog::OnEquals()
{
    SetDlgItemInt(105, GetDlgItemInt(101)+GetDlgItemInt(102));
}

BEGIN_MESSAGE_MAP(CMainDialog, CModalDialog)
    ON_BN_CLICKED(103, OnEquals)
END_MESSAGE_MAP()
```

→

TIP If you want to use floating point numbers instead of integers, you can read values using GetDlgItemText( ) and convert them to floating point with the atof( ) function. Then you can use ftoa( ), which converts floating point values to text, along with SetDlgItemText( ) to display the result.

And that's it. The rest of the program is much like what we've seen before, and only serves to put the calculator on the screen:

```
#include <afxwin.h>
#define IDM_DIALOG    1000
#define IDM_EXIT      2000

class CMainDialog : public CModalDialog
{
public:
    CMainDialog(UINT resource_number, CWnd* parentWnd);
    afx_msg void OnEquals();

    DECLARE_MESSAGE_MAP()
};

CMainDialog::CMainDialog(UINT resource_number, CWnd* parentWnd) :
        CModalDialog(resource_number, parentWnd)
{

}

void CMainDialog::OnEquals()
```

```
{
    SetDlgItemInt(105, GetDlgItemInt(101)+GetDlgItemInt(102));
}

BEGIN_MESSAGE_MAP(CMainDialog, CModalDialog)
    ON_BN_CLICKED(103, OnEquals)
END_MESSAGE_MAP()

class CMainWindow : public CFrameWnd                ←
{
public:
    CMainWindow();
    afx_msg void OnDialog();
    afx_msg void OnExit();

    DECLARE_MESSAGE_MAP()
};

CMainWindow::CMainWindow()                           ←
{
    LoadAccelTable("MainAccelTable");
    Create(NULL, "Dialog Box Application",
        WS_OVERLAPPEDWINDOW, rectDefault, NULL, "MainMenu" );
}

void CMainWindow::OnDialog()                         ←
{
    CMainDialog dialog_box(100, this);
    dialog_box.DoModal();
}

void CMainWindow::OnExit()                           ←
{
    DestroyWindow();
}

BEGIN_MESSAGE_MAP(CMainWindow, CFrameWnd)            ←
    ON_COMMAND(IDM_DIALOG, OnDialog)
    ON_COMMAND(IDM_EXIT, OnExit)
END_MESSAGE_MAP()

class CTheApp : public CWinApp                       ←
{
public:
    BOOL InitInstance();
};
```

```
BOOL CTheApp::InitInstance()                          ←
{
    m_pMainWnd = new CMainWindow();
    m_pMainWnd->ShowWindow( m_nCmdShow );
    m_pMainWnd->UpdateWindow();

 return TRUE;
}


CTheApp theApp;                                       ←
```

That completes calc.cpp. The resource file, calc.rc, appears in Listing 9-6, calc.dlg appears in Listing 9-7, calc.def in Listing 9-8, and the makefile in Listing 9-9.

Listing 9-6. Calc.rc

```
#include <windows.h>
#include <afxres.h>
#define IDM_DIALOG 1000
#define IDM_EXIT   2000

MainMenu MENU
{
  POPUP         "&File"
  {
    MENUITEM "&Calculator...\tF1", IDM_DIALOG
    MENUITEM "E&xit", IDM_EXIT
  }
}


MainAccelTable ACCELERATORS
{
  VK_F1,      IDM_DIALOG,  VIRTKEY
}

rcinclude calc.dlg
```

Listing 9-7. Calc.dlg

```
100 DIALOG 68, 26, 115, 114
STYLE DS_MODALFRAME | WS_POPUP | WS_VISIBLE | WS_CAPTION |
    WS_SYSMENU
```

Listing 9-7. *(continued)*

```
CAPTION "Calculator"
FONT 8, "Helv"
BEGIN
    EDITTEXT        101, 38, 8, 32, 12, ES_AUTOHSCROLL
    EDITTEXT        102, 38, 47, 32, 12, ES_AUTOHSCROLL
    PUSHBUTTON      "=", 103, 38, 67, 32, 14
    LTEXT           "+", 106, 51, 29, 9, 8
    CONTROL         "", 104, "Static", SS_BLACKFRAME, 40, 88, 30, 15
    LTEXT           "0", 105, 41, 90, 27, 11
END
```

Listing 9-8. Calc.def

```
NAME            Calc
DESCRIPTION     'Calculator Example'

EXETYPE         WINDOWS
STUB            'WINSTUB.EXE'

CODE            PRELOAD MOVEABLE DISCARDABLE
DATA            PRELOAD MOVEABLE MULTIPLE

HEAPSIZE        1024
STACKSIZE       4096
```

Listing 9-9. Calc.exe's Makefile

```
CPPFLAGS= /AS /W3 /Zp /GA /GEs /G2

calc.exe:     calc.obj calc.def calc.res
  link /NOD /ONERROR:NOEXE calc, calc, NUL, safxcw libw
  slibcew,calc.def;
  rc /t calc.res

calc.res:  calc.dlg
```

And we're done; compile and link the program and give it a try, as in Figure 9-16. When you bring the calculator up, you can plug (integer) values into the two text boxes, click the = button, and see the answer.

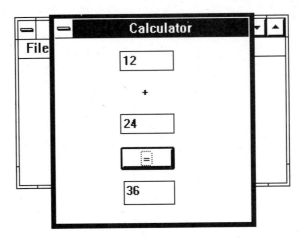

Figure 9-16. Our Calculator Example

We might also note that you can make a button inactive, graying out its caption and making it unresponsive to mouse clicks with a line like this: EnableWindow(GetDlgItem(103), FALSE), where we're assuming that 103 is the button's ID number (the GetDlgItem( ) function returns a window handle to the button — that is, buttons actually are windows). You can make it active again like this: EnableWindow(GetDlgItem(103), TRUE).

The next dialog box example will give us more experience with dialogs and will show us how to communicate with our controls. It turns out that we can rely on Window's text boxes to handle most of the details of text handling for us, and this means that we'll be able to put together a notepad example very easily, complete with word wrap and Cut and Paste capabilities. Let's turn to that now.

A Notepad Example

Start the Dialog Editor and draw a large text box, using the text box tool, as shown in Figure 9-17. Next, give this dialog box the name Notepad in the Caption box and click the text box twice to open the Edit Field Styles dialog box, as shown in Figure 9-18. To create our notepad, click the Multi-line and Vert. Scroll boxes, and then make sure that Auto HScroll is *not* clicked. Now click the OK button, making our notepad multi-line and giving it a vertical scroll bar. Add a Cancel button, setting its ID number to IDCANCEL. Finally, add two buttons labeled Cut and Paste, as shown in Figure 9-19.

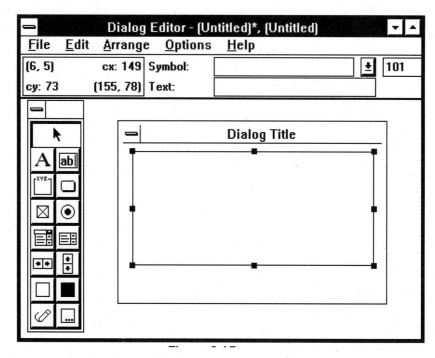

Figure 9-17. Starting Our Notepad Template

TIP By making sure automatic horizontal scroll is off in a text box, we make sure that automatic word wrap is turned on.

At this point, we're ready to integrate the new notepad into a program, so choose the Save As... item in the Dialog Editor's File menu, saving this dialog box as, say, npad.dlg. That file looks like this:

```
100 DIALOG 54, 28, 160, 114
STYLE DS_MODALFRAME | WS_POPUP | WS_VISIBLE | WS_CAPTION | WS_SYSMENU
CAPTION "Notepad"
FONT 8, "Helv"
BEGIN
    EDITTEXT        101, 5, 4, 151, 89, ES_MULTILINE | WS_VSCROLL
    PUSHBUTTON      "Cut", 102, 34, 98, 40, 14
    PUSHBUTTON      "Paste", 103, 96, 98, 40, 14
END
```

Now we can design the C++ code necessary to make it work. We start by deriving our class CMainDialog from CModalDialog and by adding two func-

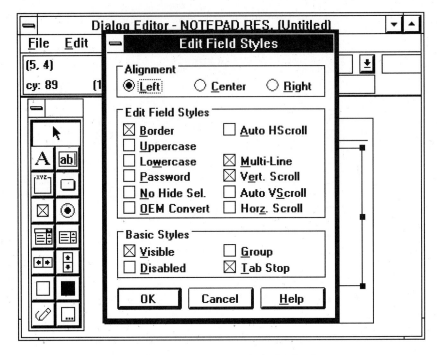

Figure 9-18. The Edit Field Styles Dialog Box

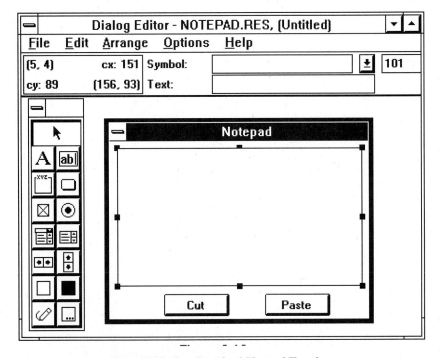

Figure 9-19. Our Completed Notepad Template

tions to take care of the Cut and Paste buttons we've added: OnCut( ) and OnPaste( ):

```
#include <afxwin.h>

class CMainDialog : public CModalDialog
{
public:
    CMainDialog(UINT resource_number, CWnd* parentWnd);
    afx_msg void OnCut();
    afx_msg void OnPaste();

    DECLARE_MESSAGE_MAP()
};

CMainDialog::CMainDialog(UINT resource_number, CWnd* parentWnd) :
        CModalDialog(resource_number, parentWnd)
{

}
```

Now we have to make our Cut and Paste buttons active by writing OnCut( ) and OnPaste( ). The text box itself will handle most of the details of text entry, and will even let the user select text (e.g., you can press the left mouse button at some location and move the cursor to another location; when you release it, the text in between will be highlighted). We can operate on the selected text (if any) with SendDlgItemMessage( ) statements like these (where the text box has control ID number 101):

```
SendDlgItemMessage(101, WM_CUT, 0, 0L);     //Cut text
SendDlgItemMessage(101, WM_COPY, 0, 0L);    //Copy text
SendDlgItemMessage(101, WM_CLEAR, 0, 0L);   //Clear text
SendDlgItemMessage(101, WM_PASTE, 0, 0L);   //Paste text
```

These statements instruct the text box to cut (to the Windows clipboard), copy (to the clipboard), clear, or paste (from the clipboard) the selected text. That means that cutting and pasting is actually very simple; any time the Cut or Paste button is clicked, we just have to send the appropriate message to the text box which handles all the details for us (note that if no text is selected, no text is cut or pasted over). That looks like this:

```
#include <afxwin.h>

class CMainDialog : public CModalDialog
{
public:
```

```
        CMainDialog(UINT resource_number, CWnd* parentWnd);
        afx_msg void OnCut();
        afx_msg void OnPaste();

        DECLARE_MESSAGE_MAP()
};

CMainDialog::CMainDialog(UINT resource_number, CWnd* parentWnd) :
        CModalDialog(resource_number, parentWnd)
{

}

void CMainDialog::OnCut()
{
        SendDlgItemMessage(101, WM_CUT, 0, 0L);
}

void CMainDialog::OnPaste()
{
        SendDlgItemMessage(101, WM_PASTE, 0, 0L);
}
```

Then we connect OnCut( ) to the Cut button (ID = 102) and OnPaste( ) to the Paste button (ID = 103) with the BEGIN_MESSAGE_MAP macro:

```
#include <afxwin.h>
#define IDM_DIALOG    1000
#define IDM_EXIT      2000

class CMainDialog : public CModalDialog
{
public:
        CMainDialog(UINT resource_number, CWnd* parentWnd);
        afx_msg void OnCut();
        afx_msg void OnPaste();

        DECLARE_MESSAGE_MAP()
};

CMainDialog::CMainDialog(UINT resource_number, CWnd* parentWnd) :
        CModalDialog(resource_number, parentWnd)
{

}

void CMainDialog::OnCut()
```

```
{
    SendDlgItemMessage(101, WM_CUT, 0, 0L);
}

void CMainDialog::OnPaste()
{
    SendDlgItemMessage(101, WM_PASTE, 0, 0L);
}

BEGIN_MESSAGE_MAP(CMainDialog, CModalDialog)
    ON_BN_CLICKED(102, OnCut)
    ON_BN_CLICKED(103, OnPaste)
END_MESSAGE_MAP()
```

To complete the program, we add a Notepad... item (ID = IDM_NOTEPAD) and an Exit (ID = IDM_EXIT) item to our File menu this way in npad.rc:

```
#include <windows.h>
#include <afxres.h>
#define IDM_NOTEPAD 1000
#define IDM_EXIT    2000

MainMenu MENU
{
  POPUP        "&File"
  {
    MENUITEM "&Notepad...\tF1", IDM_NOTEPAD
    MENUITEM "E&xit", IDM_EXIT
  }
}

MainAccelTable ACCELERATORS
{
  VK_F1,       IDM_NOTEPAD,  VIRTKEY
}

rcinclude npad.dlg
```

All that remains is to pop the notepad on the screen when the Notepad... item is clicked, and we can do that this way:

```
#include <afxwin.h>
#define IDM_NOTEPAD   1000
#define IDM_EXIT      2000

class CMainDialog : public CModalDialog
```

```
{
public:
      CMainDialog(UINT resource_number, CWnd* parentWnd);
      afx_msg void OnCut();
      afx_msg void OnPaste();

      DECLARE_MESSAGE_MAP()
};

CMainDialog::CMainDialog(UINT resource_number, CWnd* parentWnd) :
         CModalDialog(resource_number, parentWnd)
{

}

void CMainDialog::OnCut()
{
    SendDlgItemMessage(101, WM_CUT, 0, 0L);
}

void CMainDialog::OnPaste()
{
    SendDlgItemMessage(101, WM_PASTE, 0, 0L);
}

BEGIN_MESSAGE_MAP(CMainDialog, CModalDialog)
    ON_BN_CLICKED(102, OnCut)
    ON_BN_CLICKED(103, OnPaste)
END_MESSAGE_MAP()

class CMainWindow : public CFrameWnd
{
public:
      CMainWindow();
      afx_msg void OnNotepad();
      afx_msg void OnExit();

      DECLARE_MESSAGE_MAP()
};

CMainWindow::CMainWindow()
{
    LoadAccelTable("MainAccelTable");
    Create(NULL, "Notepad Application",
       WS_OVERLAPPEDWINDOW, rectDefault, NULL, "MainMenu" );
}

void CMainWindow::OnNotepad()
```

```
      {
→         CMainDialog dialog_box(100, this);
→         dialog_box.DoModal();
      }
```

The entire program npad.cpp appears in Listing 9-10, npad.dlg appears in Listing 9-11, npad.rc in Listing 9-12, npad.def in Listing 9-13, and the makefile in Listing 9-14.

Listing 9-10. Npad.cpp

```cpp
#include <afxwin.h>
#define IDM_NOTEPAD   1000
#define IDM_EXIT      2000

class CMainDialog : public CModalDialog
{
public:
    CMainDialog(UINT resource_number, CWnd* parentWnd);
    afx_msg void OnCut();
    afx_msg void OnPaste();

    DECLARE_MESSAGE_MAP()
};

CMainDialog::CMainDialog(UINT resource_number, CWnd* parentWnd) :
        CModalDialog(resource_number, parentWnd)
{

}

void CMainDialog::OnCut()
{
    SendDlgItemMessage(101, WM_CUT, 0, 0L);
}

void CMainDialog::OnPaste()
{
    SendDlgItemMessage(101, WM_PASTE, 0, 0L);
}

BEGIN_MESSAGE_MAP(CMainDialog, CModalDialog)
    ON_BN_CLICKED(102, OnCut)
    ON_BN_CLICKED(103, OnPaste)
END_MESSAGE_MAP()
```

(continued)

Listing 9-10. *(continued)*

```cpp
class CMainWindow : public CFrameWnd
{
public:
     CMainWindow();
     afx_msg void OnNotepad();
     afx_msg void OnExit();

     DECLARE_MESSAGE_MAP()
};

CMainWindow::CMainWindow()
{
    LoadAccelTable("MainAccelTable");
    Create(NULL, "Notepad Application",
        WS_OVERLAPPEDWINDOW, rectDefault, NULL, "MainMenu" );
}

void CMainWindow::OnNotepad()
{
    CMainDialog dialog_box(100, this);
    dialog_box.DoModal();
}

void CMainWindow::OnExit()
{
    DestroyWindow();
}

BEGIN_MESSAGE_MAP(CMainWindow, CFrameWnd)
    ON_COMMAND(IDM_NOTEPAD, OnNotepad)
    ON_COMMAND(IDM_EXIT, OnExit)
END_MESSAGE_MAP()

class CTheApp : public CWinApp
{
public:
    BOOL InitInstance();
};

BOOL CTheApp::InitInstance()
{
    m_pMainWnd = new CMainWindow();
    m_pMainWnd->ShowWindow( m_nCmdShow );
    m_pMainWnd->UpdateWindow();

 return TRUE;
}

CTheApp theApp;
```

Listing 9-11. Npad.dlg

```
100 DIALOG 54, 28, 160, 114
STYLE DS_MODALFRAME | WS_POPUP | WS_VISIBLE | WS_CAPTION |
    WS_SYSMENU
CAPTION "Notepad"
FONT 8, "Helv"
BEGIN
    EDITTEXT        101, 5, 4, 151, 89, ES_MULTILINE | WS_VSCROLL
    PUSHBUTTON      "Cut", 102, 34, 98, 40, 14
    PUSHBUTTON      "Paste", 103, 96, 98, 40, 14
END
```

Listing 9-12. Npad.rc

```
#include <windows.h>
#include <afxres.h>
#define IDM_NOTEPAD 1000
#define IDM_EXIT    2000

MainMenu MENU
{
  POPUP         "&File"
  {
    MENUITEM "&Notepad...\tF1", IDM_NOTEPAD
    MENUITEM "E&xit", IDM_EXIT
  }
}

MainAccelTable ACCELERATORS
{
  VK_F1,        IDM_NOTEPAD,  VIRTKEY
}

rcinclude npad.dlg
```

Listing 9-13. Npad.def

```
NAME            Npad
DESCRIPTION     'Notepad Example'

EXETYPE         WINDOWS
STUB            'WINSTUB.EXE'

CODE            PRELOAD MOVEABLE DISCARDABLE
DATA            PRELOAD MOVEABLE MULTIPLE

HEAPSIZE        1024
STACKSIZE       4096
```

Listing 9-14. Npad.exe's Makefile

```
CPPFLAGS= /AS /W3 /Zp /GA /GEs /G2

npad.exe:    npad.obj npad.def npad.res
  link /NOD /ONERROR:NOEXE npad, npad, NUL, safxcw libw
  slibcew,npad.def;
  rc /t npad.res

npad.res:  npad.dlg
```

We're ready to run. When you execute npad.exe, the main window opens. Now click the Notepad... item in the File menu, and the notepad appears, as in Figure 9-20. You can type in this notepad, and Windows automatically handles all the difficult aspects of text handling including backspaces, word wrap, and scrolling. In addition, if you select text, you can cut it with the Cut button, and paste it back in later with the Paste button.

TIP Note that our notepad is cleared every time we close it, because the notepad dialog box's destructor is invoked. If you want to change that, you can create the notepad using new in InitInstance( ) and then only use the DoModal( ) member function when you want to pop it on the screen. Another way is to store the text from the notepad (by sending a WM_GETTEXT message), override the OnInitDialog( ) function (which is called when the dialog box is placed on the screen), and restore it later (with a WM_SETTEXT message).

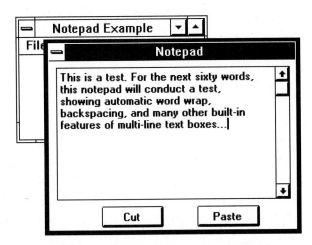

Figure 9-20. Our Notepad Program at Work

Before we finish with text boxes, it's worth noticing that there is an entire subclass of messages designed especially for them; these messages are prefaced with EM (for edit message). For example, we can find the position of the beginning and end of the selected text with EM_GETSEL (note that the first character in a text box is character 0):

```
lSelection = SendDlgItemMessage(101, EM_GETSEL, 0, 0L);
nStartPosition = LOWORD(lSelection);
nEndPosition = HIWORD(lSelection) - 1;
```

Or, we can select the start and end positions of the selected text ourselves with EM_SETSEL and the Windows MAKELONG( ) macro, which makes a long out of two integers:

```
SendDlgItemMessage(101, EM_SETSEL, 0, MAKELONG(nStart, nEnd));
```

Or, we can find the number of lines in a multi-line text box (like ours) with EM_GETLINECOUNT:

```
nLines = SendDlgItemMessage(101, EM_GETLINECOUNT, 0, 0L);
```

Overall, there are 25 text box command messages that we can send, and they appear in Table 9-3.

TIP Note that we can even undo the last edit in a text box by sending an EM_UNDO message.

Using a Dialog Box as Our Main Window

Our notepad is useful enough to be a stand-alone program instead of just a pop-up dialog box. In fact, we can use a dialog box as a program's main window (and it's often convenient to do so since we can design dialog boxes and place controls in them easily with the dialog editor). Let's see how this works with our notepad by making it into the program's main window. First, we take the earlier file notepad.dlg and make it into the program's .rc file by including windows.h and afxres.h in the beginning like this:

```
#include <windows.h>      ←
#include <afxres.h>       ←

100 DIALOG 54, 28, 160, 114
STYLE DS_MODALFRAME | WS_POPUP | WS_VISIBLE | WS_CAPTION | WS_SYSMENU
CAPTION "Notepad"
FONT 8, "Helv"
BEGIN
    EDITTEXT        101, 5, 4, 151, 89, ES_MULTILINE | WS_VSCROLL
    PUSHBUTTON      "Cut", 102, 34, 98, 40, 14
    PUSHBUTTON      "Paste", 103, 96, 98, 40, 14
END
```

EM_CANDO	Can undo occur?
EM_EMPTYUNDOBUFFER	Clear undo buffer
EM_FMTLINES	Add/remove end-of-line chars
EM_GETHANDLE	Get handle to data buffer of text
EM_GETLINE	Gets a line
EM_GETLINECOUNT	Get number of text lines
EM_GETMODIFY	Return modify flag
EM_GETRECT	Retrieve formatting rectangle
EM_GETSEL	Get start and end selected chars
EM_LIMITTEXT	Limits length (bytes) user can enter
EM_LINEFROMCHAR	Get line number of a char
EM_LINEINDEX	Get # of positions before first char on line
EM_LINELENGTH	Get length of a line
EM_LINESCROLL	Scroll lines by indicated number
EM_REPLACESEL	Replace selection with new text
EM_SETHANDLE	Set up text buffer
EM_SETMODIFY	Set modify flag
EM_SETPASSWORDCHAR	Sets char displayed in password text boxes
EM_SETRECT	Sets formatting rectangle
EM_SETRECTNP	Set formatiing rectangle, do not repaint
EM_SETSEL	Set selection
EM_SETTABSTOPS	Set tab stops
EM_SETWORDBREAK	Let application do work break
EM_UNDO	Undo last edit

Table 9-3. Text Box Command Messages

Now we have the new npad.rc. The next step is to write the C++ code. The idea here is simple; all we have to do is to create a main window out of a dialog box instead of our window class CMainWindow. Before, we created the main window and loaded it into the program in CTheApp::InitInstance( ) this way:

```
BOOL CTheApp::InitInstance()
{
    m_pMainWnd = new CMainWindow();
    m_pMainWnd->ShowWindow( m_nCmdShow );
    m_pMainWnd->UpdateWindow();

 return TRUE;
}
```

To use a dialog box as the main window, we can simply create a window of some dialog class instead of a window class like this:

```
BOOL CTheApp::InitInstance()
{
    m_pMainWnd = new CMainDialog();
    m_pMainWnd->ShowWindow(m_nCmdShow);
    m_pMainWnd->UpdateWindow();

 return TRUE;
}
```

Let's create our dialog box class now. To do that, we can derive it from the base class CDialog this way (the CModalDialog class, or classes derived from it, cannot become a program's main window; instead, we use CModalDialog's base class, CDialog):

```
#include <afxwin.h>

class CMainDialog : public CDialog
{

};
```

To create an object of type CDialog, we have to use the Create( ) member function. We cannot use CDialog's constructor here; it is protected because you have to derive your own dialog boxes from this class rather than using objects of CDialog directly. We want to create a dialog box corresponding to resource number 100, so we use CDialog::Create( ) like this:

```
        #include <afxwin.h>

        class CMainDialog : public CDialog
        {
        public:
→           CMainDialog(){Create (100);}
                :
        };
```

Next, we have to provide some way for the program to terminate. We can do that by adding code for the OnClose( ) function, which is called when the user selects the Close menu item in the dialog box's system menu (note that you cannot use your own menu bar when using a dialog box as the main window because dialog boxes cannot have menu bars). We do that like this with DestroyWindow( ):

```
        #include <afxwin.h>

        class CMainDialog : public CDialog
        {
        public:
            CMainDialog(){Create (100);}
→           afx_msg void OnClose(){DestroyWindow();}
                :
        };
```

Now we add OnCut( ) and OnPaste( ) as before, as well as the macro DE-CLARE_MESSAGE_MAP:

```
        #include <afxwin.h>

        class CMainDialog : public CDialog
        {
        public:
            CMainDialog(){Create (100);}
            afx_msg void OnClose(){DestroyWindow();}
→           afx_msg void OnCut();
→           afx_msg void OnPaste();

→           DECLARE_MESSAGE_MAP()
        };
```

The functions OnCut( ) and OnPaste( ) are exactly as before:

```
#include <afxwin.h>

class CMainDialog : public CDialog
{
public:
    CMainDialog(){Create (100);}
    afx_msg void OnClose(){DestroyWindow();}
    afx_msg void OnCut();
    afx_msg void OnPaste();

    DECLARE_MESSAGE_MAP()
};

void CMainDialog::OnCut()         ←
{
    SendDlgItemMessage(101, WM_CUT, 0, 0L);
}

void CMainDialog::OnPaste()       ←
{
    SendDlgItemMessage(101, WM_PASTE, 0, 0L);
}
    :
```

Next we connect the functions we defined to the messages we'll get with the BEGIN_MESSAGE_MAP macro:

```
#include <afxwin.h>

class CMainDialog : public CDialog
{
public:
    CMainDialog(){Create (100);}
    afx_msg void OnClose(){DestroyWindow();}
    afx_msg void OnCut();
    afx_msg void OnPaste();

    DECLARE_MESSAGE_MAP()
};

void CMainDialog::OnCut()
```

```
{
     SendDlgItemMessage(101, WM_CUT, 0, 0L);
}

void CMainDialog::OnPaste()
{
     SendDlgItemMessage(101, WM_PASTE, 0, 0L);
}

BEGIN_MESSAGE_MAP(CMainDialog, CDialog)
     ON_BN_CLICKED(102, OnCut)
     ON_BN_CLICKED(103, OnPaste)
     ON_WM_CLOSE()
END_MESSAGE_MAP()
          :
```

The last step is to make sure that we create an object of CMainDialog class and load it in:

```
#include <afxwin.h>

class CMainDialog : public CDialog
{
public:
     CMainDialog(){Create (100);}
     afx_msg void OnClose(){DestroyWindow();}
     afx_msg void OnCut();
     afx_msg void OnPaste();

     DECLARE_MESSAGE_MAP()
};

void CMainDialog::OnCut()
{
     SendDlgItemMessage(101, WM_CUT, 0, 0L);
}

void CMainDialog::OnPaste()
{
     SendDlgItemMessage(101, WM_PASTE, 0, 0L);
}

BEGIN_MESSAGE_MAP(CMainDialog, CDialog)
     ON_BN_CLICKED(102, OnCut)
```

```
        ON_BN_CLICKED(103, OnPaste)
        ON_WM_CLOSE()
    END_MESSAGE_MAP()

    class CTheApp : public CWinApp
    {
    public:
        BOOL InitInstance();
    };

    BOOL CTheApp::InitInstance()
    {
        m_pMainWnd = new CMainDialog();
        m_pMainWnd->ShowWindow(m_nCmdShow);
        m_pMainWnd->UpdateWindow();

     return TRUE;
    }

    CTheApp theApp;
```

The .def file and the makefile are just as before. When you compile and link this program, the dialog box notepad comes up as the main window as shown in Figure 9-21. Our program is a success — we've made a dialog box into our program's main window.

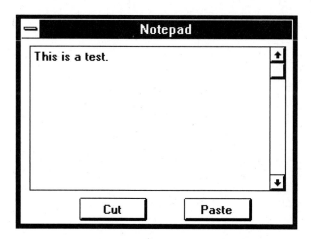

Figure 9-21. Our Notepad as Main Window

Scroll Boxes

We can go farther here, adding an additional vertical scroll bar to the side of our notepad if we wish. To do that, we can inherit our scroll bar class — CMainScroll — from the MFC class CScrollBar like this:

```
#include <afxwin.h>

class CMainScroll : public CScrollBar     ←
{
public:
     CMainScroll();
     afx_msg void OnVScroll(UINT nSBCode, UINT nPos, CScrollBar* pScrollBar);

     DECLARE_MESSAGE_MAP()
};
```

In the scroll bar's constructor, we only need to call the base class' constructor (i.e., CScrollBar's constructor). Note that we're also overriding the OnVScroll( ) function here so that we'll be notified when the scroll bar's thumb (the moveable box in the scroll bar) is moved:

```
CMainScroll::CMainScroll() : CScrollBar(){}

void CMainScroll::OnVScroll(UINT nSBCode, UINT nPos, CScrollBar* pScrollBar)
{
     SetScrollPos(nPos, TRUE);
}

BEGIN_MESSAGE_MAP(CMainScroll, CScrollBar)
     ON_WM_VSCROLL()
END_MESSAGE_MAP()
```

Here, we only move the thumb to its new position with SetScrollPos( ) in the function OnVScroll( ). That's all there is to it. Now we can add a scroll bar object of this type to our main window, CMainDialog:

```
     class CMainDialog : public CDialog
     {
     protected:
→        CMainScroll m_Scroll;
     public:
         CMainDialog(){Create (100);}
         BOOL OnInitDialog();
         afx_msg void OnClose(){DestroyWindow();}
```

```
        afx_msg void OnCut();
        afx_msg void OnPaste();

        DECLARE_MESSAGE_MAP()
    };
```

When you use scroll bars, you have to make sure that the Create( ) function is called after the scroll bar's constructor (here, the constructor is called because we've declared m_Scroll as a member of our CMainDialog class). We can call m_Scroll.Create( ) in the InitDialog( ) function, like this (note that we first set the scroll bar's size in a CRect object):

```
BOOL CMainDialog::OnInitDialog()
{
    CRect ScrollRect(6, 5, 24, 150);
→   m_Scroll.Create(WS_CHILD | WS_VISIBLE | SBS_VERT, ScrollRect, this, 104);
    m_Scroll.SetScrollRange(1, 255, TRUE);
    SetScrollPos(125, TRUE);
    return TRUE;
}
```

Now we're able to use vertical scroll bars at will. That's all for the notepad and our coverage of dialog boxes. In the next chapter, we'll start exploring Windows graphics when we create our own mouse-driven paint program.

Graphics and a
Mouse-driven Paint Program

Most of us are familiar with paint programs; using a paint program, you can draw graphics images by selecting and using graphics tools. For example, you can select a line drawing tool, press the left mouse button at the location where you want to anchor one end of the line, move to the other end of the line you want to draw, and release the mouse button. When you do, the program draws the line for you. This is the kind of program we're going to develop in this chapter. With it, we'll be able to create graphics images just like any paint program, and, more importantly, we'll get an idea of how to work with graphics in Windows.

Creating the Paint Program's Menus

We can design the paint program's menus first by setting up the file paint.rc. First, create a File menu like this:

```
#include <windows.h>
#include <afxres.h>

MainMenu MENU
```

```
      {
  →      POPUP  "File"
           {

           }
      }
```

We can place two items in that menu — New (so that the user can clear the current image and start over) and Exit:

```
   #include <windows.h>
   #include <afxres.h>

   MainMenu MENU
     {
       POPUP  "File"
         {
  →         MENUITEM "New", IDM_NEW
  →         MENUITEM "Exit", IDM_EXIT
         }
     }
```

Next, we can design a second menu which we might name Tools, which will let the user select from a set of different drawing tools. There are a variety of graphics functions available to us in Windows, so let's place some of the most popular in this menu: Point (draw a single point), Draw (freehand drawing), Line, Rectangle, Ellipse, and Fill (fill a figure with solid color):

```
   #include <windows.h>
   #include <afxres.h>

   MainMenu MENU
     {
       POPUP  "File"
         {
           MENUITEM "New", IDM_NEW
           MENUITEM "Exit", IDM_EXIT
         }
       POPUP  "Tools"
         {
  →         MENUITEM "Point", IDM_POINT
           MENUITEM "Draw", IDM_DRAW
           MENUITEM "Line", IDM_LINE
           MENUITEM "Rectangle", IDM_RECTANGLE
```

```
        MENUITEM "Ellipse", IDM_ELLIPSE
        MENUITEM "Fill", IDM_FILL
      }
   }
```

In addition, we can specify the initial state of menu items here in the .rc file, so let's give the first tool, Point, a check mark next to its name so the user knows it's the default tool. We can do that like this, with the constant **CHECKED**:

```
#include <windows.h>
#include <afxres.h>

MainMenu MENU
  {
    POPUP  "File"
      {
        MENUITEM "New", IDM_NEW
        MENUITEM "Exit", IDM_EXIT
      }
    POPUP  "Tools"
      {
        MENUITEM "Point", IDM_POINT, CHECKED
        MENUITEM "Draw", IDM_DRAW
        MENUITEM "Line", IDM_LINE
        MENUITEM "Rectangle", IDM_RECTANGLE
        MENUITEM "Ellipse", IDM_ELLIPSE
        MENUITEM "Fill", IDM_FILL
      }
  }
```

Since there are more constants here than we've used in the past (i.e., **IDM_FILE, IDM_NEW**, etc.), let's put them together into a file named paint.h so we can easily include them in both paint.rc and paint.cpp. Here is paint.h (the values given to the constants are arbitrary but unique):

```
#define IDM_FILE        1000
#define IDM_NEW         1050
#define IDM_EXIT        1100
#define IDM_TOOLS       2000
#define IDM_POINT       2050
#define IDM_DRAW        2100
#define IDM_LINE        2150
#define IDM_RECTANGLE   2200
```

```
#define IDM_ELLIPSE        2250
#define IDM_FILL           2300
```

And here's how we include it in paint.rc:

```
#include <windows.h>
#include <afxres.h>
#include "PAINT.h"          ←

MainMenu MENU
  {
    POPUP  "File"
      {
        MENUITEM "New", IDM_NEW
        MENUITEM "Exit", IDM_EXIT
      }
    POPUP  "Tools"
      {
        MENUITEM "Point", IDM_POINT, CHECKED
        MENUITEM "Draw", IDM_DRAW
        MENUITEM "Line", IDM_LINE
        MENUITEM "Rectangle", IDM_RECTANGLE
        MENUITEM "Ellipse", IDM_ELLIPSE
        MENUITEM "Fill", IDM_FILL
      }
  }
```

Now our menu system is ready to go; let's put together the program's code.

Writing the Paint Program

We can start the code by deriving our main window's class from CFrameWindow. That might look like this (note that we have included paint.h to get the definitions of IDM_NEW, IDM_EXIT, and so on):

```
#include <afxwin.h>
#include <windows.h>
#include "paint.h"

class CMainWindow : public CFrameWnd
{
public:
    CMainWindow();

};
```

All we have so far is the constructor, but we'll need other member functions and data as well. For example, when the user selects a drawing tool, it should remain active until another tool is chosen, and we can do that by setting a boolean flag. For example, if the user selects the Line option, we can set a boolean flag named bLine inside our window object and leave it set until the user chooses another drawing tool. When any part of our object needs to know what drawing tool is currently active, it can check these flags. We can define them as BOOL like this:

```
#include <afxwin.h>
#include <windows.h>
#include "paint.h"

class CMainWindow : public CFrameWnd
{
private:
    BOOL bPoint;
    BOOL bDraw;
    BOOL bLine;
    BOOL bRectangle;
    BOOL bEllipse;
    BOOL bFill;
public:
    CMainWindow();

};
```

These flags will be set when the user selects one of the drawing options (Line, Point, Ellipse, etc.). We'll need Onxxx functions to respond to menu selections and set these flags appropriately, so let's add them now:

```
#include <afxwin.h>
#include <windows.h>
#include "paint.h"

class CMainWindow : public CFrameWnd
{
private:
    BOOL bPoint;
    BOOL bDraw;
    BOOL bLine;
    BOOL bRectangle;
    BOOL bEllipse;
    BOOL bFill;
```

```
      public:
          CMainWindow();
→         afx_msg void OnNew();
:         afx_msg void OnExit();
:         afx_msg void OnPoint();
:         afx_msg void OnDraw();
:         afx_msg void OnLine();
:         afx_msg void OnRectangle();
:         afx_msg void OnEllipse();
→         afx_msg void OnFill();

          DECLARE_MESSAGE_MAP()
      };
```

In addition, we'll need to respond to mouse events, so we can include the mouse event prototypes (from afxwin.h) like this:

```
      #include <afxwin.h>
      #include <windows.h>
      #include "paint.h"

      class CMainWindow : public CFrameWnd
      {
      private:
          BOOL bPoint;
          BOOL bDraw;
          BOOL bLine;
          BOOL bRectangle;
          BOOL bEllipse;
          BOOL bFill;
      public:
          CMainWindow();
          afx_msg void OnNew();
          afx_msg void OnExit();
          afx_msg void OnPoint();
          afx_msg void OnDraw();
          afx_msg void OnLine();
          afx_msg void OnRectangle();
          afx_msg void OnEllipse();
          afx_msg void OnFill();
→         afx_msg void OnLButtonDown(UINT nFlags, CPoint point);
→         afx_msg void OnLButtonUp(UINT nFlags, CPoint point);
→         afx_msg void OnMouseMove(UINT nFlags, CPoint point);

          DECLARE_MESSAGE_MAP()
      };
```

Now let's write the functions we've just declared. We can start with the constructor, which simply creates the window and sets bPoint to TRUE, since the Point drawing tool is our default drawing tool (it's the first one in the Tools menu):

```
#include <afxwin.h>
#include <windows.h>
#include "paint.h"

class CMainWindow : public CFrameWnd
{
private:
    BOOL bPoint;
    BOOL bDraw;
    BOOL bLine;
    BOOL bRectangle;
    BOOL bEllipse;
    BOOL bFill;
public:
    CMainWindow();
    afx_msg void OnNew();
    afx_msg void OnExit();
    afx_msg void OnPoint();
    afx_msg void OnDraw();
    afx_msg void OnLine();
    afx_msg void OnRectangle();
    afx_msg void OnEllipse();
    afx_msg void OnFill();
    afx_msg void OnLButtonDown(UINT nFlags, CPoint point);
    afx_msg void OnLButtonUp(UINT nFlags, CPoint point);
    afx_msg void OnMouseMove(UINT nFlags, CPoint point);

    DECLARE_MESSAGE_MAP()
};

CMainWindow::CMainWindow()
{
    Create(NULL, "Paint", WS_OVERLAPPEDWINDOW,
        rectDefault, NULL, "MainMenu");
    bPoint = TRUE;
}
```

Now we can add the code for the two File menu items New (clear the window) and Exit. Exit, of course, simply uses DestroyWindow( ). To clear the client area, all we have to do is to declare it invalid with the CMainWindow member function InvalidateRect( ). We pass that function two parameters: NULL to indicate that we want the whole client area declared invalid, and a value of TRUE to indicate that we want the window erased before it is redrawn. Next, we can redraw the window with the UpdateWindow( ) function, which simply sends us a WM_PAINT message. Since we haven't declared a WM_PAINT handler, that message is handled by the default handler, which will simply erase the client area as we've requested, blanking the window:

```
#include <afxwin.h>
#include <windows.h>
#include "paint.h"

class CMainWindow : public CFrameWnd
{
private:
    BOOL bPoint;
    BOOL bDraw;
    BOOL bLine;
    BOOL bRectangle;
    BOOL bEllipse;
    BOOL bFill;
public:
    CMainWindow();
    afx_msg void OnNew();
    afx_msg void OnExit();
    afx_msg void OnPoint();
    afx_msg void OnDraw();
    afx_msg void OnLine();
    afx_msg void OnRectangle();
    afx_msg void OnEllipse();
    afx_msg void OnFill();
    afx_msg void OnLButtonDown(UINT nFlags, CPoint point);
    afx_msg void OnLButtonUp(UINT nFlags, CPoint point);
    afx_msg void OnMouseMove(UINT nFlags, CPoint point);

    DECLARE_MESSAGE_MAP()
};

CMainWindow::CMainWindow()
{
    Create(NULL, "Paint", WS_OVERLAPPEDWINDOW,
        rectDefault, NULL, "MainMenu");
    bPoint = TRUE;
}

void CMainWindow::OnNew()
```

```
        {
→           InvalidateRect(NULL, TRUE);
→           UpdateWindow();
        }
        void CMainWindow::OnExit()
        {
→           DestroyWindow();
        }
```

Now we can start working on the functions that respond to the Tools menu items: OnPoint( ), OnDraw( ), OnLine( ), OnRectangle( ), OnEllipse( ), and OnFill( ). The only job of those functions will be to set the boolean flags bPoint, bDraw, bLine, bRectangle, bEllipse, and bFill. Then, when the real action takes place with the mouse, we can check what type of figure we're supposed to be drawing (i.e., when the mouse button goes up, we are supposed to draw the correct graphics figure on the screen). That means that the Tools menu functions look like this:

```
        void CMainWindow::OnPoint()
        {
            bPoint = TRUE;
            bDraw = FALSE;
            bLine = FALSE;
            bRectangle = FALSE;
            bEllipse = FALSE;
            bFill = FALSE;
        }
        void CMainWindow::OnDraw()
        {
            bPoint = FALSE;
            bDraw = TRUE;
            bLine = FALSE;
            bRectangle = FALSE;
            bEllipse = FALSE;
            bFill = FALSE;
        }
        void CMainWindow::OnLine()
        {
            bPoint = FALSE;
            bDraw = FALSE;
            bLine = TRUE;
            bRectangle = FALSE;
            bEllipse = FALSE;
            bFill = FALSE;
        }
```

```
void CMainWindow::OnRectangle()
{
    bPoint = FALSE;
    bDraw = FALSE;
    bLine = FALSE;
    bRectangle = TRUE;
    bEllipse = FALSE;
    bFill = FALSE;
}
void CMainWindow::OnEllipse()
{
    bPoint = FALSE;
    bDraw = FALSE;
    bLine = FALSE;
    bRectangle = FALSE;
    bEllipse = TRUE;
    bFill = FALSE;
}
void CMainWindow::OnFill()
{
    bPoint = FALSE;
    bDraw = FALSE;
    bLine = FALSE;
    bRectangle = FALSE;
    bEllipse = FALSE;
    bFill = TRUE;
}
```

In addition, we should remove the check mark from the previous tool in the Tools menu and place it in front of the newly selected tool. We can do that with a function named CheckOnlyMenuItem( ), which takes the ID number of the new item to check. That function looks like this:

```
void CMainWindow::CheckOnlyMenuItem(int item_to_check)
{
    CMenu* pMenu = GetMenu();
    pMenu->CheckMenuItem(IDM_POINT, MF_UNCHECKED);
    pMenu->CheckMenuItem(IDM_DRAW, MF_UNCHECKED);
    pMenu->CheckMenuItem(IDM_LINE, MF_UNCHECKED);
    pMenu->CheckMenuItem(IDM_RECTANGLE, MF_UNCHECKED);
    pMenu->CheckMenuItem(IDM_ELLIPSE, MF_UNCHECKED);
    pMenu->CheckMenuItem(IDM_FILL, MF_UNCHECKED);
    pMenu->CheckMenuItem(item_to_check, MF_CHECKED);
}
```

And we can add it to each of the functions OnPoint( ), OnDraw( ), On–
Line( ), OnRectangle( ), OnEllipse( ), and OnFill( ) like this:

```
#include <afxwin.h>
#include <windows.h>
#include "paint.h"

class CMainWindow : public CFrameWnd
{
private:
    BOOL bPoint;
    BOOL bDraw;
    BOOL bLine;
    BOOL bRectangle;
    BOOL bEllipse;
    BOOL bFill;
    void CheckOnlyMenuItem(int item_to_check);
public:
    CMainWindow();
    afx_msg void OnNew();
    afx_msg void OnExit();
    afx_msg void OnPoint();
    afx_msg void OnDraw();
    afx_msg void OnLine();
    afx_msg void OnRectangle();
    afx_msg void OnEllipse();
    afx_msg void OnFill();
    afx_msg void OnLButtonDown(UINT nFlags, CPoint point);
    afx_msg void OnLButtonUp(UINT nFlags, CPoint point);
    afx_msg void OnMouseMove(UINT nFlags, CPoint point);

    DECLARE_MESSAGE_MAP()
};

CMainWindow::CMainWindow()
{
    Create(NULL, "Paint", WS_OVERLAPPEDWINDOW,
        rectDefault, NULL, "MainMenu");
    bPoint = TRUE;
}

void CMainWindow::OnNew()
{
    InvalidateRect(NULL, TRUE);
    UpdateWindow();
}
```

```
void CMainWindow::OnExit()
{
    DestroyWindow();
}
void CMainWindow::OnPoint()
{
    CheckOnlyMenuItem(IDM_POINT);          ←
    bPoint = TRUE;
    bDraw = FALSE;
    bLine = FALSE;
    bRectangle = FALSE;
    bEllipse = FALSE;
    bFill = FALSE;
}
void CMainWindow::OnDraw()
{
    CheckOnlyMenuItem(IDM_DRAW);           ←
    bPoint = FALSE;
    bDraw = TRUE;
    bLine = FALSE;
    bRectangle = FALSE;
    bEllipse = FALSE;
    bFill = FALSE;
}
void CMainWindow::OnLine()
{
    CheckOnlyMenuItem(IDM_LINE);           ←
    bPoint = FALSE;
    bDraw = FALSE;
    bLine = TRUE;
    bRectangle = FALSE;
    bEllipse = FALSE;
    bFill = FALSE;
}
void CMainWindow::OnRectangle()
{
    CheckOnlyMenuItem(IDM_RECTANGLE);      ←
    bPoint = FALSE;
    bDraw = FALSE;
    bLine = FALSE;
    bRectangle = TRUE;
    bEllipse = FALSE;
    bFill = FALSE;
}
void CMainWindow::OnEllipse()
{
    CheckOnlyMenuItem(IDM_ELLIPSE);        ←
    bPoint = FALSE;
```

```
        bDraw = FALSE;
        bLine = FALSE;
        bRectangle = FALSE;
        bEllipse = TRUE;
        bFill = FALSE;
    }
    void CMainWindow::OnFill()
    {
        CheckOnlyMenuItem(IDM_FILL);              ←
        bPoint = FALSE;
        bDraw = FALSE;
        bLine = FALSE;
        bRectangle = FALSE;
        bEllipse = FALSE;
        bFill = TRUE;
    }

    void CMainWindow::CheckOnlyMenuItem(int item_to_check)
    {
        CMenu* pMenu = GetMenu();
        pMenu->CheckMenuItem(IDM_POINT, MF_UNCHECKED);
        pMenu->CheckMenuItem(IDM_DRAW, MF_UNCHECKED);
        pMenu->CheckMenuItem(IDM_LINE, MF_UNCHECKED);
        pMenu->CheckMenuItem(IDM_RECTANGLE, MF_UNCHECKED);
        pMenu->CheckMenuItem(IDM_ELLIPSE, MF_UNCHECKED);
        pMenu->CheckMenuItem(IDM_FILL, MF_UNCHECKED);
        pMenu->CheckMenuItem(item_to_check, MF_CHECKED);
    }
```

Now when the user makes a menu selection, the check mark will appear in front of it to indicate that that tool is the current drawing tool, and the correct boolean flag will be set. Now let's see what we can do about drawing in our window.

Setting Individual Pixels in Windows

The action will take place when the user uses the mouse. For example, let's say that the user has selected our first drawing tool, Point, which sets individual points. To use it, the user only needs to move the mouse cursor to a certain location and click the (left) mouse button. When the mouse button goes up, we can draw the point at that location. To do that, we'll have to make sure that we're supposed to be drawing points (i.e., bPoint is TRUE), and then we can use the device context function SetPixel( ). We pass the x and y coordinates of the point to set to SetPixel( ) as well as the color we want our pixel to be.

We can set the color of the pixel to black with the RGB( ) macro. This macro returns a value of type COLORDEF, which is how Windows declares colors. RGB( ) takes three parameters, each of which range from 0 to 255, and each of which represent one of the primary color values: in order, red, greeen, and blue. This is the way to design colors in Windows, with separate values for the red, green, and blue components. Here, we're setting our pixel to black; i.e., all color components are 0: RGB(0, 0, 0):

```
void CMainWindow::OnLButtonUp(UINT nFlags, CPoint point)
{
    if(bPoint){
     CClientDC dc(this);
     dc.SetPixel(point.x, point.y, RGB(0, 0, 0));
    }
     :
}
```

Note that the three values RGB( ) takes can range from 0 to 255; if, for example, we wanted a red dot, we could have specified that like this: RGB(255, 0, 0). That's it for drawing points; now when the user wants to set individual pixels, they only have to select Point from the tools menu as shown in Figure 10-1 (setting bPoint TRUE) and click the mouse button when the cursor is at the desired location (generating WM_LBUTTONDOWN and WM_BUTTONUP events), drawing points as in Figure 10-2.

The next tool in the Tools menu — and the next graphics operation we'll cover — is freehand drawing.

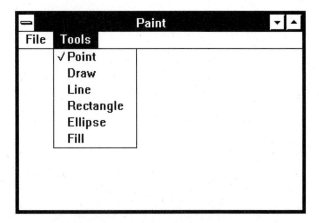

Figure 10-1. Our Paint Program's Point Item

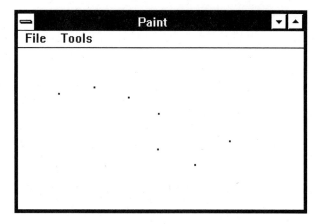

Figure 10-2. Points in Our Paint Program

Freehand Drawing in Our Paint Program

To let the user draw freehand, we should use the WM_MOUSEMOVE event. This event is generated as the mouse moves across the screen, and when it is, our function OnMouseMove( ) will be called:

```
void CMainWindow::OnMouseMove(UINT nFlags, CPoint point)
```

Here point holds the current mouse cursor position (x = point.x, y = point.y), and nFlags is encoded bit by bit to indicate what mouse buttons are down like this (MK stands for mouse key):

MK_LBUTTON	Left button is down
MK_MBUTTON	Middle button is down
MK_RBUTTON	Right button is down

That is, nFlags is made up of the appropriate combination of these constants, ORed together. When the user wants to draw, they will hold the left mouse button and move the mouse. We can check the left button and also determine whether or not the Draw tool is active by checking bDraw like this:

```
void CMainWindow::OnMouseMove(UINT nFlags, CPoint point)
{
     if((nFlags && MK_LBUTTON) && bDraw){
          :
     }
}
```

Now we have to get a device context object, which we do like this:

```
void CMainWindow::OnMouseMove(UINT nFlags, CPoint point)
{
    if((nFlags && MK_LBUTTON) && bDraw){
      CClientDC dc(this);
                    :
    }
}
```

The next step is to draw on the screen. Although you might think we should use SetPixel( ) here, mouse move events are not actually generated for every pixel we pass over. Instead, a limited number of these events are generated per second; if we simply drew a dot on the screen, we've end up with an unconnected trail of pixels. Instead, we should store the previous mouse location and draw a line from that location to our current position. The effect on the screen will be of a continuous path of set pixels, following the mouse cursor in our window.

Unlike setting individual pixels, we need two points for a line. When the user presses the left mouse button to start drawing, we can set one end of the line, which we can call the anchor point. Next, the user moves the cursor, and we should draw a line. In code, that means that we should set the anchor point, which we can store as (xAnchor, yAnchor), when the left button goes down (WM_LBUTTONDOWN) like this:

```
#include <afxwin.h>
#include <windows.h>
#include "paint.h"

class CMainWindow : public CFrameWnd
{
private:
    int xAnchor;
    int yAnchor;
    BOOL bPoint;
    BOOL bDraw;
    BOOL bLine;
    BOOL bRectangle;
    BOOL bEllipse;
    BOOL bFill;
    void CheckOnlyMenuItem(int item_to_check);
public:
    CMainWindow();
    afx_msg void OnNew();
    afx_msg void OnExit();
```

```
          afx_msg void OnPoint();
          afx_msg void OnDraw();
          afx_msg void OnLine();
          afx_msg void OnRectangle();
          afx_msg void OnEllipse();
          afx_msg void OnFill();
          afx_msg void OnLButtonDown(UINT nFlags, CPoint point);
          afx_msg void OnLButtonUp(UINT nFlags, CPoint point);
          afx_msg void OnMouseMove(UINT nFlags, CPoint point);

          DECLARE_MESSAGE_MAP()
     };
             :
             :
             :
     void CMainWindow::OnLButtonDown(UINT nFlags, CPoint point)
     {
→        xAnchor = point.x;
→        yAnchor = point.y;
     }
```

Now, in the **WM_MOUSEMOVE** event, we need to draw a line from (xAnchor, yAnchor) to (point.x, point.y). To draw lines, we use the MoveTo( ) and LineTo( ) functions. We can only pass the location of one point to LineTo( ), and it draws a line from the *current position* to that point. To set the current position, we use MoveTo( ):

```
     void CMainWindow::OnMouseMove(UINT nFlags, CPoint point)
     {
          if((nFlags && MK_LBUTTON) && bDraw){
           CClientDC dc(this);
→         dc.MoveTo(xAnchor, yAnchor);
             :
          }
     }
```

And then we can draw the line connecting the dots with LineTo( ):

```
     void CMainWindow::OnMouseMove(UINT nFlags, CPoint point)
     {
          if((nFlags && MK_LBUTTON) && bDraw){
           CClientDC dc(this);
           dc.MoveTo(xAnchor, yAnchor);
→         dc.LineTo(point.x, point.y);
             :
          }
     }
```

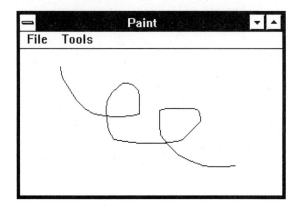

Figure 10-3. Freehand Drawing with Our Paint Program

Finally, we should update the anchor point so the next time a mouse move event is generated, we'll connect to the end of the line we just drew (note that the anchor point is only updated if bDraw is TRUE; that is, if we're drawing freehand):

```
void CMainWindow::OnMouseMove(UINT nFlags, CPoint point)
{
    if((nFlags && MK_LBUTTON) && bDraw){
    CClientDC dc(this);
    dc.MoveTo(xAnchor, yAnchor);
    dc.LineTo(point.x, point.y);
    xAnchor = point.x;
    yAnchor = point.y;
    }
}
```

And that's it; when the user selects the Draw tool, they can hold the left mouse button down and move the mouse cursor around, drawing as shown in Figure 10-3.

The next step, and the next drawing tool, is Line, which will allow the user to draw lines on the screen. Let's look into that next.

Drawing Lines

The usual way for the user to draw lines in a paint program is to select the Line tool, press the left button at one point on the screen, move the cursor to the other end of the line, and release the left button. At that time, the program connects the two points, i.e., the location where the left button went down and the location where it went up.

We already set the anchor point, which we'll use as the first end of the line, in the WM_LBUTTONDOWN event:

```
    void CMainWindow::OnLButtonDown(UINT nFlags, CPoint point)
    {
→       xAnchor = point.x;
→       yAnchor = point.y;
    }
```

Next, when the button goes back up in OnLButtonUp( ), we can complete the line. Since we want to draw a line from (xAnchor, yAnchor) to the new location, which is encoded in point as (point.x, point.y), we can draw our line like this:

```
    void CMainWindow::OnLButtonUp(UINT nFlags, CPoint point)
    {
        CGdiObject* pBackup;

        if(bPoint){
         CClientDC dc(this);
         dc.SetPixel(point.x, point.y, RGB(0, 0, 0));
        }
        if(bLine){
         CClientDC dc(this);
→        dc.MoveTo(xAnchor, yAnchor);
→        dc.LineTo(point.x, point.y);
        }
    }
```

And that's it. Now we can draw lines, as shown in Figure 10-4. We just select the Line tool (setting bLine TRUE), press the left mouse button at some location (setting the anchor point in the OnLButtonDown( ) function), move to the final location, and release the mouse button (drawing the line with MoveTo( ) and LineTo( ) in OnLButtonUp( )).

We can draw in different colors as well.

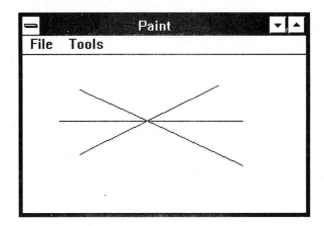

Figure 10-4. Drawing Lines in Our Paint Program

Selecting Colors and Pens

We do not specify the drawing colors for lines in the same way that we do for points (where we included a color value in the SetPixel( ) call). Instead, we have to design a new *pen*. We draw figures in Windows with pens, and, as we'll see, we can fill the figures in with *brushes*. Once you place a pen into a device context object, it stays there until changed. To change the pen in a device context object, you can use SelectStockObject( ) like this:

```
dc.SelectStockObject(STOCK_OBJECT);
```

The available stock objects are shown in Table 10-1; we can select from these three: NULL_PEN, BLACK_PEN, and WHITE_PEN. Another option is to design our own pen.

Let's say that we wanted to draw blue lines. In that case, we could create a solid blue pen, one pixel wide with the CPen member function CreatePen( ). CreatePen( ) takes three parameters: a pen style, a pixel width for the pen, and a color. The different pen styles, from solid to dotted, are shown in Figure 10-5. These are (PS stands for pen style):

PS_SOLID	Solid line
PS_DASH	Dashed line
PS_DOT	Dotted line

PS_DASHDOT	Dash-dot line
PS_DASHDOTDOT	Dash-dot-dot line
PS_NULL	Null line (does not draw)
PS_INSIDEFRAME	Draw inside boundaries

TIP The last pen type above, PS_INSIDEFRAME, is used when you're drawing closed figures with a border width greater than one pixel, but don't want to draw outside the figure. For example, if you set the pen style to **PS_IN-SIDEFRAME** and then draw a rectangle with the Rectangle( ) function (which is coming up), the border line, no matter how thick, will stay inside the rectangle's boundary. The other pen styles would overlap outside the rectangle.

Stock Object	*Means*
BLACK_BRUSH	Black brush
DKGRAY_BRUSH	Dark gray brush
GRAY_BRUSH	Gray brush
HOLLOW_BRUSH	Hollow brush
LTGRAY_BRUSH	Light gray brush
NULL_BRUSH	Null brush
WHITE_BRUSH	White brush
BLACK_PEN	Black pen
NULL_PEN	Null pen
WHITE_PEN	White pen
ANSI_FIXED_FONT	ANSI fixed system font
ANSI_VAR_FONT	ANSI variable system font
DEVICE_DEFAULT_FONT	Device-dependent font
OEM_FIXED_FONT	OEM-dependent fixed font
SYSTEM_FONT	The system font
SYSTEM_FIXED_FONT	The fixed-width system font
DEFAULT_PALETTE	Default color palette

Table 10-1. Device Context Stock Objects

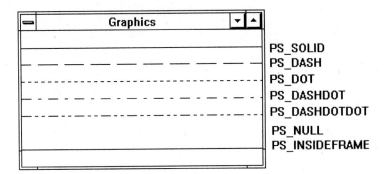

Figure 10-5. Windows Pen Styles

We want a solid blue line, so we choose PS_SOLID. In addition, we want a pen width of one pixel, so we have the first two parameters for CreatePen( ):

```
CPen* pPen = new CPen;
pPen->CreatePen(PS_SOLID, 1...);
```

Finally, we have to specify the color of the pen. To create a solid blue pen, we can do this:

```
CPen* pPen = new CPen;
pPen->CreatePen(PS_SOLID, 1, RGB(0, 0, 255));
```

RGB(255, 0, 0) would have been all red, RGB(0, 255, 0) green.

TIP You can specify white with RGB( ) like this: RGB(255, 255, 255). In addition, the standard gray in Windows is actually RGB(128, 128, 128).

Now we can use SelectObject( ) to install this pen. In general, you use SelectObject( ) like this:

```
SelectObject(pGdi)
```

Here, pGdi is a pointer to an object of class CGdiObject (a graphics device interface object), which can point to any of these classes:

CPen   Pen Object
CBrush   Brush Object
CFont   Font Object
CBitmap   Bitmap Object

SelectObject( ) returns a pointer to the object it is replacing, and it's usually a good idea to store that handle and reinstall it when you're done. We can do that by declaring a variable of type CGdiObject* which we might call pPenOld:

```
    void CMainWindow::OnLButtonUp(UINT nFlags, CPoint point)
    {
→        CGdiObject* pPenOld;

        if(bPoint){
         CClientDC dc(this);
         dc.SetPixel(point.x, point.y, RGB(0, 0, 0));
        }
        if(bLine){
         CClientDC dc(this);
→       CPen* pPen = new CPen;
→       pPen->CreatePen(PS_SOLID, 1, RGB(0, 0, 255));
→       pPenOld = dc.SelectObject(pPen);
         dc.MoveTo(xAnchor, yAnchor);
         dc.LineTo(point.x, point.y);
                 :
        }
    }
```

When we're done drawing, we can replace the original pen like this:

```
    void CMainWindow::OnLButtonUp(UINT nFlags, CPoint point)
    {
        CGdiObject* pPenOld;

        if(bPoint){
         CClientDC dc(this);
         dc.SetPixel(point.x, point.y, RGB(0, 0, 0));
        }
        if(bLine){
         CClientDC dc(this);
         CPen* pPen = new CPen;
         pPen->CreatePen(PS_SOLID, 1, RGB(0, 0, 255));
         pPenOld = dc.SelectObject(pPen);
         dc.MoveTo(xAnchor, yAnchor);
         dc.LineTo(point.x, point.y);
→        dc.SelectObject(pPenOld);
→        delete pPen;
        }
    }
```

This code would enable us to draw blue lines — now we're drawing in color. The next tool in our paint program is Rectangle, which will let us draw rectangles, a process which works much like drawing lines.

Drawing Rectangles

After the user selects the Rectangle tool, they press the mouse button at the location of one corner, move the cursor to the other corner, and release it. At that point, the program draws the rectangle. When drawing a line, we had to use two points like this:

When drawing a rectangle, we also need to specify two points, like this:

Here, however, we don't have to use MoveTo( ) to set the current position; instead, the device context Rectangle( ) member function can take the coordinates of both points at once, like this:

```
dc.Rectangle(ax, ay, bx, by);
```

This call draws a rectangle with the current pen from (ax, ay) to (bx, by). In our case, the anchor point is set when the user presses the left mouse button, and we can place the rectangle-drawing code in the WM_LBUTTONUP case. In particular, the rectangle we want to draw goes from (xAnchor, yAnchor) to (point.x, point.y). That means that we can draw rectangles like this:

```
void CMainWindow::OnLButtonUp(UINT nFlags, CPoint point)
{
    CGdiObject* pBackup;

    if(bPoint){
     CClientDC dc(this);
     dc.SetPixel(point.x, point.y, RGB(0, 0, 0));
    }
```

```
     if(bLine){
      CClientDC dc(this);
      dc.MoveTo(xAnchor, yAnchor);
      dc.LineTo(point.x, point.y);
     }
     if(bRectangle){
      CClientDC dc(this);
→     dc.Rectangle(xAnchor, yAnchor, point.x, point.y);
     }
   }
```

It looks as though this should work — we're passing the anchor point and the point at which the left button went up to Rectangle( ). However, there is a problem. When Windows draws rectangles or other closed figures, it fills them in with the background color by default, covering over what was there before. That means that when the user draws a rectangle, anything behind it will be obliterated, which is not the standard for paint programs.

Instead, we should draw figures and fill them transparently, so whatever is behind them is preserved. To do that, we have to select a new *brush.* Just as pens are used for drawing, so brushes are used for filling. And, just as there are some stock pens we can use with SelectStockObject( ), so there are stock brushes: BLACK_BRUSH, DKGRAY_BRUSH, GRAY_BRUSH, HOLLOW_BRUSH LT_GRAY_BRUSH, NULL_BRUSH, WHITE_BRUSH. For example, to load BLACK_BRUSH into the device context, and therefore to fill with black, we would use this call:

```
     pBackup = dc.SelectStockObject(BLACK_BRUSH);
```

TIP Note that you can delete text by covering it with a filled rectangle like this. You can use GetBkColor( ) to get the background color and create both a pen and solid brush of that color. Then, using GetTextMetrics( ), you can determine how high the current font is, and using GetTextExtent( ), you can determine how long the string is you want to delete. Finally, you can delete the text with Rectangle( ).

In this case, we want to use NULL_BRUSH, which insures that our figures will not be filled. Note that we save the old brush object that we're replacing (i.e., we get a pointer to the old brush from SelectStockObject( )), and restore it when we're done:

```
void CMainWindow::OnLButtonUp(UINT nFlags, CPoint point)
{
    CGdiObject* pBackup;

    if(bPoint){
     CClientDC dc(this);
     dc.SetPixel(point.x, point.y, RGB(0, 0, 0));
    }
    if(bLine){
     CClientDC dc(this);
     dc.MoveTo(xAnchor, yAnchor);
     dc.LineTo(point.x, point.y);
    }
    if(bRectangle){
     CClientDC dc(this);
     pBackup = dc.SelectStockObject(NULL_BRUSH);
     dc.Rectangle(xAnchor, yAnchor, point.x, point.y);
     dc.SelectObject(pBackup);
    }
}
```

Now we're able to draw objects in our application without disturbing what was underneath. However, there are one or two more points about brushes that we should still cover. Just as we could create pens, so we can also create brushes. In fact, there are two standard ways of creating brushes in Windows: with the CBrush member functions CreateSolidBrush( ) and CreateHatchBrush( ).

To create a solid brush (and therefore to fill with a solid color) we can use CreateSolidBrush( ), and pass it the color we want like this to create a green brush:

```
CBrush* pBrush = new CBrush;
pBrush->CreateSolidBrush(RGB(0, 255, 0));
pBackup = SelectObject(pBrush);
```

We can also create a hatch brush, which has a predefined pattern in it, with CreateHatchBrush( ). Here, we pass two parameters: the hatch style we want, and the color we want. The allowed hatch styles are (HS stands for hatch style): HS_HORIZONTAL, HS_VERTICAL, HS_FDIAGONAL, HS_BDIAGONAL, HS_CROSS, and HS_DIAGCROSS, as shown in Figure 10-6. For exam-

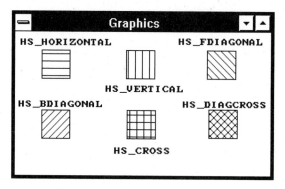

Figure 10-6. Windows Hatch Styles

ple, if we wanted to create a gray hatch brush of style HS_DIAGCROSS, we could do that like this:

```
CBrush* pBrush = new CBrush;
pBrush->CreateHatchBrush(HS_DIAGCROSS, RGB(128, 128, 128);
pBackup = SelectObject(pBrush);
```

In this way, we can fill our figures with colored patterns if we prefer.

TIP　　　You can even create your own brush patterns with the Windows functions CreatePatternBrush( ) or CreateBrushIndirect( ).

At this point, we're done with drawing rectangles. The next drawing tool in our paint program is Ellipse, and, as we'll see, drawing ellipses is very similar to drawing rectangles.

Drawing Ellipses

When the user selects the Ellipse tool, they can press the left mouse button, setting an anchor point, move the cursor to a new location, and then release the mouse button. When they release the button, we should draw an ellipse. We can do that with the Ellipse( ) function, whose arguments are identical to the Rectangle( ) function. In this case, however, an ellipse is inscribed inside the rectangle whose coordinates we pass. One corner of the rectangle will be (xAnchor, yAnchor) and the other will be (point.x, point.y). To do this, we simply check if the bEllipse flag is set in OnLButtonUp( ), and, if it is, proceed as if we were drawing a rectangle — but use Ellipse( ) instead:

```
void CMainWindow::OnLButtonUp(UINT nFlags, CPoint point)
{
    CGdiObject* pBackup;

    if(bPoint){
     CClientDC dc(this);
     dc.SetPixel(point.x, point.y, RGB(0, 0, 0));
    }
    if(bLine){
     CClientDC dc(this);
     dc.MoveTo(xAnchor, yAnchor);
     dc.LineTo(point.x, point.y);
    }
    if(bRectangle){
     CClientDC dc(this);
     pBackup = dc.SelectStockObject(NULL_BRUSH);
     dc.Rectangle(xAnchor, yAnchor, point.x, point.y);
     dc.SelectObject(pBackup);
    }
    if(bEllipse){
     CClientDC dc(this);
     pBackup = dc.SelectStockObject(NULL_BRUSH);
     dc.Ellipse(xAnchor, yAnchor, point.x, point.y);
     dc.SelectObject(pBackup);
    }
}
```

Note that we install a NULL_BRUSH before drawing the ellipse so that the background graphics is not covered over. At this point, then, we're able to add ellipses to our paint program, as shown in Figure 10-7.

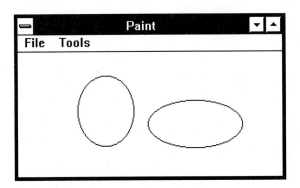

Figure 10-7. Drawing Ellipses in Our Paint Program

There is one last painting tool that we placed in our Tools menu, and that is Fill, which will allow us to fill figures in. Let's look at that next.

Filling Figures with Color

It turns out to be easy to fill in figures in Windows; all we need to do is to use the device context FloodFill( ) member function. From the user's point of view, that will work like this: They position the mouse cursor inside a figure on the screen, click it, and the figure fills with color. What's happening here is that we get the location of the mouse cursor from a point in the OnLButtonUp( ) function, and then we pass that set of coordinates on to FloodFill( ), along with a handle to our device context and a *bounding color.*

The bounding color is the color of the border of the figure that we're filling in, and we pass that color so that FloodFill( ) knows when to stop filling. For example, the figures we've drawn so far have been black, so the bounding color of our figures is black. And, to fill our figures in with black, we'll use the function SetROP2(R2_BLACK); as we'll see soon, this function specifies the *way* we draw in our device context, and here we're indicating that all pixels we draw should be black:

```
void CMainWindow::OnLButtonUp(UINT nFlags, CPoint point)
{
    CGdiObject* pBackup;

    if(bPoint){
     CClientDC dc(this);
     dc.SetPixel(point.x, point.y, RGB(0, 0, 0));
    }
    if(bLine){
     CClientDC dc(this);
     dc.MoveTo(xAnchor, yAnchor);
     dc.LineTo(point.x, point.y);
    }
    if(bRectangle){
     CClientDC dc(this);
     pBackup = dc.SelectStockObject(NULL_BRUSH);
     dc.Rectangle(xAnchor, yAnchor, point.x, point.y);
     dc.SelectObject(pBackup);
    }
    if(bEllipse){
     CClientDC dc(this);
     pBackup = dc.SelectStockObject(NULL_BRUSH);
     dc.Ellipse(xAnchor, yAnchor, point.x, point.y);
     dc.SelectObject(pBackup);
```

```
        }
        if(bFill){
        CClientDC dc(this);
→       dc.SetROP2(R2_BLACK);
            :
        }
    }
```

Next, we just fill the figure with FloodFill( ) (note that we're indicating that the bounding color is black, RGB(0, 0, 0)):

```
    void CMainWindow::OnLButtonUp(UINT nFlags, CPoint point)
    {
        CGdiObject* pBackup;

        if(bPoint){
        CClientDC dc(this);
        dc.SetPixel(point.x, point.y, RGB(0, 0, 0));
        }
        if(bLine){
        CClientDC dc(this);
        dc.MoveTo(xAnchor, yAnchor);
        dc.LineTo(point.x, point.y);
        }
        if(bRectangle){
        CClientDC dc(this);
        pBackup = dc.SelectStockObject(NULL_BRUSH);
        dc.Rectangle(xAnchor, yAnchor, point.x, point.y);
        dc.SelectObject(pBackup);
        }
        if(bEllipse){
        CClientDC dc(this);
        pBackup = dc.SelectStockObject(NULL_BRUSH);
        dc.Ellipse(xAnchor, yAnchor, point.x, point.y);
        dc.SelectObject(pBackup);
        }
        if(bFill){
        CClientDC dc(this);
        dc.SetROP2(R2_BLACK);
→       dc.FloodFill(point.x, point.y, RGB(0, 0, 0));
        }
    }
```

And that's it; now we can fill in our figures, as shown in Figure 10-8.

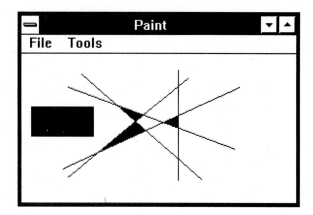

Figure 10-8. Filling with Color in Our Paint Program

Our paint program is done, except for a few embellishments that we might add. For example, it's customary for paint programs to show lines, rectangles, or ellipses as they're being sized, giving the user the illusion of "stretching" the figure into shape. And we can do that too.

"Stretching" Graphics Figures

When the user moves the mouse, we get WM_MOUSEMOVE messages, and we can give the appearance of stretching lines, rectangles, or ellipses as we do. Let's begin with lines. We'll start off at the anchor point; when the user moves the cursor, we'll draw a line from the anchor point to the new mouse position. When the cursor is moved again, we have to erase the old line and draw a new one from the anchor point to the new cursor location. This will give the impression that the user is stretching a line from the anchor point to the mouse cursor's position.

To do this, we'll have to store the end point of the previous line so that we can erase it before drawing new ones. In other words, the process will go like this:

1. Set the anchor point in OnLButtonDown( ).

2. In OnMouseMove( ), draw a line from (xAnchor, yAnchor) to (point.x, point.y), and save (point.x, point.y) as (xold, yold).

3. The next time OnMouseMove( ) is called, erase the line from (xAnchor, yAnchor) to (xold, yold), and draw a new line to the new

coordinates, (point.x, point.y). Then update (xold, yold) from (point.x, point.y).

4. Repeat step 3 as the user moves the mouse around, giving the impression of stretching the line. When OnLButtonUp( ) is called, we should draw the final line.

Note that this means we have to erase the old line before we draw the new one as the mouse cursor moves around. In addition, we should make sure that the line we're stretching is visible on the screen — if we just stretch a black line, for example, it will disappear as we move over a black filled figure. One way to do this is to specify the current pen's *drawing mode*. This indicates the way the current pen will interact with what's on the screen in a bit-by-bit fashion, and the options range from ignoring what's already on the screen entirely and simply drawing with the pen to ignoring the pen entirely and leaving the screen alone. There are 16 different options, and they appear in Table 10-2 (the R2 prefix stands for binary raster operation).

Operation	*Windows Drawing Mode*
BLACK	R2_BLACK
~(PEN | SCREEN)	R2_NOTMERGEPEN
~PEN & SCREEN	R2_MASKNOTPEN
~PEN	R2_NOTCOPYPEN
PEN & ~SCREEN	R2_MASKPENNOT
~SCREEN	R2_NOT
PEN ^ SCREEN	R2_XORPEN
~(PEN & SCREEN)	R2_NOTMASKPEN
PEN & SCREEN	R2_MASKPEN
~(PEN ^ SCREEN)	R2_NOTXORPEN
SCREEN	R2_NOP
~PEN | SCREEN	R2_MERGENOTPEN
PEN	R2_COPYPEN [the default]
PEN | ~SCREEN	R2_MERGEPENNOT
PEN | SCREEN	R2_MERGEPEN
WHITE	R2_WHITE

Table 10-2. Windows Drawing Modes

Let's use the R2_NOT drawing mode, which simply inverts what's on the screen in a bit-by-bit fashion. That is, when we draw with a R2_NOT pen, white (RGB(255, 255, 255)) will become black (RGB(0, 0, 0)), and black will become white. In addition, when we draw the same line over again with an R2_NOT pen, overwriting the first time, the original screen pixels will be restored, and that's what we want. In other words, we can rewrite our four steps above to use the R2_NOT pen like this:

1. Set the anchor point in OnLButtonDown( ).

2. In OnMouseMove( ), draw a line with a R2_NOT pen, inverting screen pixels to make sure the line is visible, from (xAnchor, yAnchor) to (point.x, point.y), and save (point.x, point.y) as (xold, yold).

3. The next time OnMouseMove( ) is called, erase the line from (xAnchor, yAnchor) to (xold, yold), simply by drawing it again with a R2_NOT pen, and draw a new R2_NOT line, inverting screen pixels, to the new coordinates, (point.x, point.y). Then update (xold, yold) from (point.x, point.y).

4. Repeat step 3 as the user moves the mouse around, giving the impression of stretching the line. When OnLButtonUp( ) is called, we should draw the final line with R2_COPYPEN.

To stretch the line, then, we can add code to OnMouseMove( ). We do that first by checking if the left mouse button is down (i.e., if (nFlags && MK_LBUTTON) is TRUE), and if we're actually drawing lines (i.e., if bLine is TRUE). If so, we create a device context object:

```
void CMainWindow::OnMouseMove(UINT nFlags, CPoint point)
{
    if((nFlags && MK_LBUTTON) && bLine){
      CClientDC dc(this);
        :
    }
}
```

Now we get the old drawing mode with the Windows function GetROP2( ) (i.e., Get binary raster operation mode) and save it in an integer variable we can call nDrawMode, then set the drawing mode to R2_NOT with SetROP2( ):

```
void CMainWindow::OnMouseMove(UINT nFlags, CPoint point)
{
    int nDrawMode;
```

```
            if((nFlags && MK_LBUTTON) && bLine){
             CClientDC dc(this);
→            nDrawMode = dc.GetROP2();
→            dc.SetROP2(R2_NOT);
                :
            }
        }
```

Next, we have to erase the old line from the previous WM_MOUSEMOVE event before drawing the new one. The old line is run from (xAnchor, yAnchor) to (xold, yold).

Note that (xold, yold) must hold a valid point from the very beginning of the drawing operation, so we set it to (xAnchor, yAnchor) when the left button orignally goes down in OnLButtonDown( ):

```
    void CMainWindow::OnLButtonDown(UINT nFlags, CPoint point)
    {
        xAnchor = point.x;
        yAnchor = point.y;
→       xold = xAnchor;
→       yold = yAnchor;
    }
```

We just erase the old line by drawing it again with the drawing mode set to R2_NOT, and draw the new line from the anchor point to our current position, like this:

```
    void CMainWindow::OnMouseMove(UINT nFlags, CPoint point)
    {
        int nDrawMode;

        if((nFlags && MK_LBUTTON) && bLine){
         CClientDC dc(this);
         nDrawMode = dc.GetROP2();
         dc.SetROP2(R2_NOT);
→        dc.MoveTo(xAnchor, yAnchor);
→        dc.LineTo(xold, yold);
→        dc.MoveTo(xAnchor, yAnchor);
→        dc.LineTo(point.x, point.y);
                :
        }
    }
```

All that remains now is to update (xold, yold) for the next time, and to reset the drawing mode:

```
void CMainWindow::OnMouseMove(UINT nFlags, CPoint point)
{
    int nDrawMode;

    if((nFlags && MK_LBUTTON) && bLine){
    CClientDC dc(this);
    nDrawMode = dc.GetROP2();
    dc.SetROP2(R2_NOT);
    dc.MoveTo(xAnchor, yAnchor);
    dc.LineTo(xold, yold);
    dc.MoveTo(xAnchor, yAnchor);
    dc.LineTo(point.x, point.y);
    xold = point.x;
    yold = point.y;
    dc.SetROP2(nDrawMode);
    }
}
```

And that's all there is to it. Now when we set the anchor point and move around the screen while drawing lines, we stretch a line from the anchor point to the current cursor position, as in Figure 10-9.

We can do the same thing for ellipses and rectangles easily; all we have to do is to set the drawing mode to R2_NOT, draw over old rectangles as the cursor

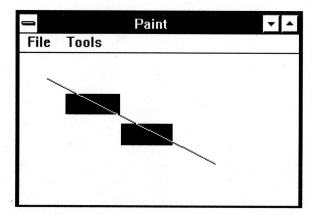

Figure 10-9. Stretching Lines in Our Paint Program

moves around the screen and draw new ones, just as we did for lines. That looks like this in OnMouseMove( ):

```
void CMainWindow::OnMouseMove(UINT nFlags, CPoint point)
{
        CGdiObject* pBackup;
        int nDrawMode;

        if((nFlags && MK_LBUTTON) && bDraw){
         CClientDC dc(this);
         dc.MoveTo(xAnchor, yAnchor);
         dc.LineTo(point.x, point.y);
         xAnchor = point.x;
         yAnchor = point.y;
        }
        if((nFlags && MK_LBUTTON) && bLine){
         CClientDC dc(this);
         nDrawMode = dc.GetROP2();
         dc.SetROP2(R2_NOT);
         dc.MoveTo(xAnchor, yAnchor);
         dc.LineTo(xold, yold);
         dc.MoveTo(xAnchor, yAnchor);
         dc.LineTo(point.x, point.y);
         xold = point.x;
         yold = point.y;
         dc.SetROP2(nDrawMode);
        }
        if((nFlags && MK_LBUTTON) && bRectangle){
         CClientDC dc(this);
         nDrawMode = dc.GetROP2();
         dc.SetROP2(R2_NOT);
         pBackup = dc.SelectStockObject(NULL_BRUSH);
→        dc.Rectangle(xold, yold, xAnchor, yAnchor);
→        dc.Rectangle(xAnchor, yAnchor, point.x, point.y);
         dc.SelectObject(pBackup);
         xold = point.x;
         yold = point.y;
         dc.SetROP2(nDrawMode);
        }
        if((nFlags && MK_LBUTTON) && bEllipse){
         CClientDC dc(this);
         nDrawMode = dc.GetROP2();
         dc.SetROP2(R2_NOT);
         pBackup = dc.SelectStockObject(NULL_BRUSH);
→        dc.Ellipse(xold, yold, xAnchor, yAnchor);
→        dc.Ellipse(xAnchor, yAnchor, point.x, point.y);
```

```
      dc.SelectObject(pBackup);
      xold = point.x;
      yold = point.y;
      dc.SetROP2(nDrawMode);
      }
  }
```

Now all our functions are complete; we can connect them to the appropriate Windows messages with the BEGIN_MESSAGE_MAP( ) macro like this:

```
BEGIN_MESSAGE_MAP(CMainWindow, CFrameWnd)
    ON_COMMAND(IDM_NEW, OnNew)
    ON_COMMAND(IDM_EXIT, OnExit)
    ON_COMMAND(IDM_POINT, OnPoint)
    ON_COMMAND(IDM_DRAW, OnDraw)
    ON_COMMAND(IDM_LINE, OnLine)
    ON_COMMAND(IDM_RECTANGLE, OnRectangle)
    ON_COMMAND(IDM_ELLIPSE, OnEllipse)
    ON_COMMAND(IDM_FILL, OnFill)
    ON_WM_LBUTTONDOWN()
    ON_WM_LBUTTONUP()
    ON_WM_MOUSEMOVE()
END_MESSAGE_MAP()
```

The rest of the code simply defines our main window and creates it as we've done many times before. The entire listing of paint.cpp appears in Listing 10-1.

Listing 10-1. Paint.cpp

```
#include <afxwin.h>
#include <windows.h>
#include "paint.h"

class CMainWindow : public CFrameWnd
{
private:
    int xAnchor;
    int yAnchor;
    int xold;
    int yold;
    BOOL bPoint;
    BOOL bDraw;
    BOOL bLine;
```

(continued)

Listing 10-1. *(continued)*

```
        BOOL bRectangle;
        BOOL bEllipse;
        BOOL bFill;
        void CheckOnlyMenuItem(int item_to_check);
public:
        CMainWindow();
        afx_msg void OnNew();
        afx_msg void OnExit();
        afx_msg void OnPoint();
        afx_msg void OnDraw();
        afx_msg void OnLine();
        afx_msg void OnRectangle();
        afx_msg void OnEllipse();
        afx_msg void OnFill();
        afx_msg void OnLButtonDown(UINT nFlags, CPoint point);
        afx_msg void OnLButtonUp(UINT nFlags, CPoint point);
        afx_msg void OnMouseMove(UINT nFlags, CPoint point);

        DECLARE_MESSAGE_MAP()
};

CMainWindow::CMainWindow()
{
        Create(NULL, "Paint", WS_OVERLAPPEDWINDOW,
                rectDefault, NULL, "MainMenu");
        bPoint = TRUE;
}

void CMainWindow::OnNew()
{
        InvalidateRect(NULL, TRUE);
        UpdateWindow();
}
void CMainWindow::OnExit()
{
        DestroyWindow();
}
void CMainWindow::OnPoint()
{
        CheckOnlyMenuItem(IDM_POINT);
        bPoint = TRUE;
        bDraw = FALSE;
        bLine = FALSE;
        bRectangle = FALSE;
```

Listing 10-1. *(continued)*

```cpp
    bEllipse = FALSE;
    bFill = FALSE;
}
void CMainWindow::OnDraw()
{
    CheckOnlyMenuItem(IDM_DRAW);
    bPoint = FALSE;
    bDraw = TRUE;
    bLine = FALSE;
    bRectangle = FALSE;
    bEllipse = FALSE;
    bFill = FALSE;
}
void CMainWindow::OnLine()
{
    CheckOnlyMenuItem(IDM_LINE);
    bPoint = FALSE;
    bDraw = FALSE;
    bLine = TRUE;
    bRectangle = FALSE;
    bEllipse = FALSE;
    bFill = FALSE;
}
void CMainWindow::OnRectangle()
{
    CheckOnlyMenuItem(IDM_RECTANGLE);
    bPoint = FALSE;
    bDraw = FALSE;
    bLine = FALSE;
    bRectangle = TRUE;
    bEllipse = FALSE;
    bFill = FALSE;
}
void CMainWindow::OnEllipse()
{
    CheckOnlyMenuItem(IDM_ELLIPSE);
    bPoint = FALSE;
    bDraw = FALSE;
    bLine = FALSE;
    bRectangle = FALSE;
    bEllipse = TRUE;
    bFill = FALSE;
}
void CMainWindow::OnFill()
```

(continued)

Listing 10-1. *(continued)*

```
{
    CheckOnlyMenuItem(IDM_FILL);
    bPoint = FALSE;
    bDraw = FALSE;
    bLine = FALSE;
    bRectangle = FALSE;
    bEllipse = FALSE;
    bFill = TRUE;
}

void CMainWindow::CheckOnlyMenuItem(int item_to_check)
{
    CMenu* pMenu = GetMenu();
    pMenu->CheckMenuItem(IDM_POINT, MF_UNCHECKED);
    pMenu->CheckMenuItem(IDM_DRAW, MF_UNCHECKED);
    pMenu->CheckMenuItem(IDM_LINE, MF_UNCHECKED);
    pMenu->CheckMenuItem(IDM_RECTANGLE, MF_UNCHECKED);
    pMenu->CheckMenuItem(IDM_ELLIPSE, MF_UNCHECKED);
    pMenu->CheckMenuItem(IDM_FILL, MF_UNCHECKED);
    pMenu->CheckMenuItem(item_to_check, MF_CHECKED);
}

void CMainWindow::OnLButtonDown(UINT nFlags, CPoint point)
{
    xAnchor = point.x;
    yAnchor = point.y;
    xold = xAnchor;
    yold = yAnchor;
}

void CMainWindow::OnLButtonUp(UINT nFlags, CPoint point)
{
    CGdiObject* pBackup;

    if(bPoint){
     CClientDC dc(this);
     dc.SetPixel(point.x, point.y, RGB(0, 0, 0));
    }
    if(bLine){
     CClientDC dc(this);
     dc.MoveTo(xAnchor, yAnchor);
     dc.LineTo(point.x, point.y);
    }
    if(bRectangle){
     CClientDC dc(this);
     pBackup = dc.SelectStockObject(NULL_BRUSH);
     dc.Rectangle(xAnchor, yAnchor, point.x, point.y);
```

Listing 10-1. *(continued)*

```
      dc.SelectObject(pBackup);
      }
      if(bEllipse){
       CClientDC dc(this);
       pBackup = dc.SelectStockObject(NULL_BRUSH);
       dc.Ellipse(xAnchor, yAnchor, point.x, point.y);
       dc.SelectObject(pBackup);
      }
      if(bFill){
       CClientDC dc(this);
       dc.SetROP2(R2_BLACK);
       dc.FloodFill(point.x, point.y, RGB(0, 0, 0));
      }
}

void CMainWindow::OnMouseMove(UINT nFlags, CPoint point)
{
      CGdiObject* pBackup;
      int nDrawMode;

      if((nFlags && MK_LBUTTON) && bDraw){
       CClientDC dc(this);
       dc.MoveTo(xAnchor, yAnchor);
       dc.LineTo(point.x, point.y);
       xAnchor = point.x;
       yAnchor = point.y;
      }
      if((nFlags && MK_LBUTTON) && bLine){
       CClientDC dc(this);
       nDrawMode = dc.GetROP2();
       dc.SetROP2(R2_NOT);
       dc.MoveTo(xAnchor, yAnchor);
       dc.LineTo(xold, yold);
       dc.MoveTo(xAnchor, yAnchor);
       dc.LineTo(point.x, point.y);
       xold = point.x;
       yold = point.y;
       dc.SetROP2(nDrawMode);
      }
      if((nFlags && MK_LBUTTON) && bRectangle){
       CClientDC dc(this);
       nDrawMode = dc.GetROP2();
       dc.SetROP2(R2_NOT);
       pBackup = dc.SelectStockObject(NULL_BRUSH);
       dc.Rectangle(xold, yold, xAnchor, yAnchor);
       dc.Rectangle(xAnchor, yAnchor, point.x, point.y);
       dc.SelectObject(pBackup);
```

(continued)

Listing 10-1. *(continued)*

```
        xold = point.x;
        yold = point.y;
        dc.SetROP2(nDrawMode);
        }
    if((nFlags && MK_LBUTTON) && bEllipse){
        CClientDC dc(this);
        nDrawMode = dc.GetROP2();
        dc.SetROP2(R2_NOT);
        pBackup = dc.SelectStockObject(NULL_BRUSH);
        dc.Ellipse(xold, yold, xAnchor, yAnchor);
        dc.Ellipse(xAnchor, yAnchor, point.x, point.y);
        dc.SelectObject(pBackup);
        xold = point.x;
        yold = point.y;
        dc.SetROP2(nDrawMode);
        }
}

BEGIN_MESSAGE_MAP(CMainWindow, CFrameWnd)
    ON_COMMAND(IDM_NEW, OnNew)
    ON_COMMAND(IDM_EXIT, OnExit)
    ON_COMMAND(IDM_POINT, OnPoint)
    ON_COMMAND(IDM_DRAW, OnDraw)
    ON_COMMAND(IDM_LINE, OnLine)
    ON_COMMAND(IDM_RECTANGLE, OnRectangle)
    ON_COMMAND(IDM_ELLIPSE, OnEllipse)
    ON_COMMAND(IDM_FILL, OnFill)
    ON_WM_LBUTTONDOWN()
    ON_WM_LBUTTONUP()
    ON_WM_MOUSEMOVE()
END_MESSAGE_MAP()

class CTheApp : public CWinApp
{
public:
    BOOL InitInstance();
};

BOOL CTheApp::InitInstance()
{
    m_pMainWnd = new CMainWindow();
    m_pMainWnd->ShowWindow(m_nCmdShow);
    m_pMainWnd->UpdateWindow();

    return TRUE;
}

CTheApp theApp;
```

NOTE To develop our paint program into a full Windows application, we'd have to handle the WM_PAINT case. That message is sent to us when part of our window is uncovered or has to be redrawn for any reason. Since we don't know exactly what the user has already drawn, we'd have to restore the entire image in our client area each time this happens. One way to do this is to set up a *bitmap* with CreateBitMap( ) and make sure that anything we draw is also drawn in the bitmap. That way, the bitmap will hold a copy of what's on the screen. When we get a WM_PAINT message, we could then transfer the image from the bitmap to the screen using the fast bit transfer function, BitBlt( ).

Adding a Program Icon

The paint program we've developed in this chapter is about as close as we've come to creating a polished Windows application; so, for that reason, let's go one step farther and give our program an icon that will appear in the Windows Program Manager. We can design our own icon with the aid of the Image Editor that comes with Microsoft C++. Open it to show the Image Editor window, as shown in Figure 10-10. Click the New... item in the File menu, and a dialog box will appear, listing the three types of images we can create: Cursors, icons, and bitmaps. Select icon and then click OK, bringing up a new dialog box called New Icon Image as shown in Figure 10-11.

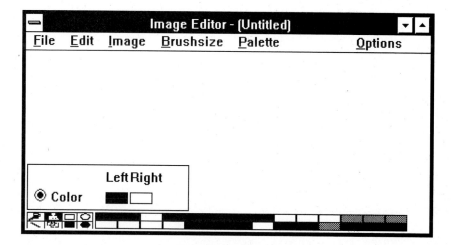

Figure 10-10. The Image Editor

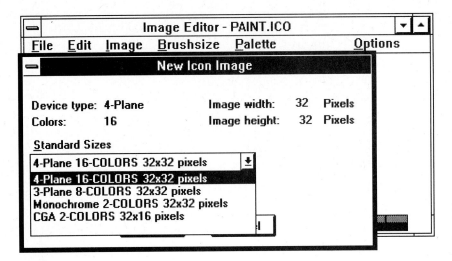

Figure 10-11. New Icon Dialog Box

Just click the OK button, indicating that we want to create a 4-Plane 16-COL-ORS 32x32 pixel icon. When you do, two new boxes appear in the Image Editor: In the left box, we can click and change pixels; in the right box, we see what our icon will look like. Since this is a paint program, let's design a paintbrush-like icon, as shown in Figure 10-12.

When done, we save the icon as the file paint.ico, using the Save As... item in the Image Editor's File menu. Now we're ready to integrate it into our pro-

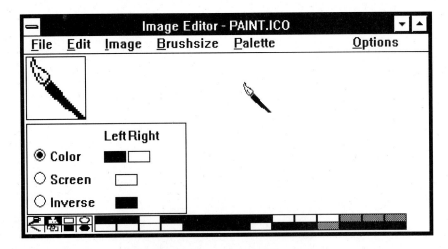

Figure 10-12. Our Paint Application's Icon

gram. Do that by adding a line that connects the icon paint.ico with the identifier AFX_IDI_STD_FRAME in paint.rc, like this:

```
#include <windows.h>
#include <afxres.h>
#include "PAINT.h"

AFX_IDI_STD_FRAME ICON paint.ico      ←

MainMenu MENU
  {
    POPUP   "File"
      {
        MENUITEM "New",  IDM_NEW
        MENUITEM "Exit", IDM_EXIT
      }
    POPUP   "Tools"
      {
        MENUITEM "Point", IDM_POINT, CHECKED
        MENUITEM "Draw",  IDM_DRAW
        MENUITEM "Line",  IDM_LINE
        MENUITEM "Rectangle", IDM_RECTANGLE
        MENUITEM "Ellipse", IDM_ELLIPSE
        MENUITEM "Fill",  IDM_FILL
      }
  }
```

Now when you create paint.exe, paint.ico will be placed inside it, and when you add paint.exe to a program group in the Windows Program Manager, that's the icon that will appear there, as shown in Figure 10-13.

For reference, paint.h appears in Listing 10-2, paint.rc in Listing 10-3, paint.def in Listing 10-4, and the associated makefile in Listing 10-5.

Listing 10-2. Paint.h

```
#define IDM_FILE          1000
#define IDM_NEW           1050
#define IDM_EXIT          1100
#define IDM_TOOLS         2000
#define IDM_POINT         2050
#define IDM_DRAW          2100
#define IDM_LINE          2150
#define IDM_RECTANGLE     2200
#define IDM_ELLIPSE       2250
#define IDM_FILL          2300
```

Figure 10-13. Our Paint Program's Icon in a Group

Listing 10-3. Paint.rc

```
#include <windows.h>
#include <afxres.h>
#include "PAINT.h"

AFX_IDI_STD_FRAME ICON paint.ico

MainMenu MENU
  {
    POPUP   "File"
      {
        MENUITEM "New", IDM_NEW
        MENUITEM "Exit", IDM_EXIT
      }
    POPUP   "Tools"
      {
        MENUITEM "Point", IDM_POINT, CHECKED
        MENUITEM "Draw", IDM_DRAW
        MENUITEM "Line", IDM_LINE
        MENUITEM "Rectangle", IDM_RECTANGLE
        MENUITEM "Ellipse", IDM_ELLIPSE
        MENUITEM "Fill", IDM_FILL
      }
  }
```

Listing 10-4. Paint.def

```
NAME          Paint
DESCRIPTION   'Paint Program'

EXETYPE       WINDOWS
STUB          'WINSTUB.EXE'

CODE          PRELOAD MOVEABLE DISCARDABLE
DATA          PRELOAD MOVEABLE MULTIPLE

HEAPSIZE      1024
STACKSIZE     4096
```

Listing 10-5. Paint.exe's Makefile

```
CPPFLAGS= /AS /W3 /Zp /GA /GEs /G2

paint.exe:      paint.obj paint.def paint.res
  link /NOD /ONERROR:NOEXE paint, paint, NUL, safxcw libw
  slibcew,paint.def;
  rc /t paint.res
```

And so we find ourselves at the end of our exploration of Microsoft C++. We've come far — from the very beginning up through classes, objects, nested classes, virtual functions, abstract classes, using pointers to objects — and now all the way up to Windows. At this point, we have a good deal of experience, and we've seen many tricks of the trade. We've seen the power of Microsoft C++ in its own environment, and we've learned what it has to offer.

However, there's much more to learn about C++, and about Windows for that matter; we cannot cover everything in a book like this. The next step is to gain more experience in programming C++ and in the Windows environment (either through books, or by programming, or both). It takes time to gain enough experience to become a professional C++ programmer, but the results are well worth the investment of time, and you've got a good leg up now with the tools and techniques we've covered here. All that remains now is the important part — putting it to work!

Using Assembly Language with C++

In this appendix, we'll start putting C++ and assembly language together for the first time. We'll do this using in-line assembly language, which Microsoft C++ supports.

Using In-Line Assembly Language

In-line assembly language used to be very primitive. In fact, in some languages, you had to type the actual bytes of machine code in (this was called in-line code). However, as speed became more and more important, languages started to improve their support of in-line assembly language. Now, in the C++, you can do practically anything that you can do in normal assembly language.

NOTE   There is one notable exception. You can't use the data directives like DB or DW in Microsoft C++. Besides that, however, you are free to do most things.

Under Microsoft C, we can preface a whole block with the keyword _asm, like this:

```
main()
{
    _asm{                    ←
        mov dl, 90
        mov ah, 2
        int 21h
    }

    return(0);
}
```

Then we just use the C++ compiler as usual. For example, this code prints the letter 'Z' on the screen. To create printz.exe in this case, we can use the cl command this way:

```
F:\>cl printz.cpp
```

Using Data in In-Line Assembly Language

Next, we can write an example program to print out the line "Hello, world.\n" using in-line assembly language. Let's start this way:

```
main()
{
    char *MSG "Hello, world.\n$";
        :
}
```

We are just setting up a string of type char in memory (a string is just a char array, and a pointer can be substituted for an array). Notice that we end it with '$' so we can use it with the string-printing DOS service, service 9. Now we can set up our in-line code:

```
main()
{
    char *MSG "Hello, world.\n$";

    _asm{
        mov dx, MSG
        mov ah, 9
```

```
        int 21h
    }

    return(0);
}
```

And that's it. Note that since MSG is a pointer — that is, the address of the beginning of MSG in memory — we are able to pass it directly to Int 21h. The normal assembly language program would have looked like this:

```
        .MODEL SMALL
        .CODE
        ORG 100H
ENTRY:  JMP HELLO
        MSG DB "Hello, world.",13,10,"$"
HELLO   PROC NEAR
        MOV DX, OFFSET MSG ←
        MOV AH, 9
        INT 21H
        INT 20H
HELLO   ENDP

        END ENTRY
```

The way we would use other types of data besides character strings is similar: The usual method is to simply declare it in C++ format so the C++ part of the code can use it as well and then refer to it in our in-line assembly language as we would if we had declared it with DB or DW.

Understanding the Internal C++ Data Formats

However, we must know the internal data format that C++ uses for its variables if we want to connect to C++ at this level — that is, we have to know how to read and work with C++ data on a byte-by-byte basis to interface with assembly language. Let's take a look at the internal representation of C++ data next.

Integers

A short int, for example, is simply a 16-bit word, so we can write the following program:

```
main()
{
    int apples = 5;            ←
    int oranges = 3;           ←
    char *msg2 = "Total fruit: $";
    _asm{
        MOV     DX, msg2
        MOV     AH, 9
        INT     21H
        MOV     DX, apples
        ADD     DX, oranges
        ADD     DX, '0'
        MOV     AH, 2
        INT     21H
    }
    return(0);
}
```

Here we have defined two ints, apples and oranges. Since they are just two one-word variables, those declarations are the same as they would be if we had used the DW directive. We can read the value in apples like this: MOV DX, apples. We add this value to the value in the variable oranges and print out the sum.

The result of this program is Total fruit: 8. Our in-line assembly language code can use the variables just as the C++ part of the code can — if we know the data format. If we wished, we could use byte-long values instead of word-long ones (note the use of DL, not DX):

```
main()
{
    char apples = 5;           ←
    char oranges = 3;          ←
    char *msg2 = "Total fruit: $";
    _asm{
        MOV     DX, msg2
        MOV     AH, 9
        INT     21H
        MOV     DL, apples     ←
        ADD     DL, oranges    ←
        ADD     DL, '0'        ←
        MOV     AH, 2
        INT     21H
    }
    return(0);
}
```

Here, we have declared apples and oranges as variables of type char, which is the same as declaring them with DB.

Long Integers

We can also look at unsigned long int format. Because of the peculiarities of the 80x86 data storage methods, long (two-word) numbers like 12345678H are stored with high and low words reversed and high and low bytes reversed. In other words, 12345678H would be stored as 78H 56H 34H 12H.

This means that our number of apples, stored as a long double, would look like this: 05 00 00 00. Since that's the case, we can just load apples into DX again because 05 00 (the low word) is the word that we are interested in and that is the first word in memory (if we had wanted the high word, we could have used a pointer to it):

```
main()
{
    long apples = 5;            ←
    long oranges = 3;           ←
    char *msg2 = "Total fruit: $";
    _asm{
        MOV     DX, msg2
        MOV     AH, 9
        INT     21H
        MOV     DX, apples          ←
        ADD     DX, oranges         ←
        ADD     DX, '0'
        MOV     AH, 2
        INT     21H
    }
    return(0);
}
```

For signed integers, C++ uses *two's complement notation*, and that's what we must learn next. Up to this point, all the numbers we've been using in assembly language have been unsigned whole numbers. A number could range from 0000H to FFFFH and that was it. Here, unsigned means positive — and positive numbers are only half the story. Temperatures run negative as well as positive, as do budgets or voltages or any number of categories. To keep track of these, any modern computer has to be able to use signed numbers.

The Sign Bit

The highest bit — the leftmost bit — in a byte or word can be used as the sign bit. In fact, what determines whether or not a number is signed is whether or not we pay attention to this bit. In unsigned bytes or words, this bit was always there, certainly — but it was only the highest bit and had no other significance. To make a number signed, we just have to treat it as signed — which means starting to pay attention to the sign bit. A 1 in the highest bit will mean that the number, if thought of as signed, is negative:

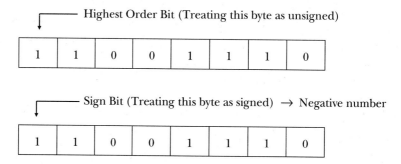

How Signed Numbers Work

The whole scheme of signed numbers in the 80x86 comes from the simple fact that $1 + (-1) = 0$. We realize that if we want to do any calculation with negative numbers in the PC, the number we choose to be -1, when added to 1, has to give 0. Yet this seems impossible. Can you think of an eight-bit number that, when added to 1, will give a result of 0? It seems as though the result must always be 1 or greater.

In fact, if we limit ourselves to the eight bits of the byte, there is an answer. If we add 255 (= 11111111B) and 1:

```
  11111111
+        1
-----------
 100000000
```

└── Carry

it yields 100000000B, that is, the eight-bit register is left holding 00000000, or 0, and there is a carry, since the 1 is in the 2^8 place (256), more than the register's capacity. This carry means that the *carry flag* will be set. If we ignore this carry, and only look at the eight bits that fit into the byte, we are left with 00000000B; in other words, FFH + 1 = 0.

Finding a Two's Complement

As a practical matter, how are these negative numbers found? For instance, if we wanted to know what -109 was, how could we find it? To find -109, we would start with 109 and find what is called its two's complement. Two's complement math is the math used in computers for dealing with negative numbers. We already know one two's complement: the two's complement of 1 is FFFFH.

We can find any number's two's complement easily. We begin by noting that, if you take a number like 5, which is 00000101B in binary, then flip all its bits, 11111010B (= FAH), and add the two together, you get all 1s:

$$
\begin{array}{rl}
00000101 & \leftarrow 5 \\
+ \quad 11111010 & \leftarrow 5 \text{ with bits flipped } [\ \text{FAH}\ ] \\
\hline
11111111 & = \text{FF}
\end{array}
$$

That is, 5 + FAH = 11111111B. This is close to what we want — adding 1 to this sum gives us 0 with a carry. If we ignore the carry, we can see that 5 + FAH + 1 = 0. In other words, adding 5 to (FAH + 1) gives 0 with the (ignored) carry:

$$
\begin{array}{r}
5 \\
+ \quad (\text{FAH} + 1) \\
\hline
0
\end{array}
$$

We know that 5 plus -5 equals zero:

$$
\begin{array}{r}
5 \\
+ \quad -5 \\
\hline
0
\end{array}
$$

And this means that -5 must equal (FAH + 1), which is FBH. This is how negative numbers are found; the rule is simple: To find any number's two's complement (and therefore to change its sign), just flip the bits and add 1. Thus, we see that -1 = Flip(1) + 1 = 11111110B + 1 = 11111111B = FFH (in byte form; it would be FFFFH in word form).

The NOT and NEG Instructions

To flip the bits in a word or byte in assembly language, you can use the NOT instruction. For example, if AX was equal to 00000000, then NOT AX would make AX equal to 11111111. If BX was equal to 01010101, then NOT BX would make it 10101010. This is just like the bitwise NOT operator in C++, ~.

If you use NOT on a word or byte and then add 1 to the result, you will have that word's or byte's two's complement. In fact, there is a special 80x86 instruction that does just this: NEG. NEG is the same as NOT, except that it adds 1 at the end to make a two's complement of the number. If AX held 1, then NEG AX would give it 1111111111111111 or FFFF.

NOTE NEG flips signs; it does not always make signs negative. For example, NEG -1 = 1.

Let's see how to use two's complement when interfacing to C++. For example, in this program:

```
main()
{
    int apples = -1;           ←
    int oranges = 3;
    char *msg2 = "Total fruit: $";
    _asm{
        MOV     DX, msg2
        MOV     AH, 9
        INT     21H
        MOV     DX, apples
        ADD     DX, oranges
        ADD     DX, '0'
        MOV     AH, 2
        INT     21H
    }
    return(0);
}
```

the number of apples, -1, is stored as FFFFH. Since we already know how to use two's complement, we are prepared for this format. That's all there is to negative numbers.

Floating Point Format

As you can see, working with integer formats is not too difficult. We can read from memory and write to it without problems. Floating point formats, however, are more difficult to decipher. We can store a floating point number like this:

```
main()
{
    float val = 10.5;          ←
        :
        :
}
```

That looks easy enough, but what is the internal representation of such a floating point number?

If we dig into the .Exe file, we will find that our number 10.5 has been stored as 41280000H. Where did it come from? The format for floating point numbers is complex and takes a little getting used to. A number like 32.1 is just $3x10^1$ plus $2x10^0$ and $1x10^{-1}$. On the other hand, the computer is a binary machine, which means it uses base 2, so a number like 10.5 must be stored as $1x2^3$ plus $1x2^1$ plus $1x2^{-1}$, which is 1010.1, where the point is a binary point. It is possible to store any number in binary that can be stored in decimal, it just might take more places. For instance, 0.75 can be broken down into 1/2 + 1/4, or $2^{-1} + 2^{-2}$, so .75 = .11B.

The numbers stored as floats are all *normalized*, which means they appear with the binary point near the beginning; so 1010.1 would appear like this: $1.0101x2^3$. To expand this, just move the binary point three places to the right, giving 1010.1 again. You can see that the first digit in any normalized binary number is always one. Under C++ floating point format, the leading 1 is *implicit*. In other words, all that is stored of the *significand* is 0101. The exponent is still three; but, to make matters even more complex, all exponents are stored after being added to some offset or *bias*.

For a float, this bias is 7FH, or 127. For doubles, this number is 3FFH, or 1023. In other words, if our number, 1010.1B, is going to be stored as a float, the exponent will be 3 + 127 = 130 = 82H. Finally, the first bit of any floating point number is the sign bit. Floating point numbers are not stored in two's complement notation. If the sign bit is 1, the number is negative; if it is 0, the number is positive. That's the only distinction between positive and negative numbers. The float format looks like this:

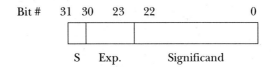

So 10.5 = 1010.1B will look like this:

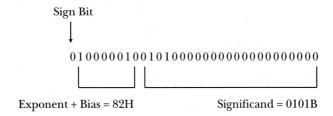

This can be made into hex by grouping every four binary digits together:

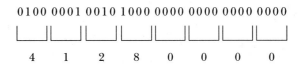

That is, 10.5 is stored as 41280000H. In fact, because the 80x86 actually stores low bytes first inside a word and then low words first, 10.5 actually shows up in memory as 00H 00H 28H 41H. These bytes are far indeed from 10.5.

TIP   If you are going to work with floating point numbers, probably the first thing you should do is write a function to translate floating point format into something you can use or let C++ do the translation for you.

The format for doubles is this:

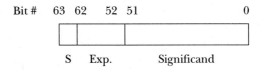

TIP   It's worth noting that this floating point format is the same format used by the 80x87 coprocessors, so you can interface with them easily.

Working directly with variables as we have been doing provides one way of communicating with a C++ program. But, in some cases we won't know the actual names of the variables we're supposed to use. For example, we might be writing an assembly language procedure to replace a ponderous C++ library function; in that case, the program that calls our function will only pass parameters to us — and it will be up to us to pick them off the stack. Let's do that next.

Passing Parameters

So far, our entire program has been in assembly language. However, it's more common to write only a few functions in assembly language (i.e., that part of the code that needs to be speeded up). To do that, we'll have to learn how to read the parameters that might be passed to us in a function. We'll start our discussion of parameter passing with a simple function that doesn't accept any parameters. That might look like this:

```
char *MSG "Hello, world.\n$";

main()
{
    print_msg();       ←

    return(0);
}

print_msg()            ←
{
    _asm{
    MOV DX, MSG
    MOV AH, 9
    INT 21H
    }
}
```

In other words, the whole program can still be written in C++, except for the function(s) we choose to write in assembly language. As you can see, it's easy to write a C++ function in assembly language — as long as we don't pass any parameters to it. (Note that we made MSG a global variable here so that print_msg( ) could have access to it.)

Now let's say we wanted to pass a parameter to our function. We could change our function to, say, print_char( ) and we could call print_char( ) with an

Language	Parameters Pushed	Parameters Passed	Return Type
BASIC	In order	As offset addresses	RET #[*]
FORTRAN	In order	As FAR addresses	RET #
→ C	In REVERSE order	As values	RET
Pascal	In order	As values	RET #

[*]Where RET # is used, # equals the total size in bytes of all pushed parameters.

Table A-1. Calling Conventions.

argument like this: print_char('Z'). The question becomes: What happens to the function's argument? To answer this question, we have to take a look at C's calling convention (see Table A-1).

That is, parameters are pushed onto the stack in reverse order in C++. In addition, C++ parameters are passed by value (not as addresses as is the case with FORTRAN or BASIC), with some exceptions (e.g., arrays). Let's give this a try. Our example with the print_msg( ) function didn't use any passed parameters:

```
char *MSG "Hello, world.\n$";

main()
{
    print_msg();        ←

    return(0);
}

print_msg()             ←
{
    _asm{
        MOV DX, MSG
        MOV AH, 9
        INT 21H
    }
}
```

That means that when we arrive at print_msg( ), the stack will look like this, depending on memory model:

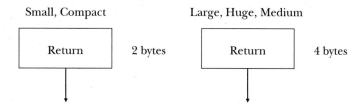

Small, Compact

Large, Huge, Medium

The size of the return address pushed on the stack depends on the memory model used in the C++ program — in the Large, Huge, and Medium models, code can be more that one segment long, so the return address is 4 bytes (2 words).

Now, however, let's change our example so that we pass two char parameters:

```
main()
{
    print_2_char('A','Z');    ←

    return(0);
}

print_2_char(char a, char b)    ←
{
    _asm{
        :
        :
    }
}
```

This time, we are passing two parameters, ASCII 65 ('A') and 90 ('Z'). The way the stack looks when we arrive at print_2_char( ) is like this:

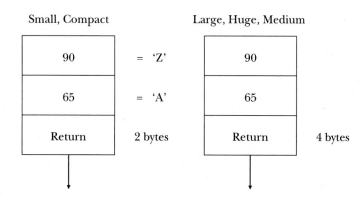

Small, Compact

Large, Huge, Medium

Note that the parameters were pushed in reverse order — first, the 'Z' was pushed, then 'A.' Notice also that each parameter takes up a full word — we cannot push byte values onto the C++ stack (unlike our C++ example). Now we need to access the parameters passed to us, and that is easy. We can simply refer to our variables as a C++ function would, like this:

```
main()
{
    print_2_char('A','Z');

    return(0);
}

print_2_char(char a, char b)
{
    _asm{
        MOV     AH, 2
        MOV     DX, 0
        MOV     DL, a       ←
        INT     21H
        MOV     DX, 0
        MOV     DL, b       ←
        INT     21H
    }
}
```

Here, C++ picks parameters off the stack for us. In other words, the instruction MOV DL, b moves the value passed as b into the DL register.

NOTE To give us access to the parameters that were passed, C++ actually substitutes the appropriate memory reference for our variables a and b. That is, since the variables are on the stack, and the stack is part of memory, their names can simply be replaced with memory addresses.

Passing Longs

It makes sense that we can pass one-byte or one-word parameters easily by pushing them. But what if we need to push more than one word? For example, look at the function my_func( ) here:

```
main()
{
    long numb = 0xaaaabbbb;
```

```
        my_func(numb);
}

my_func(long a)
{
}
```

The number passed to our function is a long value. However, we can convert it to two one-word values for use in our assembly language code like this:

```
main()
{
    long numb = 0xaaaabbbb;

    my_func(numb);

    return(0);
}

my_func(long a)
{
    int ahigh, alow;

    alow = (int) a;              ←
    ahigh = (int) a >> 16;       ←

    _asm{
        MOV     DX, ahigh   ←
        MOV     AX, alow    ←
        :
        :
    }
}
```

All we did was to put the low word into the variable alow by using a typcast of int and then load the high word by first shifting the long variable a down by 16 places (so the high word becomes the low word). Then we referred to those variables in our in-line code.

In other words, we should let C++ handle the details of manipulating the stack if we can. Now that we've gained some expertise with passing parameters, how about returning values? We can read the parameters that the calling function passes to us, but we know that real functions can return values as well. That's something we can do too — and it's as easy as reading passed parameters.

Returning	Use
char	AL
short	AL
int	AX
long	DX:AX (high word in DX, low in AX)
float	AX = Address (DX:AX for far)
double	AX = Address (DX:AX for far)
struct	AX = Address (DX:AX for far)
near pointer	AX
far pointer	DX:AX

Table A-2. Register Return Values

Returning Values from Functions

Returning values is unexpectedly easy. The convention is to use the registers in Table A-2 to return values from functions.

It's very simple. Depending on the return value expected from the function (set in the function prototype), C++ just reads return values from AL, AX, or DX:AX. To return a byte-long value, just leave the value in AL when you exit the function. If the calling function is expecting a byte-long return value, it will read that byte from AL. Word values (like short integers) are returned in AX. Double word values are simply returned in DX:AX (DX = high word; AX = low word).

Let's put this to use by writing a function named summer( ). This function will just add two integers; that is, we'll accept two ints and return an int value (in AX). Here's what it looks like under the small model:

```
main()
{
    printf("3 + 2 = %d",summer(3,2));

    return(0);
}

int summer(int a, int b)
```

```
    {
        _asm{
            MOV      AX, a
            ADD      AX, b
        }
    }
```

This program just leaves the result in AX, and this value therefore becomes the function's returns value. When we return to the calling function, we type out a message and the return value of summer( ). Here, the program types: 3 + 2 = 5. Returning values is that simple.

However, if we add two integers together, the result could be a long integer. We should adjust summer( ) to allow for such a result by returning a long integer in DX:AX. That looks like this in C++:

```
unsigned long summer(int a, int b);

main()
{
    unsigned int x = 50000, y = 60000;
    printf("%u + %u = %lu", x, y, summer(x,y));

    return(0);
}

unsigned long summer(int a, int b)
{
    _asm{
        MOV      DX, 0
        MOV      AX, a
        ADD      AX, b
        ADC      DX, 0
    }
}
```

Here we're using the instruction ADC DX, 0. This instruction places a 1 in DX if there was a carry from the addition and 0 otherwise. The output of this program is: 50000 + 60000 = 110000.

Now we have considerable expertise in writing in-line assembly language. We can use data that has been declared in C++ format, we can read parameters passed to us in a function, and now we can even return values. This means that we can write whole functions in pure assembly language, taking advantage of the improved speed and shortened size such functions can offer.

About the Diskette

The diskette that accompanies this book contains programs from the book and three additional ones not in the book. There are two types of programs: DOS programs and Windows programs. To compile and link a DOS program, use a command line like this: cl prog.cpp. To compile and link a Windows program, use the NMAKE utility that comes with Microsoft C 7+ like this: nmake /f prog.nmk (one .nmk file is provided for each Windows program). Note that since these are only example programs, the majority of Windows programs do not handle the WM_PAINT case, which means that, if you cover a part of those windows, they may not be restored later.

Microsoft C 7+ is targeted for Windows 3.1 or later versions, which means that you should install the Windows 3.1 Software Development Kit. To build Windows 3.0 programs, you must either add the line: #define WINVER 0x0300 to the source file (before the line including the file windows.h) or use the /DWINVER=0x0300 cl option in the .nmk file. In addition, use the /30 rc option when combining the .exe and .res files (i.e., where the rc /t option is used in the .nmk file, add the /30 option).

Table B-1 lists the programs and what they do.

Program	What It Does
ABSTRACT.CPP	Abstract class example.
CALC.NMK	Windows pop-up calculator example. Select Calculator... in the File menu and place integers in the top two text boxes. Click the = sign to see the result.
CARET.NMK	Windows example showing how to create and use a character-insertion caret. Type characters and the caret advances. You can also use <Enter> to move to the next line.
CHAR.NMK	Windows example that reads typed characters and echoes them in a window.
COUNTABC.CPP	Counter object example. Type various letters followed by 0 <Enter>. This program will tell you how many of each character you typed.
COUNTER.CPP	Counts x's when you type them. Type a number of x's, followed by q <Enter>. The program tells you how many x's were typed.
CSTRING.CPP	Microsoft Foundation Class example showing how to use the CString class. Compile and link like this: cl /AM cstring.cpp mafxcr.lib.
DIALOG.NMK	Windows example showing how to create and use a dialog box.
DYNAMIC.CPP	C++ dynamic initialization example. Run the program and type a single character. The program uses it to initialize a variable and then tells you what character it used.
FRIEND.CPP	Friend function example. Type characters followed by 0 <Enter>.
FWRITE.CPP	File writing example. Writes a file hello.dat that contains the string "Hello, world."
INHER.CPP	Inheritance example. Uses our stack as a base class and converts a typed integer into hex.
INLINE.CPP	Example showing how to use in-line functions in C++.
MENU.NMK	Windows example showing how to use menus. Click Hello in the File menu and "Hello world." will appear in the window.
MESSAGE.NMK	Windows example showing how to use message boxes.

Table B-1. Programs on the Diskette

Program	What It Does
MOUCARET.NMK	Windows example using mouse and character input. When the program begins, the caret is at the top-left of the window. You can move it (and so type characters anywhere in the window) by using the mouse cursor and clicking, making the caret appear there.
NPAD.NMK	Windows notepad example. Click Notepad... in the File menu. The notepad includes cut and paste capability.
PAINT.NMK	Windows paint program. Using the Tools menu, you can select from these drawing tools: Point, Draw (freehand drawing), Line, Rectangle, Ellipse, and Fill (fill the area you click with black).
PASSING.CPP	Example showing how to pass an object to a function. Type x's followed by q <Enter>; the counter object is passed to a function so that the number of x's you typed can be printed out.
PBOOK.NMK	Windows phonebook example. Type a name and spaces totalling 10 characters, followed by a phone number. The first 10 characters of what you've typed are added to the File menu. Type another name and spaces totalling 10 characters and do the same. After you've added names to the File menu, you can click them and the program will restore the name and phone number in the window. (Note: In this example, you should add all names to the File menu before retrieving them since there is no provision for erasing what's there to add more.)
PUSHME.NMK	Windows dialog box example. The dialog box has a button marked "Push Me." When you click it, "Hello, world." appears in the dialog box's text box.
SCRIBBLE.NMK	Windows example showing how to draw freehand with the mouse. To draw, simply hold down the left mouse button and move the mouse.
SERIAL.CPP	Microsoft Foundation Class example showing how to "serialize" (write to disk) objects. Two names are written to disk in this example and then they're read back in. They are stored on disk in the file friends.dat.

Table B-1. (continued)

Program	What It Does
SETF.CPP	Floating point example showing how to use setf.
STACK.CPP	Our stack example showing how to create a stack class and objects of that class. Numbers are pushed onto the stack and then popped, reappearing in reverse order.
STKREF.CPP	Stack example that shows how to pass parameters by reference.
STRING.CPP	Our string class example (as opposed to the MFC CString example above). Shows how to create a string class as well as overload the + and = operators.

Table B-1. (continued)

The diskette also contains three additional programs that do not appear in the book. They are listed in Table B-2.

Program	What It Does
CLIP.NMK	Windows example showing how to use the Windows clipboard. Type a string and then select Copy to Clipboard in the File menu, copying your text to the clipboard. To see it again, click the Paste from Clipboard item. Your text will be read from the clipboard and will reappear below the original.
QSORT.CPP	A Quicksort example showing how the Quicksort works. Some values are placed in an array and then the array is sorted.
SUMMER.CPP	In-line assembly language example. Here, we write the function summer( ) in assembly language, and add two numbers, printing the result out on the screen.

Table B-2. Additional Diskette Programs

Index

The Ultimate Computer Book!

Jim Seymour's PC Productivity Bible

The ultimate "insider's" book, from the ultimate insider, Jim Seymour. Five million people read Seymour's columns in *PC Magazine*, *PC Week*, and *PC/Computing*. Now the nation's best-known and most respected computer expert shares his best tips, tricks, and secrets, culled from years of experience as a consultant to America's top corporations.

Inside, you'll find:
- More than 100 chapter packed with no-nonsense, nuts-and-bolts advice. From taming cranky printers to finding spreadsheets' hidden mistakes, from building better databases to creating presentations that work, Seymour has the solutions you need.
- Hot tips on desktop publishing, graphics, communications, and surviving with a PC on the road.

Plus:
- Practical wisdom on today's hottest PC management issues, and memorable stories from the font lines of corporate computing.
- Free, bonus reference card—Seymour's own "cheat sheet" full of instant solutions to everyday problems.

A computer book unlike any other, *Jim Seymour's PC Productivity Bible* is the indispensable reference.

ISBN: 0-13-511080-7
Price: $24.95

Look for this and other Brady Publishing
titles at your local book or computer store.
To order directly call 1 (800) 624-0023
Visa/MC accepted

**The most comprehensive and authoritative
PC upgrade book ever published!**

The Winn L. Rosch PC Upgrade Bible

A complete "how to" guide to improving the performance of your PC system by the nation's premier technical microcomputer journalist. This book helps you define your personal strategy—costs, performance, etc.—and offers step-by-step solutions that anyone can perform to accomplish the upgrade(s).

Inside you'll find sections that:

- Define personal upgrade strategy
- Deal with every aspect of the PC system
- Extensive use of checklists to monitor specific upgrade applications
- Step-by-step easy-to-follow instructions
- Complete technical information from what works and what doesn't to toolkits—what you need and where to get them

Look for this and other Brady Publishing titles at your local book or computer store. To order directly call 1 (800) 624-0023. Visa/MC accepted.

ISBN: 0-13-922252-3
$26.95

The Only Complete Guide to
Hewlett-Packard Printers and Compatibles

The LaserJet III Companion

Virtually standard equipment in every computerized office, Hewlett-Packard LaserJet and compatible laser printers are often a mystery to their regualr users. *The LaserJet III Companion* provides much-needed solutions to the most common problems.

Devoted exclusively to HP's new LaserJet III, this book gives you everything you need to know to properly maintain your printer. You'll maximize its potential with dozens of practical tips and ideas you won't find in the manual, including important information such as how to maximize potential ozone hazards and recycle toner cartridges.

Inside you'll find:
- Step-by-step instructions covering the menu panel and its control settings
- Complete guide to printer paper selection
- Total maintenance and comprehensive troubleshooting guide
- Crash course in fonts and graphic design
- How to use the PCL 5 programming language for everyday computing

The LaserJet III Companion utility disk eliminates the need for stand-alone laser printer utilities costing as much as $125! With this disk, you can use cartridges from Hewlett-Packard and other independent sources even if their applications programs do not support the LaserJet III.

ISBN: 0-13-523861-7
Price: $34.95

Look for these and other Brady titles
at your local book or computer store.
To order directly call (800) 624-0023
Visa/MC accepted.

If your computer uses
5 1/4-inch disks...

While most personal computers use 3 1/2-inch disks to store information, some computers use 5 1/4-inch disks for information storage. If your computer uses 5 1/4-inch disks, you can return this form to Brady to obtain a 5 1/4-inch disk to use with this book. Simply fill out the remainder of this form and mail to:

Microsoft C/C++
Programming 2nd Edition

Disk Exchange
Brady
11711 N. College Ave., Suite 140
Carmel, IN 46032

We will then send you, free of charge, the 5 1/4-inch version of the book software.

Name _____   Phone _____

Company _____   Title _____

Address _____

City _____   St. _____   ZIP _____

Important! Read Before Opening Sealed Diskette
END USER LICENSE AGREEMENT

Keeping Pace With Today's Microcomputer Technology

Available at your local bookstore, or order by phone (800) 428-5331.

College Marketing Group
50 Cross Street
Winchester, MA 01890

ATT: **Cheryl Read**

DISK REPLACEMENT ORDER FORM

In the event that the disk bound in to this book is defective, Prentice Hall Computer Publishing will send you a replacement disk free of charge.

Please fill out the information below and return this card to the address listed below with your original disk. Please print clearly.

BOOK TITLE _____ ISBN _____

NAME _____ PHONE _____

COMPANY _____ TITLE _____

ADDRESS _____

CITY _____ STATE _____ ZIP _____

Prentice Hall Computer Publishing, 11711 North College Avenue, Carmel IN 46032.
ATTN: Customer Service Department.

LIMITED WARRANTY REGISTRATION CARD

In order to preserve your rights as provided in the limited warranty, this card must be on file with PHCP within thirty days of purchase.

Please fill in the information requested:

BOOK TITLE _____ ISBN _____

NAME _____ PHONE NUMBER ( ) _____

ADDRESS _____

CITY _____ STATE _____ ZIP _____

COMPUTER BRAND & MODEL _____ DOS VERSION _____ MEMORY _____ K

Where did you purchase this product?

DEALER NAME? _____ PHONE NUMBER ( ) _____

ADDRESS _____

CITY _____ STATE _____ ZIP _____

PURCHASE DATE _____ PURCHASE PRICE _____

How did you learn about this product? (Check as many as applicable.)

STORE DISPLAY _____ SALESPERSON _____ MAGAZINE ARTICLE _____ ADVERTISEMENT _____

OTHER (Please explain) _____

How long have you owned or used this computer?

LESS THAN 30 DAYS _____ LESS THAN 6 MONTHS _____ 6 MONTHS TO A YEAR _____ OVER 1 YEAR _____

What is your primary use for the computer?

BUSINESS _____ PERSONAL _____ EDUCATION _____ OTHER (Please explain) _____

Where is your computer located?

HOME _____ OFFICE _____ SCHOOL _____ OTHER (Please explain) _____

Prentice Hall Computer Publishing
11711 N. College Avenue
Carmel, IN 46032

Attn: **Order Department**